International Challenges in Investment Arbitration

As the proverbial workhorse of international economic law, investment arbitration is heavily relied upon around the globe. It has to cope with the demands of increasingly complex proceedings. At the same time, investment arbitration has come under close public scrutiny in the midst of heated political debate. Both of these factors have led to the field of investment protection being subject to continuous changes. Therefore, it presents an abundance of challenges in its interpretation and application. While these challenges are often deeply rooted in the doctrinal foundations of international law, they similarly surface during live arbitral proceedings.

International Challenges in Investment Arbitration serves not only as a collection of recently debated issues in investment law; it also deals with the underlying fundamental questions arising at the intersection of investment arbitration and international law. The book is the product of the 1st Bucerius Law Journal Conference on International Investment Law & Arbitration. It combines the current state of knowledge, new perspectives on the topic as well as practical issues and will be of interest to researchers, academics and practitioners in the fields of international investment law, international economic law, regulation and comparative law.

Mesut Akbaba, LL.B., is a Research Assistant at the Center for International Dispute Resolution at Bucerius Law School, Hamburg, Germany.

Giancarlo Capurro, LL.B., is a Law Clerk at the Higher Regional Court of Hamm, Germany.

Routledge Research in International Economic Law

Available:

Equity and Equitable Principles in the World Trade Organization
Addressing Conflicts and Overlaps between the WTO and Other Regimes
Anastasios Gourgourinis

International Investment Law and the Right to Regulate
A Human Rights Perspective
Lone Wandahl Mouyal

International Investment Law and Policy in Africa
Exploring a Human Rights Based Approach to Investment Regulation and
Dispute Settlement
Fola Adeleke

International Investment Law
A Chinese Perspective
Guiguo Wang

Culture and International Economic Law
Edited by Valentina Vadi and Bruno de Witte

WTO Trade Remedies in International Law
Their Role and Place in a Fragmented International Legal System
Roberto Soprano

Trade Facilitation in the Multilateral Trading System
Genesis, Course and Accord
Hao Wu

Forthcoming:

International Challenges in Investment Arbitration
Edited by Mesut Akbaba and Giancarlo Capurro

Defences in International Investment Law
Francis Botchway

International Challenges in Investment Arbitration

Edited by
Mesut Akbaba and Giancarlo Capurro

Routledge
Taylor & Francis Group

NEW YORK AND LONDON

First published 2019
by Routledge
52 Vanderbilt Avenue, New York, NY 10017

and by Routledge
2 Park Square, Milton Park, Abingdon, Oxon OX14 4RN

First issued in paperback 2020

Routledge is an imprint of the Taylor & Francis Group, an informa business

Library of Congress Cataloging in Publication Data
Names: Bucerius Law Journal Conference on International Investment Law & Arbitration (1st : 2016 : Bucerius Law School). | Akbaba, Mesut, editor. | Capurro, Giancarlo, editor. | Bucerius Law School, sponsoring body.
Title: International challenges in investment arbitration / edited by Mesut Akbaba and Giancarlo Capurro.
Description: Abingdon, Oxon ; New York : Routledge, 2019. |
Series: Routledge research in international economic law | Includes index.
Identifiers: LCCN 2018023010 | ISBN 9781138298729 (hbk)
Subjects: LCSH: International commercial arbitration--Congresses. |
Investments, Foreign (International law)--Congresses.
Classification: LCC K2400.A6 B83 2016 | DDC 346/.092--dc23LC record available at https://lccn.loc.gov/2018023010

ISBN 13: 978-0-36-758541-9 (pbk)
ISBN 13: 978-1-138-29872-9 (hbk)

Typeset in Galliard
by Taylor & Francis Books

Contents

Figures

Tables

Contributors

Tobias Ackermann Institute for International Law of Peace and Armed Conflict at Ruhr University Bochum, Germany

Dr Dafina Atanasova Centre for International Law at the National University of Singapore, Singapore

Dr Jola Gjuzi Kalo & Associates, Tirana, Albania

Dr Alexander Hoffmann CMS Hasche Sigle, Cologne, Germany

Neil Kaplan QC CBE SBS Self-Employed International Arbitrator, Hong Kong

Dr Sven Lange Allen & Overy LLP, Frankfurt, Germany

Javier García Olmedo Max Planck Institute Luxembourg for International, European and Regulatory Procedural Law, Luxembourg

Elsa Sardinha Centre for International Law at the National University of Singapore, Singapore and McGill University Faculty of Law, Montreal, Canada

Dr Emily Sipiorski University of Hamburg, Germany

Katarzyna Barbara Szczudlik Wardyński & Partners, Warsaw, Poland

Cees Verburg Groningen Centre of Energy Law at the University of Groningen, Netherlands

Marcus Weiler Higher Regional Court of Berlin, Germany

Sebastian Wuschka Luther, Hamburg, and Ruhr-University Bochum, Germany

Blerina Xheraj University of Geneva, Switzerland

Preface[1]

Investment arbitration is the proverbial workhorse of international economic law. It is heavily relied on around the globe and has to cope with the demands of numerous and increasingly complex proceedings. At the same time, investment arbitration has come under public scrutiny in the midst of a heated political debate. Both of these factors have led to the field of investment protection being subject to continuous challenges.

None of this has, however, led to a decrease in investment arbitration proceedings and investment law itself has been applied even throughout any purported crisis of itself. Therefore, these challenges are not obstacles to investment arbitration. Rather, they can be regarded as a driving factor for the development of this discipline and subsequently a vehicle for the study of investment law itself. This is exactly what this book seeks to portray: the continuous evolution of investment arbitration in view of its challenges.

The book is composed of papers presented at the 1st Bucerius Law Journal Conference on International Investment Law & Arbitration. The conference was organised by the editors under the patronage of Neil Kaplan QC CBE SBS and R. Doak Bishop and took place in Hamburg, Germany on 22 and 23 April 2016. It was the first international conference of the *Bucerius Law Journal*. The *Bucerius Law Journal* was established in 2007 as a cooperative effort of students and faculty of the Bucerius Law School, one of Germany's leading law schools. Since then, the *Bucerius Law Journal*'s mission has been to provide a platform for young and ambitious scholars to publish their work. In line with this goal, the conference was tailored towards international upcoming scholars and young practitioners with a research interest in investment law and arbitration.

Among all papers presented at the conference, the topics included in this book were selected with the aim to provide an illustrative array of challenges faced by investment law – from its theoretical background to its practical application:

Starting from the doctrinal foundations, Part I addresses investment law in the global framework of international law. By referring to the issues of nationality, territory, exception clauses and extraneous norms as a defense in investment

---

1 The views expressed in the chapters of this book are those of the respective authors and do not necessarily reflect the editors' views.

arbitration, the chapters in this part examine the intersection between investment law and international law. Part I concludes with an outlook on states' rights to regulate in recent Free Trade Agreements.

Part II adopts a more specific view, focusing on regulatory interactions between investment arbitration and the European legal order. Conflicts between EU law and investment law are analysed with respect to general methodological questions as well as the Energy Charter Treaty, specifically. On a policy level, the last two chapters examine the structural need for Intra-EU BITs as well as the EU Commission's proposal for an Investment Court.

Part III then deals with practical issues in investor state proceedings: With regard to arbitral procedure, effective use of bifurcation and handling mass claims are explored. As for quantum, the consequences of the political and economic situation of the host state are illustrated. Concerning the topic of costs, the final chapter of Part III explains the impact of third-party funding on a tribunal's decision on security for costs.

Continuing this topic, we included a speech on rationalising costs that Mr Kaplan gave at the conference and whose transcript he kindly provided for this book. The speech elaborates on practical issues, but relates them back to the cornerstone principles of arbitration and thus serves as a concluding remark.

The publication of this book marks the final step of our attempt to establish an international exchange between practice and academia in the field of investment arbitration at the Bucerius Law School. We thank our contributors for their outstanding work and are looking forward to continuing this concept with a 2nd Bucerius Law Journal Conference on International Investment Law & Arbitration.

Part I

The State in International and Investment Law

1 Rethinking the Relevance of Customary International Law to Issues of Nationality in Investment Treaty Arbitration

Javier García Olmedo[1]

A. Introduction

The investor-state arbitration regime is based on the principle that its protections only extend to individuals and corporations who are nationals of the home state. The nationality of the investor is therefore decisive to determine the jurisdiction *ratione personae* of arbitral tribunals and the entitlement to benefit from the treaty. However, despite being a necessary condition to enforce treaty obligations, most investment treaties contain broad nationality definitions only requiring that an individual be a national of his or her putative home state, or that a company be incorporated in that state.[2]

The often-sparse wording of nationality requirements increases the risk that investors push the boundaries of legitimate investment protection in the event of a dispute with the host state. This may occur in cases where, for instance, a company based on a third state or the host state incorporates a shell company in the home state to gain access to the dispute settlement mechanisms available in the relevant investment treaty. Broad nationality requirements may also allow an individual to benefit from treaty protection even though he or she simultaneously holds the nationality of the respondent host state (ie a dual national) and has overwhelmingly stronger links with that state. In such cases, it becomes apparent that treaty protection would ultimately be afforded to nationals that were not intended to be covered by the treaty. It should be reminded that the purpose of investment treaties is to protect *reciprocal* flows of investments made by nationals of the home state, that is to say, *foreign* investors.

In cases where the claimant's ties to its purported home state have been attenuated, respondent states have objected to the jurisdiction of arbitral tribunals. In doing so, states have argued that nationality requirements under investment treaties need to be supplemented by other sources of international law, such as the

1 Research Fellow, Max Planck Institute Luxembourg for International, European and Regulatory Procedural Law. Any errors or omissions remain the sole responsibility of the author. Translations by the author. Email: javier.garciaolmedo@mpi.lu

2 See eg Article 1 of the US-Argentina BIT, which defines a protected 'investor' as: 'b) [A]ny kind of corporation, company, association, state enterprise, or other organization, legally constituted under the laws and regulations of a Party; c) [A] natural person who is a national of a Party under its applicable law.'

rules of customary international law governing nationality in the context of diplomatic protection. These rules provide a higher threshold for the nationality of corporations and individuals by requiring, for instance, the existence of a 'genuine connection' between the home state and the corporation or by limiting protection in cases where an individual investor holds the nationality of the host state.

If the customary law principles of nationality were to be applied in investor-state arbitration, investors whose (foreign) nationality is more nominal than real would probably be denied access to international arbitration. This leads into the much-debated question of whether, and if so to what extent, the formalistic conception of nationality for juridical and natural persons employed in most investment treaties should be understood to encompass the same objectives as for the nationality rules of diplomatic protection.

All too frequently, this question has been examined by reference to the distinct nature of diplomatic protection and investor-state arbitration. In this respect, arbitral tribunals have generally considered that the rules deriving from the *inter*-state system of diplomatic protection cannot be imported into a field where investors are entitled to enforce their own rights without the intervention of states. That is, investment treaties constitute a *lex specialis* which, by enabling investors to directly access dispute settlement in the form of arbitration, departs from the customary law of diplomatic protection.

A recent example of arbitrators' general reluctance to import the customary rules of nationality into the investment regime includes a claim brought by Turkish national Cem Cengiz Uzan against Turkey under the Energy Charter Treaty (ECT).[3] In that case, unsurprisingly, Turkey objected the tribunal's jurisdiction on the grounds that, pursuant to the customary international law of diplomatic protection, a natural person is precluded from bringing a treaty claim against a state of which he is a national. The tribunal rejected this objection and found that, since there was no explicit provision in the ECT expressly excluding claims against the state of nationality, Mr Uzan was entitled to sue his own state. In other words, the tribunal considered that the determination of nationality for investment treaty purposes should be examined solely by reference to the terms of the treaty.

This article argues that the time has come to provide a more balanced approach regarding the position of the diplomatic protection rules of nationality amidst the investment treaty regime. While it is true that the *lex specialis* language of investment treaties plays a fundamental role in resolving investment disputes, this does mean that non-treaty rules of general international law have become irrelevant. Broad nationality requirements may prove insufficient in fulfilling the objective of investment treaties to protect *foreign* investment. In this regard, the author is of the view that the (more restrictive) customary rules on nationality are better equipped to ensure compliance with this objective. When interpreting nationality definitions, arbitral tribunals may consider relying on these rules when necessary to prevent investors who have a tenuous connection to the home state from misusing the entitlements granted in the treaty.

---

3 See *Cem Cengiz Uzan v Republic of Turkey*, SCC Arbitration V 2014/023, Award on Respondent's Bifurcated Preliminary Objection, 20 April 2016.

To substantiate this proposition, this contribution attempts to show that diplomatic protection and investor-state arbitration share certain fundamental elements that integrate the rules established under both systems. For one, the right to diplomatic protection and the operation of investment treaties are both dependent upon the link of nationality between the investor and the home state. This means that investors claiming under investment treaties and those seeking diplomatic protection share a similar legal status in the international plane. More fundamentally, it will be suggested that, as with diplomatic protection, the rights asserted under investment treaties also belong to the home state of the investor. This is demonstrated, *inter alia*, by the fact that investment treaties enable states to bring diplomatic protection claims on behalf of investors.

These elements of integration show that the customary international law of diplomatic protection and international investment law co-exist in parallel. As such, derogation from the customary rules of nationality should be accepted to the extent that the contracting parties have so required in the treaty.

B. The International Recognition of Nationality: Diplomatic Protection and Investment Treaty Arbitration Compared

By way of introduction, nationality can be defined as the 'legal bond [between an individual and a state] having as its basis a social fact of attachment, a genuine connection of existence, interests and sentiments, together with the existence of reciprocal rights and duties'.[4] It follows from this definition that the primary function of nationality is to determine who is a national of a given state. In this connection, the general rule is that a state has autonomy in conferring its nationality pursuant to its own domestic legislation.[5]

Yet, in addition to linking an individual to a particular state, nationality may have international consequences. Examples include: entitlement to the exercise of diplomatic protection and the enforcement of treaty rights. The question then arises whether a nationality acquired at the domestic level is entitled to automatic recognition and effect on the international plane. Formulated differently, is the mere possession of a nationality sufficient to be protected under international law?

It is generally admitted that, whilst states are free to legislate matters concerning the attribution of nationality, it is for international law to determine the international effects of such attribution.[6] So what are the limits imposed by international law? The limitations that international law imposes on the recognition of nationality are those reflected in the reservation of Article 1 of the 1930 Hague Convention on Certain Questions Relating to the Conflict of Nationality Laws (the Hague Convention). This provision provides that the state's discretion to confer

---

4 *Nottebohm (Liechtenstein v Guatemala)*, ICJ Reports (1955) 4, 23.

5 See Article 1 of the Hague Convention.

6 See generally Alfred M Boll, *Multiple Nationality and International Law* (Nijhoff/Brill 2007), 107; Mohsen Aghahosseini, *Claims of Dual Nationals and the Development of Customary International Law* (Nijhoff/Brill 2007), 76; Olivier W Vonk, *Dual Nationality in the European Union* (Nijhoff/Brill 2012), 41–42 and Paul Weis, *Nationality and Stateless in International Law* (Brill 1979), 59.

its nationality 'shall be recognised by other States in so far as it is consistent with international conventions, international custom, and the principles of law generally recognised with regard to nationality'.[7] The efficacy of nationality on an international level is therefore contingent upon the conformity of its attribution and invocation with international law requirements.[8] The following paragraphs are confined to a brief examination of these requirements for the purposes of diplomatic protection and investment treaty arbitration.

I. Nationality and Diplomatic Protection

It is a fundamental principle of customary international law that a state is entitled to protect its nationals when harmed by wrongful acts committed by other states.[9] Before the proliferation of investment treaties, the international remedy most commonly used for the protection of aliens and their property was diplomatic protection. This remedy may be defined as 'the procedure employed by the State of nationality of the injured person to secure protection of that person and to obtain reparation for the internationally wrongful act inflicted'.[10]

It follows from that definition that a state can only protect a person, whether a natural or juridical, that holds its nationality.[11] This rule, commonly known as the nationality of claims rule, can be found in the Draft Articles on Diplomatic Protection adopted by the International Law Commission in 2006 (the ILC Draft Articles).[12] These Articles codify existing customary international law on nationality and the exhaustion of local remedies.[13] Article 3 confirms that 'the State entitled to exercise diplomatic protection is the State of nationality'.[14] For a natural person, 'the State of nationality means the State whose nationality that person has acquired, in accordance with the law of that State'.[15] For a legal person, 'the State of nationality means the State under whose law the corporation was incorporated'.[16] The ILC places particular emphasis on the bond of nationality

---

7   See Article 1 of the 1930 Hague Convention (n 4).
8   José J Caicedo-Demoulin and Juan F Merizalde-Urdaneta, 'El control de la Nacionalidad de los Inversionistas por los Árbitros Internacionales' (2009), 15 Revista Colombiana de Derecho Internacional 41, 47; Brigitte Stern, 'Les Problèmes de Nationalité des Personnes Physiques et de Nationalité et Contrôle des Personnes Morales devant le Tribunal des Différends Irano-Américains' (1984), 30 Annuaire Français de Droit International 425, 426.
9   *Mavrommatis Palestine Concessions (Greece v UK)*, PCIJ ser A, No 2 (1924), 12; Marjorie M Whiteman, *Digest of International Law* (Washington: US Department of State, 1970. Volume 7, 1968), 23–24.
10   Chittharanjan F Amerasinghe, *Diplomatic Protection* (OUP 2008), 26–27.
11   *Panevezys-Saldutiskis Railway (Estonia v Lithuania)*, PCIJ ser A/B, No 76 (1938), 16.
12   See Article 1 of the ILC Draft Articles.
13   ILC Draft Articles, Articles 4–7 (rules for natural persons) and Article 14 (exhaustion of local remedies rule). See also A Vermeer-Künzli, 'As If: The Legal Fiction in Diplomatic Protection' (2007), 18(1) European Journal of International Law 37, 40.
14   See Article 3 of the ILC Draft Articles.
15   ibid Article 4.
16   ibid Article 9.

between state and national as a fundamental requirement for the entitlement to diplomatic protection.[17]

However, the fact that a person holds the nationality of the espousing state does not always result in that state being entitled to pursue a claim. International law may render unenforceable the right to diplomatic protection if the conferral or invocation of a nationality fails to abide by the relevant rules of international law.[18] The ILC Draft Articles deal with the requirements for the international recognition of nationality in Articles 4 to 7 (for natural persons) and 9 to 13 (for legal persons). Space constraints naturally preclude a comprehensive examination of all of these requirements. The focus here is therefore on those designed to preserve the foreign character of the claim.

1. Continuous Nationality (Individuals and Corporations)

It is widely accepted that the link of nationality between a person (natural or legal) and the home state must exist at the date of the injury and at the date of the presentation of the claim.[19] The ILC Draft Articles 5(1) and 10(1) confirm this requirement and further provide that the bond of nationality must exist continuously between these two dates. That is, a person who seeks diplomatic protection must be a national of the claimant state when the claim arose and maintain that nationality thereafter until the claim is presented. The combination of these requirements – time of the damage, time of the presentation of the claim and continuity – reflects the customary rule of continuous nationality.[20]

Despite its status as a long-established rule of customary international law, the rule of continuous nationality has been subject to considerable criticism. In its commentary, the ILC explained that this rule might undermine the protection of the induvial under international law in cases where there is a change of nationality for purposes unrelated to diplomatic protection. However, many considered that abandoning the rule might result in an abuse of the system of diplomatic protection through 'nationality shopping' practices.[21] Accordingly, the ILC decided to retain the rule but it agreed that some exceptions should be established which accord with contemporary international law.[22]

---

17 The Commentaries to the ILC Draft Articles, text adopted by the ILC at its 58th session and submitted to the General Assembly as a part of the Commission's report covering the work of that session A/61/10 (2006), 30 (ILC Commentaries).

18 As stipulated in Article 4 of the ILC Draft Articles, a nationality conferred by state law will be recognised by other states and tribunals inasmuch as it is not 'inconsistent with international law'.

19 Project No 15: 'Responsibility of Governments' (Article VIII), YILC (1956) II, 227.

20 For a more detailed discussion on the continuous nationality rule, see Amerasinghe (n 10), 96–106 and the ILC Commentaries (n 17), 35–41 (for natural persons) and 55–58 (for legal persons).

21 The ILC Commentaries (n 17), 36, relying on *Administrative Decision No V* (*United States v Germany*), UNRIAA, vol VII (1925) 19, 141.

22 The exceptions are thoroughly described in the ILC Commentaries (n 17), 35–41 (for natural persons) and 55–58 (for legal persons).

2. Dual Nationality (Individuals)

Another condition for the international recognition of the nationality applies in cases where the individual is a national of both the claimant state and the state party to the dispute (ie dual nationals). In accordance with the ILC Draft Article 7, the home state may exercise diplomatic protection in respect of a dual national only if the individual maintains more substantial connections with that state at the date of injury and at the date of the official presentation of the claim. This requirement, also known as the rule of dominant and effective nationality, seeks to avoid making international a claim that is purely domestic, which will occur if the dominant nationality is that of the defendant state.[23]

The ILC presented a non-exhaustive list of factors that may be taken into account in deciding dominant nationality. These factors include habitual residence, the amount of time spent in each country, family and economic ties in each country, and participation in social and public life, among others.[24] The rule of dominant and effective nationality has been applied in a number of cases. The most well-known example includes the decision by the Iran/US Claims in the *Esphahanian* case, which later became Case *A/18*. [25] In that case, the claimant, a dual US–Iranian national, instituted arbitration proceedings against Iran under the Algiers Accords,[26] which do not regulate the question of dual nationality. Despite this, the tribunal held that the relevant rule of international law to resolve the question of the standing of dual nationals was that of dominant and effective nationality.[27]

3. Substantive Business Activities and Control Requirements (Corporations)

In *Barcelona Traction*, the International Court of Justice (ICJ) confirmed that, as explained earlier, incorporation is the most important criterion to determine corporate nationality for the purposes of diplomatic protection. However, the ICJ suggested that, in addition to incorporation, there was a further need for some 'permanent and close connection' between the state exercising diplomatic protection and the corporation.[28] As Staker has remarked, 'there is […] a substantial body of opinion that a State is not entitled to protect a locally incorporated

---

23 *Case concerning the loss of property in Ethiopia owned by non-residents (Eritrea v Ethiopia)*, Eritrea-Ethiopia Claims Commission, Partial Award, 19 December 2009, para 11.

24 The ILC Commentaries (n 17), 46. The ILC emphasised that these elements are by no means determinative and that tribunals and courts enjoy full discretion to ascertain the relevance of each factor.

25 *Esphahanian v Bank Tejarat*, 2 Iran-USCTR (1983). See also *Case No A/18*, 5 Iran-USCTR (1984).

26 The Algiers Accords were created to resolve the hostage crisis between Iran and the US. Pursuant to these agreements, the Iran–US Claims Tribunal was established in 1981 in order to adjudicate claims by nationals of each country following the Iranian revolution.

27 *Esphahanian* (n 25) 160–161.

28 *Case concerning the Barcelona Traction Light and Power Company Limited (Belgium v Spain)*, ICJ Reports (1970), para 71.

company in the absence of a genuine link between the company and that state'.[29] This means, he continued, that 'not only may States be *disinclined* to protect locally incorporated companies in the absence of a genuine link, but that they would also be *legally incapable* of so doing'.[30] Drawing from this principle, it has also been accepted that a state may reject a claim 'of foreign juristic persons in which nationals of the respondent State hold the controlling interest', particularly in 'the case of a juristic person whose nationality is more fictitious or nominal than real'.[31]

The ILC acknowledges these principles and provides for an exception to the place of incorporation test. The ILC Draft Article 9 stipulates that in cases where a company:

> is controlled by nationals of another State or States and has no substantial business activities in the State of incorporation, and the seat of management and the financial control of the corporation are both located in another State, that other State is to be regarded as the State of nationality.[32]

In other words, if the only link between a company and the purported home state is incorporation and that company is owed or controlled by nationals of another state, in particular by a third state or the host state, the purported home state may not be entitled to exercise diplomatic protection.

It is evident from this cursory description of the customary international law of diplomatic protection that the conferral of a nationality in accordance with state law is not always sufficient for its international recognition. There are certain additional criteria that a home state must satisfy in order to exercise diplomatic protection on behalf of a person (legal or natural) that appears to lack a genuine connection to that state. These requirements serve the purpose of avoiding claims that do not have a true international character. It could therefore be said that, as will be seen further on, in contrast to international investment law, the customary law of diplomatic protection 'takes a restrictive approach towards the possibility of a strategic use of change of nationality'.[33]

II. Nationality and Investment Treaty Arbitration

As is well known, a key difference between diplomatic protection and investor-state arbitration is that only the latter enables investors to assert direct arbitral claims against host states. However, despite this 'procedural' difference, nationality

---

29 Christopher Staker, 'Diplomatic Protection of Private Business Companies: Determining Corporate Personality for International Law Purposes' (1990), 61 British Yearbook of International Law 155, 159.

30 ibid.

31 Francisco Garcia-Amador and others, *Recent Codification of the Law of State Responsibility for Injuries to Aliens* (Nijhoff/Brill 1974), 83. See also *Monte Blanco Real Estate Corp*, Decision No 37-B (*American-Mexican Claims Commission* of 1942), reprinted in Report to the Secretary of State (1948) 191, 195.

32 The ILC Commentaries (n 17), 52.

33 P Jorun Baumgartner, *Treaty Shopping in International Investment Law* (OUP 2016), 88.

has remained a common jurisdictional threshold in both systems of dispute resolution. Indeed, as with diplomatic protection, a fundamental prerequisite for the operation of investment treaties is that the investor must be a national of one of the contracting states. Stated differently, the investor must be foreign to avail of the protection afforded in the relevant investment treaty. As one commentator has put it: 'that the investor be foreign under some objective criterion, whether nationality or otherwise, is critical to the architecture of the system of international investment arbitration: without that criterion, the system would provide an impermissible forum for purely domestic disputes'.[34]

However, most investment treaties use broad nationality requirements to define the range of natural and legal persons that qualify as protected *foreign* investors. These instruments often only require that the affected person be a national of the home state, or being incorporated therein, pursuant to the law of that state.

The China model bilateral investment treaty (BIT) offers a typical definition of an individual 'investor': 'natural persons who have nationality of either Contracting Party in accordance with the law of that Contracting Party'.[35]

The common definition used for the nationality of legal persons can be found in the US–Argentina BIT: 'any kind of corporation, company, association, state enterprise, or other organization, legally constituted under the laws and regulations of a Party'.[36]

Broad definitions of 'investor' increase the risk that investors having only a nominal connection to the home state abuse the system of international investment protection through nationality planning. The question that arises in this context is whether arbitral tribunals should resort to the more restrictive rules of diplomatic protection when determining whether the claimant has satisfied the formal nationality criteria incorporated in the treaty. This question has proven a fertile area for objections to jurisdiction in recent cases. In line with the diplomatic protection rules on nationality, respondent states have frequently alleged that a company which lacks a substantive link with its purported home state, and which is in reality a mere 'mailbox company' controlled by nationals of the host state or a third state, should not qualify as a protected foreign investor. Objections have also arisen with respect to the foreign status of natural persons in cases where claimants who hold the nationality of the respondent state bring claims against that state under the treaty, an issue that is regulated by Article 7 of the ILC Draft Articles.

In considering these objections, arbitral tribunals have mostly been reluctant to look beyond the text of the treaty, finding that the treaty rule concerning nationality must prevail over an attempt to import a diplomatic protection rule. Under this view, absent additional requirements in the relevant investment treaty, a claim of nationality by a natural or a juridical person will be determined solely by reference to the formal nationality criteria of the treaty. The argument commonly advanced in support of this approach is that the *special* regime of investment treaty

---

34 L Reed and J E Davis, 'Who is a Protected Investor?', in Marc Bungenberg and other (eds), *International Investment Law, A Handbook* (Hart Publishing 2013), 614–615.
35 See Article 1(2) of the China model BIT.
36 See Article 1 of the US–Argentina BIT.

arbitration, in which investors are entitled to bring direct arbitral claims before international tribunals, leaves no room for the application of the rules derived from the inter-state system of diplomatic protection.

To give a recent example regarding corporations, in *Niko Resources Ltd v Bangladesh*, the claimant, a company incorporated in Barbados (the home state), but controlled by Canadian nationals (a third state), brought a claim under the ICSID Convention.[37] The applicable investment agreement defined 'investor' as 'a corporation organised under the laws of Barbados'.[38] Despite this, the respondent objected that the claimant was 'just a shell' company with no 'substantial and effective connection' to Barbados and asked the tribunal to 'take a realistic look at [its] true controller'.[39] In support of its position, the respondent relied on the customary rules of diplomatic protection, as reflected in *Barcelona Traction*, and argued that allowing the claimant to proceed with its claim would amount 'to an abuse of the ICSID system'.[40] The tribunal rejected the objection, holding that:

> an additional requirement cannot be read into the text of the Convention; nor can the travaux préparatoires for the Convention justify the assumption that this had been intended. It is sufficient for a claimant to show that it has the nationality of another Contracting State by reference to one of the generally accepted criteria, in particular incorporation or seat.[41]

Similar attempts by respondents to supplement the 'place of incorporation' test of nationality in an investment treaty with rules of diplomatic protection have failed in an overwhelming number of cases.[42]

With regard to natural persons, in *Serafín García Armas et al v Venezuela*, the claimants, two dual Spanish–Venezuelan nationals, sued Venezuela under the Spain–Venezuela BIT.[43] The BIT was silent on standing of dual nationals and only

37 *Niko Resources (Bangladesh) Ltd v Bangladesh Petroleum Exploration & Production Company Limited and Bangladesh Oil Gas and Mineral Corporation*, ICSID Case No ARB/10/18, Decision on Jurisdiction, 19 August 2013.

38 ibid, para 168.

39 ibid, para 173.

40 ibid, para 198.

41 ibid, para 203.

42 See eg *KT Asia Investment Group BV v Republic of Kazakhstan*, ICSID Case No ARB/09/8, Award, 13 October 2013, para 129; *Gold Reserve Inc v Bolivarian Republic of Venezuela*, ICSID Case No ARB(AF)/09/1, Award, 22 September 2014, para 252; *RosInvestCo UK Ltd v The Russian Federation*, SCC Case No ARB V079/2005, Final Award, 12 September 2010, paras 322–333; *Yukos Universal Limited (Isle of Man) v The Russian Federation*, PCA Case No AA 227, UNCITRAL, Interim Award on Jurisdiction and Admissibility, 30 November 2009, paras 414–416; *ADC Affiliate Limited and ADC & ADMC Management Limited v Republic of Hungary*, ICSID Case No ARB/03/16, Award, 2 October 2006, paras 357–359; *Tokios Tokelès v Ukraine*, ICSID Case No 02/18, Decision on Jurisdiction, 29 April 2004, paras 77, 81–82 and 86.

43 *Serafín García Armas and Karina García Gruber v The Bolivarian Republic of Venezuela*, PCA Case No 2013–3, UNCITRAL, Decision on Jurisdiction, 15 December

required that natural persons be nationals of the home state, in this case Spain.[44] Venezuela objected to the jurisdiction of the tribunal, arguing that investors who also hold the nationality of the host state, and maintained a long-standing connection with that state, failed to qualify as protected *foreign* investors under the treaty. To substantiate its objection, Venezuela invoked the customary rule of dominant and effective nationality contained in Article 7 of the ILC Draft Articles.

The tribunal rejected Venezuela's arguments and held that the direct access of investors to international arbitration to enforce their treaty rights means that investment treaties have derogated from the customary law of diplomatic protection:[45] '*[L]a existencia de un mecanismo de solución directa de diferencias entre inversores y el Estado receptor de la inversión retira la protección diplomática del contexto de los tratados de inversión por ser inconsistente con las reglas de los TBIs*'.[46]

In the tribunal's view, therefore, the fact that the BIT contained no express restrictions regarding dual nationals was sufficient to ground its jurisdiction and to allow two Venezuelan investors to sue Venezuela.

Similar findings were made by the tribunals in *Pey Casado v Chile* and in the more recent case *Uzan v Turkey*. [47] As was noted in the introduction to this chapter, the tribunal in the latter case allowed an investor to sue his own state under the ECT, holding that, pursuant to the *lex specialis* maxim, the sole applicable nationality criterion for individual investors is that provided for in the treaty.

This jurisprudence indicates that arbitral tribunals tend to favour treaty shopping by allowing companies established in a third state or the host state to create jurisdiction under an investment treaty through incorporation in the home state. It also reveals that individual investors holding the nationality of the host state can now gain treaty protection through the acquisition of a second passport. But did states agree to protect this category of investors? Was the intention behind the investment treaty regime to hold out a unilateral offer of arbitration to an unlimited (and sometimes unidentifiable) call of investors?

It has been argued that the increasingly expansive interpretation of notions of investor 'increases the category of persons protected beyond what a host country could have anticipated at the time it signed a treaty'.[48] In this regard, it should be reminded that the purpose 'of an investment treaty is to enable foreign investment flows', and '[t]his objective is not furthered by giving protection to citizens who

---

2014. To the author's knowledge, this is the first publicly known investment treaty arbitration where a dual national has brought a claim outside the ICSID Convention Regime, which expressly excludes dual nationals.

44 See Article 1 of the Spain–Venezuela BIT.

45 ibid, paras 167–175.

46 ibid, para 173. 'The mechanism for the direct resolution of disputes between investors and the host State abandons diplomatic protection in the context of investment treaties for being inconsistent with the rules found in BITs'.

47 *Victor Pey Casado and President Allende Foundation v Republic of Chile*, ICSID Case No ARB/98/2, Award, 8 May 2008, para 415 and *Uzan v Turkey* (n 3), paras 141–144.

48 Muthucumaraswamy Sornarajah, 'A Common Crisis: Expansionary in Investment Treaty Arbitration', in Andrea K Bjorklund (ed), *Appeals Mechanism in International Investment Disputes* (OUP 2008), 57.

cycle their investments through the other State in the treaty'.[49] Nor is the objective satisfied by extending protection to individuals holding the nationality of the host state without any limitations, especially if they maintain a stronger connection with that state.[50] Allowing these types of investors to access international arbitration may amount to an artificial establishment of the jurisdiction of arbitral tribunal.

Arbitrators' common reluctance to depart from broad nationality requirements under investment treaties has raised concern recently in the context of the current European Union's policy on the conclusion of investment treaties and free trade agreements, such as the Comprehensive Economic and Trade Agreement (CETA) and the Transatlantic Trade and Investment Partnership (TTIP). The European Commission (EC) has reiterated that the purpose of investment treaties is to encourage *foreign* investment. Thus, the EC has stated that, in order to satisfy this objective, investment protections in TTIP should be limited to corporations that have 'substantial business activities' in the territory of the home state.[51]

Consistently with the EC's concerns, states have begun to include provisions in their treaties with the aim of restricting access to arbitration of companies whose home state nationality is more nominal than real. For instance, the recently con-cluded Trans-Pacific Partnership (TPP) incorporates a denial of benefit clause, thereby excluding from its scope of protection mailbox companies owned or con-trolled by either investors of non-parties or host state nationals.[52] A similar provi-sion can be found in the 2015 India Model BIT.[53]

States have also introduced limitations for individual investors. For instance, in September 2016, the Russian Government enacted a new regulation on the con-clusion of investment treaties in which it has made clear that future treaties should *not* be applicable to investors who are nationals of the host state, thereby

---

49 ibid; see also Mark Feldman, 'Setting Limits on Corporate Nationality Planning in Investment Treaty Arbitration' (2012), 27(2) ICSID Review 281, 283–284; Thomas W Walde, 'International Investment Under the 1994 Energy Charter Treaty', in T W Waelde (ed), *The Energy Charter Treaty: An East-West Gateway for Investment & Trade* (Kluwer Law International 1996), 274 and Muthucumaraswamy Sonarajah, *The International Law on Foreign Investment* (CUP 2010), 324–331.

50 Campbell McLachlan and others, *International Investment Arbitration, Substantive Principles* (OUP 2017), 185; Noah D Rubins and others, *Investor-State Arbitration* (OUP 2008), 304.

51 See eg European Commission, *Online Public Consultation on Investment Protection and Investor-to-State Dispute Settlement (ISDS) in the Transatlantic Trade and Investment Partnership Agreement (TTIP)* (2014), 18, http://trade.ec.europa.eu/doclib/docs/2014/march/tradoc_152280.pdf accessed 20 June 2017.

52 See Article 9.14(1) of the TPP:

> A Party may deny the benefits of this Chapter to an investor of another Party that is an enterprise of that other Party and to investments of that investor if the enterprise: (a) is owned or controlled by a person of a non-Party or of the denying Party; and (b) has no substantial business activities in the territory of any Party other than the denying Party.

53 See Article 20 of the 2015 India Model BIT.

foreclosing the potential for treaty claims by dual nationals.[54] One would expect more states to adopt Russia's policy as claims of this nature continue to arise.[55]

These requirements can certainly be considered as a useful tool to ensure that the benefits of investment treaties do not run to nationals of states other than the home state. However, compliance with the object and purpose of investment treaties ultimately depends on the approach arbitral tribunals adopt in the application and interpretation of nationality definitions under those instruments. As previously shown, the prevailing jurisprudence on this issue has been formalistic in the sense that nationality definitions in investment treaties apply in isolation from the inter-state rules of diplomatic protection.

This contribution takes a different view and argues that the direct settlement of disputes between investors and host states is not sufficient to show that states intended to completely depart from the law of diplomatic protection and its rules of nationality. In fact, diplomatic protection and investment treaty arbitration share certain elements that integrate the rules established under each system. One of these elements has already been identified: the right to diplomatic protection and the operation of investment treaties are both dependent upon the link of nationality between the investor and the home state. Thus, far from displacing customary international law, states have decided to also limit the protection afforded in investment treaties to nationals of the home state. This means that investors seeking protection under both systems are not recognised as international persons independently of their home states.

As explained in the next section, a further, more fundamental element of integration relates to the question of who (the investor or the state) holds the substantive rights granted under investment treaties. It will be argued in this context that these rights are of a 'dual' nature, ie they belong to both the state and its national.

In the author's view, these elements show that states did not intend investment treaties to be exhaustive and complete. Therefore, as a part of customary international law, the diplomatic protection rules of nationality should apply to the extent that the applicable investment treaty contains no explicit derogation. As opposed to the sparse wording of most definitions of 'investor', these rules provide arbitrators with non-treaty based limitations to potentially abusive treaty claims by investors who are not truly foreign. They function as a gap filter in circumstances

---

54 Investment Arbitration Reporter, 'Russia sets out new guidelines for contents of future-investment treaties',www.iareporter.com/articles/russia-sets-out-new-guidelines-for-negotiation-of-future-investment-treaties/ accessed 20 June 2017. The new regulation in Russian is available at: http://pravo.gov.ru/proxy/ips/?docbody=&prevDoc=102071479&backlink=1&nd=102412234 accessed 20 June 2017.

55 See eg *Michael Ballantine and Lisa Ballantine v The Dominican Republic*, PCA Case No 2016–17, Notice of Arbitration, 11 September 2014; *Manuel García Armas and others v The Bolivarian Republic of Venezuela*, PCA Case No 2016–08, UNCITRAL; *Sergei Viktorovich Pugachev v the Russian Federation*, UNCITRAL, Notice of Arbitration, 21 September 2015 and *Dawood Rawat v The Republic of Mauritius*, PCA Case No 2016–20, UNCITRAL, Notice of Arbitration, 9 November 2015.

where the *lex specialis* of the BIT is silent and should therefore be considered by arbitral tribunals when interpreting nationality definitions.

C. The Nature of the Rights Asserted in Diplomatic Protection and the Investment Treaty Regime

The relevance of the nationality rules of diplomatic protection in investor-state arbitration has been examined by reference to the nature of investment treaties. In this regard, Douglas has famously argued that:

> [t]he contracting states to investment treaties have legislated for a new legal regime or sub-system to define the legal consequences that follow a violation of the minimum standards of treatment towards a qualified investment. In relation to the investor/state sphere, a breach of a treaty standard by the host state certainly creates new obligations upon that state. But these new obligations do not correspond to new rights of the national state of the investor because the injury is caused exclusively to the investor. This is so because the contracting states have opted out of the inter-state secondary rules of state responsibility in relation to a limited group of wrongs causing damage to a particular sphere of private interests. The national state of the investor thus has no immediate secondary rights within the investment treaty regime to challenge the commission of this breach of treaty; instead the new rights arising upon the breach of treaty vest directly in the investor.[56]

This approach assumes that, in contrast to the rights invoked through diplomatic protection, the rights asserted in an investment treaty claim belong to the claimant investor only. Under this view, since investment treaties confer no rights upon states, the customary rules of nationality should not be imported into the investment treaty regime. Further commentators and tribunals have adhered to Douglas' position, implicitly conceding that investment treaties are designed to derogate completely from the general regime of state responsibility and thus its rules on diplomatic protection.[57]

Indeed, if investment treaties only confer rights upon investors, then the investment regime should be considered as self-contained, thereby excluding the

---

56 Zachary Douglas, 'The Hybrid Foundations of Investment Treaty Arbitration' (2003), British Yearbook of International Law 190–191.
57 See eg R Aguirre Luzi and Ben Love, 'Individual Nationality in Investment Arbitration: The Tension Between Customary International Law and Lex Specialis', in Andrea K Bjorklund and others (eds), *Investment Treaty Law: Current Issues III: Remedies in International Investment Law & Emerging Jurisprudence in International Investment Law* (British Institute of International and Comparative Law 2009), 185; Ben Juratowitch, 'The Relationship between Diplomatic Protection and Investment Treaties' (2008) 23(1) ICSID Review 11–14 and *Ioan Micula, Viorel Micula, SC European Food SA, SC Starmill SR.L and SC Multipack SRL v Romania*, ICSID Case No ARB/05/20, Award on Jurisdiction, 24 September 2008, para 101.

customary law of diplomatic protection.[58] If, however, investment treaty rights are also owed on an inter-state basis, a deviation from this law can only be accepted to the extent that the state parties have clearly stated such an intention.[59]

It should be first noted that, as noted earlier, only the state has *ius standi* to bring a diplomatic protection claim on behalf of its nationals. The traditional view is that, in exercising this procedural right, the state is invoking its own substantive rights only and not those of the person who it is protecting. As the Permanent Court of International Justice held in *Mavrommatis*:

> By taking up the case of one of its subjects and by resorting to diplomatic action or international judicial proceedings on his behalf, a State is in reality asserting its own right, the right to ensure, in the person of its subjects, respect for the rules of international law.[60]

As explained earlier, unlike diplomatic protection, investment treaties grant investors the procedural right to commence arbitration proceedings against host states. The immediate question raised by this fundamental feature of investment treaties is whether, in bringing a treaty claim, the investor is enforcing its own substantive rights, those of its national state or both.

It is difficult to say that a non-state entity entitled to directly pursue an investment treaty claim does not have a substantive right under that instrument. As the entity suffering reparable injury, the investor is able not only to enforce but also to enjoy the rights enshrined in an investment treaty claim. However, this does not mean that the state which originally consented to grant those rights retains no legal interest in the claim. In seeking the integration of the customary law of diplomatic protection and international investment law, this contribution argues that states also hold the underlying rights derived from investment treaties. This is because, in addition to investor-state arbitration clauses, most investment treaties contain state-to-state dispute settlement provisions. The 2012 US model BIT provides a typical formulation:

> [A]ny dispute between the Parties concerning the interpretation or application of this Treaty, that is not resolved through consultations or other diplomatic channels, shall be submitted on the request of either Party to arbitration for a binding decision or award by a tribunal in accordance with applicable rules of international law.[61]

---

58 Tillmann R Braun, 'Globalization-driven Innovation: The Investor as a Partial Subject in Public International Law – An Inquiry into the Nature and Limits of Investors Rights' (2014), 15 Journal of World Investment and Trade 73, 77.

59 Zachary Douglas, *The International Law of Investment Claims* (CUP 2009), 11.

60 *Mavrommatis* (n 9), 12. See also Emer de Vattel, *Le Droit des Gens ou Principes de la Loi Naturelle* (1758), vol 2, para 71; The ILC Commentaries (n 17) 24–25.

61 See Article 37 of the 2012 US model BIT.

The term 'application' implies that, insofar as the investor has not previously sub-mitted a dispute to arbitration, states can bring diplomatic protection claims seeking compensation on behalf of injured investors. And this right is not pre-cluded even if the same treaty also incorporates an investor-state arbitration pro-vision. Indeed, investment treaties do not generally prioritise investor-state arbitration provisions over state-to-state arbitration provisions, nor do they expressly exclude diplomatic protection claims.[62] In fact, having diplomatic pro-tection as an alternative method to resolve investment disputes further enhances 'the object and purpose of increasing the efficacy of investment treaty obligations by increasing opportunities for enforcement by arbitration'.[63] Thus, diplomatic protection may be considered as dispute resolution mechanism that exists in par-allel to investor-state arbitration.[64] This was the point posited in *Diallo*, [65] where the ICJ saw the ICSID Convention and investment treaties in general as an alternative to diplomatic protection and not as one of its variations:

> The fact invoked by Guinea that various international agreements, such as agree-ments for the promotion and protection of foreign investments and the Washing-ton Convention, have established special legal regimes governing investment protection … is not sufficient to show that there has been a change in the customary rules of diplomatic protection; it could equally show the contrary.[66]

As Professor Roberts explains:

> given that both home states and investors have an interest in vindicating investment treaty obligations, and that both have been granted a procedural mechanism for doing so, we should presume that both have been granted substantive rights under investment treaties absent clear wording to the contrary.[67]

Further, she convincingly contends these rights should be 'best conceptualized as being shared or jointly held on an "interdependent" rather than an "independent" basis'.[68] This means that a violation of a treaty provision may entail a violation of

62 Anthea Roberts, 'State-to-State Investment Treaty Arbitration: A Hybrid Theory of Interdependent Rights and Shared Interpretive Authority' (2015), 55(1) Harvard International Law Journal 11.

63 ibid, 47.

64 J Dugard, Fifth Report on Diplomatic Protection, A/CN.4/538 20–21, 44.

65 *Case Concerning Ahmadou Sadio Diallo* (*Republic of Guinea v Democratic Republic of Congo*), ICJ Reports (2007).

66 ibid, para 90.

67 Roberts (n 62), 39; see also Robert Volterra, 'International Law Commission Articles on State Responsibility and Investor-State Arbitration: Do Investors Have Rights?' (2010), 25 ICSID Review 218, 220; James Crawford, 'The ILC's Articles on Responsibility of States for Internationally Wrongful Acts: A Retrospect' (2002), 96 (4) American Journal of International Law 874, 888.

68 Roberts (n 62), 39.

the rights of the investor and the rights of the home state as party to the treaty. As Amerasinghe has stated, 'an injury to an alien which violates international law is also a violation of his state's right'.[69]

These propositions find support in a decision rendered by an arbitral tribunal concerning a claim brought by Italy on behalf of several Italian investors under the Cuba–Italy BIT.[70] In that case, Italy invoked the state-to-state arbitration clause contained in Article 10 of the treaty, which also incorporates an investor-state dispute resolution provision in Article 9.[71] Italy argued that, in bringing the claim, it sought to enforce both its own substantive rights and those of its Italian investors who had invested in Cuba.[72] More pointedly, Italy contended that this dual nature of the claim: '*prend son origine dans l'institution de la protection diplomatique qui implique que le droit subjectif de l'Etat qui agit en protection diplomatique soit indissolublement connexe aux intérêts des personnes physiques et morales en faveur desquelles il agit*'.[73]

Cuba objected to Italy's claim, arguing that the existence of an investor-state arbitration provision in Article 9 of the BIT barred Italy from bringing a diplomatic protection claim.[74] The tribunal rejected this objection and held that the investor's home state was entitled to exercise diplomatic protection at any point before its national submitted a claim or consented to arbitration under the treaty.[75] In doing so, the tribunal drew an analogy to Article 27 of the ICSID Convention which allows a state to bring diplomatic protection claims only if the investor has not previously submitted the dispute to arbitration.[76] The tribunal considered that diplomatic espousal under investment treaties was complementary to investor-state dispute settlement.[77] It can therefore be said that by allowing Italy to pursue a claim on behalf of its nationals, the tribunal recognised that states also hold substantive rights under investment treaties.[78]

A corollary of the principle of allowing states to access international arbitration and to enforce their own substantive treaty rights is that the investment treaty regime does not automatically derogate from the customary law of diplomatic protection its rules on nationality. If the intention of the state's party in concluding investment treaties was to create a self-contained regime which excludes the

---

69   Chittharanjan F Amerasinghe, *Local Remedies in International Law* (CUP 2004), 164.

70   *Republic of Italy v Republic of Cuba*, Ad Hoc Arbitral Tribunal, Interim Award, 15 March 2005; *Republic of Italy v Republic of Cuba*, Ad Hoc Arbitral Tribunal, Final Award, 15 June 2008.

71   See Articles 9 and 10 of the Italy–Cuba BIT of 1993.

72   *Italy v Cuba*, Interim Award (n 69) paras 24–25.

73   ibid, para 25; the origin of the claim: 'was rooted in the very institution of diplomatic protection, which implies that the subjective right of the State which acts in diplomatic protection are indissolubly linked to the interests of the physical or juridical persons in whose behalf it is acting'.

74   ibid, para 47.

75   ibid, para 65.

76   ibid.

77   ibid.

78   Roberts (n 62), 40.

rules of diplomatic protection, they would have not granted themselves the pro-cedural right to espouse diplomatic protection claims on behalf of investors.

A more realistic approach is therefore to consider that the customary law of diplomatic protection co-exists in parallel with international investment law.[79] This means that the diplomatic protection rules of nationality apply in investor-state arbitration unless they are expressly excluded by the contracting states.[80] In the words of Joost Pauwelyn: '[i]t is for the party claiming that a treaty has "con-tracted out" of general international law to prove it'.[81] This was the view of the ICJ concerning the applicability of the customary law requirement for the exhaustion of local remedies in the *ELSI* case. The Court held that, absent of a clear derogation in the US–Italy Friendship, Commerce and Navigation treaty, the rule of the local remedies was applicable:

> The Chamber has no doubt that the parties to a treaty can therein either agree that the local remedies rule shall not apply to claims based on alleged breaches of that treaty; or confirm that it shall apply. Yet the Chamber finds itself unable to accept that an important principle of customary international law should be held to have been tacitly dispensed with, in the absence of any words making clear an intention to do so.[82]

This approach is consistent with the widely recognised principle that, in case of incompleteness (or silent) of the applicable investment treaty, customary inter-national law should be introduced as a lacuna-filling instrument.[83] In other words, if the treaty is silent on a particular issue, such as dual nationality, cus-tomary law remains applicable. As the tribunal in *Société Générale v Dominican Republic* has held:

> It is necessary to keep in mind that while it is true that investment law has meant in some respects a departure from the law governing diplomatic

---

79 Tarcisio Gazzini, 'The Role of Customary International Law in the Field of Foreign Investment' (2007), 8 Journal of World Investment and Trade 691, 697–698; Patrick Dumberry, 'Are BITs Representing the "New" Customary International Law in International Investment Law' (2010), 28 Penn State International Law Review 675, 676.

80 Martti Koskenniemi, 'Fragmentation of International Law: Difficulties Arising from the Diversification and Expansion of International Law', ILC, 58th Session, A/CN.4/L682 (2006), paras 184–185.

81 Joost Pauwelyn, *Conflict of Norms in Public International Law: How WTO Law Relates to Other Rules of International Law* (CUP 2003), 213.

82 *Case Concerning Elettronica Sicula SpA (United States v Italy)*, ICJ Reports (1989), 15, para 50.

83 Michael Wood, 'First Report on Formation and Evidence of Customary International Law' (2013), ILC, 68th Session, A/CN4/663, 15; Jean d'Aspremont, 'International Customary Investment Law: Story of a Paradox', in Tarcisio Gazzini and Eric De Brabandere (eds), *International Investment Law, the Sources of Rights and Obligations* (Nijhoff/Brill 2012), 5, 27.

> protection and the traditional law of international claims, this is correct largely to the extent that applicable treaties and conventions have so established by providing rules different from those of diplomatic protection … [t]he rules governing issues not addressed by the specific language of the treaty may sometimes be provided by the law of diplomatic protection, which apply as customary international law, and thus, provides for a residual role for at least some aspects of the law of diplomatic protection.[84]

Thus, the often-sparse wording of nationality requirements under investment treaties should not prevent an arbitral tribunal from applying the nationality criteria governed by customary international law. These criteria, as reflected in the ILC Draft Articles, would not be inconsistent with treaty provisions unless expressly excluded by the state's party.

D. Concluding Remarks

The function of investment treaties is to augment (rather than displace) customary international law by providing a more efficient mechanism for the protection of alien property. These instruments serve merely as an extension of the investor's options to avenge violations of international law, diplomatic protection being another remedy available to that effect. Thus, the fact that investors now enjoy a private right of action does not mean that all principles of the law of diplomatic protection have also been automatically derogated.

Despite arguments to the contrary, diplomatic protection and investment treaty arbitration share certain fundamental elements that make these two systems very similar in nature. In both systems, the possibility of an investor obtaining international protection depends on the state to which the investor is linked by nationality. Moreover, both systems allow states to enforce their own rights by means of diplomatic protection. Thus, it cannot be asserted that in bringing into force an investment treaty, a state has completely opted out of the customary rules of nationality. Arbitral tribunals are empowered, indeed bound, to rely on these rules with the aim of ensuring that investors do not 'internationalise' their claims through nationality planning. The mere possession of a nationality is not always sufficient to safeguard the purpose of the international investment regime: to encourage *foreign* investment in host states.

---

84 *Société Générale v Dominican Republic*, LCIA Case No UN 7927, Award on Preliminary Objections to Jurisdiction, September 19, 2008, para 108.

2 Investment Claims and Annexation of Territory

Where General International Law and Investment Law Collide?

Sebastian Wuschka[1]

A. Introduction

With at least eight treaty cases[2] filed against Russia over its actions in Crimea during the course of its 2014 annexation[3] and thereafter, the question to what extent its investment treaties bind a state that has put a part of another state's territory under its control by means of annexation is currently a hotly debated topic.[4] The impact which armed conflicts and military action might have on international economic relations and law has, during the last decade, already been

---

1 Sebastian Wuschka, LLM (Geneva MIDS), is an associate in the arbitration department of law firm Luther in Hamburg and a visiting lecturer at Ruhr-University Bochum's School of Law. The views in this chapter are the author's own and do not necessarily reflect the views of Luther or its clients.

2 *Aeroport Belbek and Igor Valerievich Kolomoisky v Russia*, PCA Case No 2015–07; *PrivatBank and Finilon v Russia*, PCA Case No 2015–21; *Luzgor and others v Russia*, PCA Case No 2015–29; *PJSC Ukrnafta v Russia*, PCA Case No 2015–34; *Stabil and others v Russia*, PCA Case No 2015–35; *Everest Estate and others v Russia*, PCA Case No 2015–36; *Naftogaz v Russia*, PCA Case No 2017–16; *Oschadbank v Russia* (case number not public).

3 For a chronology of the events, see *The Telegraph* online, 'Ukraine Crisis: Timeline of Major Events' www.telegraph.co.uk/news/worldnews/europe/ukraine/11449122/Ukraine-crisis-timeline-of-major-events.html accessed 31 January 2018. For a more detailed legal evaluation of these events, see C Marxsen, 'The Crimea Crisis – An International Law Perspective' (2014) 74 HJIL 367, 367–370; T D Grant, 'Annexation of Crimea' (2015) 109 AJIL 1, 68–95.

4 See eg Daniel Costelloe, 'Treaty Succession in Annexed Territory' (2016) 65 International and Comparative Law Quarterly 343; Richard Happ and Sebastian Wuschka, 'Horror Vacui: Or Why Investment Treaties Should Apply to Illegally Annexed Territory' (2016) 33 Journal of International Arbitration 245; Odysseas G Repousis, 'Why Russian Investment Treaties Could Apply to Crimea and What Would this Mean for the Ongoing Russo–Ukrainian Territorial Conflict' (2016) 32 Arbitration International 459; Patrick Dumberry, 'Requiem for Crimea: Why Tribunals should have Declined Jurisdiction over the Claims of Ukrainian Investors against Russian under the Ukraine–Russia BIT' (2018) 9 JIDS (advance article of 2 June 2018). For the argument that the law of occupation would also allow aggrieved foreign investors on the annexed territory to rely on the *de jure* sovereign's investment treaties, see Ofilio Mayorga, 'Occupants, Beware of BITs: Applicability of Investment Treaties to Occupied Territories' (2016) 19 Palestine Yearbook of International Law 136.

addressed in quite some detail.[5] Yet, the example of the so-called Crimea claims remains a novel one. The relationship between territorial changes and the territorial nexus of investment treaties is, to a large extent, *terra nullius* for international lawyers and legal scholars.

So far, five of the eight Crimea claims have (partly) passed the hurdle of jurisdiction, as revealed in press releases by the administering institution, the Permanent Court of Arbitration (PCA).[6] Russia, however, is not participating in the proceedings. It is therefore unlikely that the jurisdictional awards in these cases will be published in the near future. The PCA would need to obtain the parties' consent for the publication of the award, which Russia most certainly will not give. The challenges posed for international investment law and arbitral tribunals will, however, be discussed in this chapter. In particular, this chapter will address the potential collision between the international law principle of non-recognition and the individual's right under international law to file an investment claim. As this contribution argues, the Crimea claims represent yet another instance in which the strengthened position of the individual under international law calls for a readjustment of established international principles that better integrates the newly developed importance and role of the individual within the international legal system.

The contribution will first describe the potential collision between the obligation of non-recognition and the individual's interest of protection under international investment law (B.). In a further step, it will outline the challenges for arbitrators and parties in cases involving illegally annexed territory (C.). These are, as will be explained, most importantly the questions of which treaty could serve as a basis for an investor's claim with regard to investments in illegally annexed territories and how the obligation of non-recognition should be addressed. Additionally, the contribution will briefly touch upon the relevance of third-party interests of the state whose territory is under annexation in such cases as well as the approaches

---

5 See eg Christoph Schreuer, 'The Protection of Investments in Armed Conflicts' (2012) 3 Transnational Dispute Management 3; Ofilio Mayorga, 'Arbitrating War: Military Necessity as a Defense to the Breach of Investment Treaty Obligations', Harvard Program on Humanitarian Policy and Conflict Research, Policy Brief of August 2013; Josef Ostřanský, 'The Termination and Suspension of Bilateral Investment Treaties due an Armed Conflict' (2015) 6 JIDS 1, 3.

6 See the PCA's press releases of 9 March 2017 with regard to PCA Case No 2015–07 and PCA Case No 2015–21, of 5 April 2017 with regard to PCA Case No 2015–36, of 4 July 2017 with regard to PCA Case No 2015–34 and PCA Case No 2015–35. See further on these decisions Investment Arbitration Reporter, Full jurisdictional reasoning comes to light in Crimea-related BIT arbitration vs Russia, Investment Arbitration Reporter, 9 November 2017, www.iareporter.com/articles/full-jurisdictiona l-reasoning-comes-to-light-in-crimea-related-arbitration-everest-estate-v-russia/ accessed 1 May 2018; Investment Arbitration Reporter, Further Russia investment treaty decisions uncovered, offering broader window into arbitrators' approaches to Crimea controversy, 17 November 2017, www.iareporter.com/articles/investigation-further-russia-investm ent-treaty-decisions-uncovered-offering-broader-window-into-arbitrators-approaches-to-crimea-controversy/ accessed 1 May 2018.

arbitrators need to adopt in light of the respondent's likely non-participation in the proceedings. Finally, concluding remarks will be delivered (D.).

B. Where General International Law and Investment Law Potentially Collide: The Obligation of Non-Recognition and the Territorial Application of Investment Treaties

As always, every treaty's wording is different and, hence, exceptions to many rules might exist. However, almost all investment treaties conform to the general rule as also reflected in Article 29 Vienna Convention on the Law of Treaties[7] (VCLT) that treaties are limited in their application to the contracting parties' territories. Also the bilateral investment treaty (BIT) invoked in the Crimea cases[8] only protect investments in the 'territory' of the respondent state.[9] The classification of annexed territory is, therefore, of particular importance for tribunals in such cases. Would a tribunal consider that annexed land does not form part of the 'territory' of the annexing state under the treaty, it could not exercise its jurisdiction.[10]

The treaty requirement of 'territory' – defining the treaty's application *ratione loci* – will in most cases translate into a jurisdictional requirement *ratione personae* or *rationae materiae* (or both), depending on the applicable treaty's definitions. In case the treaty links the qualification of who is to be considered an investor to the making of an investment in the other state's territory, the territorial requirement will be part of the *ratione personae* jurisdictional assessment. To the contrary, should the treaty rather link the territorial requirement to the investment, it will be a *ratione materiae* requirement. Some treaties, such as the Energy Charter Treaty (ECT)[11], however, do not include any territorial link in their definitions of investor and investment. Instead, the dispute settlement provision of the ECT, Article 26, provides for, eg, arbitration with regard to '[d]isputes between a Contracting Party and an Investor of another Contracting Party relating to an Investment of the latter in the Area of the former'. These terminological and technical differences, however, are of less practical relevance for the present contribution. The illegality of the territorial situation in cases brought against a state

---

7 1155 UNTS. 331. Article 29 reads: 'Unless a different intention appears from the treaty or is otherwise established, a treaty is binding upon each party in respect of its entire territory.'

8 See Agreement between the Government of the Russian Federation and the Cabinet of Ministers of Ukraine on the Encouragement and Mutual Protection of Investments dated 27 November 1998, Article 1 (1): '"Investments" shall denote all kinds of property and intellectual values, which are put in by the investor of one Contracting Party on the territory of the other Contracting Party in conformity with the latter's legislation […].'

9 See further Happ and Wuschka (n 4) 251; P Tzeng, 'Investments on Disputed Territory: Indispensable Parties and Indispensable Issues' (2017) 14 Brazilian Journal of International Law 122, 123.

10 Happ and Wuschka (n 4) 251ff.

11 2080 UNTS 95.

that has annexed the land where the investment was made, on the contrary, turns it into the most important determination for these tribunals to make.

As a matter of general international law, illegal acquisition of territory must not be recognised by the international community. This obligation of non-recognition of situations created by illegal acts, in particular through the use of force, is nowadays well-accepted in general international law.[12] In the words of the UN International Law Commission (ILC), 'it not only refers to the formal recognition of these situations, but also prohibits acts which would imply such recognition.'[13] As a consequence, actions that imply recognition of legality are similarly excluded as part of the obligation of non-recognition in addition to deliberate recognition.[14]

According to Article 41 (2) of the ILC's Articles on State Responsibility[15], '[n]o State shall recognise as lawful a situation created by a serious breach within the meaning of article 40, nor render aid or assistance in maintaining that situation.' A 'serious breach' within the meaning of Article 40 is therein equated to a violation of *jus cogens*, which the VCLT defines as:

> a norm accepted and recognized by the international community of States as a whole as a norm from which no derogation is permitted and which can be modified only by a subsequent norm of general international law having the same character.[16]

The ILC, *inter alia* based on jurisprudence of the International Court of Justice (ICJ), has found that the prohibition of aggression and the illegal use of force, the prohibitions against slavery and slave trade, genocide and racial discrimination and apartheid, the prohibition against torture, the basic rules of international humanitarian law and the right of self-determination share this character.[17] The ICJ, however, does not limit the obligation of non-recognition to situations that are the direct result of a violation of *jus cogens*.[18] Rather, already in its 1971 *Namibia* Advisory Opinion, it extended the obligation of non-recognition to all illegal territorial situations, as their illegality involves an objective *erga omnes* character.[19]

Even though the line between violations of norms that trigger the obligation of non-recognition and those that do not seems to have been blurred, it is nevertheless clear that illegal acquisition of territory through the use of force must not

---

12 Cf eg UN General Assembly, UN Doc. Res 2734 (XXV), 16 December 1970; UN General Assembly, Res 3314 (XXIX), 14 December 1974.

13 Report of the ILC, 53rd Session, GAOR, 56th Session, Suppl No 10 (A/56/10), 2001, 287, para 5.

14 Happ and Wuschka (n 4) 254.

15 ILC Yearbook 2011, vol II(2) 31–143.

16 Article 53 VCLT.

17 Report of the ILC, 53rd Session, GAOR, 56th Session, Supp No 10 (A/56/10), 2001, 283–84, paras 4–5.

18 Enrico Milano, *Unlawful Territorial Situations in International Law* (Brill 2006) 184.

19 *Legal Consequences for States of the Continued Presence of South Africa in Namibia*, Advisory Opinion [1971] ICJ Reports 16, 56; see on this also Milano (n 18) 184.

be recognised as legal. Today's international law only recognises four legal modes of acquisition of territory. These are acquisition of *terra nullius*, cession, accretion, and prescription.[20] Annexation, in former times referred to as conquest, lost its statues of a fifth mode of territorial acquisition at the latest in the middle of the twentieth century. With the adoption of the Charter of the United Nations (UN Charter), the general prohibition on the use of force came into existence with its Article 2(4). Conquest and annexation have, since then, ceased to provide a basis for legally admissible acquisition of territory. The principle *ex injuria non oritur jus* mandates that annexation does not provide for a valid title to land (anymore).[21]

Non-recognition of illegal acquisition of territory, in turn, operators as a 'decentralized enforcement mechanism' of that rule.[22] It serves the purpose of a sanction,[23] the importance of which has constantly been reaffirmed through the years. In what is commonly referred to as the first application of the doctrine and explains its name as 'Stimson doctrine', US Secretary of State Henry Stimson declared already in 1932 during the Manchurian crisis that:

> the American Government deems it to be its duty to notify both the Imperial Japanese Government and the Government of the Chinese Republic that it cannot admit the legality of any situation de facto nor does it intend to recognize any treaty or agreement entered into between those Governments, or agents thereof, which may impair the treaty rights of the United States or its citizens in China, including those that relate to the sovereignty, the independence, or the territorial and administrative integrity of the Republic of China, or to the international policy relative to China, commonly known as the open door policy[24]

Although Stimson's note was followed by a declaration of the League of Nations' Assembly to the same effect,[25] the legal situation back then was less settled. Even though the Briand-Kellogg Pact,[26] which Stimson's doctrine also sought to

---

20 Rainer Hofmann, 'Annexation' in Rüdiger Wolfrum (ed), *MPEPIL – Online Edition* (OUP 2013) para 1; see also in greater detail M N Shaw, *International Law* (8th edn, CUP 2017) 367ff.

21 For a more detailed account of the evolution of the obligation not to recognise conquest or annexation of territory see Oliver Dörr, *Die Inkorporation als Tatbestand der Staatensukzession* (Duncker & Humblot 1995) 82ff.

22 Costelloe (n 4) 356.

23 Stefan Talmon, *Kollektive Nichtanerkennung illegaler Staaten* (Mohr Siebeck 2006), 262ff; Happ and Wuschka (n 4) 263.

24 Reprinted in Reginald G Bassett, *Democracy and Foreign Policy – A Case History: The Sino-Japanese Conflict, 1931–33* (Routledge 1968) 75.

25 See LNOJ, Spec Supp No 101, 1932, 87–88:

> it is incumbent upon the members of the League of Nations not to recognize any situation, treaty or agreement which may be brought about by means contrary to the Covenant of the League of Nations or to the Pact of Paris.

26 General Treaty for Renunciation of War as an Instrument of National Policy, 27 August 1928, 94 LNTS 57.

enforce, had been concluded shortly before as a step towards a general prohibition on the use of force, customary international law did not provide for the illegality of aggression at that time. Even the year after Stimson's note, in 1933, the Permanent Court of International Justice (PCIJ) itself still held in the *Eastern Greenland* case: 'Conquest ... operates as a cause of loss of sovereignty where there is war between two States and by reason of defeat of one of them sovereignty over territory passes from the loser to the victorious States'.[27]

Yet, the situation after the adoption of the UN Charter is straightforward. For instance, in 1970, the Friendly Relations Declaration reaffirmed that 'territory of a State shall not be the object of acquisition by another State resulting from the threat or use of force. No territorial acquisition resulting from the threat or use of force shall be recognized as legal.'[28] As the ICJ held in its *Nicaragua* judgment, the unanimous adoption of the resolution can be considered an indicator of the customary law status of the rules contained therein.[29] The UN General Assembly's later Definition of Aggression also had recourse to the doctrine when it recalled that '[n]o territorial acquisition or special advantage resulting from aggression is or shall be recognized as lawful.'[30] Most authoritatively, the ICJ held with regard to Israel's conduct in its 2004 *Palestinian Wall* Advisory Opinion that,

> [g]iven the character and the importance of the rights and obligations involved, [...] all States are under an obligation not to recognize the illegal situation resulting from the construction of the wall in the Occupied Palestinian Territory, including in and around East Jerusalem. They are also under an obligation not to render aid or assistance in maintaining the situation created by such construction.[31]

For the particular case of Crimea, the General Assembly made reference to the obligation of non-recognition in its Resolution 68/262. It called upon:

> all States, international organizations and specialized agencies not to recognize any alteration of the status of the Autonomous Republic of Crimea and the city of Sevastopol [...] and to refrain from any action or dealing that might be interpreted as recognizing any such altered status.[32]

---

27 *Legal Status of Eastern Greenland (Norway v Denmark)* [1933] PCIJ ser A/B, No 53, 29.

28 UN General Assembly, UN Doc Res 2734 (XXV), 16 December 1970.

29 *Case Concerning Military and Paramilitary Activities In and Against Nicaragua (Nicaragua v United States of America)*, Merits [1986] ICJ Reports 14, 100, para 188.

30 UN General Assembly, Res 3314 (XXIX), 14 December 1974.

31 *Legal Consequences of the Construction of a Wall in the Occupied Palestinian Territory*, Advisory Opinion [2004] ICJ Reports 136, para 159.

32 UN General Assembly, *Territorial Integrity of Ukraine*, UN Doc A/RES/68/262, 27 March 2014, para 6.

Even though the obligation of non-recognition is first and foremost only binding upon states, it is also the mandate of investment tribunals to decide their cases in accordance with international law. They are, therefore, confronted with the obligation of non-recognition as a potential obstacle to their jurisdiction. Should a tribunal, for that reason, apply a strict reading of the territorial requirements of investment treaties, it would be bound to dismiss the claims. The individual's interest, protected by international investment law, to receive reparation for the harm suffered conflicts with the international community's interest to sanction illegal acquisition of territory. International investment law and general international law collide.

C. Challenges for Arbitrators in Cases Involving Illegally Annexed Territory

Tribunals but also parties to cases dealing with territory under annexation are faced with a variety of – in many instances – unique legal issues, which can only be discussed in summary here. The first (I.) is the question of which treaty a wronged investor could rely on when seeking redress: the investment treaty between the investor's home state and the *de jure* sovereign over the occupied territory or the treaty between the investor's home state and the aggressor state, the *de facto* sovereign, over the annexing territory? A different question then is whether the *Monetary Gold* doctrine, which the ICJ has developed with regard to necessary third-party interests, might have a bearing on the tribunals' decisions as the *de jure* sovereign is generally not a party to the proceedings (II.). Last, as respondent states will most likely not defend themselves by relying on their own illegal conduct (or not participate in the proceedings at all), the question also arises whether tribunals could not simply side-step the problems discussed in this chapter in reliance on the respondent's omission to object (III.).

I. Which Investment Treaty Could Potentially Apply?

The Crimea claims are of a peculiar nature as investors having originally made domestic investments are suddenly in a position – at least factually – to file an investment claim.[33] In these cases, only one BIT is of relevance, namely the Ukraine–Russia BIT of 1998. Generally, however, investors from third states could – to stay within the realm of the Crimea example – try to file their claim against Russia under the investment treaty their home state has concluded with Ukraine or the one it has concluded with Russia. For the purposes of this contribution, only claims against the annexing state – and hence the question under which treaty Russia could be held liable – will be addressed. That being said, there might also be situations in which a claim against the *de jure* sovereign over an

---

33 In this regard, one could also ask whether such investments, which were initially purely domestic investments, should at all benefit from the protection of international investment law. This question, however, exceeds the scope of the present contribution.

annexed territory could be brought, eg with regard to a failure to comply with the applicable treaty's full protection and security clause.

1. *The Investment Treaty Between the Investor's Home State and the* De Jure *Sovereign*

For claims against the *de facto* sovereign, the investment treaty between the investor's home state and the *de jure* sovereign over the annexed territory, however, cannot serve as a valid basis.

First, as a matter of general treaty law and of the law of state succession – assuming that the acquisition of territory had been lawful – both the Vienna Convention on Succession of States in respect of Treaties[34] (VCST) and customary international law[35] would generally operate in a way that the treaties of the state that newly acquires territory extend to that territory. This so-called moving treaty frontiers rule is best explained by Article 15 of the VCST, which deals with succession in relation to parts of territory:

> When part of the territory of a State [...] becomes part of the territory of another State:

a   treaties of the predecessor State cease to be in force in respect of the territory [...] from the date of the succession of States; and
b   treaties of the successor State are in force in respect of the territory to which the succession of States relates from the date of the succession of States, unless it appears from the treaty or is otherwise established that the application of the treaty to that territory would be incompatible with the object and purpose of the treaty or would radically change the conditions for its operation.

Of course, the law of state succession cannot apply here. It is limited to situations of territorial changes in accordance with international law.[36] Nevertheless, as it prescribes that it is generally the treaties of the state acquiring territory which are deemed applicable in the acquired territory, it shows that a transfer of obligations to the state acquiring the territory along with that territory is not foreseen. If that is already not

---

34   1946 UNTS 3.

35   The customary law character of the relatively sparsely ratified VCST was affirmed by the 1999 Summary of Practice of the Secretary-General as Depositary of Multilateral Treaties, UN Doc ST/LEG/7/Rev 1, para 287: '*the Convention [on the Succession of States in respect of Treaties] in many of its aspects codifies established customary law on the matter.*'

36   See Article 6 VCST, according to which the convention 'applies only to the effects of a succession of States occurring in conformity with international law and, in particular, [...] the Charter of the United Nations'. See generally on the law of state succession in relation to investment law Patrick Dumberry, *A Guide to State Succession in International Investment Law* (Edward Elgar 2018).

the case for acquisition of territory in accordance with international law, this logic must all the more apply with regard to illegal acquisition of territory. Even though it is clear that the *de jure* sovereign's treaties remain in force for the annexed territory, the state having annexed the territory and exercising *de facto* control can, consequently, not be bound by any agreements it has never entered into itself.

Second, the argument has been made that the law of occupation would lead to a different result.[37] Indeed, Article 43 of the 1907 Hague Regulations[38] could speak in favour of the application of the *de jure* sovereign's treaty to the annexed territory. This norm reads:

> The authority of the legitimate power having in fact passed into the hands of the occupant, the latter shall take all the measures in his power to restore, and ensure, as far as possible, public order and safety, while respecting, unless absolutely prevented, the laws in force in the country.

The first question in this regard is whether a state's investment treaties are 'laws in force' in the sense of Article 43. This has been accepted by scholars, *inter alia*, for human rights treaties[39] and other international instruments.[40] As one of the ideas[41] behind the law of occupation is the continuity of the occupied state's legal order, investment treaties will most likely also have this status (either directly – in monist countries – or indirectly – through the law implementing the treaty – in dualist countries). What remain unclear under the law of occupation, however, are the consequences of this classification in the field of investment law, in particular with regard to dispute settlement.

Only one scholarly article has so far addressed this issue, arguing that an occupant would also be bound by the dispute settlement clauses of the *de jure* sovereign's investment treaties by way of a 'derivative' consent to jurisdiction.[42] This argument, however, seems questionable already on the basis that the obligation under Article 43 does not render investment treaties themselves applicable. Rather it obliges the occupying power to observe its substantive norms that form part of the law of the territory's *de jure* sovereign. Further, and *e contrario*, international dispute settlement is always dependent on the respective state's own consent to the jurisdiction of a certain forum. An argument of derivative consent would, ultimately, render all dispute settlement clauses the territory's *de jure* sovereign has

---

37 Mayorga (n 4).
38 Regulations Concerning the Laws and Customs of War on Land, The Hague, 18 October 1907, annexed to Hague Convention II of 1899 and Hague Convention IV of 1907.
39 Eyal Benvenisti, 'Occupation, Belligerent' in Rüdiger Wolfrum (ed), *MPEPIL – Online Edition* (OUP 2009) para 14.
40 Theodor Meron, 'Applicability of Multilateral Conventions to Occupied Territories' (1978) 72 *AJIL* 542, 550; Naomi Burke, 'A Change in Perspective: Looking at Occupation Through the Lens of the Law of Treaties' (2008–2009) 41 NYU J Int'l L & Pol 103, 115.
41 Cf. Eyal Benvenisti, *The International Law of Occupation* (2nd ed., Oxford University Press 2012), para. 252
42 Mayorga (n 4) 161.

ever signed applicable to the occupant. This cannot be what the law of occupation intends to provide for as a matter of legal logic.

2. The Investment Treaty Between the Investor's Home State and the De Facto *Sovereign*

In case claimants would rely on the investment treaty between their host state and the *de facto* (but not *de jure*) sovereign over the territory in which the investment is located, the obligation of non-recognition – as explained earlier – would present the main jurisdictional obstacle. The tribunal's decision will depend on its interpretation, in accordance with Article 31 and 32 VCLT, of the treaties' territorial nexus.

For investment treaties, apart from a limited number of scholarly writings, their territorial application has not been much discussed.[43] Also only a handful of arbitral awards had to deal with this matter, mainly related to the territorial nexus of financial instruments.[44] Nevertheless, good arguments can be made that an investment treaty's territorial nexus should be interpreted as including illegally annexed territories.[45] In particular, even though the wording of most investment treaties and their reference to 'territory' could be read as a reference to sovereign territory only, the object and purpose of investment treaties mandates a different conclusion.

A case to the point in this regard is *Sanum v Laos*. There, the arbitrators had to assess whether the China–Laos BIT was to extend to Macao, a special administrative region and autonomous territory of China. Macao had been taken over by China from Portugal after the BIT had been concluded. When answering whether an investor from Macao could enjoy the protection of the BIT, the tribunal found that the:

> purpose [as stated in the BIT's Preamble] is twofold: to protect the investor and develop economic cooperation. The Tribunal does not find—and no element has been provided by the Respondent to that effect—that the extension of the PRC/Laos BIT could be contrary to such a dual purpose. In fact, the larger scope the Treaty has, the better fulfilled the purposes of the Treaty are in this case: more investors—who could not otherwise be protected—are

43 Eg Christina Knahr, 'The Territorial Nexus between an Investment and the Host State', in Marc Bungenberg and others (eds), *International Investment Law: A Handbook* (Nomos/Hart Publishing/CH Beck, 2015) 590; Christian J Tams, 'State Succession to Investment Treaties: Mapping the Issues' (2016) 31 ICSID Review – Foreign Investment Law Journal 314.

44 *Bayview Irrigation District and others v Mexico*, ICSID Case No ARB(AF)/05/1, Award of 19 June 2007; *Canadian Cattlemen for Fair Trade v United States*, NAFTA/UNCITRAL, Award on Jurisdiction of 28 January 2008; *Sanum Investments Limited v Laos*, PCA Case No 2013–13, Award on Jurisdiction, 13 December 2013; *World Wide Minerals v Republic of Kazakhstan*, UNCITRAL, Decision on Jurisdiction, 2015 (unpublished).

45 See, in greater detail, Happ and Wuschka (n 4).

internationally protected, and the economic cooperation benefits a larger territory that would otherwise not receive such benefit.[46]

The object and purposes of international investment treaties that the *Sanum* tribunal identified is presumably the same for every single one of them. In line with this object and purpose, it would also only be fair to read the territorial nexus of investment treaties – as long as the relevant treaty's wording does not provide for the contrary – as encompassing illegally annexed territory as well.

Another instructive case is a commercial arbitration, ICC Case 6474. There, a tribunal acting under the auspices of the Court of Arbitration of the International Chamber of Commerce (ICC) had to decide a jurisdictional objection by a respondent that rested on the argument it was a state the recognition of which was contrary to international public policy.[47] The respondent in that case argued further that 'international arbitration of commercial dealings' with it constituted a violation of international public policy.[48]

The ICC tribunal rejected this argument. It considered non-recognition of states or foreign governments 'generally irrelevant in private international law'[49], on the basis of which it operated. The tribunal further argued that non-recognition policies were even in public international law not adhered to strictly, leaving sometimes room for provisional or *de facto* authority of the non-recognised entity.[50] As a consequence, the tribunal concluded, the question of non-recognition was not decisive; in particular, as the respondent had itself entered into the contract comprising the arbitration agreement with the claimant.[51]

Admittedly, this ratio cannot be directly transferred to investment arbitrations under BITs. Here, the territorial scope of the state's offer to arbitrate contained in the treaty is the relevant yardstick. Still, the ICC tribunal's reasons can serve as good guidance for investment treaty arbitration. In particular, the tribunal also had to address the respondent's contention that its courts were open to the claimant and were 'indeed '*the natural judges*' of the dispute'.[52] The tribunal found it was 'difficult to reconcile such assertion with the alleged "general duty of non-recognition of illegal situations", in particular the so-called *jus cogens* argument.'[53] It therefore held:

> Referring the claimant to submitting its case to the Courts of the territory would appear to involve a much greater degree of 'recognition' than can possibly be conveyed or imagined under ICC international arbitration in

---

46 *Sanum Investments Ltd v Laos*, PCA Case No 2013–13, Award on Jurisdiction, 13 December 2013, para 240.
47 ICC case No 6474 of 1992 (2000) Yearbook Commercial Arbitration XXV, 279–311.
48 ibid para 7.
49 ibid para 18.
50 ibid para 19.
51 ibid para 20.
52 ibid para 21.
53 ibid.

Switzerland, involving the entity calling itself the Republic of the territory as a defending party.[54]

As the ICC tribunal rightly pointed out, the main aim of the obligation of non-recognition is to ensure that an aggressor state would not benefit from its illegal conduct. Its character as a sanction and the principle of *ex injuria jus non oritur* mandate that the aggressor, the annexing state, must not enjoy any greater rights as a result of its annexation. If, however, the obligation of non-recognition leads to the inapplicability of dispute settlement under BITs, it actually benefits the *de facto* sovereign over the territory, the aggressor.[55] To allow a state to escape judicial proceedings would run counter to the obligation of non-recognition's purpose.[56] It is, therefore, all the more true for investment disputes that accepting jurisdiction over a claim with regard to investments on illegally annexed territories would serve the obligation of non-recognition better than to leave the claimants with the option to seek recourse in local courts.

On the conceptual level, investment treaty arbitration with regard to annexed territories, in this sense, presents yet another instance where the traditional rules of public international law – based on a perception of international law governing solely inter-state relations – and the more recently established rights for individuals on the international plane need to be better aligned. In such instances, the strengthened position of the individual under international law makes a readjustment of established international principles that better integrates the newly developed importance and role of the individual within the international legal system necessary. While the obligation of non-recognition posed fewer problems in an exclusively state-centred system of international law, its application needs to be adjusted now that it benefits aggressors and operates to the detriment of individuals.[57]

According to trustworthy media coverage[58], the tribunal in the cases *PJSC Ukrnafta v Russia* and *Stabil et al v Russia* adopted a similar approach to the one

---

54 ibid para 22.
55 For the opposing view, see (n 4) 26, arguing that 'any such 'benefit' enjoyed by Russia may only be in the short term. This is because foreign investors may be under the obligation to not continue doing business in Crimea under sanction regimes imposed by many States.'
56 See also Happ and Wuschka (n 4) 262ff. Dumberry (n 4) 27, however, argues that 'the better solution remains adopting the strict application of the non-recognition principle and, consequently, refusing to extend Russian BITs to the territory of Crimea. This seems like the most efficient way to 'sanction' the illegal action of Russia.' Yet, this solution unnecessarily puts the relevant investors at a disadvantage. On the contrary, their rights could be protected through arbitral proceedings and Russia could – should their claim have merit – be held liable and thereby sanctioned at the same time if one accepts the application of Russia's investment treaties to Crimea.
57 See also Happ and Wuschka (n 4) 264.
58 Investment Arbitration Reporter, Further Russia investment treaty decisions uncovered, offering broader window into arbitrators' approaches to Crimea controversy, 17 November 2017, www.iareporter.com/articles/investigation-further-russia-investm

suggested here. It was reportedly persuaded that, under the Ukraine–Russia BIT, *de facto* control was sufficient for its exercise of jurisdiction. These two jurisdictional decisions are currently challenged before the Swiss Federal Tribunal. It will therefore be interesting to see whether the court will concur with the tribunal's approach and will give effect to an interpretation that reconciles the individuals' interest under international law to have their investments protected and the international community's interest to sanction illegal acquisition of territory

II. The Monetary Gold *Rule*

In addition to the problems posed by the obligation of non-recognition in terms of treaty interpretation, a further obstacle to an investment claim with regard to illegally annexed territory could be the ICJ's indispensable third-party rule. In reliance on this so-called *Monetary Gold* doctrine, the argument could be made that investment tribunals were prevented from making any determination on the territorial situation in the absence of the *de jure* sovereign as an indispensable third party. As established by the ICJ in the *Monetary Gold* case, indispensable third-party interests present a bar to a claim if the legal interests of a state that is not party to the proceedings 'would not only be affected by a decision, but would form the very subject-matter of the decision.'[59] In subsequent jurisprudence, the Court has added further precision to the rule,[60] requiring for its application that the Court would need to make a 'prerequisite determination'[61] with regard to the third state's international responsibility.

It can already be questioned whether or not the *Monetary Gold* doctrine only applies in inter-state disputes and should, therefore, not be used in the investor-state arbitration context.[62] Ultimately, even if the rule applied in the investment context, the determination a tribunal would make with regard to annexed territory will not necessarily involve the *de jure* sovereign's legal interest as the 'very subject-matter of the decision'. It is true that the determination of whether or not annexed territory can be considered territory of the annexing state is still necessary and could be a 'prerequisite determination' for the tribunal's exercise of jurisdiction. Yet, the tribunal could limit any affirmative decision with regard to the fulfilment of the territorial nexus of an investment treaty to precisely that – the

ent-treaty-decisions-uncovered-offering-broader-window-into-arbitrators-approaches-to-crimea-controversy/ accessed 31 January 2018.

59 *Monetary Gold Removed from Rome in 1943 (Italy v France, UK, US)*, Judgment [1954] ICJ Reports 19, 32.

60 In greater detail on this point see Tzeng (n 9) 124ff; see also Noam Zamir 'The Applicability of the Monetary Gold Principle in International Arbitration' (2017) 33 Arbitration International 523, 526ff.

61 *East Timor (Portugal v Australia)* [1995] ICJ Reports 90, para 35; *Certain Phosphate Lands in Nauru (Nauru v Australia)* (Preliminary Objections) [1992] ICJ Reports 240, para 55; *Obligations Concerning Negotiations Relating to Cessation of the Nuclear Arms Race and to Nuclear Disarmament (Marshall Islands v United Kingdom)* (Dissenting Opinion of Judge Crawford) [2016] ICJ Reports, para 32.

62 Against the principle's application in arbitral proceedings Zamir (n 58).

determination of specific treaty requirements. It would not need to make a pronouncement on the issue of actual territorial sovereignty. 'Territory' under an investment treaty, and as defined by it, is not necessarily the same thing as a state's sovereign territory under international law. In particular in light of the obligation of non-recognition, tribunals would, in any event, be well-advised to render any decision under the caveat that it only relates to the specific treaty's requirements. To that end, however, the *Monetary Gold* rule does not bar investment tribunals from entertaining the kind of claims discussed here.[63]

At this point, it is interesting to note that Ukraine, for instance, participated in probably all known Crimea cases and made submissions as a non-disputing party. In *Everest Estate et al v Russia*, this reportedly led the tribunal to side-step the delicate debate whether or not Crimea constituted Russian *territory* under the Ukraine–Russia BIT. It simply noted that Russia and Ukraine both agreed that the BIT applied to Crimea as the latter 'presently' constituted Russian territory under the treaty.[64]

III. Jurisdictional Assessments on the Tribunals' Own Motion, Default Proceedings and the Potential to Side-Step Delicate Questions

Last, it is unlikely that a state will raise its own illegal conduct as a defence in international legal proceedings. It is also likely barred from doing so as a matter of good faith. It could, therefore, fall to the arbitrators to decide whether or not they consider the obligation of non-recognition as a jurisdictional obstacle on their own motion. As the example of the Crimea claims shows, however, respondent states in such proceedings might choose not to take part in the arbitration at all. The arbitrators will then need to conduct default proceedings. Such default proceedings and the lack of objections could also be seen by the arbitrators as a possibility to side-step the illegal territorial situation.

Yet, in general, investment tribunals, for instance in *Metal-Tech v Uzbekistan*, have held that '*it is the duty of a tribunal established on the basis of a treaty to verify its jurisdiction under that treaty, even if the parties have not objected to it.*'[65] Both

---

63 For a more detailed discussion, see Tzeng (n 9) 125–127.

64 Investment Arbitration Reporter, Full jurisdictional reasoning comes to light in Crimea-related BIT arbitration v Russia, Investment Arbitration Reporter, 9 November 2017, www.iareporter.com/articles/full-jurisdictional-reasoning-comes-to-light-in-crimea-related-arbitration-everest-estate-v-russia/ accessed 31 January 2018.

65 *Metal-Tech Ltd v Republic of Uzbekistan*, ICSID Case No ARB/10/3, Award, 4 October 2013, para 123; see also *Wintershall Aktiengesellschaft v Argentine Republic*, ICSID Case No ARB/04/14, Award, 8 December 2008, para 68ff; see also *Ioan Micula, Viorel Micula, SC European Food SA, SC Starmill SRL and SC Multipack SRL v Romania*, ICSID Case No ARB/05/20, Decision on Jurisdiction and Admissibility, 24 September 2008, para 65.

   an obligation to reject a claim if the record shows that jurisdiction is lacking. Or, put differently, a tribunal can rule on and decline its jurisdiction even where no objection to jurisdiction is raised if there are sufficient grounds to do so on the basis of the record.

in arbitrations under the auspices of the International Centre for Settlement of Investment Disputes (ICSID) and outside the ICSID framework, tribunals are required to ensure their decision's compatibility with (mandatory norms of) general international law. In ICSID proceedings this is because the system is 'rooted in international law'.[66] ICSID tribunals simply must not render awards which conflict with international public policy, including the obligation of non-recognition. In non-ICSID proceedings, tribunals must observe similar (international) public policy considerations, as these will play a role at the stage of recognition and enforcement of any award.

Despite that, in both ICSID and non-ICSID proceedings, a review of the tribunal's jurisdiction is a discretionary power on the part of the tribunal as long as both parties participate in the proceedings.[67] The tribunal may interpret the lack of jurisdictional objections as a basis for a *forum prorogatum*. It would, in such a case, not even need to make any (ancillary) determination with regard to the case's underlying territorial dispute to hear the case on the merits. In default proceedings, however, the tribunal cannot circumvent this determination. It is under a duty to review its jurisdiction *ex officio* in both the ICSID and the non-ICSID investment arbitration framework and must ensure that its decision is in the end well-founded in fact and in law.[68]

In practice and again in the Crimea cases, Russia's non-participation renders any discussion about a *forum prorogatum* a hypothetical. Reportedly, the first tribunals that have rendered awards with regard to the Crimea claims have approached their jurisdictional decisions, which remain non-public, accordingly. In two parallel cases, both heard by the same tribunal, the arbitrators are reported[69] to have followed an approach that strictly ensures the Russian side's right to be heard. In *PJSC Ukrnafta v Russia* and *Stabil et al v Russia*, the tribunal, according to the reporting, assumed it had a duty to satisfy itself that it had jurisdiction in the case in Russia's absence, which could include the application of *iura novit curia*, subject to due process considerations. It later on even appointed its own quantum expert to be able to have the claimants' quantum assessment tested by a neutral.[70]

---

66 Christoph Schreuer and others, *The ICSID Convention: A Commentary* (2nd edn, CUP 2009) Article 42, para 49.

67 Cf ICSID Arbitration Rule 41(2) for ICSID proceedings.

68 See only ICSID Arbitration Rule 42(4) and for arbitration outside the ICSID framework generally Gary B Born, *International Commercial Arbitration*, vol 2 (Kluwer Law International 2009) 1867–1868; Simon Greenberg, Christopher Kee and J Romesh Weeramantry, *International Commercial Arbitration: An Asia-Pacific Perspective* (CUP 2011) 208; see also Wolfgang Kühn 'Defaulting Parties and Default Awards in International Arbitration' in Arthur W Rovine (ed), *Contemporary Issues in International Arbitration and Mediation: The Fordham Papers 2014* (Nijhoff/Brill 2015) 400, 403.

69 Investment Arbitration Reporter, Further Russia investment treaty decisions uncovered, offering broader window into arbitrators' approaches to Crimea controversy, 17 November 2017, www.iareporter.com/articles/investigation-further-russia-investment-treaty-decisions-uncovered-offering-broader-window-into-arbitrators-approaches-to-crimea-controversy/ accessed 31 January 2018.

70 See PCA Press Release of 19 February 2018 with regard to PCA Cases No 2015–35 & 2015–35.

D. Conclusion

As this contribution has shown, arbitral proceedings with regard to investments in illegally annexed territories present one instance of situations in which general international law – here in the form of the obligation of non-recognition – and the individuals' interest as protected by investment law potentially collide. The obligation of non-recognition mandates that illegally annexed territory must not be recognised as territory of the annexing state. If investment tribunals would strictly adhere to this rule, this would, however, be to the detriment of the individual, the foreign investor, under international law. The tribunals would need to decline jurisdiction because they could not establish the necessary territorial nexus that almost all, if not all, investment treaties require under the treaty between the investor's home state and the *de facto* sovereign over the annexed territory. Reliance on the investment treaty, if any, between the home state of the investor and the *de jure* sovereign is, as has further been lined out, not possible with regard to claims against the *de facto* sovereign.

As the analysis has also shown, however, there are ways for investment tribunals to allow such claims to proceed. Should a respondent state participate in the proceedings, the tribunal could rely on a *forum progogatum* on the basis that the state will not object to its illegal acquisition of territory. This is not possible in case the respondent state decides not to participate in the proceedings, as the tribunal would then be under an obligation to satisfy itself that the claim has merit both in fact and in law. Nevertheless, in that case it could still establish its jurisdiction on the basis of an interpretation of the relevant investment treaty's requirement according to its object and purpose. This object and purpose is to protect foreign investments from illegal state conduct. The larger scope the treaty has, the better it is served.

The obligation of non-recognition does, in this instance, not warrant a different result. Its character as a sanction and the principle of *ex injuria jus non oritur* mandate that the aggressor, the annexing state, must not enjoy any greater rights as a result of the annexation. In case the obligation of non-recognition led to the inapplicability of dispute settlement under investment treaties, this would actually benefit the *de facto* sovereign over the territory, the aggressor. To allow a state to escape judicial proceedings would, however, frustrate the obligation of non-recognition's purpose. It is, therefore, all the more true for investment disputes that accepting jurisdiction over a claim with regard to investments on illegally annexed territories would serve the obligation of non-recognition better than to leave the claimants with the option to seek recourse in local courts. It would further also reflect the strengthened position of the individual under international law better. For these reasons, the obligation of non-recognition's application needs to be adjusted in case it benefits aggressors and operates to the detriment of individuals' rights under international law. As the decision in ICC case 6474 succinctly explained, any other decision would 'involve a much greater degree of "recognition"' of the illegal territorial situation.

3 Exception Clauses in International Investment Agreements

A Case for Systemic Integration?

Tobias Ackermann

A. Introduction

Recent criticism of international investment law and arbitration, *inter alia*, sees states' regulatory freedom as being unfairly restricted by a legal system that allegedly overemphasises investment protection at the expense of public policy interests.[1] Investors could, it is worried, sue states for measures taken in the pursuit of legitimate regulatory purposes or create a 'chilling effect' on governments, who refrain from taking such measures out of fear for lawsuits. Some states seem to share part of these concerns and have begun to reconsider their treaty practice. The recent innovations of the European Commission are one of many emblematic steps in this direction.[2] Yet, as large-scale reforms of a system that is set up by a vast number of bilateral and plurilateral international investment agreements (IIAs) are difficult to achieve, states have turned towards smaller options to realign the protection of foreign investments and secure their regulatory space.[3]

---

1 See eg Claire Provost and Matt Kennard, 'The Obscure Legal System that Lets Corporations Sue Countries' *The Guardian* (London, 10 June 2015) www.theguardian.com/business/2015/jun/10/obscure-legal-system-lets-corportations-sue-states-ttip-icsid accessed 18 June 2018; Peter Muchlinski and others, 'Statement of Concern about Planned Provisions on Investment Protection and Investor-State Dispute Settlement (ISDS) in the Transatlantic Trade and Investment Partnership (TTIP)' (14 July 2014) www.kent.ac.uk/law/isds_treaty_consultation.html accessed 18 June 2018; Gus van Harten and others, 'Public Statement on the International Investment Regime' (31 August 2010) www.osgoode.yorku.ca/public-statement-international-investment-regime-31-august-2010/ accessed 18 June 2018.

2 See Catharine Titi, 'The European Union's Proposal for an International Investment Court: Significance, Innovations and Challenges Ahead' (2017) 14(1) TDM, www.transnational-dispute-management.com/journal-advance-publication-Article.asp?key=1619 accessed 18 June 2018; Sebastian Wuschka, 'Ein Investitionsgerichtshof – Der große Wurf der EU-Kommission?' (2016) 19 Zeitschrift für Europarechtliche Studien 153.

3 See Lars Markert, 'The Crucial Question of Future Investment Treaties: Balancing Investors' Rights and Regulatory Interests in Host States' in Marc Bungenberg, Jörn Griebel, and Steffen Hindelang (eds), *European Yearbook of International Economic Law – Special Issue: International Investment Law and EU Law* (Springer 2011), 170; Suzanne A Spears, 'The Quest for Policy Space in a New Generation of International Investment Agreements' (2010) 13 J Int'l Econ L 1037, 1044.

One of these options may be the inclusion of exception clauses in IIAs. They are to secure states' regulatory space by allowing deviation from treaty obligations when certain interests are at play.[4] While by far not all IIAs feature exceptions, a study of the United Nations Conference on Trade and Development (UNCTAD) observed in 2006 that the number of bilateral investment treaties (BITs), which include treaty exceptions, has increased.[5] Some of these exceptions are tailored to specific obligations and thus restricted in their scope of application, whereas others are applicable to the respective treaty as a whole.

The best-known example of these latter provisions certainly is the infamous non-precluded measure (NPM) clause of the BIT between the United States (US) and Argentina. It reads:

> This Treaty shall not preclude the application by either Party of measures necessary for the maintenance of public order, the fulfillment of its obligations with respect to the maintenance or restoration of international peace or security, or the Protection of its own essential security interests.[6]

While other treaties include similarly worded exemptions, states have apparently begun to incorporate more detailed exceptions into their IIAs that cover a wide range of issues. As no overview of the proliferation of such clauses within recently concluded IIAs exists, this contribution first presents a comprehensive survey of recent IIAs. It will be shown that a significant majority of the examined treaties indeed contains exception clauses, most of which are not merely limited to security concerns. What is more, comparative examination reveals that many of these clauses strongly resemble the exceptions found in the law of the World Trade Organisation (WTO), ie Articles XX and XXI of the 1994 General Agreement on Tariffs and Trade (GATT)[7] and Articles XIV and XIV*bis* of the General Agreement on Trade in Services (GATS)[8], respectively. While this may not be entirely surprising for the case of free trade agreements (FTAs), where there is significant

---

4   See Levent Sabanogullari, 'The Merits and Limitations of General Exception Clauses in Contemporary Investment Treaty Practice' (2015) 6(2) Investment Treaty News 3, 3–4, www.iisd.org/sites/default/files/publications/iisd-itn-may-2015-en.pdf accessed 18 June 2018; Kenneth J Vandevelde, 'Rebalancing Through Exceptions' (2013) 17 Lewis & Clark L Rev 449, 454; Jeswald W Salacuse, *The Law of Investment Treaties* (OUP 2010), 342–343.

5   UNCTAD, 'Bilateral Investment Treaties 1995–2006: Trends in Investment Rule-making' (2007) UN Doc UNCTAD/ITE/IIT/2006/5, 81.

6   US–Argentina BIT (signed 14 November 1991, entered into force 20 October 1994) Article XI. See William W Burke-White and Andreas von Staden, 'Investment Protection in Extraordinary Times: The Interpretation and Application of Non-Precluded Measures Provisions in Bilateral Investment Treaties' (2008) 48 Va J Int'l L 307.

7   General Agreement on Tariffs and Trade 1994 (signed 15 April 1994, entered into force 1 January 1995) 1867 UNTS 187 (GATT).

8   General Agreement on Trade in Services (signed 15 April 1994, entered into force 1 January 1995) 1869 UNTS 183 (GATS).

overlap with world trade law, a number of BITs, too, contain 'WTO-like' exceptions.

Investment tribunals are yet to decide on such clauses and it is unclear which interpretive approach they will choose. The principle of 'systemic integration', rooted in Article 31(3)(c) of the Vienna Convention on the Law of Treaties (VCLT),[9] might serve as the doctrinal vehicle to open investment law to the influence of trade law. Yet, the appropriateness of such undertaking remains unclear. To illustrate, this contribution focuses on a key element of WTO-like exceptions, namely the 'necessary' nexus requirement between the measure in question and that measure's purpose. It suggests that tribunals should indeed strongly rely on WTO jurisprudence to inform the interpretation of IIA exception clauses, while paying regard to relevant differences in the two legal regimes during the interpretive process.

B. Stocktaking: Exception Clauses in Recent IIAs

The necessary empirical groundwork is laid through a survey of recently signed IIAs, for practical reasons limited to the span from 1 January 2013 to 1 June 2017 and to treaties whose full texts are available at UNCTAD's 'Investment Policy Hub'.[10] Treaties without comprehensive investment protection rules are not included. Accordingly, a total of 107 IIAs form the basis of the survey. They can be grouped into 82 BITs and 25 other treaties with investment provisions (TIPs), especially FTAs.

The treaties were surveyed for their use of clauses that expressly establish exceptions to IIA obligations, which apply to the treaty as a whole ('all-encompassing exceptions'). These exceptions typically indicate their unlimited scope of application by stating that 'nothing' prevents or that 'the agreement' does not prevent a state from taking specific measures. They can be divided into 'security' and 'general exceptions'. A security exception is understood as allowing measures taken in the pursuit of (essential) security interests, including the maintenance of international peace and security; a general exception is understood as establishing exemptions for broader policy issues, such as public order, health, or safety.

I. Overall Results

Figure 3.1 depicts the overall use of all-encompassing exception clauses in the surveyed IIAs, distinguishing between the different cases of exceptions. Figures 3.2 and 3.3 illustrate the results for the respective type of IIA.

A broad majority of the surveyed IIAs (68.2%) uses overall exception clauses. When taking the type of IIA into account, it transpires that all TIPs include

---

9 Vienna Convention on the Law of Treaties (signed 22 May 1969, entered into force 27 January 1980) 1155 UNTS 331 (VCLT).

10 UNCTAD, 'Investment Policy Hub', http://investmentpolicyhub.unctad.org/IIA/MostRecentTreaties accessed 18 June 2018.

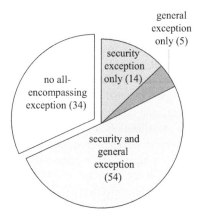

Figure 3.1 All-Encompassing Exceptions in IIAs

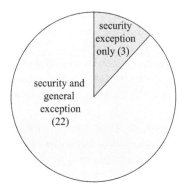

Figure 3.2 All-Encompassing Exceptions in TIPs

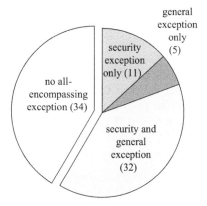

Figure 3.3 All-Encompassing Exceptions in BITs

exception clauses and that, albeit not omnipresent, still a majority of BITs follows this example (58.5%). In contrast, 34 BITs do not contain an all-encompassing exception.

Following the differentiation between security and general exceptions, 14 of the 73 IIAs that envisage all-encompassing exceptions cover security interests only, whereas 54 know both security and general exceptions. Only five cases exist where there is a general, but no security exception. Almost all TIPs contain exemption provisions for security as well as non-security policy interests. In BITs, the proliferation of general exceptions is significant (45.1%), but not as high as in TIPs.

II. Security Exceptions

1. Security Exceptions and the WTO Model

When comparing the 68 out of 107 treaties with security exceptions, it becomes apparent that the respective clauses have a lot more in common than their security motif. A large majority bears strong resemblance to the security exceptions of WTO law. Article XIVbis(1) GATS, which is nearly identical with Article XXI GATT, reads:

> Nothing in this Agreement shall be construed:

> a   to require any Member to furnish any information, the disclosure of which it considers contrary to its essential security interests; or
> b   to prevent any Member from taking any action which it considers necessary for the protection of its essential security interests:

> > i   relating to the supply of services as carried out directly or indirectly for the purpose of provisioning a military establishment;
> > ii   relating to fissionable and fusionable materials or the materials from which they are derived;
> > iii taken in time of war or other emergency in international relations; or

> c   to prevent any Member from taking any action in pursuance of its obligations under the United Nations Charter for the maintenance of international peace and security.

A security exception has been qualified as 'WTO-like' if it adopts introductory language identical or similar to the WTO provision ('Nothing in this Agreement shall be construed …' or 'This Agreement does not …'), if a catalogue of exceptions follows, and if that catalogue contains the same key terms (ie 'essential security interests', 'necessary' action, etc.).

Figure 3.4 illustrates the relation between the security clauses found in IIAs and the provisions of trade law.

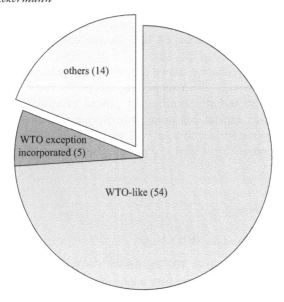

Figure 3.4 Security Exceptions and their Relation to the WTO Model

Fifty-four of the security clauses are (almost) replicas of the WTO model.[11] These 'WTO-like' clauses are in part or in whole virtually identical with the GATT/GATS provision with only minor adjustments. Five FTAs even explicitly incorporate Article XIVbis(1) GATS and/or Article XXI GATT into the respective agreement, *mutatis mutandis.*[12] This incorporation is, in all cases, done in a separate chapter of the FTA, applicable to the treaty as a whole, ie with regard to not only rules on investment protection, but also free trade and other obligations. All other TIPs entail WTO-like security exceptions, five of which are accompanied by an additional 'other' security exception.[13] These cases accordingly count double in the numbers shown earlier.

Not only TIPs, but also a majority of 33 out of 43 BITs with security exceptions adopts the WTO style. A last set of 14 security exceptions, ten of which are to be found in BITs, in contrast, is not (closely) related to the trade law model. Some of these provisions are significantly shorter and do not possess a catalogue-

11 Eg Korea–Vietnam FTA (signed 5 May 2015, entered into force 20 December 2015) Article 16.2(1); Canada–Côte d'Ivoire BIT (signed 30 November 2014, entered into force 14 December 2015) Article 17(4); Colombia–Turkey BIT (signed 28 July 2014) Article 6(2).

12 Eg Australia–China FTA (signed 17 June 2015, entered into force 20 December 2015) Article 16.3; Eurasian Economic Union–Vietnam FTA (signed 29 May 2015, entered into force 5 October 2016) Article 1.9; Japan–Mongolia Economic Partnership Agreement (EPA) (signed 10 February 2015, entered into force 7 June 2016) Article 1.10.

13 Eg Honduras–Peru FTA (signed 29 May 2015, entered into force 1 January 2017) Articles 12.1(5), 18.2; Colombia–Israel FTA (signed 30 September 2013) Articles 10.11, 14.2.

structure. For example, the Brazil–Mexico BIT contains a clause stating merely that '[n]othing in this Agreement shall be interpreted as preventing a Party from adopting or maintaining measures aimed at preserving its national security. ...'[14] Whereas thus some treaties refer to 'national security', others are still drafted in line with trade law language, in particular with regard to the term 'essential security interests'.[15]

2. Security Exceptions in Detail

When looking more closely at the design of security clauses, three details are worth comparing, namely the specific cases covered, the nexus requirement, and the level of review that is to be conducted by arbitrators.

Security exceptions are inherently limited to certain security concerns. Some provisions remain at a generic level. For example, one merely states: 'Nothing in this Agreement shall be construed to preclude a Party from applying measures that it considers necessary for ... the protection of its own essential security interests.'[16] Contrarily, as most security exceptions in recent IIAs resemble the WTO provisions, further precision is widely present. The most common specifications correspond to Article XIVbis GATS and deal with measures taken in time of war etc., trafficking in arms and related issues, the non-proliferation of nuclear weapons or fissionable and fusionable materials, as well as the maintenance of international peace and security. Other clauses are further individualised, either in a restrictive[17] or expansive way. One of the latter clauses demonstrates perfectly the common cases of application with the WTO model as well as additional individualisation:

Nothing in this Agreement shall be construed ... to prevent any Party from taking any action which it considers necessary for the protection of its essential security interest, *including but not limited to*:

i   action relating to fissionable and fusionable materials or the materials from which they are derived;

ii action taken in time of war or other emergency in domestic or international relations;

iii action relating to the traffic in arms, ammunition and implements of war and ...;

iv *action taken so as to protect critical public infrastructure ... from deliberate attempts intended to disable or degrade such infrastructure; ...*[18]

14 Brazil–Mexico BIT (signed 26 May 2015) Article 12(1) (translation of the author).
15 Eg Israel–Myanmar BIT (signed 5 October 2014) Article 7(1); Colombia–France BIT (signed 10 July 2014) Article 14.
16 Trans-Pacific Partnership Agreement (signed 4 February 2016) Article 29.2(b).
17 See Austria–Kyrgyzstan BIT (signed 22 April 2014) Article 3(4)(a).
18 Association of Southeast Asian Nations (ASEAN)–India Investment Agreement (signed 12 November 2014) Article 22(b) (emphasis added).

Second, in order to invoke a security exception successfully, taking a measure for the protection of essential security interests is generally insufficient. The overwhelmingly common and sole requirement in this regard is a 'necessary' nexus, to which exceptions are rare. Few instances exist in which the threshold is raised (eg 'strictly necessary for'[19]) or lowered (eg 'with respect to'[20] or 'aimed at'[21]).

A third and last point of interest is the level of review to be conducted when a security exception is invoked. As opposed to the objective language famously used in the US–Argentina BIT's NPM clause as well as in some recent IIAs,[22] a vast majority follows the example of trade law and uses self-judging language instead. By addressing measures the state 'considers necessary', the nexus is rendered subjective and within the state's discretion.[23] Yet, this does not mean that an investment tribunal is completely barred from reviewing the measure in question. Instead, the standard of review is lowered in the sense that arbitrators can only assess whether the party complied with its general obligation to fulfil the treaty and thus to invoke the clause in good faith.[24]

A few IIAs go even further and deem the security exception altogether non-justiciable,[25] thus precluding tribunals from undertaking even the good faith test. While the latter kind of regulation is questionable from a rule of law perspective,[26] it becomes apparent that most states do not want security-sensitive measures reviewed by arbitral tribunals in depth. For that purpose, opting for a self-judging clause and the good faith test seems to be the best way to align the state's discretion in addressing security issues with the need of preventing abusive invocation of such clauses.

19 Israel–Myanmar BIT (n 15), Article 7(1) (adding that the measure 'shall be taken and implemented … so as to minimize the deviation from the provisions of this Agreement').

20 Egypt–Mauritius BIT (signed 25 June 2014, entered into force 17 October 2014) Article 13.

21 Brazil–Mexico BIT (n 14), Article 12(1); Brazil–Colombia BIT (signed 9 October 2015) Article 12(1) ('destinadas a').

22 Eg, Israel–Myanmar BIT (n 15), Article 7(1); Belarus–Laos BIT (signed 1 July 2013) Article 11(1). See also *CMS Gas Transmission Company v Argentina*, ICSID Case No ARB/01/8, Award (12 May 2005) para 373.

23 See Roger P Alford, 'The Self-Judging WTO Security Exception' [2011] Utah LR 697; Burke-White and von Staden (n 6), 376–381; Susan Rose-Ackerman and Benjamin Billa, 'Treaties and National Security' (2008) 40 NYUJ Int'l L & Pol 437, 468, 470.

24 Salacuse (n 4), 345; Stephan Schill and Robyn Briese, '"If the State Considers": Self-Judging Clauses in International Dispute Settlement' (2009) 13 Max Planck Yrbk UN L 61, 113.

25 See, eg, Brazil–Mexico BIT (n 14), Article 12(2); ASEAN–India Investment Agreement (n 18), annex 2; Korea–Colombia FTA (signed 21 February 2013, entered into force 15 July 2016) fn to Article 21.2. See also North American Free Trade Agreement (signed 17 November 1992, entered into force 1 January 1994) 32 ILM 605 Article 1138(1).

26 See Vandevelde (n 4), 458.

III. General Exceptions

1. General Exceptions and the WTO Model

In addition to security exceptions, 53 of the 107 IIAs also incorporate exceptions of a more general nature; five IIAs even entail only general and no security exceptions. Significantly, most of the general exceptions are, again, very similar to the WTO model. A clause has been considered 'WTO-like' if it contains a precursory chapeau adopted to the investment context but otherwise (nearly) identical to trade law as well as a catalogue of public purposes that correspond at least partially to the WTO model. Article XIV GATS, similar to Article XX GATT, reads, in excerpts:

> Subject to the requirement that such measures are not applied in a manner which would constitute a means of arbitrary or unjustifiable discrimination between countries where like conditions prevail, or a disguised restriction on trade in services, nothing in this Agreement shall be construed to prevent the adoption or enforcement by any Member of measures:

a   necessary to protect public morals or to maintain public order;
b   necessary to protect human, animal or plant life or health;
c   necessary to secure compliance with laws or regulations which are not inconsistent with the provisions of this Agreement including those relating to …

  i   safety; … .

Figure 3.5 displays the relationship of general exceptions found in IIAs and the WTO model.

A majority of general exceptions bears strong resemblances to the WTO model (32 out of 58), whereby eight of these clauses can be found in TIPs and 24 in BITs. This means that 24 out of 37 BITs with general exceptions adopt the WTO model. Ten other treaties, all of which are TIPs, incorporate the general exception of the GATT and/or GATS directly. Only 19 provisions stand out as not resembling the WTO model, two of which are accompanied by an incorporation of WTO exceptions and thus count twice in the numbers shown earlier.[27]

2. General Exceptions in Detail

For the purpose of comparison, it is again useful to look at the policy concerns mentioned, the nexus requirement, and the level of review.

Article XX GATT and Article XIV GATS entail exhaustive catalogues of exceptions. Many IIAs reflect (some of) these interests, most prominently the

---

27 Eg Colombia–Costa Rica FTA (signed 22 May 2013, entered into force 1 August 2016) Articles 12.1, 21.1.

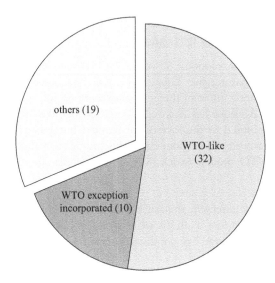

Figure 3.5 General Exceptions and their Relation to the WTO Model

protection of human, animal or plant life or health, public morals, and public order. Some provisions clarify, copying footnote 5 to Article XIV GATS, that 'the public order exception may only be invoked where a genuine and sufficiently serious threat is posed to one of the fundamental interests of society.'[28]

Other general exceptions are within the same clause as the security exceptions, thus not following the clear distinction between general and security exceptions as found in WTO law. Several of these respective treaties, mostly between Latin American countries, grasp 'public order' as a security issue, breaking off the qualification found in GATS.[29] Again other exceptions relate to interests found in WTO law, but do not display the characteristic catalogue-structure.[30]

A last group of rather peculiar clauses directly relates to the 'right to regulate'. Their purpose is not always to establish additional exceptions. Article 23 of the Morocco–Nigeria BIT, for example, affirms the right to take regulatory measures and clarifies that '[e]xcept where the rights of the host state are expressly stated as an exception', pursuing these rights 'shall be

---

28 Eg Japan–Iran BIT (signed 5 February 2016) Article 13(1)(b).
29 Eg Brazil–Colombia BIT (n 21), Article 12(1); Colombia–France BIT (n 15), Article 14; Mexico–Panama FTA (signed 3 April 2014, entered into force 1 July 2015) Article 10.2(4); Additional Protocol to the Framework Agreement to the Pacific Alliance (signed 10 February 2014, entered into force 1 May 2016) Article 18.2; Belarus–Laos BIT (n 22), Article 11(2).
30 Eg Korea–Turkey Investment Agreement (signed 26 February 2015) Article 1.16; Egypt–Mauritius BIT (n 20), 13; India–United Arab Emirates (UAE) BIT (signed 12 December 2013, entered into force 21 August 2014) Article 14(2).

understood as embodied within a balance of the rights and obligations' of the agreement.[31]

Such a clause tries to offer interpretive guidance rather than establishing exceptions and is accordingly not counted as a general exception.[32] The qualification of other 'right to regulate' provisions is less clear. The variety of clauses highlights the diverse attempts of treaty drafters to include safeguards of a state's regulatory space, but it also creates some uncertainty as to their respective operation. Article 12 of the Greece–United Arab Emirates (UAE) BIT, for example, clarifies that '[c]onsistent with the provisions of this agreement, each Contracting Party retains the right to adopt, maintain and enforce measures necessary to pursue legitimate policy objectives to protect society, the environment, public health and safety.'[33] Another clause states that the respective treaty 'shall [not] affect' the right to regulate,[34] whereas yet another provides that '[s]ubject to the provisions of this Chapter [the investment chapter], ... a Party may, on a non-discriminatory basis, adopt, maintain or enforce any measure that is in the public interest. ...'[35] As these latter examples are not formulated in typical terms of treaty exceptions, there may be some doubt as to the effects of these clauses. Yet, the cited clauses still stand, at least formally, in opposition to usually applicable obligations, show a chapeau and list diverse interests common to exceptions and have accordingly been treated as 'other' general exceptions.

Turning to the nexus requirement, most clauses again refer to the 'necessity' of the measure in question. This is true for WTO-like clauses, but also for many other general exceptions. Additionally, the necessity of the measure is generally not the only requirement. Instead, it must regularly not be 'applied in a manner that constitutes arbitrary or unjustifiable discrimination between investments or between investors, or a disguised restriction on investment.'[36] This directly echoes the chapeau of trade law, slightly adjusted to the investment context.

Third, while the self-judging language of measures 'considered necessary' is almost omnipresent in security exceptions, general exceptions are as a rule not self-judging. They regularly allow for 'measures necessary' to achieve a particular aim, thereby establishing an objective criterion arbitrators can fully review. This design corresponds again to WTO law.

Thus, while general exception clauses are prone to individualisation insofar as IIAs include or omit certain policy concerns, the examined clauses regularly stick to the same nexus requirement and the level of review as found in the WTO model. In contrast to the extraordinary character of security exceptions, general

---

31 Morocco–Nigeria BIT (signed 3 December 2016) Article 23.

32 See also Canada–European Union (EU) Comprehensive Economic and Trade Agreement (signed 30 October 2016) [2017] OJ L11/23 Article 8.9; EU–Vietnam FTA (draft) (signed 1 February 2016) Article 13bis.

33 Greece–UAE BIT (signed 6 May 2014, entered into force 6 March 2016) Article 12.

34 Argentina–Qatar BIT (signed 6 November 2016) Article 10.

35 European Free Trade Association (EFTA)–Costa Rica–Panama FTA (signed 24 June 2013) Article 5.6.

36 See, eg, Colombia–Turkey BIT (n 11), Article 6(1).

exceptions are meant to increase states' regulatory space in day-to-day governance. While an invocation is linked to arguably lower requirements established by very broad descriptions of the purpose pursued, the threshold for success and the level of review are commonly higher than in the case of security exceptions.

IV. Concluding Observations on the Survey

The survey has shown that a large number of IIAs incorporate all-encompassing exception clauses which are to a large part drafted after the exceptions of WTO law.[37]

This trend is widespread amongst states, although a few countries are over-represented in the survey. Most prominently, Canada is signatory to 12 of the BITs and three of the TIPs analysed. Each of these treaties entails WTO-like general and security exceptions. Canada has indeed taken up something like a pioneering role, as it has systematically included a comprehensive exception clause already in its 2004 model investment agreement and its subsequent IIAs. That clause constitutes a prime example of a WTO-like exception.[38] Japan (nine BITs, two TIPs) and Korea (four BITs, six TIPs) have concluded treaties that for the most part contain both types of exceptions as well. The use of all-encompassing exceptions, however, is not limited to these countries. Treaties between other countries from a range of geographical origins and with diverse economic power have included them, for example the BITs between Chile and Hong Kong, Argentina and Qatar, Nigeria and Singapore, Rwanda and Turkey, Iran and Slovakia, or Egypt and Mauritius. Other states, of course, seem to systematically not include exceptions, as demonstrated, for example, by the BITs to which Russia, Kuwait, or, for most of their treaties, the UAE are parties. Some other countries, however, have recently changed their practice in favour of all-encompassing exception clauses. The new Indian as well as the Norwegian model BIT now include general and security exceptions.[39] Thus, although some caution must be exercised, the proliferation of all-encompassing exceptions seems to increase and cover a growing number of states.

These and other states have begun to exercise some creativity in introducing regulatory interests into IIAs. Although some degree of individualisation is observable, many all-encompassing exception clauses closely follow the trade law

---

37 Cf Aikaterini Titi, *The Right to Regulate in International Investment Law* (Nomos, Dike, and Hart 2014), 173.

38 Canada, 'Model Foreign Investment Promotion and Protection Agreement' (2004), Article 10, www.italaw.com/documents/Canadian2004-FIPA-model-en.pdf accessed 18 June 2018. Already some of Canada's earlier BITs entailed similarly worded exceptions, eg Canada–Costa Rica BIT (signed 18 March 1998, entered into force 29 September 1999) annex I, s III.

39 India, 'Model Text for the Indian Bilateral Investment Treaty' (28 December 2015), Articles 32–33, www.bilaterals.org/IMG/pdf/modelbit_annex.pdf accessed 18 June 2018; Norway, 'Draft Model Agreement' (13 May 2015), Articles 24, 26, www.regjeringen.no/contentassets/e47326b61f424d4c9c3d470896492623/draft-model-agreement-english.pdf accessed 18 June 2018.

example.[40] With this growing trend, problems for interpreters arise[41] in particular with regard to the question whether they can rely on WTO law and jurisprudence to interpret provisions in investment treaties.

C. Interpreting WTO-Like Exception Clauses with Reliance on WTO Law

The relationship between investment law and other sets of rules continues to be a much-discussed topic. While Article 31(3)(c) VCLT opens the way for relying on 'any relevant rules of international law applicable in the relations between the parties' by way of 'systemic integration',[42] different approaches exist in arbitral practice on whether and how extraneous rules are to be considered. In some cases, tribunals have referred to such rules, including WTO law, when interpreting substantial obligations,[43] whereas in others, the relevance of non-investment rules was rejected.[44]

Exceptions and, in particular, their necessity nexus may be prone to systemic integration, as the notion of necessity can be found in various areas of international law. Prominently, in the Argentina cases, tribunals have dealt extensively with the interpretation of the NPM clause, with some referring to the customary necessity defence[45] and with another, namely the tribunal in *Continental*, relying on Article XX GATT.[46] Both of these approaches have received praise and rejection, rendering it unclear how investment tribunals will assess the necessity nexus in future cases.

I. The 'Necessity' Nexus in WTO Jurisprudence

Both security and general exceptions in WTO law know the 'necessity' nexus. Case law has, however, only dealt with general exceptions so far. Thereby, the WTO Appellate Body proceeds in two main steps. First, an overall view is adopted, which takes into account the importance of the measure's aim, the measure's contribution to the realisation of that aim, and the 'restrictive effects on

---

40 See also Titi (n 37), 173.
41 See Andrew Newcombe and Lluís Paradell, *Law and Practice of Investment Treaties: Standards of Treatment* (Kluwer Law International 2009), 503.
42 See International Law Commission (ILC), 'Report of the Study Group: Fragmentation of International Law' (13 April 2006) UN Doc A/CN.4/L.682, paras 413–415, 422.
43 See, eg, *Continental Casualty Company v Argentina*, ICSID Case No ARB/03/9, Award (5 September 2008) para 192; *Parkerings-Compagniet AS v Lithuania*, ICSID Case No ARB/05/8, Award (11 September 2007) paras 377–397; *Saluka Investments BV v Czech Republic*, UNCITRAL, Partial Award (17 March 2006) paras 254–255; *SD Myers v Canada*, UNCITRAL, Partial Award (13 November 2000) para 247.
44 *Occidental Exploration and Production Company v Ecuador*, LCIA Case No UN3467, Final Award (1 July 2004) para 176.
45 Eg *CMS Gas Transmission Company v Argentina* (n 22) paras 315–331.
46 *Continental Casualty Company v Argentina* (n 43) para 192.

international commerce'.[47] Second, 'reasonably available' alternative measures are assessed.[48] Additionally, the Appellate Body has claimed to exercise some 'weighing and balancing',[49] the extent of which remains unclear.[50] However, the Appellate Body has equally emphasised that it is for the state to decide on the level of protection and that it does not understand 'weighing and balancing' in the sense of a full proportionality test.[51] The necessity test in WTO jurisprudence thus facilitates a comprehensive assessment evaluating a range of factors, while paying some deference to states' regulatory freedom.

The assessment of 'necessity' in the security exception context should principally follow the same lines, as the chapeau of the general exception has no influence on the strictly separate necessity test.[52] However, as the security exceptions contain self-judging language, a tribunal will only be allowed to conduct a good faith-test, the details of which have not yet been addressed by WTO jurisprudence. The discussions surrounding the WTO's self-judging security clauses[53] could however prove informative in the investment context as well.

II. Incorporating WTO's 'Necessity' Test into IIA Exceptions

In principle, investment tribunals could follow the WTO approach to 'necessity', as they could assess the same elements of the measure in question. Such decision on the applicable standard thereby has highly important implications, as, for example, the threshold under WTO law is significantly lower than the one under the customary necessity defence.[54] However, the appropriateness of relying on WTO law is not undisputed. It certainly stands in tension with criticism levelled against reliance on WTO law in IIAs in general and *Continental's* approach to the NPM clause in particular. While arguments based on textual differences between

---

47 Eg *Korea–Measures Affecting Imports of Fresh, Chilled and Frozen Beef* (11 December 2000) WT/DS161/AB/R and WT/DS169/AB/R, paras 162–163.

48 Eg *European Communities–Measures Affecting Asbestos and Products Containing Asbestos* (12 March 2001) WT/DS135/AB/R, para 172.

49 Eg *Brazil–Retreaded Tyres* (3 December 2007) WT/DS332/AB/R, para 182.

50 See Federico Ortino, 'GATT' in Daniel Bethlehem and others (eds), *The Oxford Handbook of International Trade Law* (OUP 2009), 146.

51 Eg *Brazil–Retreaded Tyres* (n 49) paras 140, 182. See Donald H Regan, 'The Meaning of "Necessary" in GATT Article XX and GATS Article XIV: The Myth of Cost-Benefit Balancing' (2007) 6 World Trade Review 347.

52 See *US–Standards for Reformulated and Conventional Gasoline* (29 April 1996) WT/DS2/AB/R, para 22; Andrew D Mitchell and Caroline Henckels, 'Variations on a Theme: Comparing the Concept of "Necessity" in International Investment Law and WTO Law' (2013) 14 Chicago J Int'l L 93, 137; Petros C Mavroidis, *Trade in Goods: The GATT and the Other WTO Agreements Regulating Trade in Goods* (2nd edn, OUP 2012), 325–360. But see José E Alvarez and Tegan Brink, 'Revisiting the Necessity Defense: *Continental Casualty v Argentina*' in Karl P Sauvant (ed), *Yearbook on International Investment Law & Policy 2010–2011* (OUP 2012), 345–346.

53 Eg Schill and Briese (n 24), 106–110.

54 Cf Alvarez and Brink (n 52), 329–331.

IIAs and trade law are not convincing in the case of WTO-like exceptions, systemic objections may still have merit.

The relationship between trade and investment law is ambivalent.[55] Despite some scholars identifying similarities and trends towards convergence,[56] it is stressed vehemently that both regimes remain vastly different with distinct legal and institutional structures, standards, remedies, and dispute settlement procedures.[57] Scholars thus regularly advise to exercise caution when considering interpreting IIAs with reference to trade law.[58]

The caveats against merging trade and investment law are indeed valid in the context of substantial obligations,[59] but a different picture may be painted of treaty exceptions, as not only their text, but also their object and purpose are nearly identical.

The different nature of WTO inter-state and investor-state dispute settlement procedures may potentially impact procedural issues, such as the burden of proof. According to the Appellate Body, a WTO member invoking an exception must prove that the measure in question was necessary.[60] The other state merely has to show that alternative measures were reasonably available – a contention the respondent state may rebut. This is consistent with other approaches to the burden of proof and there is no apparent reason why it cannot be borrowed by investment tribunals. Investors would thus have to show that alternative measures existed when arguing against the application of an exception clause; and they could do so, if need be and without being overburdened, through experts.[61]

---

55 See generally Mary E Footer, 'International Investment Law and Trade: The Relationship That Never Went Away' in Freya Baetens (ed), *Investment Law Within International Law: Integrationist Perspectives* (CUP 2013).

56 See, eg, Sergio Puig, 'The Merging of International Trade and Investment Law' (2015) 33 Berkeley J Int'l L 1; Giorgio Sacerdoti, 'Trade and Investment Law: Institutional Differences and Substantive Similarities' (2014) 9 Jerusalem Rev Leg Stud 1, 9–10; Roger P Alford, 'The Convergence of International Trade and Investment Arbitration' (2013) 12 Santa Clara J Int'l L 35.

57 See, eg, Sacerdoti (n 56), 6–9; Mark Wu, 'The Scope and Limits of Trade's Influence in Shaping the Evolving International Investment Regime' in Zachary Douglas, Joost Pauwelyn, and Jorge E Viñuales (eds), *The Foundations of International Investment Law: Bringing Theory into Practice* (OUP 2014), 208.

58 Caroline Henckels, 'Protecting Regulatory Autonomy through Greater Precision in Investment Treaties: The TPP, CETA, and TTIP' (2016) 19 J Int'l Econ L 27, 48; Diane A Desierto, 'Public Policy in International Investment and Trade Law: Community Expectations and Functional Decision-Making' (2014) 26 Florida J Int'l L 51, 129–130; Titi (n 37), 178; Wu (n 57), 207.

59 See, eg, on national treatment, Jürgen Kurtz, 'The Use and Abuse of WTO Law in Investor – State Arbitration: Competition and its Discontents' (2009) 20 EJIL 749; Nicholas DiMascio and Joost Pauwelyn, 'Nondiscrimination in Trade and Investment Treaties: Worlds Apart or Two Sides of the Same Coin?' (2008) 102 AJIL 48.

60 *US–Measures Affecting the Cross-Border Supply of Gambling and Betting Services* (7 April 2005) WT/DS285/AB/R, para 309.

61 Mitchell and Henckels (n 52), 157–158.

A second point of divergence between trade and investment law is their different remedies.[62] In the investment context, a state is obliged to pay compensation for breaching an IIA, whereas, in trade law, states have to bring the measure into conformity with WTO law for which there may exist a variety of ways.[63] Desierto deduces from this that the WTO's necessity test is inappropriate in investment law, because a least restrictive means test 'makes no sense whatsoever' for tribunals tasked with providing compensation for IIA breaches.[64] This reasoning is not convincing. A least restrictive means test is known in many areas of domestic and international law irrespective of the remedy sought. It is not the purpose of such a test to point the acting state to ways to remedy the situation, but to ensure that the chosen measure in question did not infringe a legal right or status in a superfluously restrictive and thus unnecessary manner.

Third and last, it is argued that exceptions must always be seen in the context of the obligation to which they apply.[65] While this premise is certainly true, its impact remains unclear. The existence of exceptions in WTO law may have had some influence on the interpretation of substantive obligations,[66] but the extent of such influence remains vague. It does not necessarily follow that the exception itself must be read differently and even if it did, this may be taken into account properly during the interpretive process.

This is not to say that structural differences are unimportant or always negligible. Yet, in the particular case of WTO-like IIA exceptions, they must not be overstated. It thus seems much more compelling to take differences between the two systems into account during the interpretive process under use of Article 31(3)(c) VCLT and WTO law, rather than negating the relevance of WTO law a priori.[67]

D. Conclusion

Reliance on the GATT and GATS is often met with caution in the investment context. Investment arbitrators and scholars should, however, reconsider this reluctance in the case of WTO-like exceptions, as systemic objections are no reason to disregard the relevance of WTO jurisprudence from the outset.[68]

This is particularly compelling for FTAs that cover trade in goods and services as well as investments. When these treaties in their general parts establish exceptions

---

62 Alvarez and Brink (n 52), 349–352.

63 See *US–Sections 301–310 of the Trade Act of 1974* (22 December 1999) WT/DS152/R, paras 7.101–103.

64 Desierto (n 58), 129–130.

65 Alvarez and Brink (n 52), 344.

66 Henckels (n 58), 48–49.

67 Cf also Sacerdoti (n 56), 10; Robert Howse and Efraim Chalamish, 'The Use and Abuse of WTO Law in Investor-State Arbitration: A Reply to Jürgen Kurtz' (2009) 20 EJIL 1087, 1088–1090.

68 Cf also Mitchell and Henckels (n 52), 93–94; Andrew Newcombe, 'The Use of General Exceptions in IIAs: Increasing Legitimacy or Uncertainty?' in Armand De Mestral and Céline Lévesque (eds), *Improving International Investment Agreements* (Routledge 2013), 276; Markert (n 3), 169; Newcombe and Paradell (n 41), 504–505.

to the trade as well as the investment chapters, different interpretations may result in inconsistency within one single instrument and create a considerable amount of uncertainty. Such a result is certainly not intended by the treaty. As WTO-like exceptions in BITs, one must assume, deliberately take on the same style, renunciation of an interpretation parallel to the world trade regime would need to be substantiated with some argumentative effort, the level of which increases with the similarities of the IIA with the trade law exception.[69]

Accordingly, in the context of WTO-like exceptions, arbitrators thus should embrace Article 31(3)(c) VCLT. It is submitted that a strong presumption should be established to follow WTO jurisprudence as a source of relatively uniform and concise reasoning when interpreting exception clauses based on the GATT/GATS model. This assumption may of course be rebutted in the individual case, as divergence from WTO jurisprudence can be the result of the interpretive process. After all, Article 31 (3)(c) VCLT describes but only one element of interpretation.

This means, for example, that investment tribunals should assess a measure's necessity under a WTO-like exception based on the importance of the objective, the aptness of the measure to reach its aim, and the reasonable availability of alternative, less restrictive means. In line with WTO jurisprudence, tribunals may be best advised to pay states some deference when deciding on the importance of a public purpose and to not apply a full-scale proportionality test that could be used to question sensitive regulatory decisions by states.[70] This is true even more in the case of self-judging security exceptions, where the tribunal will be limited to a good faith-review. Beyond the issue of necessity, parallels also exist with regard to other generic terms used by exception clauses, such as 'public health' or 'essential security interests'. Here, too, international trade law should generally be used to inform the interpretation of investment law.

The investment regime currently witnesses an increasing use of these WTO-based exceptions and one can only guess whether treaty drafters were aware of the interpretive difficulties that arise from implanting a WTO provision into the investment context. The rationale behind such clauses is to widen states' regulatory powers. However, while the implementation of WTO-congruent exceptions has been praised by some,[71] others doubt the suitability of the 'copy and paste'

---

69 See also David Collins, 'The Line of Equilibrium: Improving the Legitimacy of Investment Treaty Arbitration through the Application of the WTO's General Exceptions' (2016) 32(4) Arb Int'l 575; Jürgen Kurtz, *The WTO and International Investment Law: Converging Systems* (CUP 2016), 168–228.

70 See Mitchell and Henckels (n 52), 151; Burke-White and von Staden (n 6), 370–376. See also *Continental Casualty Company v Argentina* (n 43) para 199. But see Alec Stone Sweet, 'Investor-State Arbitration: Proportionality's New Frontier' (2010) 4 Law & Ethics Hum Rts 47 (arguing in favour of a proportionality test).

71 Eg, Collins (n 69); Kurtz (n 69), 168–228; Yasuhei Taniguchi and Tomoko Ishikawa, 'Balancing Investment Protection and Other Public Policy Goals: Lessons from WTO Jurisprudence' in Julien Chaisse and Tsai-yu Lin (eds), *International Economic Law and Governance: Essays in Honour of Mitsuo Matsushita* (OUP 2016); Sabanogullari (n 4), 4–5; Markert (n 3), 168.

approach.[72] It lies outside the scope of this contribution to address this issue at length, but some scepticism seems appropriate. To name only two caveats, it stands to question whether an exception would cover expropriations and free states from liability, as expropriations for public purposes have been accompanied by a duty to compensate for centuries. It is further unclear how tribunals will align exception clauses with existing approaches to consider public interests when interpreting substantive protection standards.

There thus is reason for doubts, but there is also reason to hope that planting WTO-based exceptions will help in rebalancing the investment regime and increasing some of its legitimacy. In the end, it remains to be seen whether such clauses will bloom or wither in investment law and arbitration.

E. Annex: List of surveyed IIAs

TIPs:

Trans-Pacific Partnership Agreement
Korea–Turkey FTA
Brazil–Peru Economic and Trade
   Expansion Agreement
Australia–China FTA
Korea–Vietnam FTA
Japan–Mongolia EPA
Canada–Korea FTA
Treaty on the Eurasian Economic
   Union, Annex 16
Protocol on Trade in Services,
   Incorporation, Activities
   and Investments
Mexico–Panama FTA
Canada–Honduras FTA
Colombia–Panama FTA
Korea–Colombia FTA

China–Korea FTA
Canada–EU Comprehensive Economic
   and Trade Agreement
EU–Vietnam FTA
Honduras–Peru FTA
Korea–New Zealand FTA
ASEAN–India Investment Agreement
Australia–Japan EPA
Australia–Korea FTA
Additional Protocol to the Framework
   Agreement of the Pacific Alliance
Colombia–Israel FTA
New Zealand–Taiwan Economic
   Cooperation Agreement
Colombia–Costa Rica FTA
EFTA–Costa Rica–Panama FTA

---

72 See, eg, Barton Legum and Ioana Petculescu, 'GATT Article XX and International Investment Law' in Roberto Echandi and Pierre Sauvé (eds), *Prospects in International Investment Law and Policy: World Trade Forum* (CUP 2013), 340; Céline Lévesque, 'The Inclusion of GATT Article XX Exceptions in IIAs: A Potentially Risky Policy' in Echandi and Sauvé (eds) (n 73), 370; Andreas Kulick, *Global Public Interest in International Investment Law* (CUP 2012), 76; Alvarez and Brink (n 52), 342; Andrew Newcombe, 'General Exceptions in International Investment Agreements' in Marie-Claire Cordonier Segger, Markus W Gehring, and Andrew Newcombe (eds), *Sustainable Development in World Investment Law* (Kluwer Law International 2011), 369; Spears (n 3), 1064.

BITs:

Morocco–Nigeria
Nigeria–Singapore
Canada–Mongolia
Morocco–Russia
Mexico–UAE
Iran–Russia
Brazil–Colombia
Mauritius–Zambia
Canada–Guinea
Burkina Faso–Canada
Cambodia–Russia
Kyrgyzstan–Qatar
Canada–Mali
Japan–Kazakhstan
Canada–Serbia
Kenya–Korea
Georgia–Switzerland
Bahrain–Russia
Kenya–Turkey
Mali–Morocco
Japan–Myanmar
Netherlands–UAE
Colombia–Singapore
Japan–Mozambique
Kuwait–Mauritius
China–Tanzania
Kuwait–Mexico
Egypt–Mauritius

Chile–Hong Kong
Rwanda–Turkey
Japan–Kenya
Canada–Hong Kong
Iran–Slovakia
Kuwait–Kyrgyzstan
Azerbaijan–San Marino
Japan–Oman
Brazil–Mexico
Angola–Brazil
Japan–Ukraine
Kyrgyzstan–UAE
Canada–Senegal
Israel–Myanmar
Colombia–Turkey
Moldova–Montenegro
Greece–UAE
Belarus–Cambodia
Bahrain–Pakistan
Iraq–Jordan
India–UAE
Kenya–Kuwait
Belarus–Laos
Canada–Tanzania
Russia–Uzbekistan
Gambia–Turkey
Serbia–UAE

Argentina–Qatar
Morocco–Rwanda
Austria–Kyrgyzstan
Japan–Iran
Nigeria–UAE
Brazil–Chile
Mauritius–UAE
Guinea-Bissau–Morocco
Denmark–Macedonia
Brazil–Mozambique
Japan–Uruguay
Canada–Côte d'Ivoire
Kenya–UAE
Azerbaijan–Russia
Colombia–France
Korea–Myanmar
Canada–Nigeria
Kenya–Qatar
Cameroon–Canada
Cameroon–Korea
Guatemala–Russia
Guatemala–Trinidad
Morocco–Serbia
Japan–Saudi Arabia
Austria–Nigeria
Benin–UAE
Benin–Canada

4 International Norms

A Defence in Investment Treaty Arbitration?

Dr Dafina Atanasova[1]

A. Introduction

The right to regulate is at the centre of discussion in international investment law. This chapter tackles the question from a perspective only rarely brought forward – the right that the home state of the investor and the host state of the investment have to regulate *jointly*. It proceeds on the understanding that if a state's right to regulate at the national level is considered worthy of due consideration in investment proceedings, one would expect the same to be true to a stronger extent for the regulatory activity of *both* relevant states at the international plane.

The chapter traces the relevance of such jointly created international norms in the context of investment claims. It discusses the role they can play in investment treaty arbitration, and more specifically the conditions under which such norms (referred to as extraneous)[2] can be used as a defence in the proceedings.

The novelty of the chapter is in the general perspective it adopts, looking at the common conditions for application of extraneous norms in investment proceedings. It provides a roadmap on the common questions relevant to *all* international norms extraneous to the investment framework. Indeed, there are new fields with which investment norms will interact and conflict in the future. Rather than tackling these instances anew every time, a general study gives a starting point for their analysis. Thus, the chapter departs from current scholarly work on the integration of investment law within other branches of international law, which has mainly proceeded on an 'investment and ...' basis – focusing on the relation of investment norms and arbitration with one particular international law regime[3] at a time.

1 The chapter is based on a presentation delivered at a Conference in April 2016 organised by the Bucerius Law Journal (Hamburg, 2016) and part of a then ongoing doctoral dissertation at the University of Geneva.
2 The designation 'extraneous' mirrors the fact that the norms are subject to authoritative control of institutions or legal officials (including the state parties to them) outside of the investment legal framework.
3 The definition of regimes used in the chapter follows the one Young put forward: 'sets of norms, decision-making processes and organisations coalescing around functional issue-areas and dominated by particular modes of behavior, assumptions and biases' (p 11). The term is in no way used in order to imply as self-contained nature of such

The chapter outlines the conditions under which *any* extraneous norm could provide a viable defence for respondents in investment arbitration in a principled and internally coherent way. Grounded on research in private international law and legal theory, on occasion completed by comparative public law, the chapter presents the practically relevant insights of these sources.

The chapter moves in three sections. Section B defines the questions relevant for the integration of extraneous norms in investment arbitration. On this basis, Section C offers a conceptual framework for the place of extraneous norms in investment arbitration. Section D provides a practical example of the way in which that framework can be relevant in specific cases.

B. Defining the Questions Relevant for the Integration of Extraneous Norms in Investment Treaty Arbitration

A first step to integrating extraneous norms in investment arbitration is to identify the sequence of questions a tribunal is facing, whenever confronted with the relevance of such a norm. Identifying them seems particularly important, as the answer given to each of them is material for the extent to which extraneous norms are given effect in investment arbitration. At the same time arbitral reasoning on the topic often remains implicit, or is limited only to some of the questions identified as relevant.[4]

Consider for instance a case in which a foreign investor has begun a project for the creation of a wind power plant in State A. The investor is in the process of obtaining approval of the environmental impact assessment (EIA) for the project and has engaged substantial funds for it. It has received assurances from relevant government officials that the EIA will be approved. Consider further that State A institutes a moratorium on wind power plants in order to reassess their effect on the protected nesting areas situated in the region where the investment is made. Consider that on the basis of the stalled project, the investor then lodges a claim for breach of the fair and equitable treatment (FET) standard in an investment treaty between State A and its home state, arguing that its legitimate expectations have been violated. Now consider that the moratorium is instituted in application of a recommendation on the part of the Standing Committee to the Bern

---

structures, but rather in order to render simpler the reference to diverse structures of authority similar to the investment framework present at the international level. Margaret Young, 'Introduction: The Productive Friction between Regimes' in Margaret Young (ed), *Regime Interaction in International Law: Facing Fragmentation* (CUP 2012).

4 See eg *Bernhard von Pezold and others v Republic of Zimbabwe; Border Timbers et al v Republic of Zimbabwe*, ICSID Case No ARB/10/15&25, Procedural Order No 2, 26 June 2012; *SAUR International SA v Republic of Argentina*, ICSID Case No ARB/04/4, Decision on Jurisdiction and Liability, 6 June 2012; *Ioan Micula, Viorel Micula, SC European Food SA, SC Starmill SRL and SC Multipack SRL v Romania*, Award, 23 November 2013.

Convention,[5] which found that instituting it is necessary for the state to comply with its obligations under the Convention.

In such a case the tribunal faces a number of questions which are all material to the way in which an extraneous norm will be given effect in the arbitration. In particular: Is the extraneous norm part of the applicable law to the dispute at all? If so, how should arbitrators ascertain the meaning of the norm to decide whether it conflicts with a standard of protection in the controlling investment treaty? And if conflict is found to exist, what is the effect the extraneous norm can have on the scope of the standard of protection in question? The way in which the tribunal approaches each of these questions will play a crucial role in the outcome reached and the extent to which an extraneous norm will be integrated in investment arbitration.

The first question – asking whether the extraneous norm is part of the applicable law – relates to investment tribunals' adjudicative power, as circumscribed by the parties' will. In the hypothetical scenario earlier, the question is whether the tribunal is empowered to apply the Bern Convention. To answer it, the tribunal will search in the relevant legal instruments, ie the respective treaty and, when it is silent, the selected arbitration rules (and law) governing the arbitral procedure. Any norm *not* part of the applicable law under these instruments would be out of reach for the tribunal and thus could not be invoked as a defence in investment proceedings. Should the Bern Convention be outside the scope of applicable law the tribunal could not rule on the basis of its contents.

If the tribunal determines that the norm is applicable, how should it then answer the second question, namely how should it ascertain an extraneous norm's meaning? Should tribunals stop at the text of the norm in question or should they enquire into the way it has been interpreted; and whose interpretation is relevant? Often neglected, this question is essential for assigning to an extraneous norm its proper role *vis-à-vis* investment protection standards. In my example earlier, consider the importance of knowing whether the Bern Committee's recommendation counts as a source establishing the meaning of the Bern Convention obligations. To take a live-world example, consider also the difference it makes in the topical *Philip Morris v Uruguay* [6] of seeing the guidelines for implementation of the Framework Convention for Tobacco Control (FCTC) as an authoritative interpretative statement or not. In the latter case, the tribunal is tasked to consider whether the introduction of plain-packaging is reasonable (ie tasked to assess its regulatory soundness), in the former, as will be shown in Part C, it is expected to abstain from exactly this type of scrutiny.

Once the meaning of the relevant norms is ascertained, the tribunal must in turn assess whether that extraneous norm conflicts with the invoked investment

5 Convention on the Conservation of European Wildlife and Natural Habitats (Bern, 1979), Council of Europe.

6 *Philip Morris Brands Sàrl, Philip Morris Products SA and Abal Hermanos SA v Oriental Republic of Uruguay*, ICSID Case No ARB/10/7, Award, 8 July 2016. For the tribunal's discussion of the guidelines see paras 89–94, 396, 401, 411–412, 420.

standard in order to answer the third question. It is only when the two conflict that the extraneous norm can serve as a defence, ie as a reason not to apply the investment standard of protection. Otherwise the application of the extraneous norm cannot justify the state's actions inconsistent with the controlling investment treaty. To assert whether the two norms are in conflict, a tribunal must enquire whether both purport to regulate the case before it and if yes, whether applying them would lead to different results. This would be the case in one of the following two scenarios:[7] either the two norms create duties that cannot be complied with simultaneously, such as the respective duties of the state under the FET standard in the controlling investment treaty and the Bern Convention protection duty in the example earlier; or they create a right and a duty which contradict each other, as for instance in *UPS v Canada*, where Canada's national treatment duty under NAFTA contradicted its right to treat parcel and postal traffic differently for customs purposes under the World Customs Organization (WCO) Kyoto Conventions.[8]

Finally, if a conflict is found to exist, the tribunal must assess the effect the extraneous norm can have on the scope of application of the investment standard it conflicts with. Put differently, it must rule on which of the two norms should regulate the case before it. The panel will have to decide whether the Bern Convention duty or the right under the Kyoto Conventions or the FCTC could displace the invoked investment standard and under what conditions. If the tribunal decides that the extraneous norm prevails, the state would have succeeded in its defence – the investment standard of protection would be found inapplicable to its actions and the claim against it dismissed. Conversely, if the tribunal decides that the investment standard prevails, it will be the only controlling norm and the investor's claim would (if otherwise well-founded) be upheld.

7 The definition of conflict of norms adopted is consistent with the understanding of the phenomenon in legal theory and more recent scholarship in international law. Matthew H Kramer, *Objectivity and the Rule of Law* (CUP 2007) 125–127; Erich Vranes, 'The Definition of "Norm Conflict" in International Law and Legal Theory' (2006) 17 EJIL 395; Jorge E Viñuales, *Foreign Investment and the Environment in International Law* (CUP 2012) 44–45.

8 *United Parcel Service of America Inc v Government of Canada*, UNCITRAL, Award on the Merits, 24 May 2007 paras 87–120. The claimant, UPS, argued that the different customs treatment of parcels delivered by it and of Canada Post's non-monopoly products constituted a breach of Canada's national treatment duty under NAFTA. Canada, on its side, sustained that the different treatment was permitted under the Kyoto Convention (International Convention on the Simplification and Harmonization of Customs Procedures) (Kyoto, 1974) and the Revised Kyoto Convention (1999) of the WCO. Both contain different provisions of consignment and postal traffic, acknowledging the special character of this last type of traffic and the postal mandate more generally. The Kyoto Conventions *themselves* define postal and consignment traffic as different. They thus grant an *express* right to states to treat the two types of goods differently, at odds with Canada's national treatment obligation under NAFTA (as interpreted by the investor). The tribunal found, mainly on the basis of this international law distinction, that UPS and Canada Post were not in like circumstances and thus dismissed UPS's national treatment claim.

C. Conceptualizing the Role of Extraneous Norms in Investment Treaty Arbitration

The core argument of this chapter is that the manner in which a tribunal approaches extraneous norms and answers the questions identified in Section B should be guided by two series of considerations – the place of investment treaty norms within the broader framework of international law; and the role of investment tribunals *vis-à-vis* the relevant state parties and other international bodies tasked with interpreting and applying the relevant extraneous norms. The place of investment treaty norms is of particular relevance for answering the first question identified earlier, that of the applicability of extraneous norms in investment proceedings. The role of investment tribunals informs the answers to all other questions, illuminating what the effect should be of extraneous norms in investment disputes.

I. The Applicability of Extraneous Norms in Investment Proceedings – The Place of Investment Norms in International Law

Despite an assumption that the controlling investment treaty provides the primary source of applicable law for the merits of an investment dispute, there is no basis for limiting the sources of law a panel can apply in this way.[9] The chapter argues instead that all international norms in force between the home state of the investor and the host state of the investment are part of the international law applicable to investment disputes and as such can affect the scope of the host state's investment obligations.[10] Put in practical terms, if an investment claim is based on a factual setting involving a trade-related measure, the international trade law bearing on the issue can be applied in order to found the tribunal's reasoning on the *merits* of the investment claim.

The argument on applicability of the full range of international law norms in investment disputes is supported by the regulatory framework on applicable law

---

9 See eg A R Parra, 'Applicable Substantive Law in ICSID Arbitrations Initiated under Investment Treaties' (2001) 16 ICSID Review 20.

10 This is not to say that tribunals are competent to decide disputes having as legal basis any international law norm. There is a distinction between the norm used as a basis for the investor's claim (the cause of action) and the applicable norms in order to assess to what extent the claim is justified in law. Jurisdiction is typically determined by the terms of the controlling jurisdictional clause. On the subsidiary role which applicable law provisions can have in the determination of jurisdiction see: James Crawford, *State Responsibility: The General Part* (CUP 2013) 607; Lorand A Bartels, 'Jurisdiction and Applicable Law Clauses: Where Does a Tribunal Find the Principle Norms Applicable to the Case before It?' in Tomer Broude and Yuval Shany (eds), *Multi-Sourced Equivalent Norms in International Law* (Hart Publishing 2011) 123; Jorge E Viñuales, 'Foreign Investment and the Environment in International Law: An Ambiguous Relationship' (2010) 80 BYBIL 244, 264; Dafina Atanasova, Adrian Martinez Benoit and Josef Ostransky, 'The Legal Framework for Counterclaims in Investment Treaty Arbitration' (2014) 31 JIA 357, 374–375.

for investment disputes, as much as by core assumptions about the functioning of law at the ground level.

1. The International Law Framework on Applicable Law

The default position under the international law of treaties, if not circumscribed by the will of the relevant state parties, reveals the importance of extraneous norms. The Vienna Convention on the Law of Treaties (VCLT) expressly points to the relevance of other international norms when applying any treaty norm at several junctures. These are as much the interpretation of the norm, through Article 31 (3)(c), as its application, through Article 30, dealing with conflicting treaty-based legal norms. Other treaties are also taken into account when assessing the validity of a modification of a treaty norm (Article 41 on *inter se* modification of multi-lateral treaties) or a treaty's potential suspension or termination (Article 59), not to forget the compatibility of the norm under consideration with *jus cogens* rules (Article 53) or its possible recognition as part of international customary law (Article 38).

These instances cover the full life of any treaty norm that one purports to apply. They render international norms writ large relevant for the determination of the scope of investment standards of protection in a number of ways. Most relevant here, the existence of such references necessarily *implies* the applicability – the characterisation as formally part of the regulating legal rules – of all international norms to the relations of any two parties they are in force between.

The only real limitation of the applicability of international norms in investment arbitration is linked to the limited personal scope of certain sources of international law. International law and especially international treaty law results in something scholars compare to a 'spaghetti-bowl', due to the number of treaties simultaneously in force between variable parties. Thus, certain entitlements derived from international instruments must be disregarded on the formal ground that they are not in force between the relevant state parties, meaning the home state of the investor and the host state of the investment for investment arbitration.

The part of international law applicable in investment proceedings naturally includes all norms establishing obligations *erga omnes* and customary norms as both have by definition general personal scope of application. To the contrary, application of extraneous treaty norms is limited[11] by the *pacta tertii* rule (part of customary international law and embodied in Articles 30(4)(b) and 34 VCLT).[12] To revert to the wind power plant example, the investor's home state must be party to the Bern Convention for this one to apply to the case brought by the investor.

11 On personal scope of application of different international law norms see eg Samantha A Besson, 'Theorizing the Sources of International Law' in Samantha A Besson (ed), *The Philosophy of International Law* (OUP 2010) 168–169.

12 See eg Jean Salmon, 'Les Antinomies En Droit International Public' in Chaïm Perelman (ed), *Les Antinomies En Droit* (E Bruylant 1965); Erich Vranes, *Trade and the Environment: Fundamental Issues in International Law, WTO Law, and Legal Theory* (OUP 2009) Chapter 2.

It is important to note in this respect that the fact that one party to an investment dispute is an individual does not limit the applicability of extraneous norms. Even assuming that investors hold substantive rights under investment treaties, as the tribunal pointed out in *Electrabel v Hungary*, one 'cannot disconnect the rights of individual investors from the rights of their home states'.[13] Indeed, a reasonable construction of investment treaties suggests that investors' rights are best analysed as qualified and interdependent with those of their home state.[14] It has been convincingly demonstrated that investors' position cannot be equated to that of individuals under human rights treaties.[15] In particular, investment treaties exhibit aspects of bilateralism which suggest an important link between the investor and their home state. In addition, recent drafting practices in free trade agreements (FTAs) typically assign a subsidiary role to the investment chapter within the treaty[16] and thus confirm that investors' position is subject to limitations and linked to norms that apply at the inter-state level.

2. The Investment Law Framework on Applicable Law

At the backdrop of this general framework on applicable law, states are, subject to *jus cogens* rules, free to define the sources of law which regulate their relations. They have only rarely exercised this power in investment treaties, however. Where they have, the applicable law provisions they have provided point in the same direction as the VCLT.

Provisions regulating applicable law in investment arbitration almost invariably direct tribunals to apply international law. This is true for the limited number of treaties containing an applicable law clause,[17] with the notable exception of

---

13 *Electrabel SA v Republic of Hungary*, ICSID Case No ARB/07/19, Decision on Jurisdiction, Applicable Law and Liability, 30 November 2012, para 4.188.

14 Anthea Roberts, 'State-to-State Investment Treaty Arbitration: A Hybrid Theory of Interdependent Rights and Shared Interpretive Authority' (2014) 55 Harvard International Law Journal 1.

15 Anthea Roberts, 'Power and Persuasion in Investment Treaty Interpretation: The Dual Role of States' (2010) 104 American Journal of International Law 179, 205; Moche Hirsch, 'Investment Tribunals and Human Rights: Divergent Paths' in Pierre-Marie Dupuy, Francesco Francioni and Ernst-Ulrich Petersmann (eds), *Human Rights in International Investment Law and Arbitration* (OUP 2009); U Kriebaum, 'Is the European Court of Human Rights an Alternative to Investor-State Arbitration?' (OUP 2009) 6 *TDM*; Gus Van Harten, *Investment Treaty Arbitration and Public Law* (OUP 2007) 136–143.

16 For a sample of such provisions in treaties concluded recently see eg Korea–Colombia FTA (2013) Article 8.2; New Zealand–Taiwan Economic Cooperation Agreement (2013) Chapter 14, Article 4; Mexico–Panama FTA (2014) Article 10.2(6); Australia–Korea FTA (2014) Article 11.2; Canada–Korea FTA (2014) Article 8.2; Transpacific Partnership Agreement (2016) Article 9.3. See also CAFTA–DR (2004) Article 10.2.

17 Consider for instance that only six of the United Kingdom's bilateral investment treaties (BITs) contain an applicable law clause for investment arbitration.

India.[18] Most clauses include language directing tribunals to apply the 'rules' or 'principles' of international law.[19] Certain provisions even require them expressly to apply other treaties in force between the relevant state parties.[20] In the same vein, when the controlling treaty does not contain an applicable law provision, the relevant arbitration rules do not preclude the application of international norms. Article 42 of the ICSID Convention (and Article 55 of the ICSID Additional Facility Rules) direct tribunals to apply international law expressly.[21] Other rules, while silent on the place of international law, grant important margin of discretion to tribunals to determine the law applicable to the case before them;[22] and tribunals have generally interpreted these provisions as granting them the power to apply international law in the same terms as under the ICSID framework.[23]

Broadly termed applicable law provisions are coupled with a structural limitation on the possibility to review a tribunal's determination that any given norm (be it of domestic or international law) is applicable. As a matter of principle, a mistake in the applicable law does not constitute ground for annulment of the award.[24] Thus, concerns about the validity of the award are not pertinent for a tribunal's decision to limit itself to the application of norms contained in the controlling investment treaty either.

3. Taking Extraneous Norms Seriously

If taken seriously, the conclusions on applicable law in Sections 1 and 2 mean that international norms, as described earlier, should be part of the international

---

18 India's BITs typically require tribunals to base their award on 'the provisions of the [BIT]' only. This formulation can have the effect of limiting other international norms' applicability and rendering them relevant only to the extent they have a bearing on an investment norm's interpretation.

19 Clauses referring to one of the two (or both) seem to make up the majority of treaty language used currently.

20 See eg ASEAN–Australia–New Zealand FTA (2009), Chapter 11, Article 27(1).

21 The formulation is understood to apply to the full range of international law sources. See History of the ICSID Convention, vol 1, 192; History of the ICSID Convention, vol 2, 802; Report of the Executive Directors of the ICSID Convention, para 40.

22 Article 35(1) of the UNCITRAL Rules for International Commercial Arbitration gives to the tribunal the power to apply 'the law which it determines appropriate'. A similar provision can be found in the rules of the Arbitration Institute of Stockholm Chamber of Commerce, as well as in the Arbitration Rules of the International Chamber of Commerce, respectively at Article 22(1) SCC and Article 21(1) ICC.

23 Florian Grisel, *L'arbitrage International Ou Le Droit Contre L'ordre Juridique: Application et Création Du Droit En Arbitrage International* (Fondation Varenne 2011) 69–76.

24 Decisions upholding the tribunal's power to apply the international norms of its choice, see eg *Slovak Republic v Achmea BV (formerly Eureko BV), Higher Regional Court of Frankfurt*, Decision of 10 May 2012, 26 SchH 11/10; *The Government of the Kaliningrad Region v Republic of Lithuania*, Paris Court of Appeal Decision of 18 November 2010; *Wena Hotels Limited v Arab Republic of Egypt*, ICSID Case No ARB/98/4, Decision on Application for Annulment, 5 February 2002 para 53.

framework against which the legality of state behaviour is assessed in investment proceedings, at equal footing with the investment treaty.[25] Indeed, it is
never a norm in isolation which determines conclusively one's rights and duties
under the law.[26] The norms derived from legal sources other than the one
serving as basis for the claim presented for adjudication still affect the scope of
the rights under consideration. A decision is rather based on the full range of
legal norms of the applicable legal system which have a bearing on the factual
situation.

The fact that investment disputes typically involve the review of a domestic
governmental measure adopted by the host state of the investment does not
detract from this conclusion. When the challenged measure constitutes a good
faith implementation of an extraneous norm, one should not ignore the link
between it and the extraneous norm it implements. Ignoring this link would be
equivalent to investment tribunals giving priority to investment standards over
other international norms, by ignoring the international ground on which the
scrutinised measure was adopted.[27]

Such a *de facto* hierarchisation between the two sets of norms is not justifiable,
given that both extraneous and investment norms are situated at the plane of
international law, and satisfy equally the conditions of legality under it.[28] To argue
otherwise would reduce the scrutinised extraneous norm to a (legally unrecog-
nised) interest of the respondent state.[29] This would run against the law making
role of states in international law, by ignoring the status of their normative production as equivalent to investment norms. It would also deprive of meaning all
applicable law provisions in investment treaties which refer tribunals to other
treaties between the relevant contracting states.

II. The Effect of Extraneous Norms in Investment Disputes – The Role of Investment Tribunals in International Law

At the backdrop of the analysis earlier, what are the factors that should impact
tribunals' reasoning when determining what the relevant extraneous norms mean,
whether they conflict with an investment standard and, if they do, which one

---

25 Joseph Raz, *The Authority of Law: Essays on Law and Morality* (OUP 2009) 33.
26 ibid.
27 Jorge Viñuales, 'The Environmental Regulation of Foreign Investment Schemes under
International Law' in Pierre-Marie Dupuy and Jorge Viñuales (eds), *Harnessing Foreign Investment to Promote Environmental Protection Incentives and Safeguards* (CUP
2013) 280–285. We need to acknowledge, nevertheless, that in certain cases parties'
arguments are at the root of the conservative approach adopted by investment
tribunals.
28 Viñuales, *Foreign Investment and the Environment in International Law* (n 7) 44–48.
29 Radi refers to values recognised in law as 'meta-interests' for instance to distinguish
them from interests more generally, some of which might not be legally enforced.
Yannick Radi, 'Standardization: A Dynamic and Procedural Conceptualization of
International Law-Making' (2012) 25 LJIL 283, 268.

should prevail? The answer to these questions is not provided in the investment treaty or the treaty the extraneous norm comes from.[30] Nor do the classic international law techniques for conflict (avoidance and) resolution provide a definite answer.[31] To operationalise the available conflict resolution framework under international law, they need to be embedded in a broader understanding of the underlying institutional and regulatory structure tribunals operate in.

What follows is thus an analysis of the institutional structure investment tribunals are part of. Indeed, cases in which a state invokes an extraneous norm as a defence bring forward important questions of authority interaction.[32] That is, they bring forward the relations between three sets of 'officials' (ie individuals/entities entrusted with ensuring the functioning) of the international legal system, each claiming authority to regulate the factual circumstances in which an international law defence is brought.[33] The first is the investment tribunal, entrusted with ensuring the implementation of the investment treaty; the second – the relevant states holding the primary law-making power at the international plane; the third, because of international law's heterarchical structure – the bodies entrusted with ensuring the implementation of the extraneous norm invoked in investment proceedings. The relations of investment tribunals with the two other sets of officials should influence the proper effect of extraneous norms in investment disputes and are examined in more detail later.

1. Tribunals' Role Vis-à-Vis the Contracting Parties

In order to explain the relation between investment tribunals and states acting jointly at the international level, it is practical to refer to two revealing statements.

The first comes out of the United States pleadings in *Glamis Gold*. The United States representatives argued that international instruments 'reflect the "policy" of

---

30 Conflict clauses contained in investment treaties may sometimes offer guidance on particular instances of conflict and thus on the possibility to build a successful defence on a particular extraneous norm. Their role will, for the sake of brevity, not be addressed here.

31 In effect, while international conflict resolution principles are a testament to the need to see international law as a whole, they are not logical axioms and do not typically provide specific solutions in particular cases. For an analysis of classic conflict resolution principles in domestic and international law see eg James Crawford and Penelope Nevill, 'Relations between International Courts and Tribunals: The "Regime Problem"' in Margaret A Young (ed), *Regime Interaction in International Law: Facing Fragmentation* (CUP 2012); Vranes (n 12) 45ff; Neil MacCormick, *Rhetoric and the Rule of Law: A Theory of Legal Reasoning* (OUP 2005) 190–205; Michel van de Kerchove and François Ost, *Le Système Juridique Entre Ordre et Désordre* (Presses universitaires de France 1988) 139–141; Norberto Bobbio, 'Des Critères Pour Résoudre Les Antinomies' in Chaïm Perelman (ed), *Les Antinomies En Droit: Études* (E Bruylant 1965).

32 See Nicole Roughan, *Authorities: Conflicts, Cooperation, and Transnational Legal Theory* (OUP 2013) 45–47.

33 In this case, the officials have shared domains. Roughan (n 32).

the international community'.[34] This statement describes well the power that any two states have to define the norms applicable to their relations and to the individuals in their common regulatory space. Just as the two states define the standards in an investment treaty, they define, in the same capacity as sovereigns, the extraneous international norms applicable in investment cases.[35] Both normative acts – investment and extraneous – reflect their common policy decisions and have the same status as acts of the 'joint sovereign.'[36] Formally the two types of norms have the same normative value under international law (with the exception of *jus cogens* norms).

The second statement is authored by Jan Paulsson in a, by now, classic paper and is relevant for understanding the role of investment tribunals. According to Paulsson, 'International tribunals do not establish policy. They give effect to international agreements.'[37] While the use of the present tense may be questioned sometimes, it seems in any case accurate that international (investment) tribunals *should not* as a general rule establish policy, but should limit themselves to the extent possible to giving effect to international norms applicable to the case before them.

Indeed, it is accepted in legal theory that, outside of constitutional review, the judiciary does not have the power to review the desirability and appropriateness of legislative acts.[38] Even authors calling for judicial review of acts of the legislature consider that such a review should be very limited: 'merely to ensure conformity to the [formal] rule of law'.[39] Similarly, the role of establishing international policy should be reserved to the relevant states acting together. Investment tribunals are not the proper reviewers of the desirability of such policy choices, nor of the degree

---

34 *Glamis Gold Ltd v United States of America*, Counter-memorial of Respondent, 19 September 2006, 35.

35 See eg Samantha Besson, 'The Authority of International Law — Lifting the State Veil' (Social Science Research Network 2009) SSRN; Jeremy Waldron, 'The Rule of International Law' (2006) 30 HJLPP 15.

36 The term is borrowed from Anthea Roberts, 'Triangular Treaties: The Extent and Limits of Investment Treaty Rights' (2015) 56 Harvard International Law Journal 353.

37 Jan Paulsson, 'The Power of States to Make Meaningful Promises to Foreigners' (2010) 1 Journal of International Dispute Settlement 341, 348.

38 As Kramer points out using the example of a constitutionally permissible distinction based on ethnicity: 'In the event that a general law does favour certain people by reference to their ethnicity, any impartial implementation of that law by adjudicative or administrative officials will obviously involve their adverting to people's ethnic background.' Kramer (n 7) 177–178.

39 Raz (n 25) 217. Although the risk of certain abuse on the part of states acting jointly is certainly present, investment tribunals do not seem the proper judges of such common abuse. To refer to a domestic law analogy, potential abuse on the part of the legislator is typically avoided through the constitutional limits imposed on it. In international law, *jus cogens* norms impose narrow limits of a similar nature on the substance of states' joint sovereign will. As such, a superior role cannot be assigned to investment standards *vis-à-vis* extraneous norms, nor can investment tribunals' activity be compared to constitutional review.

to which they are the proper tools for achieving the objectives the states set for them. In this sense, investment tribunals should abstain from reviewing the common normative production of states acting in their capacity as 'joint sovereign'.

The advantage of relying on an international-law-based defence lies exactly in this relation between tribunals and states acting jointly: the right to regulate of a single state under international law is necessarily limited or the essence of international law norms as regulators of states' activities would be lost; to the contrary, the regulatory activity of states acting *together* at the international plane is not, or the essence of states' power as law making officials of the international legal system would be unduly undermined.

To go back to the hypothetical scenario from Section B, the foregoing brief remarks mean that an investment tribunal would not be justified in considering whether protecting a nesting area for migrating birds is a worthwhile objective. Nor will it be justified in assessing whether the obligations set in the Bern Convention are necessary and capable of achieving the objective of protection. Both would constitute, alongside the investment standards, legal norms it is simply bound to apply.

2. Tribunals' Role Vis-à-Vis Other Interpreting Bodies

The relation of investment tribunals with international bodies entrusted with the implementation of extraneous norms has similar implications. As a starting point, this relation is premised on equality. As there is currently no hierarchy between international law regimes, their respective institutions are in a position of equality under law.[40] In addition, to recognise the equal normative value of extraneous norms is necessarily coupled with the recognition of the competence of the bodies entrusted with interpreting and applying them.[41]

To recognise an extraneous regime and its institutions as equal can only yield effective results if the tenure of its norms is construed 'correctly' in investment cases. Otherwise the norms' meaning can be distorted, harming the perception of fairness of the conducted proceedings.[42] In any given legal system this would mean that an adjudicator is to interpret the norms 'in accordance with what would be expected by a dispassionate observer who knows those formulations and who also knows the *interpretative canons* that prevail within the system'.[43] In a

---

40 Besson (n 11) 183.
41 Tomer Broude, 'Fragmentation(s) of International Law: On Normative Integration as Authority Allocation' in Ruth Eschelbacher Lapidoth and Tomer Broude (eds), *The Shifting Allocation of Authority in International Law – Considering Sovereignty, Supremacy and Subsidiarity: Essays in Honour of Professor Ruth Lapidoth* (Hart Publishing 2008). The author demonstrates the correlation between the resistance of an adjudicator to apply a norm and the recognition of authority of the regime in which the norm originates.
42 On the need of congruence between the law in the books and the law applied for the preservation of the rule of law see: Lon Fuller, *The Morality of Law* (Yale UP 1964); Kramer (n 7).
43 Kramer (n 7) 139.

heterarchical system such as international law, the familiarity and use of the prevailing interpretative canons acquires added importance. Different regimes develop different interpretative canons over time, especially when there are adjudicative bodies within the regimes in question.[44] In such a setting tribunals need to acknowledge the legitimacy of the various interpretative techniques present across regimes and their expression in their diverse sources of law. To interpret and apply an extraneous norm correctly is to do so in accordance with the interpretative canons prevailing in the regime in which the norm originated, much in the same way private international law requires an adjudicator to apply the foreign law as if she was a judge of the particular legal system.[45]

In more practical terms, to require from investment arbitrators to interpret and apply norms from other regimes as if they were judges of those regimes means that they should take into account and give weight to secondary sources of the regime in question, such as judicial decisions, interpretative reports or regulatory acts emanating from international organisations' organs. It is those acts authored by the relevant institutions and in accordance with the applicable interpretative canons that express the meaning of the norms in the regime's founding treaty(ies). It is not a novel statement that bodies competent to ensure states' compliance with an international norm contribute through their activity to specifying the norm's tenure and ultimately to the formation of the law of the particular regime.[46]

This conclusion imposes itself whether facing a judicial controlling organ or one entrusted with 'continued' institutional control.[47] Regarding the role of the international adjudicator, it is hardy disputed that she 'does not simply resolve an individual dispute, but at this occasion, [s]he often contributes also to the specification, to the development even, of international law'.[48] In the same vein, when it comes to the role of other institutions entrusted with the effective application of a certain norm a similar specifying effect arises from their activities.[49] For instance, the recommendations of the World Heritage Committee, as well as the different reports otherwise institutionally and procedurally framed under the auspices of UNESCO, seem to provide an authoritative (albeit not binding) interpretation of the requirements of the UNESCO Conventions.[50] Returning to the wind power

---

44 See eg Richard Gardiner, *Treaty Interpretation* (OUP 2010). The author suggests as early as page 7 of the book that 'systemic use of the rules [of interpretation] as a practical means of treaty interpretation still has scope for improvement', even finding that in certain cases they are paid 'no more than lip service'.

45 Sofie Geeroms, *Foreign Law in Civil Litigation: A Comparative and Functional Analysis* (OUP 2004) 181–194.

46 Radi (n 29) 212.

47 ibid 212–224.

48 Pierre-Marie Dupuy, *Droit International Public* (Dalloz 2014) 554; Alan Boyle and Christine Chinkin, *The Making of International Law* (OUP 2007) 263–311.

49 Radi (n 29) 212–213.

50 For a presentation of the institutional procedures at UNESCO see eg Radi (n 29). For different mechanisms of control more generally see: ibid 212–8; Hélène Ruiz Fabri, LA Sicilianos and JM Sorel (eds), *L'effectivité Des Organisations Internationales: Mécanismes de Suivi et de Contrôle: Journées Franco-Helléniques 7–8 Mai 1999* (Sakkoulas/Pedone 2000).

plant example again, the same would be true with regard to the recommendations of Bern Convention Standing Committee.

The distribution of authority between investment tribunals and these various interpretative bodies suggests that investment tribunals should limit their review not only of an extraneous norm as formulated by the 'joint sovereign' discussed in the previous section, but also of the decisions of an interpretative body pertaining to it. Interpretative bodies from other fields of international law are in a better relative position to provide the interpretation of the extraneous norm than investment tribunals, as they are the extraneous norm's primary 'law-applying organs'.[51] Or put in practical terms, they are the ones whose decisions one examines to say whether a given state is complying with its obligations under the relevant instrument. Thus, tribunals should abstain from re-interpreting extraneous norms the tenure of which is already set by such interpretative bodies.

D. Extraneous Norms and the Protection of Legitimate Expectations

The insights identified earlier are not simply theoretically interesting. Recognising investment tribunals' respective position *vis-à-vis* states and other interpreting bodies can lead to an enhanced understanding of the scope of investment standards of protection. The earlier insights are thus practically relevant when analysing a specific international-based defence brought before an investment tribunal.

To illustrate this point I will refer to the Bern Convention hypothetical example again. This chapter made clear that the Bern Convention is part of the applicable law regulating the dispute between the investor and State A. It also identified the Permanent Committee's recommendation as an authoritative statement of State A's duties under the Convention. When analysed in this way, State A is under two conflicting duties – that to institute a moratorium on the building of wind power plants under the Bern Convention, and that to protect the investor's expectation to build its power plant under the relevant BIT. The remaining question is thus whether State A's obligation not to frustrate the investor's legitimate expectations under FET trumps its protection obligation under the Bern Convention.

To decide on the ultimate effect of the Bern-Convention-based duties on these investors' claims under FET, the tribunal will need to rely on reasoning by analogy, as no set rule exists in international law regulating this type of normative conflict. The most readily available source of inspiration for determining the scope of protection of legitimate expectations is comparative public law. Indeed, the protection of legitimate expectations found its way to the international (investment) plane from domestic (administrative) law.[52] To understand its appropriate

---

51 Raz (n 25) 108.

52 See eg Michele Potestà, 'Legitimate Expectations in Investment Treaty Law: Understanding the Roots and the Limits of a Controversial Concept' (2013) 28 ICSID Review 88; C Brown, 'The Protection of Legitimate Expectations as a "General Principle of Law": Some Preliminary Thoughts' (2009) 6 Transnational Dispute Management (TDM), www.transnational-dispute-management.com/article.asp?key=1303 accessed 18 March 2015; Elizabeth Snodgrass, 'Protecting Investors' Legitimate

scope one would refer to comparative domestic law and the protection that expectations are granted in different systems.

The type of institutional relations that investment tribunals have with states and other interpretative bodies identified in Section C is also relevant to this analysis. It provides the appropriate comparators for extraneous norms in domestic legal systems. Given that tribunals should abstain from substantive review of extraneous norms, the appropriate norms in domestic legal systems to compare them to are similarly norms not subject to substantive review by the courts. In domestic administrative law such a place is reserved to legislative acts. Thus, the extraneous norm, in this case the obligation to protect under the Bern Convention, should be compared to a legislative act in administrative law. In other words, to determine whether the protection of legitimate expectations should prevail over that obligation, the relevant question in administrative law terms is whether legitimate expectations protect against changes in the law and, if yes, in what circumstances.

Considering the position of the investor in the Bern Convention example, government assurances contrary to the law would not yield protection under most domestic legal systems. In effect, an examination of even the legal systems most protective of legitimate expectations (or functionally similar doctrines)[53] suggests that when a governmental agency makes a representation – individualised or not – which contradicts the law in force at the time that representation was made, such representation cannot give rise to protected expectations.[54] The rationale behind this solution is to protect the principle of legality.[55] Furthermore, this is the case whether the representation is contrary to a norm imposing a duty or granting a right.[56] If transposed to the realm of investment arbitration, this solution would give priority to the extraneous norm over investors' legitimate expectations. Host state representations contrary to an international norm in force at the time the investment was made, could not render an investor's expectation that such norm would not be complied with legitimate. Thus, State A would be able to successfully invoke its obligations under the Bern Convention as a defence against the investor's claim.

Consider also the scenario of a second investor, holder of a building permit under the law of State A, but otherwise in a position analogous to that of the first investor. This second investor, by virtue of holding a building permit, also would as a general rule hold individual rights under State A's law. This investor is in a

---

Expectations – Recognizing and Delimiting a General Principle' (2006) 21 ICSID Review 1.

53   Duncan Fairgrieve, *State Liability in Tort: A Comparative Law Study* (OUP 2003) 144–146; Søren Schønberg, *Legitimate Expectations in Administrative Law* (OUP 2003) 140–143; Jürgen Schwarze, *Droit Administratif Européen* (Bruylant 2009) 913–985.

54   German law provides an exception to this statement (Schwarze). Hector Mairal, 'Legitimate Expectations and Informal Administrative Representations' in Stephan Schill (ed), *International Investment Law and Comparative Public Law* (OUP 2010) 429–430; Schønberg (n 53) 147; Schwarze (n 53) 941.

55   Schønberg (n 53) 150.

56   ibid 147, 150.

situation which the protection of legitimate expectations in domestic legal systems has at its core, namely the protection of acquired rights. It is the most uncontroversial aspect of the doctrine. Most systems provide for the irrevocability of an act conferring a right or for compensation for its revocation, at least in certain circumstances; this even when the act has been conferred in violation of the law.[57] Authors also almost invariably consider that the prejudice suffered by an individual of frustrating their expectations in these circumstances outweighs the possible adverse effects for the community.[58] Thus the success of the second investor's claim would not be affected by State A's duties under the Bern Convention, as the investor's acquired right, albeit based on an act contrary to the state's international duties, would remain protected.

As this last passage illustrates, the suggested approach does not deprive investors of effective protection – core protections of investors' entitlements in the host state would not really be affected by other international norms' implementation. Rather it has the potential to provide a more principled framework for analysing the permissibility of states' conduct under international (investment) law, thus alleviating the liability concerns that states may have when deciding to implement a non-investment international norm.

E. Conclusion

Investment tribunals seem to adopt a rather narrow approach to the international norms that they have the power (and arguably a duty) to apply to the merits of disputes before them, considering the controlling investment treaty as the primary source of applicable law to the dispute before them. However, the framework in which investment tribunals operate does not justify limiting the application of other international norms, such as extraneous norms, in this way. Indeed, both the legal framework of applicable law in investment proceedings and the institutional position of investment tribunals in international law suggest that extraneous norms have a role to play in deciding investment disputes. For one, extraneous norms can and should be considered part of the applicable law before investment tribunals at equal footing with the controlling investment treaty. Tribunals can and should also recognise the possibility for such norms to serve as a defence in investment arbitration, thus under certain circumstances displacing the particular investment standard of protection.

---

57 ibid 64–106; Georg Notle, 'General Principles of German and European Administrative Law – A Comparison in Historical Perspective' (1994) 57 *Modern Law Review* 191, 195; Meinhard Schröder, 'Administrative Law in Germany' in René Seerden (ed), *Administrative Law of the European Union, its Member States and the United States: a Comparative Analysis* (Intersentia 2012) 116–122; Fairgrieve (n 53) 144–150.

58 Schønberg (n 53) 104–105.

5 The Right to Regulate

Towards a (Not Entirely) New Regulatory Paradigm under Recent FTA Investment Chapters

Elsa Sardinha[1]

A. Introduction

Inherent tension exists between the public nature of the interests at stake in international investment disputes and the private character of the contractual relationships between the parties to investor-state arbitrations.[2] Investment disputes often involve lucrative damage claims against states, which may require arbitrators to scrutinise a government's regulatory decisions.[3] In deciding these cases, and interpreting and applying the relevant law, arbitrators often engage in a dynamic balancing of interests between the claimant investor(s) and the respondent state. The arbitral process has come under attack by those who perceive it to unbalance the equilibrium established between the state parties and investors.[4] While several recent innovations to investment treaty drafting were prompted by criticisms in certain quarters aimed at questions of the legitimacy of investor-state arbitration,[5] these changes also acknowledge the potential uncertainties born out of competing methodological approaches to treaty interpretation. This is particularly so for

1 Research Associate and Practice Fellow, Centre for International Law, National University of Singapore. Doctoral Candidate, McGill University Faculty of Law. Barrister and Solicitor in Ontario and British Columbia, Canada (2010). Email: elsa.sardinha@gmail.com. I thank J. Christopher Thomas QC for illuminating discussions on this topic. All errors are my own.
2 William B Burke-White and Andreas von Staden, 'Private Litigation in a Public Law Sphere: The Standard of Review in Investor-State Arbitrations' (2010), 35 *Yale Journal of International Law* 283, 285.
3 Christian J Tams, 'An Appealing Option? The Debate about an ICSID Appellate Structure' (June 2006) *Essays in Transnational Economic Law* 57, 5.
4 Alex Mills, 'The Balancing (and Unbalancing?) of Interests in International Investment Law and Arbitration' in Shaheeza Lalani and Rodrigo Polanco Lazo (eds), *The Role of the State in Investor-State Arbitration* (Brill/Nijhoff 2014) 437–465, 437; Elsa Sardinha, 'Party-Appointed Arbitrators No More: The EU-Led Investment Tribunal System as an (Imperfect?) Response to Certain Legitimacy Concerns in Investor-State Arbitration' (2018), *The Law and Practice of International Courts and Tribunals* 17, 117–134.
5 Elsa Sardinha, 'The Impetus for the Creation of an Appellate Mechanism' (2017), 32 (3) *ICSID Review* 503–527.

arbitral tribunals that must contend with legal issues that remain unresolved by existing rules of customary international law or a consistent line of case law. By enshrining their inherent, and thus not entirely new, right to regulate in the public interest, defining substantive obligations to investors with far greater precision than ever before, and detailing exceptions to those protections, states are leaving less up to chance.

At a time when investor-state dispute settlement (ISDS) is facing significant opposition by some states and stakeholders, recent international investment agreements (IIAs) reflect an evolved – but not necessarily *new* – regulatory approach taken by states. IIAs negotiated in the last decade generally provide a detailed body of law within their texts, which seeks to add clarity and predictability to the current regime by reducing the discretion arbitral tribunals would otherwise enjoy when applying and interpreting broadly drafted treaty provisions. Recall that up until the mid-1990s, states tended to conclude skeletally drafted and generally worded treaties, thus leaving it open to arbitral tribunals to particularise the contours of core investment protections.[6] Early bilateral investment treaties (BITs) were short – rarely longer than a few pages – and skeletal in content with respect to the ISDS clause, substantive standards of treatment, and the definition of 'investment'. The procedural and substantive obligations included only bare-bones descriptions, which provided relatively minimal interpretative guidance to arbitral tribunals.[7]

This chapter examines the resurgent emphasis on states' inherent power to regulate for public welfare objectives, so-called 'return of the state', in the investment chapters of three free trade agreements (FTAs) – the recently signed, but not yet in force, Comprehensive Progressive Trans-Pacific Partnership (CPTPP),[8]

6 Open-textured provisions were common in the 'first generation' of investment treaties from the 1950s to the 1990s. Zachary Douglas, 'The MFN Clause in Investment Arbitration Treaty Interpretation off the Rails' (2011) 2 Journal of International Dispute Settlement 97, 99–100; Wolfgang Alschner, 'Interpreting Investment Treaties as Incomplete Contracts: Lessons from Contract Theory (18 July 2013), SSRN, http://papers.ssrn.com/sol3/papers.cfm?abstract_id=2241652 accessed 9 April 2018.

7 Karin L Kizer and Jeremy K Sharpe, 'Reform of Investor-State Dispute Settlement: The U.S. Experience' in Anna Joubin-Bret and Jean E Kalicki (eds), *Reshaping the Investor-State Dispute Settlement System, Journeys for the 21ˢᵗ Century* (Brill/Nijhoff 2015) 176; Elizabeth Boomer, 'Rethinking Rights and Responsibilities in Investor-State Dispute Settlement: Some Model International Investment Agreement Provisions' in Anna Joubin-Bret and Jean E Kalicki (eds), *Reshaping the Investor-State Dispute Settlement System, Journeys for the 21ˢᵗ Century* (Brill/Nijhoff 2015) 184.

8 The Trans-Pacific Partnership (TPP) was signed 4 February 2016, but the Donald Trump-led US Administration withdrew from the deal on 24 January 2017, in a purported effort to renegotiate the US' approach to trade and investment deals. On 11 November 2017, the TPP was renamed the Comprehensive and Progressive Agreement for Trans-Pacific Partnership (CPTPP). The final CPTPP text was released on 20 February 2018 CPTPP, was signed 8 March 2018, and will enter into force 60 days after at least six of the 11 signatories complete their respective domestic ratification procedures. The US is reportedly considering whether it will rejoin CPTPP, but Trump's rhetoric on this has been conflicting. www.mfat.govt.nz/assets/CPTPP/ Comprehensive-and-Progressive-Agreement-for-Trans-Pacific-Partnership-CPTPP-Engl ish.pdf accessed 9 April 2018.

the now in force Canada–EU Comprehensive Economic Trade Agreement (CETA),[9] and the recently revised final text of the EU–Singapore FTA Investment Protection Agreement (EUSFTA IPA or, simply, EUSFTA).[10] CPTPP, CETA, and EUSFTA are among the most complex and comprehensive trade agreements ever negotiated.[11] A dissection of these treaties reveals a common trend towards addressing relatively new issues which have not been explicitly addressed previously in treaty-making practices. While the structure of these treaties is akin to that of the 1992 North American Free Trade Agreement (NAFTA),[12] the normative content is much expanded.[13]

Section B deals with the genesis of states' concerns about preserving their policy space. Section C deconstructs the suggestion in some circles of a 'return of the state' regulatory approach to ISDS. Section D undertakes a comparative analysis of the latest developments in the investment chapters of CPTPP, CETA, and EUSFTA, with a view to identifying convergences and divergences between these agreements with respect to the right to regulate. The discussion in this section traces back the origins of the language employed in the four principle investment protections: (1) fair and equitable treatment (FET); (2) expropriation; (3) national treatment; and (4) most-favoured nation (MFN) treatment. The discussion also attempts to elucidate what effect, in practice, the more detailed language employed in these treaties can hope to have in investor-state awards

9 Canada–EU Comprehensive Economic and Trade Agreement (CETA), final text 29 February 2016, signed 30 October 2016, provisionally in force 21 September 2017 (investment chapter not yet in force), http://ec.europa.eu/trade/policy/in-focus/ceta/ceta-chapter-by-chapter/ accessed 26 March 2018.

10 EU–Singapore FTA Investment Protection Agreement (EUSFTA), final text April 2018, http://trade.ec.europa.eu/doclib/press/index.cfm?id=961 accessed 23 June 2018.

11 Armand de Mestral, 'When Does the Exception Become the Rule? Conserving Regulatory Space under CETA' (2015) Journal of International Economic Law 18, 641 (arguing that CETA is the most complex and lengthy FTA ever drafted).

12 North American Free Trade Agreement, 8–14 December 1992, 32 ILM 289 (1993), www.international.gc.ca/trade-commerce/trade-agreements-accords-commerciaux/agr-acc/ceta-aecg/text-texte/toc-tdm.aspx?lang=eng accessed 1 May 2018; Nathalie Bernasconi-Osterwalder, 'How the Investment Chapter of the Trans-Pacific Partnership Agreement Falls Short' *International Institute for Sustainable Development* (6 November 2015), www.iisd.org/commentary/how-investment-chapter-trans-pacific-partnership-agreement-falls-short accessed 1 May 2018.

13 Interestingly, the approach of the US and the EU remains similar with respect to the structure and content of its investment chapters. Whilst all three agreements bear some resemblance, CPTPP is remarkably similar to the 2012 US Model BIT, which in turn is based on NAFTA's investment chapter. Given the strong bargaining power of the US in the original TPP, the similarities are not particularly surprising. The investment chapters in CETA and EUSFTA, both in terms of their procedural and substantive provisions, are modelled on the Canadian Model Foreign Investment Protection Agreement (FIPA), which purports to reflect Canada's 20 years of arbitral experience under Chapter 11 of NAFTA (which, of course, followed the US Model BIT current at that time).

rendered pursuant to these terms, and forecasts broader implications about the future of international investment law.

Section E concludes that while these agreements help better define the scope of *bona fide* regulation by providing guidance to arbitral tribunals, through the use of exceptions and caveats in the treaty text, the catchphrase 'return of the state' is misleading. The state never left. It has always had the right to regulate for legitimate public welfare objectives, and arbitral tribunals have generally recognised this in exercising their decision-making mandate. Host state discretion in such areas as public health, environment, and safety have, with few exceptions in outlier cases, long been areas where international jurists have exercised caution and deference. Therefore, while CPTPP, CETA, and EUSFTA display some innovations in drafting, these developments are not revolutionary. It is also far from certain whether the repeated reiterations of states' right to regulate will influence the outcome of the arbitral awards rendered pursuant to these treaties (although arbitrators will likely be even more careful to note such considerations in their reasons). That said, it behoves all international investment lawyers, arbitrators, academics, and governments to be aware of the changes to investment protections contained in CPTPP, CETA, and EUSFTA, and to consider how a renewed paramountcy on states' right to regulate might alter the threshold for establishing certain breaches under these treaties.

If not new or revolutionary, then what are the state parties trying to achieve? Most importantly, states are codifying existing rules of international law and guidance on their interpretation in their treaties. States' acknowledgement that they are the driving force for reform, and the perception in some circles that the pendulum has swung too far in favour of investors on regulatory issues, has led states to reinterpret, clarify, and revise treaty language to further enshrine their right to regulate for public purposes. More generally, states are re-evaluating the costs and benefits of their trade relations with foreign investors.[14] In more certain terms than ever before, states are attempting to agree, in their treaty texts, how arbitral tribunals should deal with specific substantive issues – (FET), indirect expropriation, national treatment, MFN treatment, and exception clauses – as opposed to leaving its core investment protection obligations open to interpretation. One of the principal advantages in the formulation of this new generation of treaties lies in the clarified, and arguably improved, articulation of the standards of protection, in order to leave less room for unwarranted interpretations by arbitral tribunals.

Conversely, CPTPP, CETA, and EUSFTA also reject specific approaches taken by tribunals on certain issues, which reflects an internalisation of hard lessons learned from past mistakes in NAFTA and other treaties with more open-textured provisions. Recent arbitral awards provide states with insight into treaty text formulations that could preserve policy space, which might help prevent similar

---

14 Detlev Vagts, 'Foreword to the Backlash against Investment Arbitration', in Michael Waibel and others (eds), *The Backlash Against Investment Arbitration: Perceptions And Reality* (Kluwer Law International 2010), xxiii.

disputes from arising again. More and more states therefore have an ever-increasing awareness of potential issues of interpretation at the time of negotiation of their investment treaties, and accept that 'an obvious and effective way to prevent tribunals from adopting an "off-track" interpretation is to specify, to the maximum extent possible, the scope of application of the clause in the text.'[15] These new treaties signal a clear shift in practice towards careful drafting as states take a more 'active role in interpreting treaty provisions by influencing the interpretation by tribunals'.[16]

   With this context in mind, states' evolving understanding of the scope and content of their BITs should not merely be characterised as protectionist or reactionary. Rather, these changes should be viewed as a measured response to lessons learned as a result of the recent proliferation of investment treaties and jurisprudence on the meaning of key BIT provisions, when weighed in the balance between foreign investors' rights and states' regulatory autonomy. A study of investment treaty awards suggests that '[t]he more vaguely drafted treaties are, the higher the delegation to arbitrators.'[17] CPTPP, CETA, and EUSFTA make serious attempts to limit the otherwise wide discretion conferred upon arbitral tribunals to evaluate states' regulatory decisions in the context of arbitration claims by foreign investors. For example, this narrowing of arbitral discretion is achieved by linking certain protections to the customary international law standard (eg CPTPP does this with the FET standard) and by setting out in greater detail what constitutes 'prompt, adequate, and effective compensation', and elaborating on the 'rare circumstances' that are relevant to determining whether an indirect expropriation has occurred. Another rationale behind greater precision in treaty drafting is that it is more likely to encourage compliance with a norm, because it allows those subject to the rule to foresee the probable consequences of their actions.[18] The test of time will reveal whether these enviable aims come true after these treaties enter into force and start to be used in practice.

B. The Impetus for Moving Towards Greater Precision in Treaty Drafting

The extant ISDS system has been criticised by some for permitting:

> vague and indeterminate obligations [to be] interpreted behind closed doors by private, *ad hoc* tribunals, resulting in inconsistent and unpredictable decisions that drain state coffers, create uncertainty about the scope of a

---

15 Tomoko Ishikawa, 'Keeping Interpretation in Investment Treaty Arbitration "on Track": The Role of State Parties' in Anna Joubin-Bret and Jean E Kalicki (eds), *Reshaping the Investor-State Dispute Settlement System, Journeys for the 21st Century* (Brill/Nijhoff 2015), 139.

16 ibid.

17 ibid 22.

18 Caroline Henckels, 'Protecting Regulatory Autonomy through Greater Precision in Investment Treaties: The TPP, CETA, and TPP' (2016) Journal of International Economic Law (advance access publication date 8 March 2016) 4.

government's authority to regulate, and chill legitimate efforts to promote human rights, the environment, health, safety and other important public welfare objectives.[19]

A more nuanced and analytical perspective suggests that states will continue to include ISDS in their IIAs if the costs of constraining regulatory sovereignty do not exceed the expected net benefits.[20] A notable shift towards greater precision in treaty drafting is an attempt by states to recalibrate the arbitration system in favour of the preservation of public policy space and transparency in the arbitral proceedings. This section focuses on *why* states have reached the conclusion that reforms to ISDS can be achieved through the negotiation of more detailed and carefully drafted IIAs.

One of the realities of the system is that *ad hoc* arbitral tribunals can, and sometimes do, come to conflicting decisions on similar or even identical points of law. Sometimes this is the result of impartial arbitrators, however such an allegation is very difficult to prove. More often, it is conflicting approaches to arbitral interpretative methodology that has led to varying levels of quality in the coherence of investment treaty arbitration and has diminished the predictability of ISDS. After all, ISDS is a flat system, with no centralised form of review to resolve inconsistencies in the application of treaties or in the application of general rules and principles of international law. Aside from the appellate body included in the EU-led two-tier investment tribunal system (adopted in CETA and EUSFTA IPA, but not yet operationalised),[21] investor-state arbitral awards afford no possibility of

19 Karin L Kizer and Jeremy K Sharpe, 'Reform of Investor-State Dispute Settlement: The U.S. Experience' in Anna Joubin-Bret and Jean E Kalicki (eds), *Reshaping the Investor-State Dispute Settlement System, Journeys for the 21ˢᵗ Century* (Brill/Nijhoff 2015), 172. See also Pia Eberhardt and Cecilia Olivet, 'Profiting from Injustice – How Law Firms, Arbitrations and Financiers are Fuelling an Investment Arbitration Boom' (27 November 2012), www.tni.org/files/download/profitingfrominjustice.pdf accessed 1 May 2018.

20 Anne van Aaken, 'Delegating Interpretative Authority in Investment Treaties' in Anna Joubin-Bret and Jean E Kalicki (eds), *Reshaping the Investor-State Dispute Settlement System, Journeys for the 21ˢᵗ Century* (Brill/Nijhoff 2015), 21.

21 In November 2015, the European Commission (EC) released its official proposal for the establishment of an international 'Investment Court System' in the context of its Transatlantic Trade and Investment Partnership (TTIP) negotiations. The EC's Proposal was adopted by Canada, Vietnam, and Mexico in their respective treaties with the EU. *See* EC, 'Proposal of the European Union for Investment Protection and Resolution of Investment Disputes' (12 November 2015), http://trade.ec.europa.eu/doclib/docs/2015/november/tradoc_153955.pdf accessed 14 April 2018. Stephan W Schill, 'The [EC]'s Proposal of an Investment Court System for TTIP: Stepping Stone or Stumbling Block for Multilateralizing International Investment Law?' 20 *ASIL Insights* 9 (22 April 2016), www.asil.org/insights/volume/20/issue/9/european-comm issions-proposal-investment-court-system-ttip-stepping#_edn4 accessed 4 April 2018; Elsa Sardinha, 'The New EU-Led Approach to Investor-State Arbitration: The Investment Tribunal System in the Comprehensive Economic Trade Agreement (CETA) and EU-Vietnam FTA' (2017), 32(3) ICSID Review 625–672; Elsa Sardinha, 'Towards a New Horizon in Investor-State Dispute Settlement? Reflections on the Investment

review for errors of law under Article 52 of the ICSID Convention[22], and rarely pursuant to judicial review at the place of arbitration for non-ICSID arbitrations. Therefore, arbitral awards that are wrong on the law are essentially unchallengeable, and the consequences of defending such a claim, let alone losing or having to settle one, puts enormous strain on a state's financial resources. Changes to treaty drafting are therefore aimed at reducing the leeway for arbitrators to get it wrong on the law, by providing them with detailed guidance on each of the substantive standards of investment protection.

In historical context, a rethinking of treaty models has been underway since at least 2004, after the first series of cases arising under NAFTA.[23] The initial NAFTA experience reflected arbitral tribunals' efforts at grappling with the core obligations of FET, national and MFN treatment, and expropriation, and were viewed by some 'to pose a threat to governments' powers to impose new regulations designed to protect the environment.'[24] Take the *Methanex v USA* [25] arbitration, for instance. This case involved Canadian company Methanex, which produced an additive to motor vehicle fuels, known as MTBE, that purportedly diminished air pollution compared to straight gasoline. It turned out that MTBE had the potential to contaminate underground water supplies if it were to leak from a fuel storage tank. In response to this apparent risk, California introduced regulation that ended Methanex's MTBE programme. In turn, Methanex sued the US for USD 970 million in damages. Notwithstanding that Methanex's claims were rejected, this arbitration 'set off alarm bells' for NAFTA state parties, and they soon gathered and agreed a joint interpretation of NAFTA that attempted to narrow the substantive protections afforded to investors under that treaty.

While NAFTA has far more extensive exceptions to substantive obligations in its Chapter 11 investment provisions in comparison to earlier, more skeletally drafted and generally worded BITs, the NAFTA ISDS experience sometimes suggested a pragmatism on the part of its arbitrators that tended 'to give short shrift to objections based on noncompliance with the chapter's procedural requirements'. Canada and the US' shock at being sued under NAFTA's ISDS provisions was not eased by the intensity of the public interest in the inner workings of NAFTA's tribunals and demands for more transparency in the arbitral process. Issues that seemed clear to the state parties at the time of drafting were not clear to all

Tribunal System in CETA' (2017), 54 Canadian Yearbook of International Law 311–365.

22 Convention on the Settlement of Investment Disputes between States and Nationals of Other States, 18 March 1965, 575 UNTS 159 (ICSID Convention).

23 J Christopher Thomas QC, 'Introductory Comments: The Pacific Rim and International Economic Law: Opportunities and Risks of the Pacific Century' TDM 1 (2015), www.transnational-dispute-management.com/article.asp?key=2168 accessed 29 July 2018.

24 Detlev Vagts, 'Foreword to the Backlash against Investment Arbitration', in Michael Waibel and others (eds), *The Backlash Against Investment Arbitration: Perceptions And Reality* (Kluwer Law International 2010), xxv.

25 *Methanex Corp v USA*, UNCITRAL, Final Award on Jurisdiction and Merits (3 August 2005), IIC 167.

tribunals. For instance, tribunals were inundated with questions about what constitutes an 'investment', what are the conditions precedent to bring a claim, what amounts to an indirect expropriation, and how should regulatory measures be distinguished from expropriatory measures. These are but a sampling of the many types of interpretive issues which arose in the NAFTA context, which were not foreseen at the time of drafting. As such, the NAFTA and post-NAFTA experience served as the impetus driving calls for more detailed and perspective treaties.[26]

To date, over 3,300 IIAs have been concluded.[27] This increase in the number of IIAs in force has been accompanied by a gradual change in the nature of investment disputes. Most present-day claims engage FET and indirect expropriation standards of protection, rather than more straight-forward claims of nationalisation or direct expropriation. Such claims often challenge states' regulatory measures taken in relation to environmental, energy, health, privatisation, subsidy, taxation, natural resource management and exploitation policies, and responses to economic crises.[28] The potentially extensive political, financial, legal, and social implications of investment tribunal awards on governance makes ISDS – disconnected as it is from domestic court and administrative law processes – particularly prone to scrutiny and criticism. The right of states to regulate commercial activities, in a way that is compatible with both their domestic obligations to their citizenry and treaty obligations to investors, can compete with investors' claims to treatment required by international treaties. It is in this way that the outcomes in individual investor-state arbitrations have the potential to influence states' policies beyond the immediate disputes they resolve.[29] The importance of such arbitral decisions on domestic law-making has therefore been seen by some commentators to have a chilling effect on states' regulatory powers, that has led some states to include text in their treaties that clarifies and constrains the bounds of FET and provides greater direction to tribunals for distinguishing between an indirect expropriation and *bona fide* regulatory measures.[30]

The continued negotiation and conclusion of IIAs, notwithstanding the criticisms facing ISDS and questions about its future,[31] suggests that states have not

26 Thomas, *supra* note 23.
27 UNCTAD, *World Investment Report 2015: Reforming International Investment Governance* (UNCTAD, 2015) 106, http://unctad.org/en/PublicationsLibrary/wir2015_en.pdf accessed 8 September 2016.
28 Joachim Karl, 'Investor-State Dispute Settlement: A Government's Dilemma' (18 February 2013), *Columbia Center on Sustainable Development*, http://justinvestment.org/2013/02/investor-state-dispute-settlement-a-governments-dilemma/ accessed 1 May 2018.
29 ibid, 1113, 1186, 1203–1204.
30 Caroline Henckels, 'Protecting Regulatory Autonomy through Greater Precision in Investment Treaties: The TPP, CETA, and TTIP' (2016) Journal of International Economic Law (advance access publication date 8 March 2016), 1.
31 Eg Kaj Hobér, 'Does Investment Arbitration have a Future?' in Marc Bungenberg and others (eds), *International Investment Law* (Hart Publishing 2015), 1873; Muthucumaraswamy Sornarajah, 'After Neo-Liberalism: The Future Course of International

turned their backs on ISDS. Rather, states are engaged in a process of recalibration, elaboration, and restatement of the procedural and substantive aspects of their trade initiatives.

C. Deconstructing the so-called 'Return of the State'

The right to regulate in recent treaties has been written about extensively by various scholars.[32] But can it be said that ISDS and investment treaty-making has entered a new age, which features the 'return of the state'? This phraseology implies that the state left, or assumed lesser importance in the international investment legal framework, which is not the case. The state's right to regulate has always existed, and is recognised under customary international law. States enter into treaties freely. While investment treaties limit governments' ability to expropriate foreign investments and/or treat foreign investors in an arbitrary or discriminatory manner, they do not limit (and, in fact, are intended to safeguard) states' sovereign right to regulate in the public interest in a fair, reasonable, and non-discriminatory manner. Hence, is enshrining states' right to regulate really necessary and will it make any difference in the outcomes of arbitral awards?

Even the phrase 'right to regulate' is misleading, for it glosses over key distinctions in how international trade and investment law rules affect domestic regulation, and ignores essential nuances in the debate. For instance, arbitral tribunals have long accepted that not all state measures interfering with property amount to expropriation. Conversely, an intrusion by arbitral tribunals into domestic regulatory decisions *is* justified in rare circumstances where states' measures are found to be discriminatory. Nevertheless, recent treaty-making trends reveal that it might be wise to set out, in detail, precisely which regulatory areas may or may not be considered to be a violation of the relevant treaty. A measure of arbitral discretion will, however, always be required, and not all potential situations can possibly be accounted for in the already quite detailed language of these treaties.

Investment Law' (Columbia-Vale Symposium on International Investment Law 2012); Muthucumaraswamy Sornarajah, 'The Past, Present and Future of the International Law' in Wenhua Shan (ed), *China and International Investment Law* (Martinus Nijhoff 2014), 24–57.

32 Eg David A Gantz, 'Increasing Host State Regulatory Flexibility in Defending Investor-State Disputes: The Evolution of U.S. Approaches from NAFTA to the TPP' (5 June 2017). 50 International Lawyer 231 (2017); Arizona Legal Studies Discussion Paper No 17–09, SSRN, https://ssrn.com/abstract=2974428 accessed 1 April 2018. Martins Paparinskis, 'Masters and Guardians of International Investment Law: How to Play the Game of Reassertion' in Andreas Kulick (ed), *Reassertion of Control over the Investment Treaty Regime* (CUP 2016), 30–52; Mavulda Sattorova, 'Reassertion of Control and Contracting Parties' Domestic Law Responses to Investment Treaty Arbitration: Between Reform, Reticence and Resistance' in Andreas Kulick (ed), *Reassertion of Control over the Investment Treaty Regime* (CUP 2016), 53–80; Eleni Methymaki and Antonios Tzanakopoulos (2016), 'Masters of Puppets? Reassertion of Control through Joint Investment Treaty Interpretation' in Andreas Kulick (ed), *Reassertion of Control over the Investment Treaty Regime* (CUP 2016), 151–181.

D. Convergences and Divergences between the Investment Chapters of CPTPP, CETA, and EUSFTA

I. The Right to Regulate in the Preambles to the Treaty and the Investment Chapter

Although the right to regulate is intrinsic to state sovereignty, the inclusion of language in treaty preambles that explicitly recognises this inherent regulatory power is a notable trend in international investment law, followed in varying degrees in CPTPP, CETA, and EUSFTA. Reference to a right to regulate is innovative as compared to EU Member States' traditional approach in their BITs, which largely included reference only to economic imperatives and the promotion and protection of investments. With this latest generation of investment treaties, governments are attempting to clarify the bounds of their regulatory space, not only through carve-outs in certain substantive investment protections and general exception clauses, but also by way of general reference to this right in the treaty preamble. While introductory preambles do not normally create binding commitments, their content provides arbitrators with the broader context in which all cases must be considered under that treaty. Tribunals which face ambiguity in interpreting particular treaty provisions, or inconsistent authority argued by the parties, may look to these preambular statements and prefer interpretations that advance the fair and predictable treatment of foreign investments, while being careful not to displace states' ability to regulate in the public interest.

Table 5.1 sets out the right to regulate language in the preambles to the treaty, in the investment chapter itself, if any, and in the Joint Declaration to CPTPP, signed between New Zealand, Canada and Chile.[33]

The explicit reference in CETA's preamble to the right to regulate gives important interpretative guidance to arbitrators in assessing investors' claims brought under the investment chapter. Similarly, CETA's investment chapter 'reaffirms' the state parties' right to regulate in nearly identical terms at Article 8.9(1).

Note the different, and arguably stronger pro-right to regulate, formulation of Article 8.9(2) as compared to the 2014 draft version of the same provision, before CETA underwent legal scrubbing:

> For greater certainty, the provisions of this section shall not be interpreted as a commitment from a Party that it will not change the legal and regulatory framework, including in a manner that may negatively affect the operation of covered investments or the investor's expectations of profits.

---

33 Joint Declaration on ISDS, signed 8 March 2018 between New Zealand, Canada and Chile, https://www.mfat.govt.nz/assets/CPTPP/CPTPP-Joint-Declaration-ISDS-Final.pdf accessed 23 June 2018.

Table 5.1 Preambles

CPTPP	CETA	EUSFTA IPA
REAFFIRM the importance of promoting corporate social responsibility, cultural identity and diversity, environmental protection and conservation, gender equality, indigenous rights, labour rights, inclusive trade, sustainable development and traditional knowledge, as well as the importance of preserving their right to regulate in the public interest;	RECOGNISING that the provisions of this Agreement preserve the right of the Parties to regulate within their territories and the Parties' flexibility to achieve legitimate policy objectives, such as public health, safety, environment, public morals and the promotion and protection of cultural diversity;	REAFFIRMING each Party's right to adopt and enforce measures necessary to pursue legitimate policy objectives such as social, environmental, security, public health and safety, promotion and protection of cultural diversity;
TPP's Preamble (expressly incorporated in CPTPP):	AFFIRMING their commitments as parties to the UNESCO Convention on the Protection and Promotion of the Diversity of Cultural Expressions, done at Paris on 20 October 2005, and recognising that states have the right to preserve, develop and implement their cultural policies, to support their cultural industries for the purpose of strengthening the diversity of cultural expressions, and to preserve their culturalidentity, including through the use of regulatory measures and financial support;	
RECOGNISE their inherent right to regulate and resolve to preserve the flexibility of the Parties to set legislative and regulatory priorities, safeguard public welfare, and protect legitimate public welfare-objectives, such as public health, safety, the environment, the conservation of living or non-living exhaustible natural resources, the integrity and stability of the financial system and public morals;	RECOGNISING that the provisions of this Agreement protect investments and investors with respect to their investments, and are intended to stimulate mutually beneficial business activity, without undermining the right of the Parties to regulate in the public interest within their territories;	
RECOGNISE further their inherent right to adopt, maintain or modify health care systems;	REAFFIRMING their commitment to promote sustainable development and the development of international trade in such a way as to contribute to sustainable development in its economic, social and environmental dimensions;	

CPTPP	CETA	EUSFTA IPA
Investment Chapter: none	Investment Chapter: Art. 8.9 Investment and regulatory measures	Ch. 2, Art. 2.2 Investment and Regulatory Measures
Joint Declaration in ISDS (New Zealand, Canada and Chile) Reaffirm the right of each Party to regulate within its territory to achieve legitimate policy objectives such as safety; the protection of health, the environment or public morals; social or consumer protection; or the promotion and protection of cultural diversity;	1. For the purpose of this Chapter, the Parties reaffirm their right to regulate within their territories to achieve legitimate policy objectives, such as the protection of public health, safety, the environment or public morals, social or consumer protection or the promotion and protection of cultural diversity.	1. The Parties reaffirm their right to regulate within their territories to achieve legitimate policy objectives, such as the protection of public health, social services, public education, safety, environment or public morals, social or consumer protection privacy and data protection and the promotion and protection of cultural diversity.
Recognise the strong procedural and substantive safeguards that are included in the Investment Chapter of CPTPP; Recognise the important role of civil society and other interested groups on public policy matters relating to ISDS; Intend to consider evolving international practice and the evolution of ISDS including through the work carried out by multilateral international fora; Intend to promote transparent conduct rules on the ethical responsibilities of arbitrators in ISDS procedures, including conflict of interest rules that prevent arbitrators from acting, for the duration of their appointment, as counsel or party appointed expert or witness in other proceedings, pursuant to Article 9.22.6 of CPTPP.	2. For greater certainty, the mere fact that a Party regulates, including through a modification to its laws, in a manner which negatively affects an investment or interferes with an investor's expectations, including its expectations of profits, does not amount to a breach of an obligation under this Section.	2. For greater certainty, the mere fact that a Party regulates, including through a modification to its laws, in a manner which negatively affects an investment or interferes with an investor's expectations, including its expectations of profits, does not amount to a breach of an obligation under this Chapter.

The final version of CETA's right to regulate provision does not create any new right to regulate; rather, it simply 'reaffirms' a right that is assumed to already exist.[34] CETA's final text appears to be weaker than its previous formulation and that advocated by the EU in its TTIP proposal, which, at Article 2(1), provides that:

> the provisions of this section *shall not affect the right of the Parties to regulate* within their territories through measures necessary to achieve legitimate policy objectives, such as the protection of public health, safety, environment or public morals, social or consumer protection or promotion and protection of cultural diversity.[35]

While official summaries released by the European Commission (EC) and Singapore indicate that the text of the EUSFTA reaffirms the right of the treaty parties to regulate and to pursue legitimate public policy objectives, language to that effect is slightly more subtle in the preamble to the EUSFTA IPA and in the preamble to its investment chapter, which both simply reaffirm 'each Party's right to adopt and enforce measures necessary to pursue legitimate policy objectives such as social, environmental, security, public health and safety, promotion and protection of cultural diversity'. The investment chapter also reinforces the right to regulate in the area of 'social or consumer protection privacy and data protection'. The right to regulate is, however, reflected in more pronounced terms in its investment chapter *vis-à-vis* FET and indirect expropriation.[36]

CPTPP reflects a greater emphasis placed on states' right to regulate in the public interest. In comparison to the preambles in CETA and EUSFTA, CPTPP's preamble is more descriptive and employs stronger language – recognising not just a right, but an 'inherent' right, to regulate. CPTPP also affirms the parties' resolve to preserve their flexibility to set legislative and regulatory priorities, safeguard public welfare, and protect legitimate public welfare objectives, and goes on to detail that these will include, but therefore not be limited to, such things as 'public health, safety, the environment, the conservation of living or non-living exhaustible natural resources, the integrity and stability of the financial system and public morals'.

CPTPP's arguably stronger preservation of appropriate regulatory space for host states to promote public welfare objectives reflects a revision and clarification upon the US' BIT programme which, since the 1980s, has focused on: (i) protecting American investments abroad, (ii) encouraging open, transparent, and non-discriminatory market-based domestic policies, and (iii) supporting the development

---

34 Ante Wessels, 'CETA: Who Pulled the Plug on the Right to Regulate' (14 March 2016), https://blog.ffii.org/ceta-who-pulled-the-plug-on-the-right-to-regulate/ accessed 14 April 2016.
35 TTIP Proposal Article 2(1) (emphasis added).
36 EUSFTA Investment Protection Agreement (IPA), Chapter 2, Article 2.4 (Standard of Treatment) and Article 2.6 (Expropriation). Chapter 4, Annex 1 (Expropriation)

of international law standards consistent with these objectives.[37] The rationale behind such language in the preamble is, in part, that it might deter corporations from using ISDS as a way to challenge basic, progressive law-making. Over the past two decades, the US has been a respondent in over a dozen claims under NAFTA's Investment Chapter 11, of which the US has never had a monetary damage award ordered against it. Nevertheless, this enhanced right to regulate may prove useful to other states, as well as to the US in the event that it rejoins the CPTPP fold, in future claims brought under these new treaties.

II. Definitions

In comparison to older treaties, all three agreements have tightened key definitions in the hopes of avoiding unwarranted interpretations. Aside from similar definitions being placed in slightly different parts of the chapter,[38] the definitions in the two EU agreements and CPTPP are congruent, with only a few subtle differences. If anything, CPTPP's definitions are more detailed, with additional qualifications provided in the footnotes. The definitions of 'investment' and 'investors' are broad in all three treaties, and are nearly identically worded.

An 'investment' is defined as every kind of asset that an investor owns or controls, directly or indirectly, that has the characteristics of an investment, which features the commitment of capital or other resources, the expectation of gain or profit, or the assumption of risk. Forms that an investment may take include property, enterprise, shares, stocks, bonds, concessions, claims to money, contracts, intellectual property rights, and licenses. CPTPP's list of possible investments is slightly more descriptive than that of CETA and EUSFTA, but effectively appears to cover the same areas and types of investments. For instance, footnote 3 to CPTPP's definition of 'investment' clarifies that a loan by one party to another party is not an investment. However, unlike CETA and EUSFTA, CPTPP does not specify that 'licenses, authorisations, permits and similar rights' include concessions to search for, cultivate, extract or exploit natural resources (although these types of investments are mentioned under CPTPP's definition of 'investment agreement'). Instead, a footnote attempts to clarify this provision as follows:

---

37 Karin L Kizer and Jeremy K Sharpe, 'Reform of Investor-State Dispute Settlement: The U.S. Experience' in Anna Joubin-Bret and Jean E Kalicki (eds), *Reshaping the Investor-State Dispute Settlement System, Journeys for the 21st Century* (Brill/Nijhoff 2015), 174; US Department of State, *Bilateral Investment Treaties and Related Agreements*, www.state.gov/e/eb/ifd/bit/ accessed 1 May 2018; Office of the United States Trade Representative, *Bilateral Investment Treaties*, https://ustr.gov/trade-agreements/bilateral-investment-treaties accessed 1 May 2018.

38 In EUSFTA, a definitions section appears at Articles 9.1 under Section A Investment Protection and further ISDS specific definitions appear at Article 9.11 under Section B ISDS. In CETA and TPP, all the relevant definitions applicable to the investment chapter appear at the beginning of the chapter.

Where a particular type of licence, authorisation, permit or similar instrument (including a concession to the extent that it has the nature of such an instrument) has the characteristics of an investment depends on such factors as the nature and extent of the rights that the holder has under the Party's law. Among such instruments that do not have the characteristics of an investment are those that do not create any rights protected under the Party's law. For greater certainty, the foregoing is without prejudice to whether any asset associated with such instruments has the characteristics of an investment.[39]

One of the questions which frequently occupies arbitral tribunals is the situation of an investor which claims that a license, permit, or authorisation of some kind granted by the state under its local law is affected by a measure attributable to the state. Through its definition of investment, CPTPP resolves this scenario by providing that such types of interest can be investments for the purposes of the treaty, that the tribunal has then to establish what these rights mean and, in so doing, it must look at the local law pursuant to which these rights were created. However, wouldn't tribunals intuitively look to the local law anyway to find out how the interest is defined? Most likely. But once again, this example illustrated states' reluctance to leave such determinations to chance, and instead provides further guidance to arbitral tribunals. There is no corresponding direction given under CETA or EUSFTA.

It is noteworthy that the footnotes to the definition of 'investment agreement' in CPTPP contain several public sector exclusions meant to further enshrine states' 'right to regulate' – eg any agreement pertaining to land, water, radio, healthcare, education, childcare, and welfare services does not qualify as an investment agreement.

III. Substantive Provisions

CPTPP, CETA, and EUSFTA promote and protect – through more precise drafting, the codification of customary international law, and the use of exceptions – states' regulatory autonomy far more than earlier treaties. In so doing, these treaties 'precisely define the contours of States' obligations towards foreign investors and investments',[40] and provide guidance to tribunals on how to construe these obligations against the backdrop of how states regulate in the public interest and govern foreign investments.[41] This section will examine how and why these treaties are the first of their kind to incorporate significantly more detailed

---

39 Emphasis added.
40 Caroline Henckels, 'Protecting Regulatory Autonomy through Greater Precision in Investment Treaties: The TPP, CETA, and TPP' (2016) Journal of International Economic Law (advance access publication date 8 March 2016), 1.
41 Karin L Kizer and Jeremy K Sharpe, 'Reform of Investor-State Dispute Settlement: The U.S. Experience' in Anna Joubin-Bret and Jean E Kalicki (eds), *Reshaping the Investor-State Dispute Settlement System, Journeys for the 21st Century* (Brill/Nijhoff 2015), 180.

guidance to arbitrators in the treaty text of the following provisions: (1) FET; (2) indirect expropriation; (3) national treatment; and (4) MFN treatment.

One commentator observed that these new provisions:

> continue to grant broad discretion to arbitrators through the use of evaluative language such as 'manifestly arbitrary', 'rare circumstances', 'excessive', and 'necessary', and that their content 'might not go far enough towards ensuring that non-discriminatory public welfare measures do not attract liability'.[42]

However, while states might continue to draft such provisions with more precision, too much precision might have the effect of unduly constraining arbitrators' discretion. Drafters of both domestic and international legal orders:

> simply cannot anticipate all the situations in which a rule might be applied and, consequently, cannot be expected (and often do not attempt) to explicate in legislation, or in legislative guidance materials, the precise application of the law in all circumstances.[43]

As is acknowledged by a proponent of the view that these treaties are not detailed *enough*, '[m]ore precise norms fetter adjudicators' discretion to make evaluative judgments by narrowing the degree of interpretive discretion entrusted to them and placing greater constraints on the decision-making criteria that they employ'.[44] Too much precision can actually 'narrow the scope for reasonable interpretation',[45] and is self-defeating to the objectives greater precision in treaty drafting aims to achieve.

1. Fair and Equitable Treatment (FET)

The minimum standard of treatment granted under most investment treaties requires states to accord to covered investments FET and full protection and security. The immense room given for interpretation of the FET standard,

---

42 ibid, 4.
43 N Jansen Calamita, 'International Human Rights & the Interpretation of International Investment Treaties – Constitutional Considerations', in Freya Baetens (ed), *The Interaction of International Investment and Other Fields of Public International Law* (CUP 2013), 169.
44 ibid 4–5, citing Duncan Kennedy, 'Form and Substance of Private Law Adjudication' (1976) 89 Harvard Law Review 1688, 1701; Kathleen M Sullivan, 'The Justices of Rules and Standards' (1992) 106 Harvard Law Review 58–59; Louis Kaplow, 'Rules Versus Standards: An Economic Analysis' (1992) 42 Duke Law Journal 557, 560; Pierre Schlag, 'Rules and Standards' (1986) 33 UCLA Law Review 386; Cass Sunstein, 'Problems with Rules' (1995) 83 California Law Review 974–976; Isaac Erlich and Richard A Posner, 'An Economic Analysis of Legal Rulemaking' (1974) 3 Journal of Legal Studies 261, 265.
45 Kenneth W Abbott and others, 'The Concept of Legalization', in Beth A Simmons and Richard H Steinberg (eds), *International Law and International Relations: An International Organization Reader* (CUP 2007), 115, 124.

sometimes referred to as the minimum standard of treatment, has made it the most frequently invoked provision in investor-state disputes.[46] For some time now, treaty parties have tried to define more clearly the contested scope of this standard.[47] FET provisions in treaties are typically quite brief and understated as to their normative content. Whilst FET is most often understood to require that the host state refrain from adopting a conduct towards investors that is arbitrary, grossly unfair, unjust or idiosyncratic, discriminatory, or that involves a lack of due process or a lack of transparency,[48] most treaties do not provide further guidance for tribunals' value judgments in this regard.[49] The phrase 'full protection and security', which is included in each of the relevant agreements' FET standard, encompasses the obligation to ensure that the assets and individuals connected with a qualifying investment are free from physical harm in the host state.

The key provisions of the FET provisions in CPTPP, CETA, and EUSFTA are given in Table 5.2.

Unlike CPTPP, neither CETA nor EUSFTA explicitly link FET to the standard in customary international law, but instead establish FET as a standard independent of customary international law, and cite guidance from a closed list of protection categories developed in arbitral practice. There are a couple of notable differences between the lists in CETA and EUSFTA, which will be discussed later, but the types of conduct described appear to have been heavily influenced by Judge James Crawford's statement in *Waste Management v Mexico*[50] on the kinds of things that could constitute a treaty breach.

In a celebratory press release prior to the conclusion of negotiations on the main achievements of the new agreement, the EC noted that: 'for the *first time ever*, the CETA agreement provides for a *precise definition of* "[FET]". This will avoid too wide interpretations and provide clear guidelines to tribunals.'[51] Similarly, the Canadian government described its FET standard as a 'robust and

---

46 Stephan W Schill, 'Fair and Equitable Treatment, the Rule of Law, and Comparative Public Law' in Stephan W Schill (ed), *International Investment Law and Comparative Public Law* (OUP 2010), 151.

47 ibid.

48 Allen & Overy '*Protection of Investments Under the Trans-Pacific Partnership*', Allen & Overy News (16 October 2015), www.allenovery.com/news/en-gb/articles/Pages/Protection-of-investments-under-the-Trans-Pacific-Partnership.aspx accessed 1 May 2018.

49 Stephan W Schill, 'Fair and Equitable Treatment, the Rule of Law, and Comparative Public Law' in Stephan W Schill (ed), *International Investment Law and Comparative Public Law* (OUP 2010), 152, 156–157; Caroline Henckels, 'Protecting Regulatory Autonomy through Greater Precision in Investment Treaties: The TPP, CETA, and TPP' (2016) Journal of International Economic Law (advance access publication date 8 March 2016) 7.

50 *Waste Management Inc v United Mexican States*, ICSID Case No ARB(AF)/00/3, Award, 30 April 2004, paras 98–99.

51 EC Press Release, 'Investment Provisions in the EU-Canada Free Trade Agreement' (12 March 2013), 2, http://trade.ec.europa.eu/doclib/docs/2013/november/tradoc_151918.pdf accessed 1 May 2018 (emphasis in original).

Table 5.2 FET

CPTPP	CETA	EUSFTA IPA
Art. 9.6 Minimum Standard of Treatment	Art. 8.10 Treatment of investors and of covered investments	Art. 2.4 Standard of Treatment
2. For greater certainty, paragraph 1 prescribes the customary international law minimum standard of treatment of aliens as the standard of treatment to be afforded to covered investments. The concepts of "fair and equitable treatment" and "full protection and security" do not require treatment in addition to or beyond that which is required by that standard, and do not create additional substantive rights. The obligations in paragraph 1 to provide: (a) "fair and equitable treatment" includes the obligation not to deny justice in criminal, civil or administrative adjudicatory proceedings in accordance with the principle of due process embodied in the principal legal systems of the world; and (b) "full protection and security" requires each Party to provide the level of police protection required under customary international law. ...	2. A Party breaches the obligation of [FET] referenced in paragraph 1 if a measure or series of measures constitutes: (a) denial of justice in criminal, civil or administrative proceedings; (b) fundamental breach of due process, including a fundamental breach of transparency, in judicial and administrative proceedings; (c) manifest arbitrariness; (d) targeted discrimination on manifestly wrongful grounds, such as gender, race or religious belief; (e) abusive treatment of investors, such as coercion, duress and harassment; or (f) a breach of any further elements of the fair and equitable treatment obligation adopted by the Parties in accordance with paragraph 3 of this Article. ...	2. A Party breaches the obligation of [FET] referenced in paragraph 1 if its measure or series of measures constitute: (a) denial of justice[9] in criminal, civil and administrative proceedings; (b) a fundamental breach of due process; (c) manifestly arbitrary conduct; (d) harassment, coercion, abuse of power or similar bad faith conduct; 3. In determining whether the fair and equitable treatment obligation, as set out in paragraph 2, has been breached, a Tribunal may take into account, where applicable, whether a Party made specific or unambiguous representations[10] to an investor so as to induce the investment, that created legitimate expectations of a covered investor and which were reasonably relied upon by the covered investor, but that the Party subsequently frustrated.[11] ... 5. For greater certainty, "full protection and security" only refers to a Party's obligation relating to physical security of covered investors and investments.

CPTPP	CETA	EUSFTA IPA
4. For greater certainty, the mere fact that a Party takes or fails to take an action that may be inconsistent with an investor's expectations does not constitute a breach of this Article, even if there is loss or damage to the covered investment as a result. ... Annex 9–A Customary International Law The Parties confirm their shared understanding that "customary international law" generally and as specifically referenced in Article 9.6 (Minimum Standard of Treatment) results from a general and consistent practice of states that they follow from a sense of legal obligation. The customary international law minimum standard of treatment of aliens refers to all customary international law principles that protect the investments of aliens.	4. When applying the above fair and equitable treatment obligation, the Tribunal may take into account whether a Party made a specific representation to an investor to induce a covered investment, that created a legitimate expectation, and upon which the investor relied in deciding to make or maintain the covered investment, but that the Party subsequently frustrated. 5. For greater certainty, "full protection and security" refers to the Party's obligations relating to the physical security of investors and covered investments. ... 7. For greater certainty, the fact that a measure breaches domestic law does not, in and of itself, establish a breach of this Article. In order to ascertain whether the measure breaches this Article, the Tribunal must consider whether a Party has acted inconsistently with the obligations in paragraph 1.	6. Where a Party, itself or through any entity mentioned in paragraph 7 of Article 1.2 (Definitions), had given a specific and clearly spelt out commitment in a contractual written obligation[12] towards a covered investor of the other Party with respect to the covered investor's investment or towards such covered investment, that Party shall not frustrate or undermine the said commitment through the exercise of its governmental authority[13] either: (a) deliberately; or (b) in a way which substantially alters the balance of rights and obligation in the contractual written obligation unless the Party provides reasonable compensation to restore the covered investor or investment to a position which it would have been in had the frustration or undermining not occurred. ... fn: 9 For greater certainty, the sole fact that the covered investor's claim has been rejected, dismissed or unsuccessful does not in itself constitute a denial of justice.[10] For greater certainty, representations made so as to induce the investments include the representations made in order to convince the investor to continue with, not to liquidate or to make subsequent investments.[11] For greater certainty, the frustration of legitimate expectations as described in this paragraph does not, by itself, amount to a breach of paragraph 2, and such frustration of legitimate expectations must arise out of the same events or circumstances that give rise to the breach of paragraph 2.

innovative provision on minimum standard of treatment', which is 'substantively the same as NAFTA (that is, substantively the same as the customary international law minimum standard of treatment).'[52] However, this statement is somewhat misleading, as Article 8.10 of CETA sets out a limitative definition of FET. In CETA, there is no link to customary international law and the FET standard is defined by way of examples of treatment, not by reference to an underlying international law standard.

As distinct from EUSFTA and CPTPP, CETA refers to 'transparency' in the due process provision of FET. It also makes explicit that due process extends not only to administrative, but also judicial, proceedings. Moreover, CETA appears to have expanded the definition of a breach of the obligation of host governments to provide FET to include: 'targeted discrimination on manifestly wrongful grounds, such as gender, race or religious belief'. The effect of specifically singling out these kinds of discrimination is unclear, but it could be assigned some importance by arbitral tribunals who attribute this ground greater significance due to its explicit inclusion in the treaty's text. Some commentators have queried whether this attempt to broaden the scope for complaints should be a cause for concern.[53] Some view the closed list of prohibited measures under CETA's FET as too broad and more investor-friendly than, for instance, NAFTA's previously controversial minimum standards of treatment clause. It might have been wiser for CETA's FET clause to at least specify that the closed list of proscribed government conduct does not go beyond the customary international law standard on the treatment of aliens, to be proven by the claimant.

CETA is explicit that a tribunal may take into account whether the host state made a specific representation to an investor to induce a covered invest-ment, that created a legitimate expectation, and upon which the investor relied in deciding to make the covered investment, but that the host state subsequently violated. This clarification arguably tilts the balance in favour of the investor and might pose a clear threat to the rights of governments to regulate, and especially to alter and strengthen regulatory approaches in response to changing circumstances, new knowledge, investor behaviour, public perceptions of risk, and democratic decision-making. It singles out the 'legitimate expectations' that investors may hold for their investments as an interpretive issue that tribunals may consider – even above issues relating to the public interest.[54]

---

52 Foreign Affairs, Trade, and Development Canada, 'Canada-European Union: Com-prehensive Economic and Trade Agreement (CETA): Technical Summary of the Final Negotiated Outcomes (October 2013)' (10 November 2013), www.international.gc. ca/trade-commerce/trade-agreements-accords-commerciaux/agr-acc/ceta-aecg/ index.aspx?lang=eng accessed 1 May 2018.

53 Simon Lester, 'An Equal Protection Clause for Investment' (6 February 2014), *Interna-tional Economic Law and Policy Blog*, http://worldtradelaw.typepad.com/ielpblog/ 2014/02/an-equal-protection-clause-for-investment.html accessed 1 May 2018.

54 Government of Canada, '(2013) Technical Summary of Final Negotiated Outcomes: Canada European Union Comprehensive Economic and Trade Agreement', www.

Nearly identical to CETA, EUSFTA also provides a clear, closed list of types of behaviour that can constitute a breach of the 'standard of treatment' provision. Notice that it is not entitled FET or even a 'minimum' standard of treatment. While a breach of legitimate expectations based on a specific representation may in and of itself constitute a breach of FET under EUSFTA, legitimate expectations appear to play a less significant role in CETA, and may only be taken into account by the tribunal in determining whether a breach has occurred of any category in the closed list. EUSFTA requires that legitimate expectations be based on an unambiguous representation reasonably relied upon by the investor, whereas CETA refers to legitimate expectations stemming from specific representations.

The inclusion in both CETA and EUSFTA of strong adjectival modifiers is also worth noting. For instance, rather than simply unfair, the impugned measure must be 'grossly unfair', 'unjust or idiosyncratic', 'targeted' discrimination, a 'fundamental' breach of due process, and exhibit 'manifest' arbitrariness. This drafting arguably limits an investor's protection, as compared to an openly worded FET standard clause. EUSFTA uses the term 'similar bad faith conduct' regarding harassment and coercion, whilst CETA employs the more generic term 'abusive treatment'. It is unclear whether these differences in syntax will lead to different interpretations by arbitral tribunals.

In contrast to CETA and EUSFTA, CPTPP narrows the scope of application of the FET standard to which qualifying investors are entitled as equivalent to the minimum standard of treatment provided under customary international law.[55] CPTPP's approach is in line with NAFTA Chapter 11, as well as the investment chapters in more recent FTAs by the US. CPTPP provides for a customary international law standard that is not limited. Indeed, CPTPP Article 9.6(2) uses inclusive, not exclusive, language, and provides that states are under no obligation to afford treatment 'in addition to or beyond that which is required by' the customary international law standard, and stipulates that its FET provisions do not 'create additional substantive rights'.[56]

CPTPP's FET provision and Annex 9-A also reflect an effort by the treaty parties to reign in some of the risky provisions that have caused problems for states wanting to implement environmental and other public interest measures. Perhaps as a reaction to the *Clayton v Canada* (Bilcon)[57] decision, which struck down a permit denial by the government for the operation of a quarry on environmental grounds, the novel, negative formulation of the minimum standard of treatment

---

international.gc.ca/trade-agreements-accords-commerciaux/assets/pdfs/ceta-aecg/ceta-technicalsummary.pdf accessed 1 May 2018.

55 Herbert Smith Freehills, 'TPP Deal Reached: Investment Arbitration Survives', Herbert Smith Freehills Dispute Resolution Arbitration Notes (5 October 2015), http://hsfnotes.com/arbitration/2015/10/05/tpp-deal-reached-investment-arbitration-survives/ accessed 1 May 2018.

56 CPTPP Article 9.6 and Annex 9-A.

57 *William Ralph Clayton, William Richard Clayton, Douglas Clayton, Daniel Clayton and Bilcon of Delaware Inc v Government of Canada*, UNCITRAL (NAFTA), PCA Case No 2009–04, Award on Jurisdiction and Liability, 17 March 2015, Dissenting Opinion of arbitrator Donald McRae, para 2.

may limit investor claims of legitimate expectations. Similar to the provision at Article 8.9(2) of CETA, Article 9.6(4) of CPTPP provides as follows:

> For greater certainty, the mere fact that a Party takes or fails to take an action that may be inconsistent with an investor's expectations does not constitute a breach of this Article, even if there is loss or damage to the covered investment as a result.

Notwithstanding the above-mentioned efforts to draft a more exacting standard of treatment, some commentators note that CPTPP's FET provisions are unlikely to assuage problems arising from arbitral tribunals' interpretive discretion because of the 'lack of consensus concerning what the customary minimum standard of treatment actually requires of states in the regulatory context.'[58]

CPTPP's legitimate expectations formulation is different from CETA (where legitimate expectations are supposed to be 'taken into account') and EUSFTA (where legitimate expectations appear to be sufficient for a finding of a breach of FET). This fine-tuning of CPTPP's language could be a response to a fear that the concept of legitimate expectations will be applied inconsistently in some investment awards. It is an attempt to redress the oscillating standard which has been fundamental to the success of investors in such claims. Such wording aims at limiting the scope of this standard of protection, in line with the *ad hoc* intervention of the NAFTA Free Trade Commission, which paved the way for a conservative case law after the interim award in *Pope & Talbot v Canada*.[59] Outside the NAFTA regime, FET has been construed on some occasions as going much beyond this minimal approach,[60] significantly reducing the host state's margin of manoeuvre. By anchoring the mention of FET to the customary minimum standard of treatment, CPTPP goes a long way towards protecting the state's regulatory power. The wording adopted might prevent extensive interpretation and do away with the use of 'legitimate expectations' as an autonomous ground of investment protection.[61] This choice might 'increase the threshold of state liability and thus limit exposure to investor claims.'[62]

---

58 Caroline Henckels, 'Protecting Regulatory Autonomy through Greater Precision in Investment Treaties: The TPP, CETA, and TPP' (2016) Journal of International Economic Law (advance access publication date 8 March 2016), 10.

59 For a brief summary of *Pope & Talbot, Inc v Government of Canada* and its relevant legal documents, see *NAFTA - Chapter 11 - Investment*, CANADA (20 May 2014), www.international.gc.ca/trade-agreements-accords-commerciaux/topics-domaines/disp-diff/gov.aspx?lang=eng accessed 1 May 2018.

60 Stephen Vasciannie, 'The Fair and Equitable Treatment Standard in International Investment Law and Practice' (1999), 70 Brit YB Int'l L 99, 102–105.

61 Stephen Fietta, 'Expropriation and the "Fair and Equitable" Standard: The Developing Role of Investors' "Expectations" in International Investment Arbitration' (2006) 23 J Int'l Arb 375, 398.

62 Sergey Ripinsky and Diana Rosert, 'European Investment Treaty Making: Status Quo and the Way Forward (A Development Perspective)' (2013), 10 TDM 19.

2. Indirect Expropriation

Expropriation provisions in all investment agreements require that the state's measures be for a public purpose, conducted under due process of law, on a non-discriminatory basis, and with prompt and adequate payment of compensation. Indirect expropriation is the second most commonly invoked breach against a host state, after the failure to afford FET. It is trite law that 'the fact that a regulatory measure affects an investment, increases its cost of doing business due to increased costs of compliance, or results in reduced profitability does not *ipso facto* mean that the State has engaged in an expropriation.'[63] However, older investment treaties generally do not provide specific guidance to arbitrators on how to distinguish an unlawful expropriation from states' inherent 'police powers' to regulate or take actions significantly affecting an investment, without the measure constituting an indirect expropriation. Customary international law is similarly uncertain.[64]

The most notable aspects of the indirect expropriation clauses and related annexes of the subject treaties are given in Table 5.3.

CPTPP, CETA, and EUSFTA reflect the recent trend by states of including a comprehensive definition of indirect expropriation, which, in turn, reflects a concerted effort on the part of the state parties to distinguish indirect expropriation from non-compensable *bona fides* regulatory measures taken by the state in pursuit of legitimate public welfare objectives. Both CETA Article 8.12 and EUSFTA IPA Article 2.6 provide detailed guidance to arbitrators on how to decide whether or not a government measure constitutes indirect expropriation, such as the economic impact, character, and duration of the measure(s) and the interference with distinct, reasonable investment-backed expectations.[65] When the state is protecting the public interest in a non-discriminatory way, the right of the state to regulate prevails over the economic impact of those measures on the investor.[66] In *Methanex v USA*, the tribunal found that:

> as a matter of general international law, a non-discriminatory regulation for a public purpose, which is enacted in accordance with due process and, which affects, *inter alios*, a foreign investor or investment, is not deemed expropriatory and compensable unless specific commitments had been given by the

---

63 Expert Report of J Christopher Thomas QC, 130, in *Hupacasath First Nation v Canada (Foreign Affairs and International Trade Canada)*, 2015 FCA 4, 379 DLR (4th) 737.

64 Caroline Henckels, 'Protecting Regulatory Autonomy through Greater Precision in Investment Treaties: The TPP, CETA, and TTIP' (2016) 19 Journal of International Economic Law 27–50, 14.

65 Following the language of the 2012 US Model BIT, Annex B(4)(a) and of the Canadian Model BIT, Article 13 and Annex B.13(1).

66 EU-Singapore Free Trade Agreement and Investment Protection Agreement (April 2018), http://trade.ec.europa.eu/doclib/docs/2018/may/tradoc_156885.pdf accessed 23 June 2018 ('governments remain free to change their laws in the future, even if that means the investor can expect to make less profit as a result.').

Table 5.3 Expropriation

CPTPP	CETA	EUSFTA IPA
Art. 9.8 (Expropriation and Compensation)	Art. 8.12 Expropriation	Art. 2.6 Expropriation
Fn [16]: Article 9.8 ... shall be interpreted in accordance with Annex 9-B ... Fn [17]: For greater certainty, for the purposes of this Article, the term "public purpose" refers to a concept in customary international law. Domestic law may express this or a similar concept by using different terms, such as "public necessity", "public interest" or "public use".	For greater certainty, this paragraph shall be interpreted in accordance with Annex 8-A.	Fn [14]: For greater certainty, this Article shall be interpreted in accordance with Annexes 1 to 3.
Annex 9-B Expropriation The Parties confirm their shared understanding that:	Annex 8-A Expropriation The Parties confirm their shared understanding that:	Annex 1 Expropriation The Parties confirm their shared understanding that:
1. An action or a series of actions by a Party cannot constitute an expropriation unless it interferes with a tangible or intangible property right or property interest in an investment. 2. Article 9.8.1 (Expropriation and Compensation) addresses two situations. The first is direct expropriation, in which an investment is nationalised or otherwise directly expropriated through formal transfer of title or outright seizure.	1. Expropriation may be direct or indirect: (a) direct expropriation occurs when an investment is nationalised or otherwise directly expropriated through formal transfer of title or outright seizure; and (b) indirect expropriation occurs if a measure or series of measures of a Party has an effect equivalent to direct expropriation, in that it substantially deprives the investor of the fundamental attributes of property in its investment, including the right to use, enjoy and dispose of its investment, without formal transfer of title or outright seizure.	1. Article 2.6 (Expropriation) addresses two situations. The first is direct expropriation where a covered investment is nationalised or otherwise directly expropriated through formal transfer of title or outright seizure. The second is indirect expropriation where a measure or series of measures by a Party has an effect equivalent to direct expropriation in that it substantially deprives the covered investor of the fundamental attributes of property in its covered investment, including the right to use, enjoy and dispose of its covered investment, without formal transfer of title or outright seizure.

CPTPP	CETA	EUSFTA IPA
3. The second situation addressed by Article 9.8.1 (Expropriation and Compensation) is indirect expropriation, in which an action or series of actions by a Party has an effect equivalent to direct expropriation without formal transfer of title or outright seizure. (a) The determination of whether an action or series of actions by a Party, in a specific fact situation, constitutes an indirect expropriation, requires a case-by-case, fact-based inquiry that considers, among other factors: (i) the economic impact of the government action, although the fact that an action or series of actions by a Party has an adverse effect on the economic value of an investment, standing alone, does not establish that an indirect expropriation has occurred; (ii) the extent to which the government action interferes with distinct, reasonable investment-backed expectations;[36] and (iii) the character of the government action. (b) Non-discriminatory regulatory actions by a Party that are designed and applied to protect legitimate public welfare objectives, such as public health,[37] safety and the environment, do not constitute indirect expropriations, except in rare circumstances.	2. The determination of whether a measure or series of measures of a Party, in a specific fact situation, constitutes an indirect expropriation requires a case-by-case, fact-based inquiry that takes into consideration, among other factors: (a) the economic impact of the measure or series of measures, although the sole fact that a measure or series of measures of a Party has an adverse effect on the economic value of an investment does not establish that an indirect expropriation has occurred; (b) the duration of the measure or series of measures of a Party; (c) the extent to which the measure or series of measures interferes with distinct, reasonable investment-backed expectations; and (d) the character of the measure or series of measures, notably their object, context and intent. 3. For greater certainty, except in the rare circumstance when the impact of a measure or series of measures is so severe in light of its purpose that it appears manifestly excessive, non-discriminatory measures of a Party that are designed and applied to protect legitimate public welfare objectives, such as health, safety and the environment, do not constitute indirect expropriations.	2. The determination of whether a measure or series of measures by a Party, in a specific situation, constitutes an indirect expropriation requires a case-by-case, fact-based inquiry that considers, among other factors: (a) the economic impact of the measure or series of measures and its duration, although the fact that a measure or a series of measures by a Party has an adverse effect on the economic value of an investment, standing alone, does not establish that an indirect expropriation has occurred; (b) the extent to which the measure or series of measures interferes with the possibility to use, enjoy or dispose of the property; and (c) the character of the measure or series of measures, notably its object, context and intent. For greater certainty, except in the rare circumstance where the impact of a measure or series of measures is so severe in light of its purpose that it appears manifestly excessive, non-discriminatory measure or series of measures by a Party that are designed and applied to protect legitimate public policy objectives such as public health, safety and the environment, do not constitute indirect expropriation.

CPTPP	CETA	EUSFTA IPA
Fn [36] For greater certainty, whether an investor's investment-backed expectations are reasonable depends, to the extent relevant, on factors such as whether the government provided the investor with binding written assurances and the nature and extent of governmental regulation or the potential for government regulation in the relevant sector. [37] For greater certainty and without limiting the scope of this subparagraph, regulatory actions to protect public health include, among others, such measures with respect to the regulation, pricing and supply of, and reimbursement for, pharmaceuticals (including biological products), diagnostics, vaccines, medical devices, gene therapies and technologies, health-related aids and appliances and blood and blood-related products.		

regulating government to the then putative foreign investor contemplating investment that the government would refrain from such regulation.[67]

The statement on indirect expropriation from *Methanex* was later reflected in American and Canadian treaty making, and underlies the annexes to all three agreements. CETA Annex 8-A, EUSFTA IPA Annex 1, and CPTPP Annex 9-B reserve regulatory space to protect legitimate public welfare objectives such as public health, safety, and the environment for the host state. Each of the three agreements employs the wording: 'except in rare circumstances' will a regulatory measure that is non-discriminatory and 'designed and applied to protect legitimate public welfare objectives' translate to an indirect expropriation. Whilst the possibility of finding an indirect expropriation is not completely barred, it will be a rare case in which a *bona fide* regulation could constitute an indirect expropriation. Therefore, this language creates a sort of presumption *against* the finding of an indirect expropriation in cases in which regulatory power is exercised. The consequence is evidently that an investor would not be entitled to compensation, *unless* he manages to overcome the burden of proof and demonstrates that those 'rare circumstances' have in fact materialised.[68] This is a clear example of recalibration on the party of states in an attempt to codify a general rule of international law (which tribunals and parties may or may not take notice of otherwise), thereby reducing it to a treaty text which the tribunal is then directed to apply.

CETA is unique in that it propounds a proportionality test for the determination of 'rare circumstances', which requires that the impact of the measure be 'so severe in light of its purpose that it appears manifestly excessive'. CPTPP does not provide any further guidance with respect to rare circumstances.

3. National Treatment

The national treatment standard ensures that foreign investors are not placed in a competitive disadvantage compared to domestic ones. The obligation is to treat the investor and investment no less favourably than a local investor and investment in 'like situations' (CPTPP and EUSFTA) or 'like circumstances' (CETA). All of the discussed treaties protect the pre- and post-establishment phases of the investment. It must be a justified distinction if the investor is treated differently from others in comparable circumstances. This provision directs tribunals to look for like situations/circumstances. In so doing, this national treatment formulation directs tribunals to allow different treatment when the distinction is based on a legitimate policy regulation, rather than on nationality.[69]

---

67 *Methanex Corp v USA*, UNCITRAL, Final Award on Jurisdiction and Merits (3 August 2005), IIC 167, pt IV, ch D, para 7.

68 Filippo Fontanelli and Giuseppe Bianco, 'Converging Towards NAFTA: An Analysis of FTA Investment Chapters in the European Union and the United States' (2014) 50 *Stan J Int'l L* 211, 223.

69 Karin L Kizer and Jeremy K Sharpe, 'Reform of Investor-State Dispute Settlement: The U.S. Experience' in Anna Joubin-Bret and Jean E Kalicki (eds), *Reshaping the Investor-State Dispute Settlement System, Journeys for the 21ˢᵗ Century* (Brill/Nijhoff

Table 5.4 sets out the key features of the national treatment provisions in each of treaty.

Recent FTA investment chapters increasingly reflect an elevation of public welfare and state regulatory interests. Note the additional clarification in the footnote to CPTPP's national treatment provision, which provides guidance to arbitral tribunals on 'like circumstances'. The level of detail included in this reservation for *bona fide* regulatory reasons to the normal application of the national treatment obligation is a novel feature in recent investment treaties, and one which reflects US practice. All US agreements include an exception to ensure that treaties are not construed to preclude actions that it considers necessary to protect the enactment of legitimate regulations in the public interest.

The inclusion of the phrase 'for greater certainty' in CPTPP could easily be exchanged for the wording 'as has always been the case'; for states appear to be stating the obvious for good measure, so as to curb discretion by arbitral tribunals to apply a different test. CPTPP's use of the above-mentioned footnote, as well as its (presumably non-binding) Drafter's Note[70] serves as guidance to arbitrators on the application of the national treatment rule for determining the basis of the distinction and how it relates to the impugned regulation. This relates back to the treaty preamble language that recognises states' inherent right to regulate; a right which, like the inherent right of states to make local choices which safeguard their public interests, has, of course always existed, but is being accentuated in these treaties.

In contrast, the EU's treaties with Canada and Singapore expressly set out the grounds of justification for what would otherwise be considered discriminatory treatment. This tool effectively exempts from ISDS certain types of core government activities and sectors, such as taxation and financial services, which can broadly affect the economic activities of the host state. EUSFTA exempts certain economic activities from national treatment, such as matters of public security or morals, of human, animal or plant life or of exhaustible natural resources.[71] Interestingly, CETA explicitly incorporates the exceptions to national treatment found at Article XX of GATT, and EUSFTA spells out the GATT grounds of justification within the agreement. It is noteworthy that CPTPP contains GATT Article XX type exceptions for other chapters of the agreement, just not in the investment chapter. The implications of this divergence between CPTPP's

---

2015), 180; *SD Meyers v Government of Canada*, NAFTA/UNCITRAL, Partial Award, para 250: 'The assessment of "like circumstances" must also take into account circumstances that would justify governmental regulations that treat them differently in order to protect the public interest.'

70 'Drafter's Note on Interpretation of "In Like Circumstances" under Article II.4 (National Treatment) and Article II.5 (Most-Favoured-Nation Treatment)', www.tpp. mfat.govt.nz/assets/docs/Interpretation%20of%20In%20Like%20Circumstances.pdf accessed 14 April 2016.

71 EUSFTA IPA, Chapter 2, Article 2.3(3) (National Treatment).

Table 5.4 National Treatment

CPTPP	CETA	EUSFTA IPA
Art. 9.4	Art. 8.6	Art. 2.3(3)
Fn[14] For greater certainty, whether treatment is accorded in "like circumstances" under Article 9.4 (National Treatment) or Article 9.5 (Most-Favoured-Nation Treatment) depends on the totality of the circumstances, including whether the relevant treatment distinguishes between investors or investments on the basis of legitimate public welfare objectives.	Standard formulation	3. Notwithstanding paragraphs 1 and 2, a Party may adopt or enforce measures that accord to covered investors and investments of the other Party less favourable treatment than that accorded to its own investors and their investments, in like situations, subject to the requirement that such measures are not applied in a manner which would constitute a means of arbitrary or unjustifiable discrimination against the covered investors or investments of the other Party in the territory of a Party, or is a disguised restriction on covered investments, where the measures are: (a) necessary to protect public security, public morals or to maintain public order[6]; (b) necessary to protect human, animal or plant life or health; (b) relating to the conservation of exhaustible natural resources if such measures are applied in conjunction with restrictions
	But see Chapter 2, Art. 2.3(1): Each Party shall accord national treatment to the goods of the other Party in accordance with Article III of the GATT 1994. To this end Article III of the GATT 1994 is incorporated into and made part of this Agreement.	on domestic investors or investments; (c) necessary for the protection of national treasures of artistic, historic or archaeological value; (d) necessary to secure compliance with laws or regulations which are not inconsistent with the provisions of this Chapter including those relating to: (i) the prevention of deceptive or fraudulent practices or to deal with the effects of a default on a contract; (ii) the protection of the privacy of individuals in relation to the processing and dissemination of personal data and the protection of confidential individual records and accounts; (iii) safety; (f) aimed at ensuring the effective or equitable[7] imposition or collection of direct taxes in respect of investors or investments of the other Party.
See Drafters' Note on Interpretation of "In Like Circumstances" Under Article 9.4 (National treatment)		

'footnote guidance' on national treatment versus CETA and EUSFTA's broader exceptions remains to be seen.

Some commentators propound the view that the inclusion of Article XX GATT exceptions 'is not well-suited to the international investment law regime to pursue sustainable development goals or provide "balance" in the regime', and that states should instead focus on clarifying their primary obligations.[72] One key distinction between investment law and international trade is that they engage fundamentally different regimes and types of commitment issues – investment treaties are aimed at providing minimum standards of protection to foreign investors, whilst GATT's purpose is primarily the reduction of tariffs and the elimination of protectionist treatment.[73] This difference results in uncertainty in how general exceptions will be applied. Further, it is uncertain how these general exceptions guide arbitrators in determining how to balance states' right to regulate with investors' rights under the relevant treaty.

4. Most-Favoured Nation (MFN) Treatment

In the same vein as national treatment, the MFN clause contains a comparative standard aimed at protecting against discrimination between foreign investors from different countries. It is meant to secure a level playing field for investors and their investments, along with compensation in the event of discrimination. The host state, in addition to not discriminating against foreign investors in favour of domestic competitors in like circumstances, must not treat foreign investors any less favourably than it treats competitors from another state party or any third-party state.[74]

Table 5.5 sets out the MFN clauses in the treaties under discussion. Note that EUSFTA excludes an MFN clause altogether from its treaty text.

Since the MFN clause means that the highest standard applicable in any BIT entered into by each state will apply to it, '[t]he adoption of such a clause may, if the states involved have already entered into previous BITs with stronger standards of investment protection, [might] render any detailed negotiation of the standards of treatment in the particular BIT somewhat redundant.'[75] CPTPP Article 9.5(3) and CETA Article 8.7(4) attempt to avoid this potential pitfall by employing language specifically aimed at resolving the

72 Elizabeth Boomer, 'Rethinking Rights and Responsibilities in Investor-State Dispute Settlement: Some Model International Investment Agreement Provisions' in Anna Joubin-Bret and Jean E Kalicki (eds), *Reshaping the Investor-State Dispute Settlement System, Journeys for the 21ˢᵗ Century* (Brill/Nijhoff 2015), 194.

73 Andrew Newcombe, 'The Use of General Exceptions in IIAs: Increasing Legitimacy or Uncertainty?' in Armand de Mestral and Celine Levesque (eds), *Improving Investment Agreements* (Routledge Research in International Economic Law 2013), 282, fn 52.

74 Allen & Overy 'Protection of Investments under the Trans-Pacific Partnership', News (16 October 2015), www.allenovery.com/news/en-gb/articles/Pages/Protection-o f-investments-under-the-Trans-Pacific-Partnership.aspx accessed 9 April 2018.

75 Mills (n 4), 439.

Table 5.5 MFN Treatment

CPTPP	CETA	EUSFTA IPA
Art. 9.5	Art. 8.7	none
1. Each Party shall accord to investors of another Party treatment no less favourable than that it accords, in like circumstances, to investors of any other Party or of any non-Party with respect to the establishment, acquisition, expansion, management, conduct, operation, and sale or other disposition of investments in its territory.	1. Each Party shall accord to an investor of the other Party and to a covered investment, treatment no less favourable than the treatment it accords in like situations, to investors of a third country and to their investments with respect to the establishment, acquisition, expansion, conduct, operation, management, maintenance, use, enjoyment and sale or disposal of their investments in its territory.	
2. Each Party shall accord to covered investments treatment no less favourable than that it accords, in like circumstances, to investments in its territory of investors of any other Party or of any non-Party with respect to the establishment, acquisition, expansion, management, conduct, operation, and sale or other disposition of investments.	2. For greater certainty, the treatment accorded by a Party under paragraph 1 means, with respect to a government in Canada other than at the federal level, or, with respect to a government of or in a Member State of the [EU] treatment accorded, in like situations, by that government to investors in its territory, and to investments of such investors, of a third country.	
3. For greater certainty, the treatment referred to in this Article does not encompass international dispute resolution procedures or mechanisms, such as those included in Section B (Investor-State Dispute Settlement).		
Fn [14] to National Treatment: For greater certainty, whether treatment is accorded in "like circumstances" under … Article 9.5 (Most-Favoured-Nation Treatment) depends on the totality of the circumstances, including whether the relevant treatment distinguishes between investors or investments on the basis of legitimate public welfare objectives.		
Drafters' Note on Interpretation of "In Like Circumstances" Under Article 9.5 (Most-Favoured Nation Treatment)		

CPTPP	CETA	EUSFTA IPA

CPTPP

2. When a claimant challenges a measure as inconsistent with … Article 9.5 (Most-Favoured-Nation Treatment), the claimant bears the burden to prove that the respondent failed to accord to the claimant or the claimant's covered investment treatment no less favourable than it accords, in like circumstances … (b) to investors of any other Party or of any non-Party, or their investments, in its territory (Article 9.5). Article … 9.5 do not prohibit all measures that result in differential treatment. Rather, they seek to ensure that foreign investors or their investments are not treated less favourably on the basis of their nationality.

3. The phrase "in like circumstances" ensures that comparisons are made only with respect to investors or investments on the basis of relevant characteristics. This is a fact-specific inquiry requiring consideration of the totality of the circumstances, as reflected in paragraphs 4 and 5. Such circumstances include not only competition in the relevant business or economic sectors, but also such circumstances as the applicable legal and regulatory frameworks and whether the differential treatment is based on legitimate public welfare objectives. Accordingly, the Parties agreed to include a new footnote in the text: "For greater certainty, whether treatment is accorded in 'like circumstances' depends on the totality of the circumstances, including whether the relevant treatment distinguishes between investors or investments on the basis of legitimate public welfare objectives."

4. In considering the phrase "in like circumstances", NAFTA tribunals have held that investors or investments that are "in like circumstances" based on the totality of the circumstances have been discriminated against based on their nationality. See, eg, *Archer Daniels Midland, et al v United Mexican States*, ICSID Case No ARB(AF)/04/05, Award, (21 November 2007), para. 197, (finding a breach of the national treatment obligation after taking into account "all 'circumstances' in which the treatment was accorded . . . in order to identify the appropriate comparator").

CETA

3. Paragraph 1 does not apply to treatment accorded by a Party providing for recognition, including through an arrangement or agreement with a third country that recognises the accreditation of testing and analysis services and service suppliers, the accreditation of repair and maintenance services and service suppliers, as well as the certification of the qualifications of or the results of or work done by those accredited services and service suppliers.

4. For greater certainty, the "treatment" referred to in paragraphs 1 and 2 does not include procedures for the resolution of investment disputes between investors and states provided for in other international investment treaties and other trade agreements. Substantive obligations in other international investment treaties and other trade agreements do not in themselves constitute "treatment", and thus cannot give rise to a breach of this Article, absent measures adopted or maintained by a Party pursuant to those obligations.

CPTPP	CETA	EUSFTA IPA
5. NAFTA tribunals have also accepted distinctions in treatment between investors or investments that are plausibly connected to legitimate public welfare objectives, and have given important weight to whether investors or investments are subject to like legal requirements. See, eg, *Grand River Enterprises Six Nations Ltd et al v United States of America*, UNCITRAL, Award (12 January 2011), at paras 166–167 ("NAFTA tribunals have given significant weight to the legal regimes applicable to particular entities in assessing whether they are in 'like circumstances' under Article... 1103 [Most-Favoured-Nation Treatment].... The reasoning of these cases shows the identity of the legal regime(s) applicable to a claimant and its purported comparators to be a compelling factorin assessing whether like is indeed being compared to like for purposes of Articles 1102 and 1103."); UNCITRAL, Award (15 November 2004), at paras 111–115 (holding that foreign investor was not "in like circumstances" with domestic investors because the difference in treatment was "plausibly connected with a legitimate goal of policy . . . and was applied neither in a discriminatory manner nor as a disguised barrier to equal opportunity"); *Pope & Talbot Inc. v Canada*, UNCITRAL, Award on the Merits of Phase 2 (10 April 2001), at paras 78–79 (the tribunal's assessment included whether the difference in treatment had a "reasonable nexus to rational government policies" and was not based on nationality).		

live issue of whether the MFN clause of a treaty applies to its dispute settlement provisions. Both treaties attempt to bar 'cherry-picking' under the MFN clause by stating that it does not apply to dispute settlement arising under its Agreement. Recall that the MFN issue commonly arises where, for example, the claimant investor fails to fulfil a requirement in the dispute resolution provisions of the applicable treaty (such as to refer a dispute to domestic procedures before commencing international arbitration) that does not bind investors from third states under the host state's other BITs.

The clarifications adopted in both CPTPP and CETA are an important advancement for international investment law, and likely result from the jurisdictional holding in *Maffezini v Spain*,[76] where it was argued by the claimant investor that the MFN clause should apply to pre-conditions to arbitration and dispute resolution clauses more widely.[77] The question in that case – which was also addressed in *Salini v Jordan*[78] and *Plama v Bulgaria*[79] – was whether, and if so in what circumstances, it is permissible for investors to invoke the MFN provision in the applicable BIT as a means of establishing jurisdiction for an arbitral tribunal where jurisdiction could not otherwise be established. In addressing this issue, the tribunal in *Maffezini* stated that a clear distinction must be drawn between the 'legitimate extension of rights and benefits by means of the operation of the [MFN] clause, on the one hand, and disruptive treaty-shopping that would play havoc with the policy objectives of underlying specific treaty provisions, on the other hand.' CPTPP and CETA take this advice to heart, and their respective formulations of the MFN protection limits its application regarding privileges given to third countries under public international law. CPTPP goes one step further and provides guidance for arbitral tribunals on how to determine 'like circumstances'.[80]

E. Conclusion

CPTPP, CETA, and EUSFTA focus on balancing investment protection provisions with the host state's right to regulate. CPTPP's investment chapter is hailed by some as the 'gold standard'[81] in international investment law, and is currently

---

76 *Emilio Agustín Maffezini v The Kingdom of Spain*, ICSID Case No ARB/97/7, Decision on Jurisdiction, 25 January 2000.

77 Herbert Smith Freehills, 'Leaked Investment Chapter of the TPP: Broad Similarities to the US Model BIT, A Nod to the Ongoing Debate and Some Outstanding Issues', *PIL Notes* (2 April 2015), http://hsfnotes.com/publicinternationallaw/2015/04/02/leaked-investment-chapter-of-the-tpp-broad-similarities-to-the-us-model-bit-a-nod-to-the-ongoing-debate-and-some-outstanding-issues/ accessed 9 April 2018.

78 *Salini Costruttori SpA and Italstrade SpA v The Hashemite Kingdom of Jordan*, ICSID Case No ARB/02/13, Decision on Jurisdiction, 15 November 2004.

79 *Plama Consortium Ltd v Republic of Bulgaria*, ICSID Case No ARB/03/24, Decision on Jurisdiction, 8 February 2005.

80 CPTPP fn 14, provided earlier at Table 5.5 MFN.

81 Allen & Overy, '*Protection of Investments under the Trans-Pacific Partnership*', Allen & Overy News (16 October 2015), www.allenovery.com/news/en-gb/articles/Pages/Protection-of-investments-under-the-Trans-Pacific-Partnership.aspx, http://business.

informing the redrafting of NAFTA 2.0, notwithstanding US President Donald Trump's withdrawal from and condemnation of CPTPP, as well as the China-led Regional Comprehensive Economic Partnership (RCEP). CETA and EUSFTA similarly reflect this touchstone in treaty drafting. This chapter analysed how the preambles, definitions, substantive protections, and accompanying carve-outs and footnotes in the respective treaty texts are being used to further enshrine states' right to regulate in the public interest. These FTAs undoubtedly tighten the rules and articulate more elaborate exceptions meant to preserve regulatory discretion in sensitive areas such as public health, safety, environmental protection, and labour standards. In so doing, they elevate the relative importance of states' right to regulate, which although always an inherent and underlying premise in trade agreements, features prominently in the core substantive obligations in these new treaties. This process of recalibration, elaboration, and restatement of the substantive aspects in states' trade initiatives is, in turn, promoting harmonisation, and a sort of 'treaty propagation',[82] in the international investment law regime. That said, this latest generation of treaties, and other BITs and mega-regionals presently under negotiation, should not deter states and the ISDS community from addressing these issues independently if there is a broader desire to avoid further criticisms and fragmentation.

financialpost.com/news/economy/forget-nafta-the-tpp-is-the-new-gold-standard-of-global-trade accessed 1 May 2018, www2.itif.org/2012-ensuring-tpp-gold-standa rd-trade-agreement.pdf accessed 1 May 2018, www.iisd.org/itn/2012/01/12/investment-developments-in-the-trans-pacific-partnership-agreement/ accessed 1 May 2018.

82 J Christopher Thomas QC, 'Introductory Comments, The Pacific Rim and International Economic Law: Opportunities and Risks of the Pacific Century' (2015) TDM 1, www.tra nsnational-dispute-management.com/article.asp?key=2168 accessed 12 April 2016 (observing that the NAFTA FTC's 2001 Interpretation have been mirrored in many subsequent treaties, which shows a kind of '"treaty propagation" whereby an expression of a substantive obligation in one bilateral treaty finds its way into other treaties not necessarily being negotiated by the states who agreed the original text.'

Mark Feldman, Rodrigo M Vignolo and Cristián R Chiffelle, 'The Role of Pacific Rim FTAs in the Harmonisation of International Investment Law: Towards a Free Trade Area of the Asia-Pacific' (March 2016) *E15 Task Force on Investment Policy, International Centre for Trade and Sustainable Development* (ICTSD) (Geneva, Switzerland), 13, http://e15initiative.org/wp-content/uploads/2015/09/E15-Investm ent-Feldman-Monardes-Rodriguez-Chiffelle-Final.pdf accessed 12 April 2016.

Part II

Investment Arbitration and the European Legal Order

1 A Comparative Law Approach as a Technique for Solving Conflicts between EU Law and Investment Arbitration

The Case of the ECtHR

Blerina Xheraj[1]

A. Introduction

The impact of European Union (EU) law over investment treaty obligations represents a relatively new topic in international legal scholarship. The academic input on this issue started to develop mainly in the aftermath of the first known investment treaty dispute challenging the validity of the investor-state arbitration clause in an intra-EU Bilateral Investment Treaty (BIT), for reasons related to a member state's (MS) accession to the EU.[2] The last 14 years of investment arbitration practice were, consequently, dominated by polemics on alleged conflicts between EU law and International Investment Agreements (IIAs).

This chapter proposes a framework for solving these conflicts based on a comparative law approach. It identifies the relevant '*tertium comparationis*' in the field of fundamental human rights, as represented by the legal framework of the European Convention on Human Rights (ECHR) and the case law of the European Court of Human Rights (ECtHR).

The chapter analyses the jurisprudence of the ECtHR dealing with the interplay between EU law and the ECHR. This analysis focuses on two aspects of that interaction: i) the determination of 'the existence of a conflict' between the ECHR and EU law; and ii) the determination of 'the existence of international responsibility' of EU MS for violations of international human rights obligations under the ECHR. It identifies the patterns of the relationship between EU law obligations and international human rights obligations of EU MS and compares the approach of the ECtHR with the reasoning of investment arbitral tribunals

1 Blerina Xheraj (PhD, University of Geneva; LLM, Queen Mary University of London; JD, University of Siena; Diploma in Legal Studies, University of Oxford) can be contacted at blerina.xheraj@graduateinstitute.ch. The author would like to thank Valentina Vadi for valuable comments on an earlier draft of this contribution, and Marc Bungenberg for the feedback in the aftermath of the Bucerius Law School Conference (Hamburg, April 2016).
2 *Eastern Sugar BV v The Czech Republic*, SCC No 088/2004 (UNCITRAL), Notice of Arbitration 22 June 2004.

dealing with 'like' matters in the investment context. The chapter concludes that the ECtHR and investment arbitral tribunals follow partially different approaches when addressing the intersection with EU law, and that the relationship between EU law and investment treaty law should be determined by following the patterns found in the case law of the ECtHR.

B. Comparative Law as a Method for Solving Conflicts

The use of comparative method for the study of international law has received broad support in international legal scholarship.[3] Martti Koskenniemi highlights that the comparative study of international law addresses issues pertaining to debates on fragmentation and conflicts of international law.[4] In the context of international arbitration, the need for a comparative law approach was initially advocated by the late Pierre Lalive. He sustained that comparative law should be promoted through legal teaching because knowledge of other regimes may help avoid clashes of legal cultures.[5] In the specific area of investment treaty law, Stephan Schill also suggests that comparative public law should be adopted as the 'appropriate method of interpretation'.[6] Other authors opine that a comparative perspective is key to identify general principles of law, and can play an important role in improving the perceived legitimacy of the system.[7]

Applying comparative methods to the study of international law is challenging. The first challenge consists in the identification of the proper *tertium comparationis*, ie the legal system with more similarities to the system of reference. In this case, the proper legal comparator is the framework of the ECHR, and the system of reference is investment arbitration. These systems share many similarities. First, treaty rights protected under these regimes have similar nature and private parties may exercise those rights to sue states before international courts/arbitral tribunals for violations of the respective treaty obligations.[8] Second, from a substantive law perspective, the subject matter of the ECHR overlaps with EU treaties; both frameworks regulate fundamental human rights. It is basically for these reasons that the ECtHR is often

---

3 Martti Koskenniemi, 'The Case for Comparative International Law' (2009) 20 Finnish Yearbook of International Law; Valentina Vadi, 'Critical Comparisons: The Role of Comparative Law in Investment Treaty Arbitration' (2010) 39 Denver Journal of International Law and Policy; Stephan Schill, 'Comparative Public Law Methodology in International Investment Law'. www.ejiltalk.org/comparative-public-law-methodology-in-international-investment-law/ accessed 1 May 2018; Anthea Roberts, 'Comparative International Law? The Role of National Courts in Creating and Enforcing International Law' (2011) 60 International & Comparative Law Quarterly; Sarah Dookhun, 'Q&A with Professor Pierre Lalive' (2008) Global Arbitration Review; Stephan Schill (ed), *International Investment Law and Comparative Public Law* (OUP 2010).
4 Koskenniemi (n 3) 6.
5 Dookhun (n 3).
6 Schill, 'Comparative Public Law Methodology in International Investment Law' (n 3).
7 Vadi (n 3) 71.
8 Zachary Douglas, *The International Law of Investment Claims* (CUP 2009) 7.

used as an alternative venue to hear investment disputes[9] at a substantive or at the enforcement stage.[10] Besides, there is an extensive case law of investment tribunals already referring to the jurisprudence of the ECtHR confirming that there is already in place some form of judicial dialogue between investment arbitral tribunals and the ECtHR in relation to other issues.[11]

The second challenge of the comparative approach is the identification and application of the proper method. 'Methodology' is a *sine qua non* of comparative law studies,[12] but different views exist on what constitutes the best comparative law method. Some authors suggest the 'functional method' as the most appropriate method for the study of comparative law.[13] The functional method concentrates on functionality problem solving, which means that although the legal regime that we choose as a legal *tertium* may be different from our own legal regime, it remains functionally equivalent to the former because it addresses the same problem. Functional comparative law starts with the identification of the *tertium comparationis*, ie the compared legal order, continues with the evaluation phase and ends with the attempt to uniform the law at a regional or international level. This chapter relies on the functional method.

C. Overlaps between the ECHR and EU Law

I. The Existence of Conflicts

Provisions of the ECHR have often clashed with EU law obligations. The ECHR was adopted in 1950 by the Council of Europe in order to guarantee the

9 Christian Tomuschat, 'The European Court of Human Rights and Investment Protection', in Christina Binder and others, *International Investment Law for the 21st Century: Essays in Honour of Christoph Schreuer* (OUP 2009).

10 Leonila Guglya, 'International Review of Decisions Concerning Recognition and Enforcement of Foreign Arbitral Award: A Threat to the Sovereignty of the States or an Overestimated Hazard (so Far)? (With Emphasis on the Developments within the International Investment Arbitration Setting)' (2011) Czech Yearbook of International Law 96–100.

11 For a detailed overview of legal reasoning of investment tribunals and the use of ECtHR jurisprudence, please refer to James D Fry, 'International Human Rights Law in Investment Arbitration: Evidence of International Law's Unity' (2007) 18 Duke Journal of Comparative & International Law. Examples include: *Lauder v Czech Republic* on expropriation standards; *Tecmed* on the standard of proportionality and legitimate public interest; Separate Opinion of Walde in *Thunderbird Gaming* on the concept of legitimate expectations; *Saipem* tribunal on expropriated awards and the capacity of judicial acts to expropriate an investor (jurisdictional decision); *Amco Asia v Indonesia* and *ADC v Hungary* on assessment of damages; and *Mondev* on non-retroactivity of laws. See also, UNCTAD, 'Selected Recent Developments in IIA Arbitration and Human Rights' (United Nations 2009) IIA Monitor No 2 UNCTAD/WEB/DIAE/IA/2009/7.

12 Simone Glanert, 'Method?', in Pier G Monateri (ed), *Methods of Comparative Law* (Edward Elgar 2012) 63; For a more general overview, see John C Reitz, 'How to Do Comparative Law' (1998) 46 The American Journal of Comparative Law.

13 Konrad Zweigert and Hein Kötz, *Introduction to Comparative Law* (OUP 1998).

protection of fundamental human rights and freedoms between contracting parties. There are 47 signatories to the ECHR nowadays and that number includes all existing 28 EU MS. The EU is currently not a member of the ECHR.[14] The protection of fundamental human rights under the ECHR is guaranteed by the ECtHR, while the Court of Justice of the European Union (CJEU)[15] guarantees the correct application and interpretation of EU law, which includes protection of human rights and fundamental freedoms. Therefore, the subject-matter 'human rights' is regulated by two different legal regimes. The existence of overlapping regimes for the protection of human rights in the EU territory increases the potential for conflicts between them.

The ECtHR has often decided disputes concerning substantive law conflicts between EU law and the ECHR.[16] In *POVSE v Austria*, [17] the alleged conflict was one between the enforcement of a return order required under EU law by the EU Regulation 2201/2003 (Brussels IIa Regulation) on one hand, and Article 8 ECHR on the right to respect for family life, on the other hand. The object of the dispute was the enforcement of a return order issued by the Venice Youth Court and the decision of an Austrian Court to enforce that return order, in a dispute concerning the custody of an Italian born child holding dual Austrian/Italian citizenships.

The First Section of the ECtHR addressed the issue of conflicting obligations deriving from EU law and the ECHR and resolved the alleged conflict by using the interpretative technique of conflict avoidance. The ECtHR argued in favour of the principle of 'presumption of compliance'[18] and 'presumption of equivalent protection' between the two regimes. According to the ECtHR: 'the protection of fundamental rights afforded by the European Union **is in principle equivalent** to that of the Convention system as regards both the **substantive guarantees** offered and the **mechanisms controlling their observance**'.[19]

---

14 However, the changes introduced by the Treaty of Lisbon (ToL) and Protocol No 14 impose on the EU an obligation to accede to the ECHR. The EU has already taken steps towards its accession to the ECHR, although unsuccessfully. For more, see Opinion 2/13 of the Court (Full Court) of 18 December 2014, available at: http://curia.europa.eu/juris/document/document.jsf?docid=160882&doclang=EN accessed 1 May 2018. In this Opinion, the CJEU gave its negative opinion on the latest proposed accession agreement of 2013. It is not clear whether the EU will present another modified version of that agreement to the court for its approval and whether it will finally join the ECHR in the near future.

15 Previously referred to as the European Court of Justice (ECJ).

16 Interestingly, jurisdictional law conflicts between the ECHR and EU law have never been decided by the ECtHR.

17 *Sofia POVSE and Doris POVSE v Austria*, ECtHR Application No 3890/11 of 18 June 2013.

18 Gilles Cuniberti, 'Povse v. Austria: Taking Direct Effect Seriously?', http://conflictoflaws.net/2013/povse-v-austria-taking-direct-effect-seriously/ accessed 1 May 2018; Gilles Cuniberti, 'Gascon on Povse: A Presumption of ECHR Compliance When Applying the European Civil Procedure Rules', http://conflictoflaws.net/2013/gascon-on-povse-a-presumption-of-echr-compliance-when-applying-the-european-civil-procedure-rules/ accessed 1 May 2018.

19 *POVSE v Austria* (n 16), para 77 (emphasis added).

The ECtHR had established the principle of presumption of compliance in its previous landmark *Bosphorus* case.[20] In *Bosphorus*, the alleged conflict was one between Article 1 of Protocol No 1 to the ECHR and Article 8 of Regulation (EEC) No 990/93, which was adopted by the EU in order to implement the United Nation Security Council Resolution 820 of 1993. The applicant in that case was a Turkish company and the object of the dispute concerned a lease contract and the impounding of an aircraft in Ireland. Before getting to the ECtHR, the question on applicability of Article 8 to the aircraft under lease was referred by the Irish Supreme Court to the European Court of Justice (ECJ) for a preliminary ruling. The ECJ issued the ruling and decided that Article 8 would apply, thus driving the applicant to seek protection of his fundamental rights before the ECtHR.

The ECtHR justified the state behaviour adopted to comply with an international organisation legal obligations, based on the argument that the organisation affords protection of fundamental rights which is 'at least equivalent to that for which the Convention provides'.[21] The Court clarified the content of that protection in 'substantive terms' and in relation to 'the mechanism controlling their observance'. Moreover the ECtHR made the observance of control mechanisms a necessary condition for the effectiveness of substantive protection.[22]

The Court elaborated on the meaning of 'equivalent' as encompassing 'comparable' protection, to the exclusion of 'identical' protection. Only after these conditions were fulfilled, a presumption arose against alleged violations of the ECHR by the EU MS.[23] Yet, the ECtHR opted for a qualified presumption, ie a presumption that could be rebutted when certain requirements were not respected. For example, the ECtHR referred to the 'manifest deficiency' of the protection as a cause for invalidating the presumption.[24]

In a similar vein, the ECtHR in *POVSE* explained the conditions under which the presumption of compliance could apply. One of those conditions was identified in the absence of discretion for the EU MS when implementing obligations deriving from EU law.[25] The argument of the Court continued with observations regarding the 'exercise' and the 'existence' of such discretion[26] and concluded by stating that 'the presumption ... of compliance with the Convention has not been rebutted'.[27] Finally, the Court decided that there was a violation of Article 8 of the Convention,[28] but rejected the application based on other considerations.

---

20 *Bosphorus Hava Yollari turizm ve ticaret Aninim Sirketi v Ireland*, ECtHR Application No 45036/98 of 30 June 2005.
21 *Bosphorus* (n 20), para 155.
22 *Bosphorus* (n 20), para 160.
23 *Bosphorus* (n 20), para 156.
24 ibid.
25 *POVSE v Austria* (n 17), para 78.
26 *POVSE v Austria* (n 17), para 82.
27 *POVSE v Austria* (n 17), para 87.
28 *POVSE v Austria* (n 17), para 70–71.

II. The Bosphorus Test and Its Application

The ECtHR in *Bosphorus* established that the presumption of equivalent protection applies to acts of MS. Later the Court extended the application of the presumption to procedures of the ECJ.[29] In the case *Cooperatieve*, the applicant claimed violation of Article 6 ECHR by an order of the ECJ that denied to the applicant the permission to submit a written response to the Advocate General's Opinion during the proceedings.[30] The dispute concerned mechanical cockle fishing in the Netherlands waters of the Wadden Sea, and the annulment of the Cooperatieve's cockle-fishing licenses on the ground that it violated the Habitats Directive. The ECtHR in *Cooperatieve* concluded that: 'the **presumption applies** not only to actions taken by a contracting party but also **to the procedures** followed within such an international organisation and hence to the procedures of the ECJ'.[31]

Ultimately the ECtHR did not rebut the presumption because it did not find a 'manifestly deficient protection'. In doing so, the ECtHR analysed Rules and Procedures of the ECJ, especially Rule 61 on reopening of oral proceedings[32] and the case law related to its application.

Notwithstanding the previously stated considerations, the ECtHR has – on other occasions – rebutted the presumption of compliance based on the principle of equivalent protection. One example is the decision of the ECJ in *Michaud v France*.[33] Here the Strasbourg Court considered whether Article 8 of the Convention was in conflict with an obligation to report suspicions regarding money laundering posed on French lawyers as a result of transposition of an EU Directive in the French legal system. The ECtHR underlined differences that existed between obligations imposed on MS by an EU Regulation on one hand, and obligations deriving from an EU Directive on the other hand. As the ECtHR put it, only the former legal act is 'directly and fully applicable in the Member States… and leaves no margin of manoeuvre at all in the execution of the obligation'.[34] The latter instead, 'are binding on the member states as regards the results to be achieved but leave it to them to choose the means and manner of achieving it'.[35]

The ECtHR therefore departs from its previous decision in *Bosphorus*, based on the differences that exist between types of EU legal obligations and the amount of discretion applicable to the MS. Moreover, the circumstance by which the Conseil d'Etat denied to the party the possibility to refer the question to the ECJ for a preliminary ruling was considered crucial for denying effect to the presumption of

---

29 *Cooperatieve Producentenorganisatie van de Nederlandese Kokkelvisserij UA v the Netherlands*, ECtHR Application No 13645/05 of 8 April 2005.

30 *Cooperatieve* (n 29), 16.

31 *Cooperatieve* (n 29), 20 (emphasis added).

32 Article 61 of the Rules of Procedure of the Court of Justice says the following: 'The Court may after hearing the Advocate General order the reopening of the oral procedure'.

33 *Michaud v France*, ECtHR Application No 12323/11 of 6 December 2012.

34 *Michaud* (n 33), para 113.

35 ibid.

equivalent protection.[36] In the reasoning of the ECtHR, this meant that contrary to *Bosphorus*,[37] the control mechanism was not fully brought into play.

Another example of rebuttal is found in *MSS v Belgium and Greece*.[38] The applicant (an Afghan citizen who asked the Court not to have his name publicly displayed) lodged an application against both Belgium and Greece for violations of Articles 2, 3 and 13 of the ECHR, while acting in conformity of the EU asylum rules under Dublin Regulation II. Similarly, the ECtHR analysed obligations of MS and confirmed that the presumption of equivalent protection was rebutted because Belgium should have known of the treatment afforded to asylum seekers in Greece and it had the means to do so.[39] In addition, the Dublin Regulation contained a 'sovereignty clause', which allowed a MS to derogate from the general regime and handle a request for asylum by a third-country national. The ECtHR concluded that Belgium could have derogated from the general regime, given the risk faced by the applicant of having his rights violated in Greece. This confirms that although a Regulation – as compared to a Directive – is binding in its entirety, it finally depends on the language used in the Regulation whether the obligation on the MS is derogatory or non-derogatory in nature. Only in the latter case the presumption can survive a rebuttal.

III. Determining the International Responsibility of EU MS

The *Michaud* judgment clarified a number of other aspects related to the interaction between EU law and the ECHR. With respect to principles of international responsibility, *Michaud* confirmed that the MS (not the EU) remains internationally responsible for the acts they undertake in order to comply with international obligations, 'even when those obligations stem from their membership of an international organisation to which they have transferred part of their sovereignty'.[40] In *Michaud*, Ireland was held responsible, even though it was recognised that the conduct of the state was 'dictated by acts of the EU'.[41]

In *Cantoni v France*,[42] again, the ECtHR confirmed its position that an act of the MS taken in order to fulfil obligations of EU law remained an act of the MS with no direct consequences of attribution on the EU itself.[43] The case concerned French criminal proceedings constituted against Mr Cantoni for unlawfully selling pharmaceutical products and alleged violations of Article 7 of the ECHR. The

---

36 *Michaud* (n 33), para 115.
37 *Michaud* (n 33), para 114.
38 *MSS v Belgium and Greece*, ECtHR Application No 30696/09 of 21 January 2011.
39 For more see *MSS* (n 38), paras 340, 345, 352, 353 and 358.
40 *Michaud* (n 33), para 102.
41 Enzo Cannizzaro, 'Beyond the Either/Or: Dual Attribution to the European Union and to the Member State for Breach of the ECHR', in Malcolm Evans and Panos Koutrakos (eds), *The International Responsibility of the European Union* (Hart Publishing 2013) 340.
42 *Cantoni v France*, ECtHR Application No 17862/91 of 11 November 1996.
43 Cannizzaro (n 41) 303.

argument made by the ECtHR in this case was in line with Advocate General Jacobs' opinion in *Bosphorus*, who expressed the view that 'community law cannot release Member States from their obligations under the Convention'.[44] This conclusion has been interpreted as a confirmation of the role of consent in international relations.[45] Still, the EU Commission intervened in support of the case that Ireland could not be held liable in the circumstances where it had no discretion, because of the binding force of the ruling of the ECJ on the Irish Supreme Court.[46]

Even when a MS transfers competences to the EU, the state remains internationally responsible for its acts in that area of competence. This is confirmed by the ECtHR's decision in *Matthews v United Kingdom.* [47] The dispute in *Matthews* concerned an alleged conflict between the ECHR and the European Community (EC) Act on Direct Elections of 1976. The dispute questioned the responsibility of the UK for non-application of the Election Act in Gibraltar, a dependent territory of the United Kingdom. The contested EC Act is an international treaty between MS of the EU, and like many other treaties it constitutes a primary source of the EU legal order. In that case the ECtHR clarified that the Act was a 'treaty within the Community legal order', not an act of the Community.[48] As such, the Act could not be challenged before the ECJ.[49] As a result, the state remained internationally responsible for the legal act deemed to be in conflict with the ECHR.[50]

The *Matthews* judgment confirms that when dealing with EU primary sources, as it may be the case with EU Treaty provisions, the ECtHR can scrutinise in full the contested EU legislation. This is so because the provisions of EU treaties cannot be reviewed by the ECJ. To the contrary, EU secondary law can be subject to the ECJ's scrutiny. Based on this peculiarity of EU law, the ECtHR has distinguished between primary and secondary EU law, in the sense that it has adopted either a higher, or a lower threshold, for finding a violation of fundamental human rights. The threshold for finding a violation is lower in the case of primary EU law, and higher in the case of secondary EU law. In a different context, some authors have included in the list of provisions, which can be fully reviewed by the ECtHR, the provisions of the EU treaties on market freedoms, including provisions on free movement of capital.[51]

44 *Bosphorus* (n 20), para 46.
45 Cannizzaro (n 41) 303–304.
46 *Bosphorus* (n 20), para 125.
47 *Matthews v United Kingdom*, ECtHR Application No 24833/94 of 18 February 1999, para 32.
48 *Matthews* (n 47), para 33.
49 ibid.
50 For a contrary view, see Cuniberti, 'Povse v. Austria: Taking Direct Effect Seriously?' (n 18). The author states that: 'it is not coherent to admit the direct effect of EU law and, at the same time, to hold the MS liable for a breach of ECHR arising out of the application of EU law'.
51 Franz C Ebert and Marie Walter, 'Cross-Border Collective Action: Jurisprudential Conflicts between European Courts over the Right to Strike' (International Labour Office 2013) Discussion Paper No 16, 24–26.

Overall, and despite the fact that *Bosphorus* and *POVSE* differ from *Matthews* in relation to the nature of the legislative act (*Bosphorus* and *POVSE* deal with secondary EU legal acts, while *Matthews* deals with a primary legal act), it is submitted that in both cases the same rule on international responsibility applies, ie the MS remains internationally responsible – not the EU.

D. Overlaps between EU Law and Investment Treaty Law

I. *The Existence of Conflicts*

A survey of arbitral awards dealing with the relationship between EU law and investment treaty law reveals that investment tribunals constantly deny the existence of conflicts between these two legal orders.[52] When faced with alleged incompatibilities on substantive rights such as the free movement of capital, the arbitral tribunal in *Eastern Sugar* declared that 'free movement of capital and protection of the investment are different, but complementary things.'[53] In the tribunal's reasoning, if rights under two regimes are not equal, it does not mean they are incompatible:

> If the EU Treaty gives more rights than does the BIT, then all EU parties, including the Netherlands and Dutch investors, may claim those rights. If the BIT gives rights to the Netherlands and to Dutch investors that it does not give other EU countries and investors, it will be for those other countries and investors to claim their equal rights. But **the fact that these rights are unequal does not make them incompatible**. [54]

The tribunal in *Eureko* confirmed that there is no incompatibility between EU law and BIT's legal rights.[55] The tribunal suggested that the substantive rights under EU law are not as broad as those provided by the BIT. It stated that 'there are rights that may be asserted under the BIT that are not secured by EU law',[56] and added the following:

> the BIT establishes extensive legal rights and duties that are neither duplicated in EU law nor incompatible with EU law. **The protections afforded to investors by the BIT are**, at least potentially, **broader than those available under EU law** (or, indeed, under the laws of any EU Member State).[57]
>
> …

---

52 Investment awards decided after July 2016 – the time this contribution was finalised – are not reflected in this chapter.
53 *Eastern Sugar BV (Netherlands) v The Czech Republic*, UNCITRAL SCC Case No 088/2004, Partial Award of 27 March 2007, para 168.
54 *Eastern Sugar* (n 53), para 170 (emphasis added).
55 *Eureko BV v The Slovak Republic*, UNCITRAL, PCA Case No 2008–13, Award on Jurisdiction, Arbitrability and Suspension of 26 October 2010, para 245.
56 *Eureko* (n 55), para 262.
57 *Eureko* (n 55), para 245 (emphasis added).

Thus, a treaty provision guaranteeing non-discrimination does not have, even indirectly, the 'same subject-matter' as a treaty provision guaranteeing fair and equitable treatment, even if on the facts of a particular case a claim might be raised under either provision and the claimant might be able to recover compensation for the entire loss under either provision. In this respect the notion of the same 'subject-matter' has certain common features with the notions of 'identity' that operate in the context of the doctrine of res judicata.[58]

The final award in *Micula v Romania* also excluded the existence of 'real conflicts' between treaties[59] and likewise, the tribunal in *AES v Hungary* denied that this is a case of conflict between EU law and the Energy Charter Treaty (ECT).[60] The same was confirmed by the arbitral tribunal in the *Electrabel* award, where it stated that it 'has decided that there is no material inconsistency between the ECT and EU law.'[61]

The tribunal in *Electrabel* addressed the hierarchy between legal orders and sustained that there was no inconsistency between them. Because it did not find any inconsistency, the tribunal did not need to rely on harmonious interpretation techniques in order to reconcile the obligations of Hungary under the ECT with its obligations under EU law.[62] The tribunal stated, nonetheless, in *obiter dicta*, that should a material inconsistently be found, EU law would prevail over the ECT.[63] Finally, the tribunal in *Electrabel* confirmed that the substantive protection in Part III of the ECT and EU law do not cover the same subject-matter. Because the subject-matter differs, Article 16 ECT, ie the conflict clause provision of the ECT, could not apply.[64] It follows that with respect to the level of protection of substantive rights, arbitral tribunals deny the following: i) the existence of conflicts; ii) the existence of the same subject-matter; and iii) the existence of the presumption of equivalent protection between EU law and investment treaty law.

The existence of conflicts between EU law and investment treaty law has also been argued with regard to mechanism controlling the observance of those substantive rights. MS and the EU have often objected to the validity of arbitration clauses in intra-EU BIT-based disputes, and intra-EU disputes based on mixed agreements like the ECT. On 6 March 2018, this issue has been finally resolved by the CJEU, at least from a purely EU law perspective.[65] Responding to a request

---

58 *Eureko* (n 55), para 258.
59 *Ioan Micula, Viorel Micula, SC European Food SA, SC Starmill SRL and SC Multipack SRL v Romania*, ICSID Case No ARB/05/20, Final Award of 11 December 2013, para 319.
60 *AES Summit Generation Limited and AES-Tisza Erömü Kft v The Republic of Hungary*, ICSID Case No ARB/07/22, para 7.6.8
61 *Electrabel SA v Republic of Hungary*, ICSID Case No ARB/07/19, para 4.167.
62 *Electrabel* (n 61), para 4.146.
63 *Electrabel* (n 61), para 4.191.
64 *Electrabel* (n 61), para 4.176.
65 *Slovak Republic v Achmea BV*, Case C-284/16, Judgment of the Court (Grand Chamber) of 6 March 2018, available at: http://curia.europa.eu/juris/document/document.jsf?text=&docid=199968&pageIndex=0&doclang=EN&mode=req &dir=& occ=first&part=1&cid=404057 accessed 1 May 2018.

for a preliminary ruling from the German Supreme Court in the *Achmea* dispute, the Grand Chamber decided that there is an incompatibility between the investor-state dispute settlement (ISDS) provision of the Netherlands–Czech and Slovak Republic BIT, and EU law. The CJEU declared that Article 8 of the BIT 'has an adverse effect on the autonomy of EU law'.[66]

From an investment arbitration perspective, the situation is very different. Arbitral tribunals have constantly denied the existence of inconsistencies between ISDS provisions in intra-EU BITs (and mixed agreements like the ECT) and EU law.[67] If the case concerns an intra-EU BIT dispute, arbitral tribunals argue that the accession of a state to the EU does not, *per se*, invalidate the ISDS provision contained in the intra-EU BIT.[68] If the dispute concerns a mixed agreement to which the EU itself is a contracting party, arbitral tribunals argue that the EU cannot object to the investor-state arbitration option that it has previously agreed to.[69]

Notwithstanding the earlier, the presence of an ISDS provision in investment agreements makes the procedural guarantees of these legal instruments very different from the guarantees offered under EU law. According to arbitral tribunals, the fact that some rights are broader under one regime makes them unequal but does not make them incompatible. According to the tribunal in *Eureko*, even if there was some kind of duplication of rights between EU law and the BIT, it would not undermine the jurisdiction of the tribunal.[70]

II. The International Responsibility of EU MS

EU law may preclude international wrongfulness of a MS in accordance with Article 23, 24 and 25 of the ILC Draft Articles on Responsibility of States for Internationally Wrongful Acts. Regardless, this objection has never been used in investment arbitration proceedings and arbitral tribunals have not had the chance to rule on that issue.[71] Instead, tribunals have ruled on whether acts of the MS taken pursuant to the dictate of EU law were exempted from its scrutiny of legitimacy. For example, arbitral tribunals questioned whether EU MS enjoyed discretion when they adopted the specific acts required by EU law and alleged to be in violation of investment treaty obligations.

The tribunal in *Eastern Sugar* analysed the Czech Republic's First Sugar Decree of 2000, Second Sugar Decree of 2001 and Third Sugar Decree of 2003. The First Decree contained a flexible system of reserve quotas and the Czech Republic claimed that this quota system was required by an EU Regulation which did not give discretion to the government. Nonetheless, the tribunal concluded that in

---

66 ibid para 59.
67 *Electrabel* (n 61), para 4.146.
68 For some examples, see the awards in *Eastern Sugar* (n 53), *Eureko* (n 55) and *Micula* (n 59).
69 *Electrabel* (n 61), para 4.164
70 *Eureko* (n 55), para 249.
71 *Micula* (n 59), para 329.

that case the government enjoyed full discretion.[72] That discretion, the ineffective implementation and the insufficient legislative basis were, however, not sufficient to determine a violation of the BIT's fair and equitable treatment (FET).[73] In other words a finding in favour of discretion did not lead to a finding of investment treaty violation.

In *Electrabel* the arbitral tribunal addressed the discretion exercised by Hungary when enforcing the Decision of the EU Commission. The claimant did not contest the enforcement in itself, but the way it was performed which, according to the claimant, was not in conformity with the discretion afforded by EU law to the EU MS. The argument of the claimant was that Hungary had a 'margin of appreciation' when enforcing that decision. The question posed to the tribunal was whether Hungary breached the ECT when it exercised that discretion.[74] The tribunal excluded the violation of the ECT by referring to the decision of another tribunal in the *AES* award.[75]

In international investment law, the debate about the exercise of discretion by an EU MS is strictly linked to the FET standard of protection. The tribunal in *AES* considered whether Article 10(1) ECT was violated by Hungary's acts. According to the tribunal, those acts should be reasonable in order to avoid a violation of the FET. Said differently, one should prove the existence of a 'rational policy' and that the measure was taken 'in pursuit of that policy'.[76] Consequently, the nature of the measure and the way it is implemented is important for the establishment of an appropriate correlation between the measure on one side, and the achievement of the public policy objective on the other side.[77] Moreover a violation of the FET is related to a potential violation of legitimate expectations. When this is the case, one may question 'who bares the risk of the regulatory change, the state or the investor'?[78]

In *Micula*, after acknowledging the state's right to regulate,[79] the tribunal engaged in the analysis of the role of EU law in determining violations of reasonable legitimate expectations. The tribunal agreed that for a certain period (between 1998 and 2003), the claimant believed the scheme would be qualified as regional operating aid which would be exempted from the general prohibition under EU law.[80] Once it became clear in 2002 that the schemes constituted prohibited aid covered by the prohibition of EU law, Romania thought that they could be turned into compatible aid. The EU Commission initially asked Romania to 'align' the aids to the acquis – and not to terminate them[81] – but later, it adopted a stronger position.

---

72 *Eastern Sugar* (n 53), para 261.
73 *Eastern Sugar* (n 53), para 274.
74 *Electrabel* (n 61), para 4.168.
75 *Electrabel* (n 61), para 4.169.
76 *AES* (n 60), para 10.3.7.
77 *AES* (n 60), para 10.3.9.
78 *Micula* (n 59), para 665.
79 *Micula* (n 59), para 666.
80 See *Micula* (n 59), para 691 (referring to the Guidelines on Regional Aid of 1998).
81 *Micula* (n 59), paras 767, 777.

In view of that EU request, the tribunal concluded that the repeal of incentives was motivated by EU's demand[82] and they were not unreasonable.[83]

In *AES* the respondent declared that the reason for introducing the Price Decrees was also due to the 'pressure from the EU Commission's investigations and the foreseeable obligation to correct state aid that the Commission's decision would impose'.[84] For the tribunal, that circumstance constituted a rational public policy. However, the tribunal concluded that because no binding decision was issued by the EU Commission, Hungary was not yet under any obligation of EU law to behave as it did.[85] Still, in cases similar to *AES*, EU law may play a role in assessing the state conduct[86] and more importantly, the decision in *AES* seems to exclude that possibility for a state to shield its acts behind EU law dictate. The tribunal remained of the opinion that MS cannot exclude international responsibility for their own acts.

The situation in *AES* differs from the one concerning the dispute in *Electrabel*. In the latter dispute, a binding EU Commission decision was already rendered against the respondent state. Only in similar situations the host state can use EU law as a shield to its responsibility under investment agreement. In this case the EU act was binding on the MS and the latter did not exercise any margin of discretion. For that reason, the tribunal in *Electrabel* considered is absurd to find Hungary liable for acts required under EU law.[87]

Last, if the tribunal concludes that the EU did not afford discretion to the MS and that act violated the BIT, can the tribunal review the legality of EU law? In *Eureko* the tribunal ruled that, although it may apply EU law in the merits phase in order to determine the scope of rights and obligations under the BIT, it cannot rule on 'breaches of EU law as such'.[88] In many awards, tribunals have been careful and have expressly assured the EU that they are not reviewing the legality of EU legal acts by engaging in interpretation and application of EU law.[89]

E. Comparative Observations

According to investment arbitral tribunals, EU law and BITs cover different subject-matters and there is no conflict between the EU legal order and investment

---

82 *Micula* (n 59), para 796.
83 *Micula* (n 59), para 811.
84 *AES* (n 60), para 10.3.15.
85 *AES* (n 60), paras 10.3.16–10.3.18.
86 See *AES* (n 60), paras 7.6.8–7.6.9:

> The question of whether Hungary was, may have been, or may have felt obliged under EC law to act as it did, is only an element to be considered by this Tribunal when determining the 'rationality,' 'reasonableness', 'arbitrariness' and 'transparency' of the reintroduction of administrative pricing and the Price Decrees.

87 *Electrabel* (n 61), para 6.72.
88 *Eureko* (n 55), para 290.
89 *Electrabel* (n 61), para 4.198.

arbitration. To the contrary, the ECtHR recognizes that EU law and the ECHR cover partially the same subject-matter, and overlap with each other. The analysis of the case law shows that the assumptions applied by the ECtHR and investment arbitral tribunals when addressing alleged conflicts with EU law are very different; investment tribunals start their reasoning by denying the existence of conflicts, while the ECtHR applies a presumption against its existence.

The presumption of the ECtHR is based on the fact that EU law and the ECHR offer equivalent protection in the field of fundamental human rights. The application of the presumption of equivalent protection between EU law and the ECHR requires that the protection offered by both legal orders be at least 'comparable', although it need not be 'identical'. This presumption applies only when the protection covers both substantive law and its controlling mechanisms. When one regime does not provide for controlling mechanisms equivalent to the ECHR, the ECtHR denies the existence of the equivalent protection and consequently that presumption ceases to apply (ie rebuttable presumption). In these cases, a conflict can arise between EU law and the ECHR.

The reasoning of arbitral tribunals behind the denial of conflict in investment arbitration practice is different. Investment tribunals do not consider the difference in procedural rights – such as the existence of ISDS – as a reason to confirm the existence of conflicts. According to investment tribunals, a conflict does not exist, even when the protection is not 'equal'. Protection may be more extensive under one regime, but it may not be considered incompatible with the protection under the other regime. Therefore investment arbitral tribunals do not consider the concept of 'inequality' of protection as the determining factor for accepting the existence of a conflict.

As mentioned earlier, when reaching a decision on equivalent protection the ECtHR refers to equivalent 'substantive guarantees' and equivalent 'mechanisms controlling their observance'. And although the presumption may cover all types of EU law sources, the threshold applied to find a violation of the ECHR varies, depending on the type of EU legal act involved (eg EU primary law versus EU secondary provision). The ECtHR distinguishes among different EU secondary sources (eg Regulations versus Directives) depending on the amount of discretion left to the MS. This Court also distinguishes between legal acts of the same category, based on the derogatory or non-derogatory language contained in that legal act.

Investment tribunals, to the contrary, apply these considerations only in order to determine the responsibility of the MS for violations of specific standards of protection. And even in that case, tribunals do not always distinguish between different sources of EU law, and do not engage in analysing the derogatory or non-derogatory language of an EU law obligation. While this is often done in order to avoid any form of review of EU legal acts, the same is not true for the ECtHR. This court reviews acts of the EU. The ECtHR reviews even primary EU sources, as it is the case with treaties concluded between MS. Since these acts are not reviewable before the ECJ, sometimes the ECtHR scrutinises them in full. When the object of review are secondary EU legal acts, the threshold applied by the ECtHR is lower, because those acts can be reviewed and challenged also before EU courts.

The ECtHR constantly holds EU MS internationally responsible for their acts, even when they have transferred their competence to an international organisation. The act of a MS remains its own act, irrespective of whether it is fulfilling an EU law obligation. To the contrary, investment tribunals tend to deny the responsibility of EU MS when their acts are required by EU law. In doing so investment tribunals tend to take a formalistic approach by relying more on the form of the EU act, rather than on its substance.

F. Conclusions

The approach of investment arbitral tribunals differs from the approach of the ECtHR when addressing alleged conflicts with EU law. This chapter highlights that when deciding on the relationship between EU law and investment arbitration, there is no need for investment tribunals to reinvent the wheel; the jurisprudence of the ECtHR in the field of human rights provides satisfactory solutions that can be transposed to the context of investment arbitration.

Investment arbitral tribunals should follow the patterns identified in the case law of the ECtHR when addressing the relationship between EU law and the ECHR, in order to determine the relationship between EU law and investment arbitration. These patterns consist in: a) the application of a rebuttable presumption against conflict between the EU legal order and investment arbitration (ie the ECtHR conflict test); and b) the allocation of international responsibility to EU MS (not the EU) for violations of investment treaty obligations for reasons related to EU law (ie the ECtHR international responsibility test). MS should bare international responsibility even when they have conferred a competence to the EU.

Moreover, the patterns identified in the ECtHR case law on the relationship between the ECHR and EU law have a substantive nature and do not necessarily support the superiority of EU law. In other words, the approach of the ECtHR is not formalistic, but takes into account the substance of EU law obligations.[90] It is also for that reason that arbitral tribunals should follow the example of the ECtHR when dealing with similar questions of law in the area of investment protection.

90 Tobias Lock, *The European Court of Justice and International Courts* (OUP 2015) 202.

2 The Energy Charter Treaty and European Union Law

Mutually Supportive Instruments for Economic Cooperation or Schizophrenia in the '*Acquis*'?

Cees Verburg[1]

A. Introduction

The relationship between international investment agreements (IIAs) and European Union (EU) law increasingly receives academic attention. This chapter deals specifically with the relationship between the Energy Charter Treaty (ECT), an IIA that applies to the energy sector, and EU law. Since the EU is a contracting party to the ECT and the ECT is, therefore, part of the *acquis communautaire*, one might expect that no difficulties arise in this relation. Unfortunately, practice has proven otherwise. For example, EU competition law might require the termination of contracts, such as power purchasing agreements (PPAs), if these contracts were concluded on terms that are very favourable for the investor since they might constitute unlawful state-aid while these contracts might be protected under the ECT.[2]

This chapter will analyse some of these difficulties by reference to the ECT *Electrabel v Hungary* case. This chapter will primarily adopt the perspective of

1 PhD Researcher at the Groningen Centre of Energy Law, University of Groningen. E-mail: c.g.verburg@rug.nl. The author would like to thank Prof Dr M M T A Brus, Prof Mr Dr M M Roggenkamp, and Dr R C Fleming for their valuable feedback. Any errors and omissions remain my own. Also, the author wants to acknowledge that this research has benefitted from the support of the Dutch Energy Law Association (NeVER) and Stibbe. After the completion of this chapter a 'Decision on Jurisdiction' was rendered in the *RREEF Infrastructure (GP) Limited and RREEF Pan-European Infrastructure Two Lux SARL v Kingdom of Spain* case that also addressed the issue of the relationship between the ECT and EU law. The Decision seems to support some of the points made in this chapter. Therefore, reference to the *RREEF* case will be made in the footnotes. In addition, the *RREEF* Decision makes reference to and seems to follow an ECT Award rendered in the *PV Investors v Spain* case, which is currently not publicly available.
2 See for instance *EDF International SA v Republic of Hungary*, UNCITRAL. *Electrabel SA v Republic of Hungary*, ICSID Case No ARB/07/19. *AES Summit Generation Limited and AES-Tisza Erömü Kft v Republic of Hungary*, ICSID Case No ARB/07/22. Note: Hungary is not bound by the umbrella clause of the ECT, nevertheless, these cases demonstrate the potential conflict between EU law and the ECT.

public international law to this issue since it is to be expected that investor-state dispute settlement (ISDS) Tribunals that derive their jurisdiction from the ECT will adopt this approach.[3] The *Electrabel* Award is chosen as a reference since the Tribunal elaborated extensively on the relationship between the ECT and EU law.

Section B will introduce the *Electrabel v Hungary* case and describe and analyse some of the findings of the Tribunal. These findings concern the text of the ECT regarding the relationship with other international agreements, the interpretation of the ECT in the light of EU law, the international responsibility and liability of EU member states for implementing EU law, and the conclusion of the *Electrabel* Tribunal that EU law prevails over the ECT in cases of inconsistency. Section C will contain recommendations regarding the procedure that should be followed when there might be a substantive conflict between the ECT and EU law. Finally, this chapter will end with a conclusion.

B. *Electrabel v Hungary*

The *Electrabel v Hungary* case concerned the termination of a PPA and the introduction of a fixed price regime for electricity tariffs by Hungary. Electrabel incurred damage as a consequence of the reduced electricity tariffs and therefore initiated ISDS proceedings against Hungary on the basis of the ECT. Hungary had been 'under serious pressure from the [European Commission] to take action at least to minimize the effects of what the EC considered to be unlawful state aid, if not to terminate the PPAs outright.'[4] At various points in its 'Decision on Jurisdiction, Applicable Law and Liability' does the *Electrabel* Tribunal touch upon the relationship between the ECT and EU law; some of these points will be addressed in turn.

I. The ECT Text

The first point relates to the text of the ECT and whether it contains any guidance as to how conflicts should be resolved between various international agreements. Article 16 ECT addresses the relation of the ECT to other international agreements and provides for the following:

3 It has to be noted that this problem can also be analysed from the perspective of EU law. When adopting this approach other issues might become relevant, such as the primacy of the EU law, the role of the ECJ, and the division of competences between the EU and its Member States. The point of view that any conflict between the ECT and EU law has to be examined from the perspective of public international law in ECT cases is supported by the 'Decision on Jurisdiction' in the *RREEF Infrastructure (GP) Limited and RREEF Pan-European Infrastructure Two Lux SARL v Kingdom of Spain* case. See: *RREEF Infrastructure (GP) Limited and RREEF Pan-European Infrastructure Two Lux SARL v Kingdom of Spain*, ICSID Case No ARB/13/30, Decision on Jurisdiction (2016), para 75.

4 This quote is taken from the – factually very similar – *AES* case. *AES Summit Generation Limited and AES-Tisza Erömü Kft v Republic of Hungary*, ICSID Case No ARB/07/22, Award (2010), para 9.2.13.

Where two or more Contracting Parties have entered into a prior international agreement, or enter into a subsequent international agreement, whose terms in either case concern the subject matter of Part III or V of this Treaty,

1   nothing in Part III or V of this Treaty shall be construed to derogate from any provision of such terms of the other agreement or from any right to dispute resolution with respect thereto under that agreement; and
2   nothing in such terms of the other agreement shall be construed to derogate from any provision of Part III or V of this Treaty or from any right to dispute resolution with respect thereto under this Treaty,

where any such provision is more favourable to the Investor or Investment.

As becomes clear from the first paragraph, Article 16 applies in relation to Part III (Investment Promotion and Protection) and Part V (Dispute Settlement) of the ECT. According to Bamberger and Wälde, Article 16 is 'designed to ensure that an investor will enjoy the most favourable treatment available to him under any treaty'.[5] However, it is clear from Article 16 that this article can only be applied in case subsequent agreements concern the same subject matter. It is for this reason that the *Electrabel* Tribunal refused to apply Article 16: while the ECT and EU law have much in common, especially in relation to the protection of foreign investors, both bodies of law do so from a very different perspective.[6] Hence, they do not 'share the same subject-matter.'[7] Arguably, the Tribunal hereby adopted a rather narrow interpretation of 'subject matter': indeed, one will not find a 'fair and equitable treatment' (FET) standard in EU law, but it does contain rules that can provide protection to investors investing abroad. Nevertheless, similar views were held by investment tribunals constituted under other IIAs.[8] The *AES v Hungary* Tribunal concluded that Article 16 ECT was only applicable in case of a dispute between the ECT and EU law, which it considered was not the case.[9]

---

5   Craig Bamberger and Thomas Wälde, 'The Energy Charter Treaty' in Martha M Roggenkamp and others (eds), *Energy Law in Europe: National, EU and International Regulation* (OUP 2007) 158.
6   *Electrabel SA v Republic of Hungary*, ICSID Case No ARB/07/19, Decision on Jurisdiction, Applicable Law and Liability (2012), para 4.177.
7   ibid para 4.176.
8   *Eastern Sugar BV v the Czech Republic*, SCC Case No 088/2004, Partial Award (2007), para 159. *Eureko BV v the Slovak Republic*, PCA Case No 2008–13, Award on Jurisdiction, Arbitrability and Suspension (2010), paras 254–263.
9   *AES Summit Generation Limited and AES-Tisza Erömü Kft v Republic of Hungary*, ICSID Case No ARB/07/22, Award (2010), paras 7.6.7–7.6.9. The Tribunal in the *RREEF v Spain* case noted the following about Article 16 ECT:

> [...] the Tribunal would have to insure the full application of its '*constitutional*' instrument, upon which its jurisdiction is founded. This conclusion is all the more

Perhaps more interesting to note is not so much what is in the ECT text, but what is *not* in the ECT; namely a so-called 'disconnection clause.'[10] According to Klabbers, this is the 'oldest and most well-known technique for safeguarding the *acquis*.[11] For instance, Article 27 of the 1989 European Convention on Transfrontier Television, that was concluded before the ECT negotiations were held, states:

> In their mutual relations, Parties which are members of the European Community shall apply Community rules and shall not therefore apply the rules arising from this Convention except in so far as there is no Community rule governing the particular subject concerned.

The purpose of this clause is clear: EU relations *inter se* shall be governed by EU law and the relations *vis-à-vis* third states shall be governed by the treaty.[12] However, since the ECT does not contain a disconnection clause it could be argued that the ECT was also intended to govern intra-EU relations, otherwise the drafters could have easily inserted a disconnection clause. In fact, during the negotiations of the ECT the European Commission proposed to include a disconnection clause into the current Article 24 of the ECT.[13] Given the current text of the ECT, this proposal was rejected. In the *Charanne v Spain* and *RREEF v Spain*

> compelling given that Article 16 of the ECT expressly stipulates the relationship between the ECT and other agreements – from which there is no reason to distinguish EU law.

Nevertheless, the *RREEF* Tribunal endorsed that the provisions concerned a different subject-matter, a point seemingly supported by the Tribunal in the *PV Investors v Spain* case. See: *RREEF Infrastructure (GP) Limited and RREEF Pan-European Infrastructure Two Lux SARL v Kingdom of Spain*, ICSID Case No ARB/13/30, Decision on Jurisdiction (2016), paras 75, 79.

10 Christian Tietje, 'The Applicability of the Energy Charter Treaty in ICSID Arbitration of EU Nationals vs EU Member States' (2008) 78 Beiträge zum Transnationalen Wirtschaftsrecht 11, http://papers.ssrn.com/sol3/papers.cfm?abstract_id=1625323& download=yes accessed 2 March 2016. Richard Happ and Jan A Bischoff, 'Role and Responsibility of the European Union Under the Energy Charter Treaty' in Graham Coop (ed), *Energy Dispute Resolution: Investment Protection, Transit and the Energy Charter Treaty* (JurisNet 2011) 178.

11 Jan Klabbers, 'Safeguarding the Organization *Acquis*: The EU's External Practice' (2007) 57 *Int'l Org L Rev* 57, 70.

12 ibid.

13 The proposed clause provided for the following:

> In their mutual relations, Contracting Parties which are members of the EC shall apply Community rules and shall not therefore apply the rules arising from this Agreement except insofar as there is no Community rule governing the particular subject concerned.

See: Letter by Secretary-General Clive Jones to Ambassador Rutten dated 19 February 1993 (CLJ/jal). Source: Archives of the Energy Charter Secretariat.

cases, Spain argued that the ECT nevertheless contains an 'implicit' disconnection clause.[14] While the *Charanne* Tribunal did acknowledge that the presence of a disconnection clause could resolve a conflict between the ECT and the EU treaties, it did not rule on this argument since the Tribunal was of the opinion that there was no conflict between the two in the case at hand.[15] Taking into account that the disconnection clause was explicitly rejected during the negotiations, any arbitrator that would read such a non-existing clause into the treaty would arguably – *de facto* – be amending the treaty; something well beyond the powers of an arbitrator to do. Also, according to Article 216(2) of the Treaty on the Functioning of the European Union (TFEU), international agreements concluded by the EU, such as the ECT, are binding upon the EU institutions and on its member states. Thus, in the absence of a specific provision to the contrary, the EU and its member states are bound by the ECT as is any other contracting party.

II. Interpreting the ECT in the Light of EU Law

The second point relates to the method with which the *Electrabel* Tribunal interpreted the ECT, since the Tribunal interpreted the ECT in the light of EU law while not all ECT contracting parties are a member state of the EU.

One of the striking features of the ECT's chapter on investment protection is the potentially high level of investment protection that it offers to investors. Contrary to many recent IIAs, the ECT's protection standards are largely unqualified and poorly defined. Every ECT Tribunal will thus have to give substance to the provisions of the ECT while taking into account the specific facts of each case. In the process of interpreting the ECT, Tribunals often rely on the Vienna Convention on the Law of Treaties (VCLT).[16] One way of avoiding conflict between the ECT and EU law is by interpreting the ECT provisions in the light of EU law. The *Electrabel* Tribunal stated that 'the ECT's historical genesis and its text are

---

14 *Charanne BV and Construction Investments SARL v Spain*, SCC Case No 062/2012, Award (2016), paras 433–439. *RREEF Infrastructure (GP) Limited and RREEF Pan-European Infrastructure Two Lux SARL v Kingdom of Spain*, ICSID Case No ARB/13/30, Decision on Jurisdiction (2016), para 81.

15 *Charanne BV and Construction Investments SARL v Spain*, SCC Case No 062/2012, Award (2016), para 438. The *RREEF* Tribunal was not convinced by Spain's argument that there is an 'implicit disconnection clause.' The Tribunal stated that: '[...] given that there is no disharmony or conflict between the ECT and EU, as noted above, there is simply no need for a disconnection clause, implicit or explicit.' Considering the consequences of a disconnection clause, the Tribunal considers that a reservation or unequivocal disconnection clause is necessary. Therefore, an attempt to read an implicit disconnection clause into the ECT would be 'untenable.' See: *RREEF Infrastructure (GP) Limited and RREEF Pan-European Infrastructure Two Lux SARL v Kingdom of Spain*, ICSID Case No ARB/13/30, Decision on Jurisdiction (2016), paras 81–87.

16 See for instance *Plama Consortium Ltd v Republic of Bulgaria*, ICSID Case No ARB/03/24, Decision on Jurisdiction (2005), para 117.

such that the ECT should be interpreted, if possible, in harmony with EU law.'[17] Article 31(3)(c) VCLT allows a Tribunal to take into account '[a]ny relevant rules of international law applicable in the relations between the parties.' However, the fact that the ECT is a multilateral treaty and includes many non-EU contracting parties, distinguishes the ECT from intra-EU bilateral investment treaties (BITs). In the case of the latter it could be argued that, since both the home state of the investor and the respondent state are an EU member state, EU law contains relevant rules of international law applicable in the relations between the parties.[18] In the case of the ECT, the situation is slightly more complicated. The main question is, what is meant by 'the parties' in Article 31(3)(c) VCLT?[19] In relation to this question, a Panel of the World Trade Organization (WTO) considered the following:

> [...] Article 31(3)(c) indicates that it is only those rules of international law which are 'applicable in the relations between the parties' that are to be taken into account in interpreting a treaty. This limitation gives rise to the question of what is meant by the term 'the parties'. [...] It may be inferred from these elements that the rules of international law applicable in the relations between 'the parties' are the rules of international law applicable in the relations between the States which have consented to be bound by the treaty which is being interpreted, and for which that treaty is in force. This understanding of the term 'the parties' leads logically to the view that the rules of international law to be taken into account in interpreting the WTO agreements at issue in this dispute are those which are applicable in the relations between the WTO Members.[20]

This statement reinforces the argument that interpreting intra-EU BITs in line with EU law is possible on the basis of Article 31(3)(c) VCLT, but that this is more complicated in ECT cases since nearly half of the ECT constituency is not an EU Member. According to the WTO Appellate Body 'a delicate balance must', therefore, be struck:

17 *Electrabel SA v Republic of Hungary*, ICSID Case No ARB/07/19, Decision on Jurisdiction, Applicable Law and Liability (2012), para 4.130. The *RREEF v Spain* Tribunal also considers that the ECT and EU law should, to the extent possible, be interpreted 'in such a way not to contradict each other.' See: *RREEF Infrastructure (GP) Limited and RREEF Pan-European Infrastructure Two Lux SARL v Kingdom of Spain*, ICSID Case No ARB/13/30, Decision on Jurisdiction (2016), paras 76–77.
18 Hanno Wehland, 'Intra-EU Investment Agreements and Arbitration: Is European Community Law an Obstacle?' (2009) 58 ICLQ 297, 307. Thomas Eilmansberger, 'Bilateral Investment Treaties and EU Law' (2009) 46 CMLR 383, 421.
19 Panos Merkouris, *Article 31(3)(c) VCLT and the Principle of Systemic Integration: Normative Shadows in Plato's Cave* (Nijhoff/Brill 2015) 18, 46–48.
20 WTO, *European Communities – Measures Affecting the Approval and Marketing of Biotech Products* (29 September 2006) WT/DS291/R, WT/DS292/R, WT/DS293/R, para 7.68.

An interpretation of 'the parties' in Article 31(3)(c) should be guided by the Appellate Body's statement that 'the purpose of treaty interpretation is to establish the common intention of the parties to the treaty.' This suggests that one must exercise caution in drawing from an international agreement to which not all WTO Members are party. [...] In a multilateral context such as the WTO, when recourse is had to a non-WTO rule for the purposes of interpreting provisions of the WTO agreements, a delicate balance must be struck between, on the one hand, taking due account of an individual WTO Member's international obligations and, on the other hand, ensuring a consistent and harmonious approach to the interpretation of WTO law among all WTO Members.[21]

There are some good arguments in favour of this 'balanced approach' as suggested by the Appellate Body, since it allows for a coherent interpretation of a single legal document in the wider context of international law but which does not lead to a situation in which contracting parties are bothered with legal obligations that they did not enter into. In my view, the Tribunal in the *Electrabel v Hungary* case did not adopt this balanced approach. Instead, when considering whether or not the claimants could have had legitimate expectations, the Tribunal considered the following:

[...] the Tribunal concludes that the objectives of the ECT and EU law were and remained similar as regards anti-competitive conduct, including unlawful State aid. Foreign investors in EU Member States, including Hungary, cannot have acquired any legitimate expectations that the ECT would necessarily shield their investments from the effects of EU law as regards anti-competitive conduct.[22]

The Tribunal adopted this reasoning by reference to Article 6 ECT and EU (competition) law. While Article 6 ECT does address the issue of competition, and unilateral and concerted anti-competitive conduct in particular, it can hardly be said that this provision contains anything more than hortatory obligations. Therefore, for the following reasons I find the reasoning of the Tribunal problematic.

First, Article 6 ECT speaks of anti-competitive conduct, but the words 'state aid' are not mentioned. It is clear that the Tribunal equates unlawful state aid with anti-competitive conduct, but even in EU law both concepts are treated differently.[23] Therefore, the Tribunal might have oversimplified matters in this case by classifying unlawful state aid as uncompetitive conduct. Interestingly,

---

21 WTO, *European Communities and Certain Member States – Measures Affecting Trade in Large Civil Aircraft* (18 May 2011), WT/DS316/AB/R, para 845.

22 *Electrabel SA v Republic of Hungary*, ICSID Case No ARB/07/19, Decision on Jurisdiction, Applicable Law and Liability (2012), para 4.141.

23 Anti-competitive conduct falls within the scope of Articles 101 & 102 TFEU whereas State aid is addressed by Article 107 TFEU.

early drafts of the ECT contained a separate provision addressing state aid.[24] However, in the final version of the ECT the state aid provision would be omitted while the competition provision is included. Thus, while the negotiators of the ECT were aware of the difference between the two concepts, they decided to incorporate one into the treaty while disregarding the other. In light of this, the Tribunal's approach to simply merge the two concepts becomes even more untenable.

Second, in a hypothetical but similar case as *Electrabel* between an investor from a non-EU ECT state and another non-EU ECT party, it would be remarkable for a Tribunal to make reference to EU competition law since both the home state of the investor and the host State are not bound by it. Moreover, in the absence of an international competition law regime for such a State to rely on, it would be much more difficult for a respondent state to rely on its domestic competition law, since Article 27 VCLT states that a 'party may not invoke the provisions of its internal law as justification for its failure to perform a treaty.' Hence, both the legal certainty and the reciprocity of the ECT would be undermined if the ECT is interpreted in the light of EU law. Legal certainty might be impaired since different levels of investment protection may be offered by the ECT: EU member states can refer to EU competition law which, in turn, would lead to a lower level of investment protection, while other ECT parties cannot refer to their competition law as easily and a higher level of investment protection would be provided for in those states.[25] As a consequence, the reciprocity of the ECT would also be undermined: in the EU foreign investors receive less investment protection than those in non-EU jurisdictions. This would probably be an unacceptable situation.

24 See for example: Article 10, BA 6, Basic Agreement, 21 January 1992. www.energy charter.org/fileadmin/DocumentsMedia/ECT_Drafts/4_-_BA_6__21.01.93_.pdf accessed 3 April 2017. Article 13, BA 4, Basic Agreement, 31 October 1991. www. energycharter.org/fileadmin/DocumentsMedia/ECT_Drafts/3_-_BA_4__31.10. 91_.pdf accessed 3 April 2017.

25 This argument can be exemplified by reference to the *AES v Kazakhstan* case. In this case, the Dutch investor advanced a FET claim regarding the amendments to and application of Kazakh competition law. The Tribunal merely said 'that the nature of the changes made to the Kazakh competition legislation are not of a nature to breach the FET standard under Article 10(1) of the ECT' without enunciating on the special nature of competition law by reference to Article 6 ECT in the same way as the *Electrabel* Tribunal did. Contrary to the *Electrabel* Tribunal, the *AES v Kazakhstan* Tribunal did not explicitly preclude the possibility that the investor could have acquired legitimate expectations that would have shielded their investment from the effects of the application of competition laws, but rather that it did not consider that 'the successive amendments of the competition law were of such a nature to violate any legitimate expectations under the ECT'. Reference was made by the Tribunal to competition law 'practices in other European countries and emerging economies.' See *AES Corporation and Tau Power BV v Republic of Kazakhstan*, ICSID Case No ARB/10/16, Award (2013), paras 283, 289, 317.

III. International Responsibility and Liability

A third interesting deliberation of the *Electrabel* Tribunal is related to the issues of international responsibility and liability. According to the Tribunal:

> Where Hungary is required to act in compliance with a legally binding decision of an EU institution, recognized as such under the ECT, it cannot (by itself) entail international responsibility for Hungary. Under international law, Hungary can be responsible only for its own wrongful acts. The Tribunal considers that it would be absurd if Hungary could be liable under the ECT for doing precisely that which it was ordered to do by a supranational authority whose decisions the ECT itself recognizes as legally binding on Hungary.[26]

This statement of the Tribunal could be interpreted as an implicit recognition that EU decisions are to be treated somewhat different from the acts of states by stating that they are 'recognized as such under the ECT.' However, there is nothing in the text of the ECT that seems to justify such a differential treatment of the EU as a 'Regional Economic Integration Organization' (REIO). As noted by Happ and Bischoff, the only differentiations that the ECT make between REIOs and states are related to the definition of the 'Area' of a contracting party, the rules regarding voting in the Energy Charter Conference, and entrance into force of the ECT.[27] A 'contracting party' is defined as a state or a REIO in Article 1(7) ECT, thereby explicitly putting states and REIOs on an equal footing for the purpose of the ECT. Also, the investment protection chapter of the ECT and its ISDS provision only refer to 'contracting parties.' Therefore, a textual reading of the ECT leads to the conclusion that the EU has the same obligations under the ECT *vis-à-vis* investors as states. Another reading of the earlier quote could suggest that the investors initiated ISDS proceedings against the wrong respondent, since Hungary cannot be held responsible for it, and that the EU should be respondent in cases involving EU law.

Regardless, the earlier statement touches upon some of the most complicated issues that may arise in international relations involving the EU. Namely, who is responsible for what and how should this be determined? In my view, the statement of the *Electrabel* Tribunal is incorrect, both from the perspective of public international law as well as EU law, for the following reasons.

As to the perspective of public international law, it has to be noted that the issue of international responsibility of international organisations is far from clear. For instance, in relation to international litigation practice concerning the EU and EU

---

26 *Electrabel SA v Republic of Hungary*, ICSID Case No ARB/07/19, Decision on Jurisdiction, Applicable Law and Liability (2012), para 6.72.

27 Richard Happ and Jan Asmus Bischoff, 'Role and Responsibility of the European Union Under the Energy Charter Treaty' in Graham Coop (ed), *Energy Dispute Resolution: Investment Protection, Transit and the Energy Charter Treaty* (JurisNet 2011) 163–165.

measures, at least two different approaches can be adopted. For example, under the European Convention on Human Rights (ECHR), the European Court of Human Rights (ECtHR) reached the opposite conclusion as the *Electrabel* Tribunal. For instance, in the *Bosphorus v Ireland* case, the ECtHR considered the following:

> [...] establishing the extent to which a State's action can be justified by its compliance with obligations flowing from its membership of an international organisation to which it has transferred part of its sovereignty, the Court has recognised that absolving Contracting States completely from their Convention responsibility in the areas covered by such a transfer would be incompatible with the purpose and object of the Convention; the guarantees of the Convention could be limited or excluded at will, thereby depriving it of its peremptory character and undermining the practical and effective nature of its safeguards. The State is considered to retain Convention liability in respect of treaty commitments subsequent to the entry into force of the Convention.[28]

It has been said that the Draft Articles on the Responsibility of International Organizations of the International Law Commission follow a similar approach as the ECtHR, although these draft articles have attracted criticism.[29] What makes the statement of the *Electrabel* Tribunal problematic is that it allows for a circumvention of international obligations of both the EU and its member states: Although both are bound by the ECT, the EU often acts through its member states since they apply EU law through their national authorities, which the EU has acknowledged within the WTO.[30] After all, EU law has to be implemented by the member states in order to be applied and enforced. Thus, if EU member states cannot be liable for violations of the ECT if EU law requires them to breach their ECT obligations, and if all Tribunals would interpret the ECT in the light of EU law as the *Electrabel* Tribunal did, it will be difficult to establish a breach of the ECT by the EU or its member states.

It has to be noted, however, that litigation practice under the WTO takes a different direction, with the EU acting as the main litigant in nearly all cases that concern the EU and its member states. According to Eeckhout, the European Commission is 'most eager' to act as respondent in WTO cases stressing that it has

---

28 *Bosphorus Hava Yollari Turizm v Ireland*, ECtHR (Application No 45036/98), Judgment (2005), paras 152–154.

29 Thomas Roe and Matthew Happold, *Settlement of Investment Disputes under the Energy Charter Treaty* (CUP 2011) 182–184. Frank Hoffmeister, 'Litigating Against the European Union and Its Member States – Who Responds Under the ILC's Draft Articles on International Responsibility of International Organizations' (2010) 21 EJIL 723, 728. See also: Articles 16(1) & 19 Draft Articles on the Responsibility of International Organizations, 2011. The commentary to Article 16 refers to the *Bosphorus v Ireland* case of the ECtHR.

30 WTO, *European Communities – Protection of Trademarks and Geographical Indications for Agricultural Products and Foodstuffs* (15 March 2005) WT/DS174/R, paras 7.98, 7.725. Thomas Roe and Matthew Happold, *Settlement of Investment Disputes under the Energy Charter Treaty* (CUP 2011) 173.

'full international responsibility under a mixed agreement', even when 'Member State measures are in issue.'[31] It has been said that WTO jurisprudence has accepted that member states act '*de facto* as organs of the Community, for which the Union would be responsible under WTO law and international law in general.'[32] Contrary to the ECtHR, however, a WTO Panel did not provide a reasoning that logically leads to this conclusion. In the *EC – Biotech Cases*, for instance, the Panel merely considered the following:

> [...] the European Communities as a whole is the responding party in respect of the member State safeguard measures. This is a direct consequence of the fact that the Complaining Parties have directed their claims against the European Communities, and not individual EC member States. The European Communities never contested that, for the purposes of this dispute, the challenged member State measures are attributable to it under international law and hence can be considered EC measures.[33]

Thus, contrary to the ECtHR's doctrinal reasoning why EU member states retain responsibility under international law for implementing EU law under the ECHR, the WTO Panel accepted the EU's responsibility because of practical reasons or the absence of objections. Of course, a relevant consideration is that, contrary to the WTO, the EU cannot directly be a respondent at the ECtHR since it is not (yet) a contracting party to the ECHR. Nevertheless, there are good reasons why the 'Strasbourg' approach should be adopted in ISDS cases.

First of all, I find the reasoning behind the approach of the ECtHR more persuasive since it can hardly be said that there is any legal reasoning involved in the WTO cases at all. Second, what international human rights law and investment law have in common is that both bodies of law are aimed at providing effective protection to individuals. In both cases, those individuals that are protected under international law can enforce the states' obligations on an international level, either through the ECtHR or ISDS. International trade law, on the other hand, usually does not have direct effect in the national legal order of contracting parties nor does it allow standing for individuals through a mechanism like ISDS.[34] Article 30.6 of the Comprehensive Economic and Trade Agreement (CETA) between

31 Piet Eeckhout, *EU External Relations Law* (OUP 2011) 263.

32 Frank Hoffmeister, 'Litigating Against the European Union and Its Member States – Who Responds under the ILC's Draft Articles on International Responsibility of International Organizations' (2010) 21 *EJIL* 723, 728. WTO, *European Communities – Protection of Trademarks and Geographical Indications for Agricultural Products and Foodstuffs* (15 March 2005) WT/DS174/R, paras 7.98, 7.725.

33 WTO, *European Communities – Measures Affecting the Approval and Marketing of Biotech Products* (29 September 2006) WT/DS291/R, WT/DS292/R, WT/DS293/R, para 7.101.

34 Hélène Ruiz Fabri, 'Is There a Case – Legally and Politically – for Direct Effect of WTO Obligations?' (2014) 25 EJIL 151, 151–153.

the EU and Canada, for instance, is quite unequivocal by stating that the agreement only contains obligations between the parties under public international law. Finally, for very practical reasons I consider it unlikely that the EU would be as 'eager' to be a respondent in ISDS cases as it is in trade disputes. For instance, in WTO law it is common practice that when the Dispute Settlement Body establishes that a WTO Member has violated its WTO obligations, the WTO Member concerned is obliged to bring its national policy in conformity with the WTO Agreements.[35] Monetary compensation is therefore rare in WTO practice.[36] Practice in ISDS is completely the opposite: monetary compensation is usually awarded when a IIA breach has been established but rarely will ISDS Tribunals order a state to amend its legislation. In fact, Article 26(8) ECT specifically provides for 'monetary damages in lieu of any other remedy.' This argument is also supported by the EU's Financial Responsibility Regulation that it adopted in the wake of its newly gained competence over FDI with respect to the common commercial policy.[37] The preamble states that it would be 'inequitable if awards and costs of arbitration were to be paid from the budget of the Union where the treatment was afforded by a Member State, unless the treatment in question is required by Union law.'[38]

The statement of the *Electrabel* Tribunal can also be questioned from a European perspective. The ECT is a 'mixed agreement' from the perspective of EU law, meaning that both the EU and its member states are a contracting party.[39] The reason for this lies in the division of competences between the EU and its member states.[40] Thus, when a treaty involves issues over which the EU does not have exclusive competence, the involvement of the member states is required.[41] The declaration that the EU made upon ratification of the ECT makes a reference to this division of competences: 'The European Communities and their Member States have both concluded the Energy Charter Treaty and are thus internationally responsible for the fulfillment of the obligations contained therein, in accordance with their respective competences.'[42]

---

35 Article 19 Dispute Settlement Understanding, Annex 2 of the WTO Agreement.
36 David Palmeter and Petros C. Mavroidis, *Dispute Settlement in the World Trade Organization: Practice and Procedure* (CUP 2004) 266.
37 Article 3 Regulation (EU) No 912/2014 of the European Parliament and the of the Council of 23 July 2014 establishing a framework for managing financial responsibility linked to investor-to-state dispute settlement tribunals established by international agreements to which the European Union is party (2014) L 257/121.
38 ibid Preamble Recital 5.
39 To complicate matters further, since 1 January 2016, Italy has withdrawn from the ECT. Therefore, not all EU Member States are bound by the Treaty.
40 Piet Eeckhout, *EU External Relations Law* (OUP 2011) 213.
41 ibid.
42 Statement submitted by the European Communities to the Energy Charter Secretariat pursuant to Article 26(3)(b)(ii) of the Energy Charter Treaty, OJ 1998 L 69, 9 March 1998, 115.

The text of the ECT is nevertheless silent on the division of competences between the EU, or a REIO more generally, and its member states.[43] However, the European Court of Justice (ECJ) acknowledges that, in the absence of a specific treaty provision that describes the division of competences between the EU and its member states, 'the Community and its Member States [...] are jointly liable to those latter States [the other contracting parties] for the fulfilment of every obligation arising from the commitments undertaken[...].'[44]

The ECT Tribunal in the *AES v Hungary* case adopted a diverging, yet more maintainable position:[45]

> Regarding the Community competition law regime, it has a dual nature: on the one hand, it is an international law regime, on the other hand, once introduced in the national legal orders, it is part of these legal orders. It is common ground that in an international arbitration, national laws are to be considered as facts. Both parties having pleading that the Community competition law regime should be considered as a fact, it will be considered by this Tribunal as a fact, always taking into account that a state may not invoke its domestic law as an excuse for alleged breaches of its international obligations.[46]

The reasoning of the *AES* Tribunal is more persuasive since it does not allow a host state to avoid international responsibility by making reference to EU law, which seems to be possible under the reasoning of the *Electrabel* Tribunal. In that regard, the position of the *AES* Tribunal is more in line with public international law as described earlier. However, having these two opposing statements by Tribunals that are both constituted under the ECT and adjudicating on factually very similar cases is problematic since it is hard to imagine more diverging views on this matter.

---

43 Richard Happ and Jan Asmus Bischoff, 'Role and Responsibility of the European Union Under the Energy Charter Treaty' in Graham Coop (ed), *Energy Dispute Resolution: Investment Protection, Transit and the Energy Charter Treaty* (JurisNet 2011) 168. Thomas Roe and Matthew Happold, *Settlement of Investment Disputes under the Energy Charter Treaty* (CUP 2011) 172.

44 Case C-361/91 *European Parliament v Council* (EDF) (1994) I-062, para 29.

45 The *Electrabel* Tribunal also recognised the possibility to take EU law into account in this manner as well:

> Accordingly, where a binding decision of the European Commission is concerned, even when not applied as EU law or international law, EU law may have to be taken into account as a rule to be applied as part of a national legal order, as a fact.

> *Electrabel SA v Republic of Hungary*, ICSID Case No ARB/07/19, Decision on Jurisdiction, Applicable Law and Liability (2012), para 4.129

46 *AES Summit Generation Limited and AES-Tisza Erömü Kft v Republic of Hungary*, ICSID Case No ARB/07/22, Award (2010), para 7.6.6.

IV. Conclusion of the Electrabel Tribunal

The fourth remark is related to the conclusion that the *Electrabel* Tribunal draws regarding the relationship between the ECT and EU law: 'In summary, from whatever perspective the relationship between the ECT and EU law is examined, the Tribunal concludes that EU law would prevail over the ECT in case of any material inconsistency.'[47] This conclusion, however, cannot possibly be correct and is contradicted in the more recent 'Decision on Jurisdiction' of the *RREEF v Spain* Tribunal.[48]

First of all, there is absolutely nothing in the ECT that would suggest that this statement is correct. In fact, Article 1(2) ECT defines a 'Contracting Party' as 'a state or Regional Economic Integration Organization which has consented to be bound by this Treaty and for which the Treaty is in force.' Thus, under the ECT, REIOs such as the EU are a contracting party to the treaty as any other state. Nothing in the text of the ECT would suggest that REIOs have diverging ECT obligations in comparison with 'regular' states. In fact, even if there was a conflict between the ECT and EU law regarding the promotion and protection of investments or dispute settlement, Article 16 ECT makes clear that both regimes continue 'to apply equally, unaffected by the other and an investor may seek to rely on the substantive or procedural provisions of' the regime that contains the most favourable provisions.[49] Second, as stated before, according to Article 216(2) TFEU, international agreements concluded by the EU are binding upon the EU institutions and its member states. Thus, even under the TFEU, EU law will not 'prevail' over the ECT.

Upon ratification of the ECT the EU submitted the following statement to the Energy Charter Secretariat:

> The European Communities and their Member States have both concluded the Energy Charter Treaty and are thus internationally responsible for the fulfillment of the obligations contained therein, in accordance with their respective competences.

47 *Electrabel SA v Republic of Hungary*, ICSID Case No ARB/07/19, Decision on Jurisdiction, Applicable Law and Liability (2012), para 4.191.

48 *RREEF Infrastructure (GP) Limited and RREEF Pan-European Infrastructure Two Lux SARL v Kingdom of Spain*, ICSID Case No ARB/13/30, Decision on Jurisdiction (2016), paras 75, 87. The Tribunal concludes that if a 'hierarchy' of norms is to be determined by the Tribunal (as is the case in instances of a conflict between the ECT and EU law), this must be 'determined from the perspective of international law, not of EU law. Therefore, the ECT prevails over any other norm (apart from those of *ius cogens* – but this is not an issue in the present case).' In addition, in case of a conflict the *RREEF* Tribunal considers that an ECT Tribunal should apply the ECT: 'EU law does not and cannot "*trump*" public international law.'

49 Thomas Roe and Matthew Happold, *Settlement of Investment Disputes under the Energy Charter Treaty* (CUP 2011) 34. This point seems to be supported by the *RREEF v Spain* Tribunal: Decision on Jurisdiction, *RREEF Infrastructure (GP) Limited and RREEF Pan-European Infrastructure Two Lux SARL v Kingdom of Spain*, ICSID Case No ARB/13/30, 2016, para 75.

The Communities and the Member States will, if necessary, determine among them who is the respondent party to arbitration proceedings initiated by an Investor of another Contracting Party. In such case, upon the request of the Investor, the Communities and the Member States concerned will make such a determination within a period of 30 days. [The statement then contains a footnote which provides for: This is without prejudice to the right of the investor to initiate proceedings against both the Communities and their Member States.][50]

This statement acknowledges that the EU is responsible for fulfilling the obligations under the ECT and that investors can initiate ISDS proceedings under the ECT pursuant to Article 26. Thus, for an ECT Tribunal that is constituted on the basis of Article 26 ECT to make the statement that EU law would prevail simply does not make sense. Therefore, I fully endorse the position adopted by the *RREEF v Spain* Tribunal which held that 'EU law does not and cannot "*trump*" public international law.'[51]

C. Recommendations

How should conflicts between EU law and the ECT be resolved? One should start with acknowledging that EU law and policy have great potential for conflict with the ECT. Since the EU is a contracting party to the ECT as any other contracting party, this means that the EU should be held accountable for violations of its international obligations: one should not strive to reconcile the irreconcilable. There is nothing in the ECT that suggests that the conduct of REIOs should be measured according to a different standard than the conduct of states, since both are considered 'contracting parties.'[52] Moreover, is not EU law to the EU what domestic law is for states? Under international law, Article 27 VCLT states that 'a party may not invoke the provisions of its internal law as justification for its failure to perform a treaty.' If the EU is simply one of the 54 ECT contracting parties, its conduct should be measured according to the same standards as all other contracting parties. Therefore, I fully endorse the conclusion of the *AES v Hungary* Tribunal that EU law should be considered as a fact, at least in those cases where the EU is respondent. Considering EU law as a fact is completely in line with the recent

---

50 Statement submitted by the European Communities to the Energy Charter Secretariat pursuant to Article 26(3)(b)(ii) of the Energy Charter Treaty, OJ 1998 L 69, 9.3.1998. P. 115.

51 *RREEF Infrastructure (G.P.) Limited and RREEF Pan-European Infrastructure Two Lux S.A.R.L v Kingdom of Spain*, ICSID Case No ARB/13/30, 2016, decision on Jurisdiction, para 87.

52 Richard Happ and Jan Asmus Bischoff, 'Role and Responsibility of the European Union Under the Energy Charter Treaty' in Graham Coop (ed), *Energy Dispute Resolution: Investment Protection, Transit and the Energy Charter Treaty* (JurisNet 2011) 163–165.

EU IIA practice. For instance, Article 8.31(2) CETA explicitly states that 'the domestic law of the disputing party' should be considered as a fact.[53] It must be emphasised, however, that in all the ECT cases where the potential conflict between EU law and the ECT became most apparent, the home state of the investor was also an EU member state. One could wonder why claimants in these cases only initiated proceedings against Hungary and not against the EU, or both. This question is very much related to admissibility: who is allowed to bring a claim against whom? Non-EU investors may of course bring claims against the EU and/or its member states.[54] In addition, as recently reaffirmed by the *Charanne v Spain* Tribunal and thereby explicitly rejecting the submission of the European Commission, investors from EU member states may also initiate proceedings against other EU member states when the claims do not involve EU measures.[55] Whether investors from EU member states may also initiate proceedings against the EU itself remains unclear. However, scholars have actually argued both ways, although the scenario that EU investors could initiate proceedings against the EU was probably not envisioned at the time the ECT was negotiated.[56]

Recently, the *Charanne v Spain* Tribunal touched upon this issue without making a determination on it. On the one hand, the Tribunal acknowledged that:

> although the EU is a Contracting Party of the ECT, the States that compose it have not ceased to be Contracting Parties as well. Both the EU, as its Member States, may have legal standing as Respondent in an action based on the ECT.[57]

On the other hand, the Tribunal argued that an investor from an EU member state that is initiating proceedings against the EU might not be investing in the 'area' of another contracting party in the sense of Article 26 ECT, the ECT's ISDS provision, since both the territory of the home state and the host state

---

53 See also Chapter 2 Section 3 Article 16(2) EU–Vietnam Free Trade Agreement (2016).

54 Richard Happ and Jan Asmus Bischoff, 'Role and Responsibility of the European Union Under the Energy Charter Treaty' in Graham Coop (ed), *Energy Dispute Resolution: Investment Protection, Transit and the Energy Charter Treaty* (JurisNet 2011) 178.

55 *Charanne BV and Construction Investments SARL v Spain*, SCC Case No 062/2012, 2016, Award, paras 427–432.

56 Richard Happ and Jan Asmus Bischoff, 'Role and Responsibility of the European Union Under the Energy Charter Treaty' in Graham Coop (ed), *Energy Dispute Resolution: Investment Protection, Transit and the Energy Charter Treaty* (JurisNet 2011) 178, 180–181. Markus Burgstaller, 'European Law and Investment Treaties' (2009) 26 J Int'l Arb 181, 207–208. Jan Kleinheisterkamp, 'The Next 10 Year ECT Investment Arbitration: A Vision for the Future – From a European Law Perspective' (VERLAG 2011) 15, www.lse.ac.uk/collections/law/wps/WPS2011-07_Kleinheis terkamp.pdf accessed 7 April 2016.

57 *Charanne BV and Construction Investments SARL v Spain*, SCC Case No 062/2012, Award (2016), para 429.

are considered part of the 'area' of the EU.[58] Hence, EU member state investors would not be able to invoke the ECT's ISDS provision to bring claims against the EU.

Instead of trying to reconcile any conflicts between the ECT and EU law, the proper respondent in a dispute should be determined prior to arbitral proceedings. If the EU is the proper respondent, the threshold to establish liability under the ECT should not differ merely because the EU is the respondent. This is supported by the fact that there is nothing in the text of the ECT that seems to justify a differential treatment for the EU as a REIO in comparison to any other contracting party.[59] By making an adequate determination of who the proper respondent should be, EU member states will no longer be in the awkward position where they have to prioritise between their obligations under the ECT and those under EU law.

In relation to the determination of the proper respondent, the earlier quoted statement submitted by the European Communities upon depositing its instrument of approval of the ECT is of interest;[60] although the statement does not clearly define which circumstances are decisive to determine the proper respondent.[61] In that regard, recent EU IIA practice provides more guidance. For instance, Article 8.21 CETA states that if the investor has not been informed of the determination within a specified time limit:

a if the measures identified in the notice are exclusively measures of a member state of the European Union, the member state shall be the respondent.
b if the measures identified in the notice include measures of the European Union, the European Union shall be the respondent.[62]

This procedure contains a clear indication that is in line with the EU's ISDS Financial Responsibility Regulation: in those cases where the contested measures include EU measures (thus implementation of Directives or Decisions), the EU should be (co-)respondent and bear financial responsibility.[63] This is in line with

---

58 ibid para 431. According to Article 1(10) second paragraph ECT, the 'Area' of the EU comprises the 'Areas of the Member States'.
59 Richard Happ and Jan A Bischoff, 'Role and Responsibility of the European Union Under the Energy Charter Treaty' in Graham Coop (ed), *Energy Dispute Resolution: Investment Protection, Transit and the Energy Charter Treaty* (JurisNet 2011) 163–165.
60 ibid (n 42).
61 Graham Coop, 'Energy Charter Treaty and the European Union: Is Conflict Inevitable?' (2009) 27 J Energy & Nat Resources L 404, 417.
62 It has to be noted that the wording of similar procedures in other recent IIAs of the EU varies. Compare for instance: Article 9.15 of the EU–Singapore Free Trade Agreement (2014) and Chapter 8 Article 6 of the EU–Vietnam Free Trade Agreement (2016).
63 Article 3 Regulation (EU) No 912/2014 of the European Parliament and of the Council of 23 July 2014 establishing a framework for managing financial responsibility linked to investor-to-state dispute settlement tribunals established by international agreements to which the European Union is party (2014) L 257/121.

the reasoning of the ECJ that the EU and its member states 'are jointly liable for the fulfilment of every obligation arising from the commitments undertaken.'[64] Of course, once a determination of the respondent has been made by the EU and the member state, this respondent should, on the basis of the principle of estoppel, not be allowed to argue that it is not the proper respondent.[65]

In cases where the EU is the respondent, EU law should be considered as a fact. Thus, it should not be taken into account in the process of treaty interpretation on the basis of Article 31(3)(c) VCLT, because EU law is not binding on all ECT states and the national law of other ECT parties will not be taken into account in this way either. Nor should EU law be applied by a Tribunal as 'applicable rules and principles of international law' on the basis of Article 26(6) ECT, because this would also give EU law a more prominent role in ECT ISDS cases than the domestic law of other contracting parties.[66] Instead, EU law should be dealt with in the same way as domestic law in cases where a state is respondent; merely as fact.

D. Conclusion

Tribunals have been struggling with the exact relationship between the EU and the ECT. In some of the ECT cases where Tribunals dealt with this issue, it has been a complicating factor that the home state of the investor and the host state were both EU members, the EU was only indirectly involved in the proceedings, and the parties to the dispute continually stressed that EU law was either not involved or not the reason that proceedings were initiated.

Instead of adopting awkwardly reasoned awards that either deny that there is any conflict between the ECT and EU law or that try to reconcile both bodies of law, the EU should be respondent in ECT cases involving EU law and EU law should be treated as facts by ECT Tribunals. In cases brought by non-EU investors, this should not be problematic. For EU-investors this might become problematic if it is decided that EU investors cannot bring claims against the EU. Once the EU is (co-)respondent, EU law should merely be treated as a fact since this would be the case for the domestic laws of all other ECT states and this is supported by recent EU IIA practice. Thus, EU law should not have a more prominent role either by taking it into account when interpreting the ECT or by applying it as 'applicable rules and principles of international law' as described in Article 26(6) ECT.

To return to the title of this chapter, are the ECT and EU law mutually supportive instruments for economic cooperation in the energy sector or is it a case of

---

64 Case C-361/91 *European Parliament v Council* (EDF) (1994) I-0625, para 29.
65 Thomas Roe and Matthew Happold, *Settlement of Investment Disputes under the Energy Charter Treaty* (CUP 2011) 174.
66 The *Electrabel* Tribunal did find that EU law is part of the applicable law on the basis of Article 26(6) ECT. See Decision on Jurisdiction, Applicable Law and Liability, *Electrabel SA v Republic of Hungary*, ICSID Case No ARB/07/19, 2012, para 4.195.

schizophrenia in the *acquis*? Probably the former. The EU and EU law have developed significantly over the last 20 years, with the EU increasingly gaining competences and developing a sophisticated body of legislation and case law in many fields that can have an influence on investors in the energy sector.[67] At the same time, the ECT has largely remained unchanged. Nevertheless, the ECT offers a form of investment protection that is not available under EU law. Moreover, investors have become increasingly aware of their ECT rights and are increasingly willing to invoke them. However, to do justice to all ECT contracting parties and avoid undermining legal certainty and the reciprocity of the ECT, EU law should be treated as the domestic law of any other ECT contracting party. This also means that the EU should be (co-)respondent in all cases that involve EU measures. For investors from EU member states, however, this might mean that their claims are not admissible. Nevertheless, I am sure that the first ECT claim brought against the EU, especially when initiated by an EU investor, will be followed with great interest by many.

---

67 Ernesto Bonafé and Gökçe Mete, 'Escalated Interactions between EU Energy Law and the Energy Charter Treaty' [2016] J World Energy Law Bus first published online May 17, 2016 doi:10.1093/jwelb/jww011. P. 15.

3 The Need for Intra-EU Investment Protections[1]

Dr Emily Sipiorski

A. Introduction

The organisation of intra-European Union (EU) investment protection has been uneasily on the verge of substantial change since the implementation of the Lisbon Treaty. It is widely discussed in the field that the Treaty on the Functioning of the European Union (TFEU) included foreign direct investment in the Common Commercial Policy. Discussions have ensued regarding the EU's control over investment agreements, as evidenced by the now-defunct Transatlantic Trade and Investment Partnership discussions and the EU–Canada Comprehensive Economic and Trade Agreement, which provisionally entered into force in September 2017. The EU's actions prior to the European Court of Justice's (ECJ) decision in *Slovak Republic v Achmea*, however, mostly concerned the relationship between the EU investment protection and third states, that is, non-EU member states. Following the *Achmea* decision, it has become clear that the transformation in the EU's competence also affects the protection of intra-EU investments – namely that the right for investors from one EU state to bring a dispute against another state adversely affects the autonomy of EU law.[2] This decision, however, does not account for the changes in protections for investors, concerns that were widely identified in the opinion of the Advocate General prior to the ECJ decision;[3] the ECJ instead focuses on the internal impacts on the EU.

Both prior to and after the conclusion of the TFEU in 2009, disputes were brought to investment tribunals based on the substantive protections included in intra-EU Bilateral Investment Treaties (BITs). The earliest such dispute was *Eastern Sugar v the Czech Republic*, followed by *Achmea v the Slovak Republic, AES v Hungary, Binder v the Czech Republic*, and *Oostergetel and Laurentius v the Slovak*

1 This chapter was originally written in June 2017, and was updated in May 2018 with respect to the ECJ decision in *Slovak Republic v Achmea* and Advocate General Wathelet's opinion in the case.
2 *Slovak Republic v Achmea BV* (Case C-284/16), Decision of 6 March 2018, para 59.
3 *Slovak Republic v Achmea BV* (Case C-284/16), Opinion of Advocate General Wathelet, 19 September 2017, para 199 (noting that '[a] number of legal rules of the BIT have no equivalent in EU law. These are the MFN clause, the clause whereby the Parties undertake to observe their contractual obligations, the sunset clause, and the ISDS mechanism').

Republic, amongst others.[4] Following the TFEU, the European Commission has participated by submitting *amicus curiae* to arbitral tribunals, challenging both the jurisdiction of the tribunal to decide the dispute and arguing that the subject matter falls within EU competence.

Leaving aside the issue of whether intra-EU BITs, already existing at the enactment of the Lisbon Treaty, have been *de facto* terminated by the TFEU or by the *Achmea* decision, the question stands whether there remains a need for intra-EU BITs, or at least protection for investors and investments from other member states. Are the protections provided by these agreements absent from what the courts and laws of the individual member states would provide for investors? Are the protections for free movement and non-discrimination under EU law sufficient? Would a substantial gap be left by forcing member states to eliminate BIT protections?

Until 2009, most of the intra-EU investment disputes applied BITs concluded during the opening of Central and Eastern European economies in the 1990s. The *Achmea* dispute was brought under one such treaty.[5] Disputes were also brought under the Energy Charter Treaty, filling a similar gap in protections.[6] To an extent, it could be surmised that investors were protecting themselves against the realities of still-developing, post-communist legal systems. Since 2011, however, increasing numbers of intra-EU disputes have been between older member states[7] or between newer member states.[8] To an extent, member states brought before proceedings as responding states have not challenged the validity of the BITs – possibly in part because of the continued use of the treaties by their own

---

4 *Achmea BV v The Slovak Republic*, UNCITRAL, PCA Case No 2008–13, Decision on Jurisdiction, Arbitrability and Suspension (26 October 2010), paras 217–292; *Rupert Binder v the Czech Republic*, UNCITRAL, Award on Jurisdiction (6 June 2007), paras 59–67; *Eastern Sugar BV v the Czech Republic*, SCC Case No 088/2004, Partial Award (27 March 2007), Final Award (12 April 2007); *Electrabel SA v the Republic of Hungary*, ICSID Case No ARB/07/19, Decision on Jurisdiction, Applicable Law and Liability (30 November 2012), paras 4.111–5.60; *Micula v Romania*, ICSID Case No ARB/05/20, Award (11 December 2013); *European American Investment Bank AG (EURAM) v the Slovak Republic*, UNCITRAL, PCA Case No 2010–17.

5 Netherlands–Slovakia BIT (1991).

6 The Energy Charter Treaty holds a particular role in the discussion as a mixed agreement, which includes the member states in addition to the EU as signatories.

7 See Matteo Barra, 'The Use of the ECT in Intra-EU Disputes' (Presentation at Conference: The EU and investment arbitration under the Energy Charter Treaty, Queen Mary University of London, 11–12 February 2016) 6; European Commission, 'Investor-to-State Dispute Settlement (ISDS): Some Facts and Figures' (12 March 2015), http://trade.ec.europa.eu/doclib/docs/2015/january/tradoc_153046.pdf accessed on 23 May 2016. See, for example, the recent influx of cases against Spain, *inter alia*: *NextEra Energy Global Holdings BV and NextEra Energy Spain Holdings BV v Kingdom of Spain*, ICSID Case No ARB/14/11, 23 May 2014, Notice of Arbitration; *Charanne BV and Construction Investments SÀRL v Kingdom of Spain*, SCC Arb No 062/2012, Final Award (21 January 2016).

8 See for example, Andrej Arpa, 'Intra-EU Investment Protection: Up the Creek without a Paddle' [2017] Investment Treaty News (referring to *Spółdzielnia Pracy Muszynianka v Slovak Republic* (UNICTRAL)).

investors.[9] Thus, the previous justifications for the use of BIT protections cannot be substantiated. Instead, this trend highlights a level of deficiency under EU law: investors from member states do not have the same protection outside the BIT regime.

This chapter first addresses some background issues regarding the current state of the intra-EU scope of investment protection, including the most recent case law. The second section contrasts the protections offered in BITs with the protections available under EU law. In particular, some of the characteristic protections in BITs are compared to protections under EU law should the BITs be terminated without a replacement developed. The results are varied, and in certain areas – particularly from the perspective of pre-investment protections – the protections offered by EU law exceed those included in the BIT. These distinctions are assessed in light of the extent of changes that would need to be implemented into EU law in order to create a system that parallels the level of protection that investors have under the current investor-state regime. The next section considers the proposal offered by five member states for a solution to phasing-out the current intra-EU BITs and implementing a multilateral, EU-wide compromise. The final section offers brief preliminary conclusions on the issue.

B. Background

In the past years, the EU has assumed authority over certain aspects of investment protection and specifically indicated an intention to control investor-state disputes. With regard to disputes between member states and third states, the TFEU included foreign direct investment in the exclusive competence of the EU.[10] Following the conclusion of this treaty, the member states are restricted from concluding agreements providing for resolution of investment disputes.

The European Commission has indicated that BITs between two member states are no longer valid following the implementation of this treaty. In June 2015, the European Commission requested that five member states, namely Austria, the Netherlands, Romania, Slovakia, and Sweden terminate their BITs with other

---

9 With regard to the Energy Charter Treaty, and more specifically, the International Energy Charter, the independence of the member states in regard to protections has been reaffirmed by the European Council.

10 Treaty on the Functioning of the European Union, Article 207(1):

> The *common commercial policy shall be based on uniform principles*, particularly with regard to changes in tariff rates, the conclusion of tariff and trade agreements relating to trade in goods and services, and the commercial aspects of intellectual property, *foreign direct investment*, the achievement of uniformity in measures of liberalisation, export policy and measures to protect trade such as those to be taken in the event of dumping or subsidies. The common commercial policy shall be conducted in the context of the principles and objectives of the Union's external action.

> [emphasis added]

member states.[11] This request, however, failed to be clear, and there is nothing decisive in the treaty that obliges member states to terminate their existing treaties, including the BITs with other EU member states. Problematically, the request was only made to five of the 28 EU member states. Moreover, in essence by requesting the termination of the treaties, the European Commission acknowledged that they remain valid treaties within public international law. No transition out of the current intra-EU investment regime was proposed, no detailed suggestions regarding the sunset clauses were included, no recognition was made by the proposal of the vast network of protection and the impact that termination could have on investors who had relied on the treaties. By early 2017, Romania and Poland both began the process of terminating intra-EU BITs, at least partially in response to the Commission's actions.[12]

Previously in *amicus curiae* submissions, the European Commission insisted that the courts of the EU had control over disputes arising out of these treaties based on various provisions of the Lisbon Treaty, including Article 344 providing that 'Member States undertake not to submit a dispute concerning the interpretation or application of the Treaties to any method of settlement other than those provided for therein.'[13] Article 351 further indicates that 'Member State or States concerned shall take all appropriate steps to eliminate the incompatibilities established [by previously existing agreements].' Other incompatibilities highlighted by the Commission included the discriminatory character of the treaties – often considered inherent in most-favoured nation clauses – as inconsistent with the EU's internal market standards,[14] as well as incompatibilities resulting from the overlap in free transfer of funds and free movement of capital clauses.[15]

---

11 European Commission, 'Commission Asks Member States to Terminate their Intra-EU Bilateral Investment Treaties' (Press Release 18 June 2015), http://europa.eu/rapid/press-release_IP-15-5198_en.htm accessed on 22 May 2016.

12 Crina Baltag, 'Green Light for Romania to Terminate its Intra-EU Bilateral Investment Treaties' [2017] Kluwer Arbitration Blog, http://kluwerarbitrationblog.com/2017/03/14/green-light-for-romania-to-terminate-its-intra-eu-bilateral-investment-treaties/ accessed on 20 June 2017.

13 Recent tribunals have disregarded any conflict arising out of this provision of the TFEU, noting that the article applies 'literally' between two member states. A controversy between an investor and a member state would thus be inapplicable. See *Charanne BV and Construction Investments SÀRL v Kingdom of Spain*, SCC Arb No 062/2012, Final Award (21 January 2016) para 441, http://res.cloudinary.com/lbresearch/image/upload/v1453825171/laudo_final_arb_062_2012_260116_1618.pdf accessed on 2 May 2016. (In the original Spanish: 'Literalmente, dicha norma se a acuerdos relativos a controversias entre los Estados Miembros, y no entre una privada y un Miembro.')

14 See generally Dominik Moskvan, 'Is There an Alternative to Intra-European Bilateral Investment Treaties Framework under European Law?' [2011] Business Law Forum 2012, 353–398, http://ssrn.com/abstract=2221905 accessed on 2 May 2016, 368.

15 See for example, *Achmea BV v The Slovak Republic*, UNCITRAL, PCA Case No 2008–13, Decision on Jurisdiction, Arbitrability and Suspension, 26 October 2010, para 20.

Now, following the *Achmea* decision, the position under EU law is clear. By way of background, the arbitral tribunal had assumed jurisdiction over the intra-EU dispute,[16] and the Slovak Republic responded by challenging that decision in the German Courts, the seat of the arbitration. The Higher Regional Court took an affirmative decision on the role of arbitral tribunals in EU disputes.[17] The Bundesgerichtshof, tasked with deciding on the validity of the lower court's decision, submitted the question to the ECJ in this regard.[18] The Advocate General submitted an opinion several months before the ECJ's final decision, indicating that the BIT was 'not incompatible' with EU law.[19] The Court did not follow the position. The ECJ's decision in *Achmea* was based on the incompatibility of the investor-state settlement clause with the uniformity of application of EU law, which Articles 267 and 344 TFEU were intended to protect.[20] The ECJ dismissed the idea that an investment arbitration tribunal was a court of the EU within the meaning of the TFEU, and was thus incapable of referring a question of EU law to the Court of Justice. In short, the ECJ concluded that the dispute settlement clause of the BIT adversely affected the autonomy of EU law.[21]

The EU has been cautious in implementing decisive action to create a uniform role in intra-EU investment protection following the TFEU, and now, following the *Achmea* decision, the need is even greater. There is a lack of proposals to provide tangible answers as to how the institutions of the EU are used to protect intra-EU investment – beyond, of course, the assumption that investors would be protected by the treaties of the EU and by the national courts. A leaked non-paper submitted to the Council of the European Union, Trade Policy Committee by Austria, Finland, France, Germany, and the Netherlands made the first substantive

---

16 *Achmea BV v the Slovak Republic*, UNCITRAL, PCA Case No 2013–12 (Number 2), Decision on Jurisdiction and Admissibility, 20 May 2014.
17 *Achmea BV v the Slovak Republic*, Judgment of the Higher Regional Court of Frankfurt (Oberlandesgericht Frankfurt am Main), Beschluss, 18 December 2014 (26 Sch 3/13).
18 Bundesgerichtsfhof (BGH), Beschluss, 3 March 2016 (I ZB 2/15), published on 11 May 2016, available at http://juris.bundesgerichtshof.de/cgi-bin/rechtsprechung/document.py?Gericht=bgh&Art=pm&Datum=2016&Sort=3&nr=74612&linked=bes&Blank=1&file=dokument.pdff accessed on 22 May 2016; see also Richard Happ and Georg Scherpf, 'The Door is Open for the ECJ to Rule on Intra-EU BIT Arbitration' (19 May 2016), www.luther-lawfirm.com/en/news/the-door-is-open-for-the-ecj-to-rule-on-intra-eu-bit-arbitration.html accessed on 22 May 2016; Anne-Karin Grill and Sebastian Lukic, 'The End of Intra-EU BITs: Fair Accompli or Another Way Out?' [2016] Kluwer Arbitration Blog, available at http://kluwerarbitrationblog.com/2016/11/16/the-end-of-intra-eu-bits-fait-accompli-or-another-way-out/ (detailing the progress in the issue of intra-EU BITs and concluding that a decision by the ECJ will provide clarity on the issue).
19 *Slovak Republic v Achmea BV* (Case C-284/16) Opinion of Advocate General Wathelet, 19 September 2017, para 181.
20 *Slovak Republic v Achmea BV* (Case C-284/16), Decision of 6 March 2018, paras 49, 60.
21 ibid para 59.

acknowledgment of the gap that would be left by eliminating all BITs between EU member states.[22]

C. Contrasting Protections

The substantive protections offered in BITs are recognised as providing investors with options when an investment has been impacted by a host state's actions – whether a partial loss of investment or a complete expropriation. The majority of these protections may be referred to as post-investment protections. In essence, the BIT regime allows a certain amount of protection at the pre-investment stage, but focuses its strength in the phase after the investment has been pursued or established. As noted by Bernasconi-Osterwalder, 'the EU already could negotiate and has negotiated investment liberalization elements. What the EU has not done so far is negotiate post-establishment investment protection.'[23]

Some protections – for example, national treatment – are sufficiently protected under the EU; national treatment under EU law in fact provides a higher level of protection since an investor would not be required at the pre-investment stage to prove the benefit of the project or secure a right of entry.[24] Other protections, however, are either different or nonexistent. The following section explores some of these more pronounced distinctions. Depending on the language of the BIT or the relevant investment protection instrument, these protections include the right to bring the dispute to an arbitral tribunal (1); expropriation (2); substantive protections, including fair and equitable treatment, full protection and security, and legitimate expectations (3); and compensation (4). Essentially, protections

22 Council of the European Union, General Secretariat, Trade Policy Committee (Services and Investment), 'Intra-EU Investment Treaties', Non-paper from Austria, Finland, France, Germany, and the Netherlands (7 April 2016) www.s2bnetwork.org/wp -content/uploads/2016/05/Intra-EU-Bits2-18-05.pdf accessed on 22 May 2016.

23 Nathalie Bernasconi-Osterwalder, 'European Parliament Hearing on Foreign Direct Investment' (November 2010), www.iisd.org/pdf/2010/eu_parliament_hearing_investment.pdf accessed on 23 May 2016, at 2.

24 Dominik Moskvan, 'Is There an Alternative to Intra-European Bilateral Investment Treaties Framework under European Law?' [2011] Business Law Forum 2012, 353–398, http://ssrn.com/abstract=2221905 accessed on 2 May 2016, 364–365:

> Adoption of national treatment at the pre-entry stage would imply that the country would cease to test whether the intended investment would possess a benefit to the local economy, would prove otherwise harmful or would create environmental damages. [...] This so called pre-entry and post-entry model differentiation of national treatment thus proves to create a disadvantageous condition under international investment law when compared to the legal background governing such matter under European law.

> See also Dominik Moskvan, 'The Clash of Intra-EU Bilateral Investment Treaties with EU Law: A Bitter Pill to Swallow' (2015–2016), 22 Columbia Journal of European Law 101, 116ff.

under EU law are limited to the EU provisions on the free movement of capital[25] as well as provisions included in the Charter of Fundamental Rights of the European Union.[26] These protections are far less extensive than the protections offered by the BIT regime and offer none of the procedural protections regarding dispute resolution. In the following section, several of these protections are considered, contrasting the BIT protection with the protections currently available under EU law.

I. Right to Bring a Dispute to an Arbitral Tribunal

The right to pursue investor-state dispute resolution has always been considered one of the central provisions of BITs.[27] Advocate General Wathelet reaffirmed this element as 'most essential'.[28] Allowing an investor to independently bring a claim against a state was integral to distinguishing the development of the BIT regime from the protections offered to investors under the previous Friendship, Commerce and Navigation Treaties (FCNs).[29] Previously, investors would have needed their home state to bring a claim on their behalf. This system would have been significantly more burdensome as well as lacking the assurance that the home state would in fact pursue the claim, thus substantially less secure in terms of stability and reliability.

This protection in the BITs has been identified in arbitral decisions as an essential distinction from EU law. In the earliest of the intra-EU decisions, the tribunal in *Eastern Sugar v the Czech Republic* identified the arbitration clause as the 'most essential provision of the Bilateral Investment Treaties' and noted that 'EU law does not provide such a guarantee'.[30] It concluded with regard to the Czech Republic's arguments on the equivalence of protections that the lack of 'possibility for an investor to sue a host state directly'[31] distinguished the protections.

25 Treaty on the Functioning of the European Union, Articles 64–65; see also Anna De Luca, 'New Developments on the Scope of the EU Common Commercial Policy Under the Lisbon Treaty: Investment Liberalization vs. Investment Protection?' in Karl P Sauvant (ed), *Yearbook on International Investment Law & Policy 2010/2011* (OUP 2012), 165–215.

26 Charter of Fundamental Rights of the European Union, Official Journal of the European Communities (2007/C 303/01).

27 Cf Shen Wei, 'Is This a Great Leap Forward? A Comparative Review of the Investor-State Arbitration Clause in the ASEAN-China Investment Treaty: From BIT Jurisprudential and Practical Perspectives' (2014), 27(4) Journal of International Arbitration 379, 381–382.

28 *Slovak Republic v Achmea BV*, Case C-284/16, Opinion of Advocate General Wathelet, 19 September 2017, para 77.

29 Christian Tietje and Emily Sipiorski, 'The Evolution of Investment Protection Based on Public International Law Treaties: Lessons to be Learned' in Andrea Bjorklund and August Reinisch (eds), *International Investment Law and Soft Law* (Cheltenham/ Northampton 2012), 192–237.

30 *Eastern Sugar v the Czech Republic*, Partial Award, 27 March 2007, para 165.

31 ibid para 180.

As the system of protection currently stands in the EU, should the BIT protections be removed without an immediate replacement, an investor's alternative would be to bring the dispute to the national court. As clearly a court pursuant to Article 267 TFEU, any questions of EU law could be submitted to the Court of Justice of the EU for a preliminary ruling. This idea of bringing the dispute instead to the national courts has significant historical context, but has also been implemented by Australian investment policies.[32]

Beyond the mere right to take the dispute to arbitration, this approach undermines one purpose of BITs to ensure a neutral forum. A key aim of investor-state dispute settlement (ISDS) is to prevent a denial of justice to a foreign investor that results from discrimination in the local courts.[33] Eliminating this more direct access to justice, although assuring non-discrimination pursuant to Article 18 TFEU, may not ensure a neutral forum to the same extent as provided by the BIT or investment agreement – or would require additional steps of litigation to manage any discrimination that occurs.

This investor-state dispute resolution provision, however, stands as one of the most controversial elements of the BIT regime. In particular, in the recent EU–Canada trade agreement, the investor-state provision has been modified, recommending a 'new approach' to the system,

> notably with full transparency of proceedings and clear and unambiguous investment protection standards. [...] [considering it] a clear break from the old Investor to State Dispute Settlement (ISDS) approach and demonstrates the shared determination of the EU and Canada to replace the current ISDS system with a new dispute settlement mechanism and move towards establishing a permanent multilateral investment court. This revised CETA text is also a clear signal of the EU's intent to include this new proposal on investment in its negotiations with all partners.[34]

This introduction of a permanent multilateral investment court of 15 members parallels the European Commission's insistence on an investment court in the

---

32 Leon Trakman, 'Investor State Arbitration or Local Courts: Will Australia Set a New Trend?' (2012) 46(1) Journal of World Trade 83–120, http://ssrn.com/abstract= 2000361 accessed on 2 May 2016.

33 Francesco Francioni, 'Access to Justice, Denial of Justice and International Investment Law' (2009), 20 European Journal of International Law 729, http://ejil.oxfordjourna ls.org/cgi/reprint/20/3/729 accessed on 2 May 2016; Jürgen Kurtz, 'Access to Justice, Denial of Justice and International Investment Law: A Reply to Francesco Francioni' (2009), 20(4) European Journal of International Law 1077–1085, www. ejil.org/pdfs/20/4/1947.pdf accessed on 2 May 2016; *Loewen Group, Inc and Raymond L Loewen v United States of America*, ICSID Case No ARB(AF)/98/3, www. italaw.com/cases/632#sthash.VYK9iXtC.dpuf accessed on 23 May 2016.

34 European Commission, 'CETA: EU and Canada Agree on New Approach on Investment in Trade Agreement' (Press Release 29 February 2016), http://europa.eu/rap id/press-release_IP-16-399_en.htm accessed on 23 May 2016.

Transatlantic Trade and Investment Partnership (TTIP) negotiations.[35] The Commission noted that its proposal for a standing investment court included significant advantages, including an appeals process, highly qualified judges, and an assurance of a government's right to regulate.[36]

These proposals, potentially establishing a new era of investor-state dispute resolution, have yet to be tested. This means that a potential gap remains in the level of protection, aside from taking a dispute to the national courts and thus facing the limitations of domestic litigation. In addition, the implementation of this system may prove unfavourable to parties, and may be significantly difficult to implement in a comprehensive manner, in particular with regard to the negotiations with the United States, a treaty partner unlikely to agree to such a system considering its comparative success under the NAFTA regime and unpredictable success rate in the WTO context.

II. Substantive Protections

The BITs contain extensive protections often based in the principle of legitimate expectations that ensure a certain guarantee for the maintenance of the investments.

1. Fair and Equitable Treatment

Fair and equitable treatment, although lacking a certain precision in its intended scope,[37] is often understood as requiring that the state provide a certain level of substantive and procedural conduct. Schreuer considers the essential nature of the standard to include 'transparency, stability and the investor's legitimate expectations, compliance with contractual obligations, procedural propriety and due process, action in good faith and freedom from coercion and harassment.'[38] This somewhat malleable standard has the advantage for investors of covering a wide range of government action.[39] The principle of good faith has also been widely linked to the standard, providing even less clarity in its application.[40]

---

35 European Commission, 'Commission Proposes New Investment Court System for TTIP and other EU Trade and Investment Negotiations' (Press Release 16 September 2015), http://europa.eu/rapid/press-release_IP-15-5651_en.htm accessed 23 May 2016.

36 ibid.

37 Christoph Schreuer, 'Fair and Equitable Treatment', www.univie.ac.at/intlaw/wordpress/pdf/99_fair_equit_treatm_zuerich.pdf accessed on 23 May 2016, 125.

38 ibid 126.

39 See for example, *MTD v Chile*, Award (25 May 2004), 12 ICSID Reports 6 (finding a breach of the standard because of inconsistent action by two branches of the government); *CMS Gas Transmission Company v Argentina*, Award (12 May 2005), 44 ILM (2005), 1205 (finding a breach of the standard as a result of the government's failure to provide a stable legal and business environment).

40 *TECMED v Mexico*, Award (29 May 2003), 43 ILM (2003), 811, para 153; *Saluka v the Czech Republic*, Partial Award (17 March 2006), para 307.

Should the BIT protections be eliminated, such protection from a government's inconsistent action would likely not be protected – at least on the broader EU perspective. Wathelet notes that although there are commonalities in the scope of protection under EU law, the principle as such is not recognised.[41] To the contrary, many changes in legislation or legal protections could be justified by EU requirements or considered necessary for the operation of EU law.[42] National law would control how the general principles arising out of fair and equitable treatment are managed and protected. Thus, there would be a varied application of the standard, possibly resulting in a protection more favourable to the state as well as to the EU.

Other aspects of the investment, however, would be protected under EU law. The non-discrimination requirements could prove to have a far-reaching impact similar to the outcome of applying the fair and equitable treatment standard arising out of BITs. Moreover, legitimate expectations are recognised in the prohibition of applying laws retroactively where such application would have a damaging impact. Namely, where a party has relied on established case law, legitimate expectations may be considered as part of assessments with the internal market.[43]

2. Full Protection and Security

Full protection and security, closely related to the previously mentioned fair and equitable treatment standard, is also frequently included in BITs as a substantive protection. As noted by the tribunal in *Eastern Sugar v the Czech Republic*, the provision:

> concerns the obligation of the host state to protect the investor from *third* parties, in the cases cited by the Parties, mobs, insurgents, rented thugs and others engaged in physical violence against the investor in violation of the state monopoly of physical force. Thus, where a host state failure to grant full

---

41 *Slovak Republic v Achmea BV*, Case C-284/16, Opinion of Advocate General Wathelet, 19 September 2017, paras 213–215.

42 See generally, Dominik Moskvan, 'Is There an Alternative to Intra-European Bilateral Investment Treaties Framework under European Law?' [2011] Business Law Forum 2012, 353–398, http://ssrn.com/abstract=2221905 accessed on 2 May 2016, at 371:

> European law itself does not offer a fair and equitable treatment guarantee, nor does it offer a direct restriction to private property rights that accrue from expropriation. Efforts targeted on seeking for an alternative to the fair and equitable treatment under the European framework are necessarily impaired by its vague formulation. Nevertheless, the European Union cannot be deemed as a futile agent in promoting fair and equitable treatment of investors.

43 See for example, 2003/81/EC, Commission Decision of 22 August 2002, paras 43–44, http://eur-lex.europa.eu/legal-content/EN/TXT/?qid=1455022490949&uri=CELEX:32003D0081 accessed on 23 May 2016.

protection and security, it fails to act to *prevent* actions by third parties that it is required to prevent.[44]

It follows that this treaty provision protects an investor from both public and private actions.

The extent of such protection would result differently if the dispute were instead taken to a domestic court. Public actions may be viewed in a distinct light, with a level of discretion different from an impartial tribunal. Moreover, private actions, particularly of physical aggression, would most likely not be dealt with in parallel to an action for losses to the investment. Such actions would instead fall under the jurisdiction of criminal courts in the domestic context, a separation that is avoided in arbitral awards.

3. Expropriation

The right to seek recovery for expropriation of an investment drives the security of investments. Its presence in the standard language of BITs is well accepted. This, of course, does not exclude a state from expropriating an investment, but creates a breach of the treaty which leads to a potential damages claim.

At the moment and for the foreseeable future, the EU lacks competence over this issue:

> Protection of foreign investment against expropriation and other political risks has so far been completely excluded from Union agreements dealing with foreign investment, as this field has been widely considered to fall under the exclusive competence of the Member States.[45]

This draws on the restrictions provided in Article 345 TFEU providing that the EU cannot take measures that 'prejudice the rules in Member States governing the system of property ownership.' The restriction has been limited by the ECJ, noting that non-discrimination applies to any property laws applied by member states.[46] This lack in protection has been further acknowledged by the ECJ in *Annibaldi*:

> Finally, given the absence of specific Community rules on expropriation and the fact that the measures relating to the common organization of the agricultural markets have no effect on systems of agricultural property ownership, it follows from the wording of Article 222 of the Treaty that the Regional Law concerns an area which falls within the purview of the Member States.[47]

---

44 *Eastern Sugar v the Czech Republic*, Partial Award (27 March 2007) para 203.
45 Angelos Dimopoulos, *EU Foreign Investment Law* (OUP 2011), 108.
46 *Costa v ENEL*, Case 6/64 [1964] ECR 1251; *Fearon*, Case 182/83 [1984] ECR 3677.
47 ECJ, C-309/96, *Annibaldi*, EU:C:1997:631, para 23.

This limitation with regard to legislating on the matter of expropriation does not exclude the possibility of compensation for an expropriation. This matter is discussed below.

4. Compensation

The next protection integral to the investment regime in its current form is compensation for losses to investments. International investment agreements, including the agreements between current EU Member states, include the investor's right to receive compensation when there have been breaches. There are two ways that this right to compensation is limited under a regime that does not include intra-EU BITs. First, some national courts may not provide protection of basic rights to foreign-owned companies. This may result in breaches to protections not being fully compensated:

> the German constitution (the 'Grundgesetz' or 'GG') denies any protection to foreign companies. Under Art 19 (3) GG, only domestic companies enjoy the basic rights the constitution grants to natural persons (and even them only insofar as the nature of such rights allows). What is more, domestic companies owned by foreign state-owned companies are completely denied protection.[48]

Second, the EU has argued that based on the state aid provisions of the TFEU, an award could be considered state aid.[49] This, however, extends beyond denying the protections of the BIT, and includes the reality with the current BIT regime. This position, however, indicates a resistance to allowing compensation for awards that would surely extend to any decision by a national court in favour of an investor.

Nonetheless, there are protections in EU law that ensure compensation. First, although not binding on the EU, the European Convention on Human Rights provides for 'peaceful enjoyment of [...] possessions.'[50] This provision further indicates a restriction based in international law for takings in the public interest, but includes 'the right of a State to enforce such laws as it deems necessary to control the use of property in accordance with the general interest or to secure the

---

48 Richard Happ, 'Why Investors in Germany Need Investment Protections', [2016] EFILA Blog, http://efilablog.org/2016/03/29/why-investors-in-germany-need-investment-protection/ accessed on 22 May 2016.

49 Christian Tietje and Clemens Wackernagel, 'Outlawing Compliance? – The Enforcement of Intra-EU Investment Awards and EU State Aid Law' (2014), 41(6) Policy Papers on Transnational Economic Law, http://telc.jura.uni-halle.de/de/node/24 accessed on 2 May 2016; Christian Tietje and Clemens Wackernagel, 'Enforcement of Intra-EU ICSID Awards – Multilevel Governance, Investment Tribunals and the Lost Opportunity of the Micula Arbitration' (2015) 16 The Journal of World Investment & Trade 201–243; Pietro Ortolani, 'Intra-EU Arbitral Awards *vis-à-vis* Article 107 TFEU: State Aid Law as a Limit to Compliance' (2015) 6(1) Journal of International Dispute Settlement 118–135.

50 European Convention on Human Rights, Protocol No 1.

payment of taxes or other contributions or penalties.'[51] Individuals within the EU would be able to bring a claim. Such breach would require exhaustion of local remedies before the dispute could be brought before the European Court of Human Rights. This provision, although allowing for peaceful enjoyment, does not indicate any right to compensation.

These protections of property in addition to the right to compensation have been included in the Charter of Fundamental Rights of the European Union.[52] Article 17 of the Charter provides the right for fair compensation:

> Everyone has the right to own, use, dispose of and bequeath his or her lawfully acquired possessions. No one may be deprived of his or her possessions, except in the public interest and in the cases and under the conditions provided for by law, subject to fair compensation being paid in good time for their loss. The use of property may be regulated by law insofar as is necessary for the general interest.

The Charter's applicability, however, remains limited to actions associated with the EU or EU institutions. Thus, a breach by a national government – unless induced by an EU Directive – would most likely not fall under the rights for compensation provided in the Charter.

D. Procedural Limitations

The previous issues highlight several of the limitations regarding investor security should the EU effectively terminate the intra-EU BIT regime through the recent decision. In addition, BITs remain instruments of public international law, and are thus protected both by the express provisions in the treaties, pursuant to Articles 30 and 59 of the Vienna Convention on the Law of Treaties (VCLT) on termination. This means that the parties would need to terminate the treaties in most cases, and their membership in the EU could not serve as grounds to justify a failure to observe their obligations existing under those treaties, pursuant to Article 27 of the VCLT. Thus, under the requirements set in the VCLT, it appears necessary for a treaty to be implemented by all the member states that clearly assumes authority over the investment disputes arising in this area.

The second limitation to an effective termination is the sunset clause included in the BITs that provide for continued protection for a period of 15–20 years following the termination of the agreement. The purpose of these sunset clauses is clear: investors have entered the host state with the expectation of a certain level of legal protection pursuant to those treaties. It would be contrary to the investors' rights to unilaterally dismiss those protections. Thus, in essence, even if the

---

51 ibid.
52 See generally Charter of Fundamental Rights of the European Union, Official Journal of the European Communities (2007/C 303/01); see also *Slovak Republic v Achmea BV*, Case C-284/16, Opinion of Advocate General Wathelet, 19 September 2017, paras 218–219 (considering the overlap of expropriation provisions with Article 17(1) of the Charter as 'obvious' but 'partial').

EU were to effectively terminate the treaties today, the open offer to arbitrate would remain in effect for that additional period of time.

The point noted earlier regarding investor expectations and security is essential to the position that intra-EU BITs cannot be simply removed. These provisions include distinct protections that have been extensively relied upon by the EU investors entering other EU member states. The removal of the protections leaves a gap in certainty and may in fact impact the level of intra-EU investment.

E. Member State Proposal for an EU-Wide Investment Protection Mechanism

In April 2016, five member states, including Austria, Finland, France, Germany, and the Netherlands submitted a non-paper to the Trade Policy Committee (Services and Investment) of the Council of the European Union. This proposal is important in part because it is the only defined comment that has been made by member states to include a suggested path forward for intra-EU investment protection. The proposal recommends that the intra-EU BITs be terminated, in a coordinated fashion, without any remaining protection from the sunset clauses.[53] Under the proposal, no currently pending proceedings that apply intra-EU BITs would be impacted.[54] Recognising the place of the BITs within public international law, the proposal suggests the conclusion of a multilateral agreement completed among the member states to replace the intra-EU BITs and thereby fulfil the termination criteria provided in Article 59 of the VCLT.[55] Amongst its aims is the desire to 'creat[e] an investment friendly environment by providing investors with a clear, predictable and stable legal framework.'[56]

The proposal acknowledges the need for a level of unified investor protection, namely '**an appropriate level of substantive and procedural protection for EU-Investors** so that the phasing-out of intra-EU BITs do not result in any gaps in the protection of cross-border investment within the internal market.'[57] It is noted in the proposal that failure to implement a system within the EU could result in foreign investors achieving a competitive advantage over internal EU investors. One of the lingering reasons for establishing a level of EU-wide protection includes the sunset clauses, which the member states have cited as problematic both in terms of claims from investors and the need for removal of the clauses by the respective parliaments.[58] If protections were included in a replacement agreement, it is suggested that fewer of these problems would ensue.

---

53 Council of the European Union, General Secretariat, Trade Policy Committee (Services and Investment), 'Intra-EU Investment Treaties', Non-paper from Austria, Finland, France, Germany, and the Netherlands (7 April 2016), www.s2bnetwork.org/wp-content/uploads/2016/05/Intra-EU-Bits2-18-05.pdf, paras 3–4.
54 ibid para 5.
55 ibid paras 3–4.
56 ibid para 6.
57 ibid (emphasis in the original).
58 ibid para 6.

The proposal submitted further indicates that without a unified internal policy, the external EU investment policy could be affected, specifically with regard to the trade agreements that the EU is currently negotiating, as well as any other BIT currently in force with EU member states.[59] The proposal for substantive protection recognises the need, but stops short of providing specific language or policy suggestions, instead indicating that the proposal must be clear. The relevant paragraph of the non-paper states:

> Regarding the substantive protection for intra-EU investors and their investments, the Delegations note that rights of EU investors are currently not codified at the EU level in a single framework but scattered around in various legal instruments, such as the EU Treaties, the Charter of Fundamental Rights, international treaties to which Member States are parties, such as the European Convention on Human Rights, Member States' constitutions and legislations and national and European courts' jurisprudence.[60]

The member states reference the intrinsic substantive protections of BITs: 'fair and equitable treatment, full protection and security or compensation in case of expropriation.'[61] The non-paper calls for codification of these protections in order to ensure predictability and consistency. Finally, the proposal states:

> [t]he wording of such principles should be as precise as the EU investment policy developed for TTIP and should also reaffirm EU Member States' right to regulate, in line with the EU's new approach in the field of trade policy.[62]

Procedurally, the proposal appears to maintain the protections as they are currently contained in EU law, namely referral to the domestic courts.[63] The member states suggest mediation as an intermediary step and 'a binding and enforceable settlement mechanism for investment disputes, as a last resort [...].'[64] Three options are proposed, including submission to the ECJ, a system modeled on the Unified Patent Court, and finally reliance on the Permanent Court of Arbitration – and suggest the final option to be the most realistic.[65]

There are certain issues with this proposal from both the investor and member state perspective. From a policy implementation standpoint for member states, is it possible that most (or all) member states would agree to such a system of transition? The member states which have submitted this proposal are amongst the strongest economies in the EU. On the other hand, from the perspective of investors, without the same initial guarantee of a right to arbitration, the policy

59 ibid para 6.
60 ibid.
61 ibid.
62 ibid para 8.
63 ibid para 9.
64 ibid para 11.
65 ibid para 12.

cannot fully replace the protections contained in the current intra-EU BIT regime. Nonetheless, this proposal suggests a realistic compromise to the replacement of the intra-EU BIT regime.

F. Conclusion

If no replacement system is established, the termination of BITs would result, somewhat ironically, in a greater inconsistency of protection for investors throughout the EU. As noted with regard to expropriation, the fact that the EU cannot concretely act with regard to property, but instead must allow the member states to independently legislate, could result in diverse and inconsistent protections throughout the member states. One author has noted,

> [a]lthough the predictability of the standards of protection offered by Member countries was proclaimed as a substantial resort out of the peculiarities of the EU and international investment law interaction, some legal counsellors already advise their clients to consider an option for non-EU BITS legal reconstruction of their investment.[66]

This further implies that even with the ECJ determining that intra-EU investment settlement is incompatible with EU law, the EU currently lacks the power to legislate in the area to a degree that would provide the level of protections guaranteed by BITs. A multilateral agreement by all member states may be the only solution and only means of implementing a uniform system. If a replacement to the current system has not been developed, it is difficult to imagine a scenario in which investors – currently operating under a level of legal and economic guarantees – will be assured a similar level of protection. As the protections currently exist under EU law, there would be a substantial breach of legitimate expectations and procedural protections with the dissolution of the intra-EU BIT regime. The gap left by the *Achmea* decision leaves much to be determined for the future of investment protection within the EU.

66 Dominik Moskvan, 'Is There an Alternative to Intra-European Bilateral Investment Treaties Framework under European Law?' [2011] Business Law Forum 2012, 353–398, http://ssrn.com/abstract=2221905 accessed on 2 May 2016, at 357; European Commission, Directorate-General for Trade, 'Memorandum of the European Commission Q&A: Commission Launches Comprehensive European International Investment Policy' (7 July 2010), http://trade.ec.europa.eu/doclib/press/index.cfm?id=590 accessed on 2 May 2016.

4 Is One Permanent Instance Enough?

A Comparison between the WTO Appellate Body and the Proposed Investment Court System

Marcus Weiler[1]

In its most recent trade strategy, the EU Commission declared that it 'is best placed – and has a special responsibility – to lead the reform of the global investment regime'.[2] At the heart of these reform efforts has been the suggestion to replace investor-state arbitration as a means of dispute settlement by a 'public Investment Court System'.

The Commission's draft of the Transatlantic Trade and Investment Partnership (TTIP) investment chapter of November 2015 was the first specific, yet unilateral, proposal on what such an Investment Court System (ICS) could look like.[3] While the TTIP negotiations have stalled since the 2016 US presidential election and are unlikely to be resumed, the Commission's first draft has still been instrumental in serving as a blueprint for other free-trade agreements (FTAs) between the EU and third countries. In January 2016, the Commission published the investment chapter of the EU–Vietnam FTA which then constituted the first negotiated and agreed text to implement the core features of its previous TTIP proposal.[4] On 29 February 2016, the Commission and the Canadian government announced that they had agreed on including the ICS in the final CETA text by means of 'legal scrubbing'.[5] Although none of the investment courts under said agreements is

1 Legal Clerk at the Higher Regional Court of Berlin. Email: weiler.marcus@gmail.com. The chapter was presented at the *1st Bucerius Law Journal Conference on International Investment Law & Arbitration* on 22–23 April 2016 in Hamburg and has since been slightly updated to reflect recent developments on TTIP and CETA. I am grateful for comments on a previous version of this chapter by David Hu, Andrew Lang and Jonathan Lim.
2 Commission, *Trade for All – Towards a More Responsible Trade and Investment Policy*, COM (2015) 497 final, Ch 4.1.2.
3 European Union's Proposal for Investment Protection and Resolution of Investment Disputes in the Transatlantic Trade and Investment Partnership (TTIP) of November 2015 (TTIP Proposal), http://trade.ec.europa.eu/doclib/docs/2015/november/tradoc_153955.pdf accessed 1 May 2018.
4 Chapter 8: Trade in Services, Investment and E-Commerce, Section 3, Free Trade Agreement between the EU and Vietnam, agreed text of January 2016 (EU–Vietnam FTA), http://trade.ec.europa.eu/doclib/docs/2016/february/tradoc_154210.pdf accessed 1 May 2018.
5 Comprehensive Economic and Trade Agreement (CETA) between Canada, of the one part, and the EU and its member states, of the other part, final text of 14 September

operational yet at the time of writing,[6] the European proposal of an ICS is likely to be the subject of upcoming trade negotiations with other third states. It could therefore shape the future of investor-state dispute settlement involving the EU in the years ahead.[7]

By replacing arbitrators appointed to resolve individual disputes with permanent judicial bodies, the ICS marks a significant departure from the investor-state arbitration system that is currently prevalent in most international investment agreements. In doing so, the ICS takes inspiration from the WTO Dispute Settlement Body which has been renowned for its effective settlement of trade disputes since its creation in 1995.[8]

In particular, the ICS Appeal Tribunals are largely modelled after the WTO Appellate Body. Not only does the TTIP Proposal contain several references to the WTO Appellate Body[9] but some articles are adopted *verbatim* from the WTO Dispute Settlement Understanding (DSU).[10] In its earlier concept paper of 5 May 2015, the Commission explicitly suggested: 'The bilateral appellate mechanism could be modelled largely on the institutional set-up of the WTO Appellate Body, with some adaptations both to make it specific for [investor-state dispute settlement], and in light of experience in the WTO.'[11]

The first part of this chapter seeks to discuss to what extent the WTO Appellate Body can serve as a model for the ICS. To that end, I shall identify several features that have been instrumental to the WTO Appellate Body's success and that are adopted by the ICS Appeal Tribunals (A.). However, a significant difference between the two dispute settlement systems becomes apparent when we look at the lower instances. The ICS combines a permanent Tribunal of First Instance

2016, http://data.consilium.europa.eu/doc/document/ST-10973-2016-INIT/en/p df accessed 1 May 2018.

6 Note that the investment chapter is exempted from the provisional application of CETA; see http://europa.eu/rapid/press-release_MEMO-17-271_en.htm accessed 1 May 2018.

7 Although the investment courts are constituted for each bilateral agreement only (and do not form a multilateral investment court), their institutional design is almost identical. They will therefore be analysed together for the purpose of this chapter. On 21 April 2018 (after this chapter was written) the EU published another draft agreement with Mexico whose chapter on investment dispute resolution also includes the EU's new ICS; see http://trade.ec.europa.eu/doclib/docs/2018/april/tradoc_156814. pdf accessed 21 June 2018.

8 See eg Mitsuo Matsushita, The Dispute Settlement Mechanism at the WTO: The Appellate Body – Assessment and Problems, in Amrita Narlikar and others (eds), *The Oxford Handbook on the World Trade Organization* (2012 OUP) 507, 510.

9 Articles 9.12, 10.12 TTIP Proposal.

10 See eg Article 11.1 sentence 4 TTIP Proposal which is identical with Article 17.3 sentence 4 DSU, or Article 10.5 TTIP Proposal which is almost identical with Article 17.2 DSU.

11 Commission, *Investment in TTIP and Beyond – The Path for Reform. Enhancing the Right to Regulate and Moving from Current Ad Hoc Arbitration Towards an Investment Court*, concept paper of 5 May 2015, http://trade.ec.europa.eu/doclib/docs/ 2015/may/tradoc_153408.PDF accessed 1 May 2018.

with a permanent Appeal Tribunal and requires similar qualifications for judges in both instances. In contrast, the WTO Appellate Body was created as a counterbalance to the *ad-hoc* first-instance Panels that are typically composed of inexperienced trade diplomats. The WTO Appellate Body may therefore serve as a model for an ICSID Appeal Facility, as has been suggested before,[12] rather than for a permanent two-tier court system (B.).

On that basis, the second part of this chapter will discuss whether an Appeal Tribunal is indeed warranted in addition to a permanent Tribunal of First Instance. To that end, I will look at some common arguments for establishing an appeal facility in international investment law and argue that they only carry weight in conjunction with an *ad-hoc* first instance. They cannot build a strong case for having two permanent tiers instead of just one (C.). Finally, I will explain why a permanent two-tiered ICS might actually be counter-productive (D.).

This chapter will draw together the previously mentioned points to argue that the ICS goes one step too far in creating two permanent instances with similarly qualified judges. This could undermine the enforceability of awards under the ICSID Convention, the efficiency of proceedings and the acceptance of first-instance decisions and increase the risk of judicial activism of the appeal instance.

A. Parallels between the WTO Appellate Body and the ICS Appeal Tribunals

Commentators have offered various explanations for the WTO Appellate Body's success. According to McRae, the Appellate Body's clear and simple mandate, its small size but broad representativeness, its practice of random selection combined with collegiality and the introduction of time limits have shaped its institutional design and enabled it to develop a coherent and consistent jurisprudence in WTO law.[13]

The ICS Appeal Tribunals[14] adopt several of these design features that have been instrumental to the WTO Appellate Body's success. I will now go on to highlight five key similarities in the two appeal facilities' institutional design.

---

12 ICSID Secretariat, *Possible Improvements of the Framework for ICSID Arbitration*, discussion paper of 22 October 2004, https://icsid.worldbank.org/en/Documents/resources/Possible%20Improvements%20of%20the%20Framework%20of%20ICSID%20Arbitration.pdf accessed 1 May 2018; David Gantz, 'An Appellate Mechanism for Review of Arbitral Decisions in Investor-State Disputes: Prospects and Challenges' (2006) 39 Vanderbilt Journal of Transnational Law 39; Donald McRae, 'The WTO Appellate Body: A Model for an ICSID Appeals Facility?' (2010) 2 Journal of International Dispute Settlement 371.

13 McRae (n 12) 373ff.

14 I use the term 'ICS Appeal Tribunals' to denote the different appeal tribunals under TTIP, CETA and the EU–Vietnam FTA.

I. Both Appellate Bodies are Composed of Permanent Members

First, both appellate facilities are composed of a relatively small number of permanent members serving a term of several years. While there are seven permanent members on the WTO Appellate Body serving a term of four years,[15] the TTIP Proposal[16] and the EU–Vietnam FTA[17] each provide for six members serving a term of six and four years, respectively.[18] The members of the appellate bodies are not regularly employed but receive a monthly retainer fee in exchange for being available at all times.[19] In both cases, they are appointed by a selection committee.[20]

II. Both Appellate Bodies Operate on a Rotation Basis

Second, the appellate bodies both operate on a rotation basis. Cases are heard in divisions of three members with a random allocation which makes it impossible to predict who hears a certain appeal.[21] While the nationality of the sitting WTO Appellate Body members is irrelevant, the divisions in the ICS shall consist of one national of a member state of the EU, one national from the US, Canada or Vietnam respectively, and one national from a third country.

Although the division assigned to the appeal takes all decisions itself, it has become a common practice for divisions within the WTO Appellate Body to exchange views with the other members before finalising their report. This practice of collegiality serves the purpose of ensuring consistency and coherence in the decision-making.[22]

It remains to be seen whether the ICS Appeal Tribunals will adopt a similar approach. Similar to the DSU, the rules establishing the ICS Appeal Tribunals do not explicitly provide for such practice but give the Tribunals the authority to adopt their own working procedures.[23] Commentators have regarded the principle of collegiality as a crucial factor contributing to the Appellate Body's success,[24] and have recommended it as a model for other international tribunals to follow.[25]

---

15 Article 17.1, 17.2 DSU.
16 Article 10.2, 10.5 TTIP Proposal.
17 Article 13.2, 13.5 EU–Vietnam FTA.
18 The final CETA text leaves this to be decided by the CETA Joint Committee; see Article 8.28.7 (f) CETA.
19 Article 17.8 DSU; Article 13.14 EU–Vietnam FTA; Article 10.12 TTIP Proposal.
20 Article 17.2 DSU; Article 8.28.3 CETA; Article 13.3 EU–Vietnam FTA; Article 10.3 TTIP Proposal.
21 Article 17.1 DSU; Article 13.7 EU–Vietnam FTA; Article 8.28.5 CETA; Article 10.9 TTIP Proposal.
22 Rules 4.1, 4.3 of the Working Procedures for Appellate Review.
23 Article 8.3.13.10 EU–Vietnam FTA; Article 10.10 TTIP Proposal.
24 Claus-Dieter Ehlermann, 'Experiences from the WTO Appellate Body' (2003) 38 Texas International Law Journal 469, 477ff.
25 Alberto Alvarez-Jimenez, 'The WTO Appellate Body's Decision-Making Process: A Perfect Model for International Adjudication?' (2009) 12 Journal of International Economic Law 289.

As such, the ICS Appeal Tribunals might be well advised to develop a similar practice. Though not explicit, the fact that a division of the ICS Appeal Tribunals is to make every effort to reach a decision by consensus[26] may be an indication that a collegial approach is encouraged.

III. Both Appellate Mechanisms Require Their Members to Abstain from Engaging in Other Dispute Settlement Activities

Both the WTO and the ICS have similar standards regarding the incompatibility of serving as member of the appellate body and engaging in other professional activities. Members of the appellate bodies shall not be affiliated with any government and must not accept or seek instructions from any international, governmental or non-governmental organisation or any private source. WTO Appellate Body members 'shall stay abreast of dispute settlement activities and other relevant activities of the WTO.' ICS appeal judges are required to refrain from acting as counsel or as party-appointed expert in any investment protection dispute under any treaty during their term of office.[27]

IV. Both Appellate Mechanisms Set Time Limits for the Issuance of Decisions

The existence of time limits for appeal proceedings is another feature that the ICS Appeal Tribunals have in common with the WTO Appellate Body. While the WTO Appellate Body is normally required to issue its report within 60 days after the Panel report has been appealed and must not take longer than 90 days,[28] the ICS appeal proceedings should take no longer than 180 days and must not in any case exceed 270 days.[29]

Even without appeal, investment arbitral proceedings already take significantly longer on average than WTO disputes. According to varying estimates, the average length of investment proceedings is between 3.5 and 5 years.[30] Contrastingly, WTO Panel proceedings average at 15 months with appellate proceedings taking another 96 days.[31] The introduction of time limits in the ICS might therefore be inspired by the desire to provide for more predictability and efficiency as in WTO dispute settlement and avoid making the

---

26 Article 13.12 EU–Vietnam FTA; a similar provision is missing in CETA and the TTIP Proposal.

27 Article 17.3 DSU; Rule 2.3 of the Working Procedures for Appellate Review; Article 14.1 EU–Vietnam FTA; Articles 8.28.4, 8.30 CETA; Article 11.1 TTIP Proposal.

28 Article 17.5 DSU.

29 Article 28.5 EU–Vietnam FTA; Article 29.3 TTIP Proposal.

30 See EFILA, *Task Force Paper Regarding the Proposed International Court System (ICS)* (2016), http://efila.org/wp-content/uploads/2016/02/EFILA_TASK_FORCE_on_ICS_proposal_1-2-2016.pdf accessed 1 May 2018, 56ff for a comparison of the different average times.

31 Peter Van den Bossche and Werner Zdouc, *The Law and Policy of the World Trade Organization* (3rd edn, CUP 2013) 246ff.

already lengthy investment proceedings even longer by adding an appeal mechanism.

V. The Appellate Bodies' Scope of Review is Similar

Finally, both appellate mechanisms provide a similarly broad scope of appellate review. In the ICS, the appellate scope of review extends to essentially all parts of the decisions by the first-instance Tribunals. The ICS Appeal Tribunals can hear appeals on the grounds of both legal and manifest errors in the appreciation of the facts (including relevant domestic law) as well as on the annulment grounds under Article 52 ICSID Convention.[32]

At first glance, the WTO Appellate Body's scope of review seems to be narrower. Pursuant to Article 17.6 DSU, the Appellate Body is confined to hearing appeals on grounds of only legal errors. Accordingly, it has held in *EC – Hormones (1998)* that the fact-finding process 'is, in principle, left to the discretion of a panel as the trier of facts.'[33]

Yet, upon closer scrutiny, Article 11 DSU requires a Panel to make an objective assessment of the facts of the case. Whether the Panel has fulfilled this obligation has been classified by the WTO Appellate Body as a legal question.[34] Therefore, even under the DSU, the Panels' factual determinations are not exempt from appellate review. The WTO Appellate Body examines whether the Panel has failed to 'consider all the evidence presented to it, assess its credibility, determine its weight, and ensure that its factual findings have a proper basis in that evidence.'[35]

While it is yet to be seen what a manifest error in the appreciation of facts entails in practice, it is unlikely that the ICS Appeal Tribunals will revisit each and every factual question. Instead, they would determine whether the first-instance Tribunals have done a fair assessment of the presented evidence and whether their factual findings had a sufficient evidentiary basis. Arguably, this is likely to correspond to the threshold applied by the WTO Appellate Body.

VI. Interim Summary

The ICS Appeal Tribunals adopts several design features that have been instrumental to the WTO Appellate Body's legitimacy and success. These include, most prominently, the existence of permanent judges, the random composition of individual divisions and the introduction of strict standards of professional incompatibility. Their inclusion in the ICS marks a significant departure from the previous investor-state arbitration system.

---

32 Article 28.1 (b) EU–Vietnam FTA; Article 8.28.2 (b) CETA; Article 29.1 (b) TTIP Proposal.
33 WTO Appellate Body Report, *EC – Hormones (1998)*, para 132.
34 See eg ibid.
35 WTO Appellate Body Report, *Brazil – Retreaded Tyres (2007)*, para 185.

B. Differences between the WTO Panels and the ICS Tribunals of First Instance

Although the ICS Appeal Tribunals are largely modelled on the WTO Appellate Body, there remains a major difference in the institutional set-up of the two dispute settlement systems. This becomes clear when we look at the first-instance Tribunals in both systems and contrast them with their respective appeal instance. In the ICS, the Tribunals of First Instance are composed of permanent judges who need to fulfil virtually the same qualification requirements as appeal judges. The first-instance Tribunals thus mirror the structure and composition of the Appeal Tribunals. In contrast, the first-instance WTO Panels are composed of relatively inexperienced *ad-hoc* members. I will show that the WTO Appellate Body was created as a counterbalance against the pre-existent Panel system when compulsory jurisdiction with binding outcomes was introduced in the Uruguay Round. Against this background, I will argue that the WTO Appellate Body may serve as an example for an ICSID Appeal Facility rather than for an investment court with two permanent tiers.

I. The ICS Tribunals of First Instance Mirror the Structure of the ICS Appeal Tribunals

The ICS goes beyond proposals frequently voiced in the ICSID context[36] to add a permanent appeal facility to first-instance arbitral tribunals. It establishes permanent Tribunals of First Instance that share three key similarities with the Appeal Tribunals.

First, both instances are staffed with permanent, non-rotating judges who receive a monthly retainer fee in exchange for being available at any time. Second, both instances require similar qualifications for their judges. Members of both instances must have demonstrated expertise in public international law. Experience in international trade and investment law and international dispute resolution is desirable. Under the TTIP Proposal and the EU–Vietnam FTA, the only (marginal) difference is that while first-instance judges shall 'possess the qualifications required in their respective countries for appointment to judicial office, or be jurists of recognised competence', appeal judges need to be qualified for appointment to the 'highest judicial offices'. However, this supposedly higher requirement is qualified by the identical previous alternative of 'jurists of recognised competence'.[37] In fact, under the final CETA, the qualifications for judges on both instances are identical.[38] Finally, the same standards on professional incompatibility apply for first-instance and appeal judges.[39]

---

36 See n 12.
37 Articles 12.4, 13.7 EU–Vietnam FTA; Articles 9.4, 10.7 TTIP Proposal.
38 Article 8.28.4 CETA merely refers to the qualifications for first-instance judges under Article 8.27.4.
39 Article 14.1 EU–Vietnam FTA; Article 8.30 CETA; Article 11.1 TTIP Proposal.

II. Other than the WTO Appellate Body, the First-Instance Panels are Constituted on an Ad-Hoc Basis

Contrastingly, the WTO first-instance Panels distinguish themselves from the WTO Appellate Body on all three points.

First, the Appellate Body is the only permanent instance in the WTO dispute settlement system. The first-instance Panels are established on an *ad-hoc* basis for the purpose of resolving a particular dispute. After a Panel is established by the Dispute Settlement Body, the WTO Secretariat proposes nominations for the three Panellists to the parties. To that end, the Secretariat maintains an indicative list of suitable candidates.[40] While the parties are not supposed to oppose these nominations for less than compelling reasons,[41] rejections of these nominations without much justification is the norm rather than the exception in practice which often makes the composition of a Panel a lengthy and difficult process.[42]

Second, the requirements for the WTO Appellate Body members' qualifications are significantly higher than those of the *ad-hoc* Panellists. While the WTO Appellate Body comprises 'persons of recognized authority, with demonstrated expertise in law, international trade and the subject matter of the covered agreements generally',[43] the DSU merely states that Panels shall be composed of 'well-qualified governmental and/or non-governmental individuals.'[44] These individuals may include former Panellists, former WTO diplomats, senior trade policy officials and academics. However, the pool of Panellists is not limited to such individuals. It is important to note that Panellists need not have a legal background or particular legal expertise.

Finally, the standards on professional incompatibility vary between the Panels and the Appellate Body. While Appellate Body members may not be affiliated with any government and shall stay abreast of other dispute settlement activities,[45] the DSU explicitly states that Panellists may be government officials as long as their governments are not direct or third parties to the current dispute.[46] As to potentially incompatible activities, the DSU merely mentions that Panellists 'should be selected with a view to ensuring [their] independence'.[47] As long as any potential conflicts are disclosed,[48] the DSU does not prevent a Panellist from participating in other disputes in a different role.

These differences in the required qualifications are also reflected in the actual composition of both instances. As Pauwelyn has recently shown in an empirical study, Panellists tend to be relatively low-key diplomats or ex-diplomats from developing countries who have a government background but who often have

40 Article 8.4 DSU.
41 Article 8.6 DSU.
42 Van den Bossche and Zdouc (n 31) 215.
43 Article 17.3 DSU.
44 Article 8.1 DSU.
45 See n 27.
46 Article 8.1, 8.3 DSU.
47 Article 8.2 DSU.
48 See Annex 2 (b) of the WTO Rules of Conduct for the Understanding on Rules and Procedures Governing the Settlement of Disputes.

neither a law degree nor other legal expertise.[49] The majority of Panellists serve only once and therefore lack prior experience.[50]

In contrast, the Appellate Body members are far more experienced in international trade policy and law. The formal requirements of the DSU have typically been at the very least fulfilled, if not even exceeded by past personnel choices.[51] Out of the seven current Appellate Body members, three are law professors specialising in international trade law. While two of the remaining members do not have a law degree, they have served as governmental permanent representatives to the WTO. One member has been the head of the international trade practice of a large international law firm.[52]

Overall, WTO Appellate Body members are significantly more experienced and higher qualified than the first-instance Panellists.

III. The WTO Appellate Body has been Created as a Safeguard Against the Ad-Hoc *Panels*

The WTO Appellate Body draws its *raison d'être* from the *ad-hoc* nature and the composition of the Panels. This is evinced by the negotiating history of the Uruguay Round leading to the creation of the WTO and the Appellate Body. The Appellate Body was 'conceived as a standing institution in contradistinction to the ad hoc composition of GATT and now WTO panels'.[53] Its creation has been the result of a trade-off in the negotiations.[54]

Under the old consensus-based dispute settlement procedures of the General Agreement on Tariffs and Trade (GATT), the Panels performed their task of investigating the dispute and preparing their recommendations to the GATT Council independently. However, both the initiation of Panel proceedings and the adoption of a Panel report required unanimity among all GATT contracting parties including the parties to the dispute. This allowed the losing party to block any decisions directed against it.[55]

During the Uruguay Round, the negotiators did not intend to derogate from the established GATT dispute settlement procedures but decided to take the existent panel system, as developed over many years, as a basis for the DSU.[56]

---

49 Joost Pauwelyn, 'The Rule of Law Without the Rule of Lawyers? Why Investment Arbitrators are from Mars, Trade Adjudicators are from Venus' (2015) 3, http://ssrn.com/abstract=2549050 accessed 1 May 2018.

50 ibid 17.

51 Jürgen Kurtz, *The WTO and International Investment Law: Converging Systems* (CUP 2016) 233.

52 This list is as of June 2017. The current and past members' CVs are available at www.wto.org/english/tratop_e/dispu_e/ab_members_descrp_e.htm accessed 1 May 2018.

53 Kurtz (n 51) 232.

54 McRae (n 12) 372.

55 Arie Reich, 'From Diplomacy to Law: The Juridicization of International Trade Relations' (1996–1997) 17 Northwestern Journal of International Law & Business 775, 796ff.

56 ibid 801.

However, they reversed the previous consensus rule so that consensus would now be required to prevent the initiation of Panel proceedings or the adoption of a Panel report.[57] This effectively amounted to compulsory jurisdiction with binding outcomes. States, however, were only willing to accept this automatism on the condition that an appellate mechanism would be created to ensure the coherence of WTO jurisprudence and to install 'some form of safeguard against "wrong cases" or "rogue panels"'.[58]

The permanent nature of the WTO Appellate Body and its higher qualification requirements were therefore implemented to compensate for the *ad-hoc* design of first-instance Panels and the lack of experience and legal background among the Panellists. It is against this backdrop that the WTO Appellate Body might serve as a model for an ICSID Appeal Facility rather than for a permanent two-tier ICS.

IV. The Debate About Introducing Permanent Panel Body in the WTO has Produced Few Arguments on the Necessity of Two Permanent Tiers

It is worth noting that there has also been a debate in the WTO about whether a Permanent Panel Body should be introduced. This debate can shed some light on possible advantages and disadvantages of establishing a permanent two-tier system.

Initial suggestions for this date back to the 1980s[59] but the most detailed and significant proposal was made by the European Communities in March 2002.[60] According to the proposal, the Permanent Panel Body should comprise between 15 and 24 full-time Panellists with demonstrated expertise in international trade law, economy or policy or past experience as an *ad-hoc* Panellist. The EC proposal has led to both some fierce opposition among WTO members and a lively scholarly discussion (although the entire debate has recently subsided without any concrete results).[61]

It has been argued that many potential flaws of *ad-hoc* Panels, such as their delayed composition, their high workload and lack of experience, the frequent occurrence of conflicts of interest and legitimacy concerns, could be remedied by a WTO Permanent Panel Body.[62] All these arguments, however, focus entirely on the advantages of a permanent first instance over an *ad-hoc* Panel.

Notably, few arguments have been advanced for the necessity of a permanent two-tier system. This might be due to the fact that in terms of negotiation

---

57   See eg Articles 6.1, 16.4, 17.14 DSU.
58   McRae (n 12) 372.
59   See Thomas Cottier, 'The WTO Permanent Panel Body: A Bridge Too Far?' (2003) 6 Journal of International Economic Law 187, 188ff for an overview.
60   WTO, Dispute Settlement Body Special Session Document, *Contribution of the European Communities and its Member States to the Improvement of the WTO Dispute Settlement Understanding*, 12 March 2002, TN/DS/W/1.
61   See Marc Busch and Krzysztof Pelc, 'Does the WTO Need a Permanent Body of Panelists?' (2009) 12 Journal of International Economic Law 579, 581ff for an overview of the debate.
62   William Davey, 'The Case for a WTO Permanent Panel Body' (2003) 6 Journal of International Economic Law 177, 178ff.

dynamics, once two fully fledged instances have been established, returning to just one but permanent instance might be considered a step backwards rather than forwards.

Davey argues that the existence of the judicial-like Appellate Body logically calls for an equally judicialised permanent lower instance.[63] At the same time, he suggests that the extent of intervention by the Appellate Body can partly be explained 'by a desire to leave its own stamp on WTO jurisprudence'. That would mean that even if the quality of first-instance reports improved, there might not be fewer Appellate Body interventions.[64] This, however, raises the question (that I will fully address in the next section of this chapter) of what the value-added of the higher instance would then be if the lower instance were also permanent and similarly staffed.

Wasescha takes this one step further by arguing that the creation of a permanent Panel would inevitably lead to increased competition with the Appellate Body. He points to the risk of duplicating the Appellate Body, rendering one of two bodies redundant.[65]

So what does the debate within the WTO tell us about the necessity of a permanent two-tier ICS? First, merely creating a permanent appeal facility will not be the panacea to all the problems that an *ad-hoc* first instance entails (such as the slow composition, the recurring conflicts of interest or the immense workload of part-time adjudicators). Instead of making an *ad-hoc* first instance permanent *after* establishing a permanent appeal instance, it might be easier to replace the *ad-hoc* tribunals with a permanent single instance from the very outset. Second, the debate has revealed few – if any – reasons why one should prefer two permanent instances over a single one. A two-tier system rather creates the risk of overlapping functions and increasing competition between the two permanent instances.

V. The Two-Tiered ICS Would be Unprecedented in International Adjudication

While a two-tier court system might be the norm from a domestic perspective, an investment court comprising two permanent instances with similarly qualified judges would be unprecedented in the landscape of international adjudication. It would go far beyond the institutional set-up of the WTO Dispute Settlement Body.

That is not to say that the WTO approach of combining an *ad-hoc* first instance with a permanent appeal mechanism is the ideal solution. As we have seen, the creation of the WTO Appellate Body was a compromise to counterbalance the introduction of compulsory jurisdiction with binding outcomes while maintaining the GATT tradition of rather inexperienced *ad-hoc* Panels. The debate on a

---

63 ibid 183.
64 ibid 180; see also Cottier (n 59) 191.
65 Luzius Wasescha, 'Comment on a WTO Permanent Panel Body' (2003) 6 Journal of International Economic Law 224, 226.

permanent WTO Permanent Panel Body shows that it is difficult to go back on a two-tiered system once it has been successfully established.

The key difference between the WTO Appellate Body's genesis and the ICS debate is that the ICS negotiating parties are actually willing to give up on the first-instance arbitral tribunals and replace them with a permanent body. With that in mind, there is no need to counterbalance any potential flaws of the *ad-hoc* arbitral system by creating a permanent appeal mechanism. This raises the question of what purpose an appeal facility would then serve. Is it preferable to have two permanent tiers instead of just one? The remainder of this chapter will question the necessity of a permanent appeal facility and discuss whether a permanent single body, as it can be found in most international courts, would achieve the same objectives.

C. Reasons for Establishing Two Permanent Tiers

The ICS already replaces investor-state arbitral tribunals with a permanent first court instance. It is against this backdrop that I shall now discuss what can be said in favour of adding a second layer of appeal to a permanent first instance.

While there have been few reactions specifically on the two-tiered nature of the ICS proposal so far,[66] we can draw both on the experience of the WTO Appellate Body and the longstanding debate about an ICSID Appeal Facility to identify arguments in favour of an appeal mechanism. I shall focus on four key arguments that are often advanced for establishing a permanent appeal facility in addition to first-instance *ad-hoc* Panels or arbitral tribunals.[67] I will then discuss to what extent they still apply in the presence of a permanent first instance and justify having two permanent tiers instead of just one.

I. Increased Consistency and Coherence

First, an appeal facility could improve the consistency and coherence in international investment law.

As we have seen, this has been one of the key drivers for the creation of the WTO Appellate Body. It has often been said that the success of the WTO Appellate Body in ensuring coherence in the interpretation of the covered agreements cannot be duplicated in the investment context. This is because international investment law is a deeply fragmented regime of international law consisting of many different bilateral or plurilateral agreements that would not fall within the mandate of one single appellate body.[68] This would mean that the fragmentation

---

66 See eg EFILA Task Force Paper (n 30) 50; Robert Howse, *Courting the Critics of Investor-State Dispute Settlement: The EU Proposal for a Judicial System for Investment Disputes* (forthcoming) 16ff.

67 The first three arguments build upon Tams' analysis of reasons for introducing an ICSID Appeal Facility in Christian Tams, *An Appealing Option? The Debate About an ICSID Appellate Structure* (2006) 57 Essays in Transnational Economic Law 5, 17ff.

68 McRae (n 12) 383ff; EFILA Task Force Paper (n 30) 54.

is inherent in the nature of the subject matter being adjudicated and cannot be solved by structural reforms of the adjudicatory process.

It is true that the ICS Appeal Tribunals' task would be limited to ensuring a consistent jurisprudence for the respective agreements under which they were created. Yet, even within these limitations, a permanent body could arguably increase the internal consistency under one particular treaty by narrowing down the pool of judges, standardising their qualifications and enhancing coordination amongst judges. Although not as authoritative as the jurisprudence of a multi-lateral investment court,[69] it is still likely that a consistent body of case law on one treaty would influence the interpretation of similar terms under different treaties.[70]

The question is whether this could be equally achieved by a permanent single body without appeal. It might be argued that a single body is overburdened with handling the complex fact-finding, the legal analysis and the development of a coherent jurisprudence all at the same time as they would not see the wood for the trees. A second instance would be better able to fully grasp the systemic implications when confronted with specific legal challenges to a first-instance decision.

The risk of incompatible first-instance decisions might be particularly pertinent in domestic courts where there is a high caseload and there are different first-instance courts and divisions working in parallel and independent of each other. However, other than in domestic courts, both the caseload and the number of first-instance judges in the ICS will be relatively small. For the WTO Appellate Body, its small number of permanent members and their practice of collegiality have proven decisive for developing its institutional responsibility and its custodianship for the coherence of WTO law.[71] Adopting a similar tradition of exchanging views with the non-sitting judges might therefore be an effective strategy for judges of a permanent single body to avoid losing sight of the systemic implications and handing down incompatible decisions.

This leads me to conclude that even without an appeal instance, the risk of inconsistencies in the jurisprudence of the ICS is relatively small as long as there is a limited number of judges who convene and exchange views on a regular basis.

II. Increased Likelihood to Produce Correct Decisions

Apart from the systemic argument of ensuring a coherent jurisprudence, having two permanent instances could increase the likelihood of accurate decisions.

Again, one might argue that two tribunals are less likely to overlook relevant facts than just one instance because four eyes see more than two. Or one could argue that an appeal tribunal is better suited to find and rectify legal errors as it has the benefit of a previous decision and is able to spend more time on specific issues

---

69 Note that Article 15 EU–Vietnam FTA, Article 8.29 CETA and Article 12 TTIP-Proposal commit the parties to entering into negotiations on a multilateral investment court.
70 EFILA Task Force Paper (n 30) 48.
71 McRae (n 12) 374ff.

looking at them from a more distant perspective. Consequently, the appeal tribunal would be more likely to get it right on appeal than a first-instance Tribunal.

There might be something to these arguments but eventually, as Tams points out, they rest on general, speculative assumptions on the relative advantages of appeals structures.[72] One could also come up with different assumptions that would lead to different conclusions. For example, the fact that appeal tribunals predominantly look at specific legal issues might rather increase the likelihood of erroneous rulings as they know the facts less well and risk to oversee the factual implications of their decisions. In the absence of empirical evidence, it is impossible to confirm or refute these assumptions.

It is, however, clear that there remains the possibility of error. More importantly, the assumption that an appeal instance increases the likelihood of accuracy rests on the underlying notion that the higher instance is more competent to decide the case. One would expect that this higher competence is reflected by stricter qualification requirements, a more rigorous appointment process[73] or at least a promotion requirement. None of this, however, is the case in the ICS where the required qualifications for judges are almost identical for both instances.

In the end, the expectation of better judgments rests entirely on the assumption that a second body of equal jurists will get it right more often than just one body. In consequence, the accuracy argument is insufficient to establish the necessity of two permanent instances.

III. Increased Authority and Legitimacy

Even if the creation of an appeal mechanism does not lead to more consistency and less erroneous rulings, it could at least enhance the authority of the rulings and increase the overall legitimacy of the dispute settlement system.

In that vein, Howse argues that an appeal might be able to calm the waves and avoid potential systemic crises where there has been a highly controversial first-instance decision that is perceived as fundamentally unbalanced. He points to cases in the WTO where some modest corrections of approach by the Appellate Body have sufficed to convince the losing party that its concerns have been heard and properly considered. That leads him to conclude that there is a case for a second permanent instance in the ICS.[74]

While there is some truth in the smoothing effect of a well-reasoned and considerate appeal decision upholding the initial finding, I would not overestimate this effect in the context of investment proceedings. In the WTO, disputing parties are more used to looking ahead because remedies are largely prospective. As governments merely need to withdraw or modify the disputed measure, they might experiment with different options and be satisfied with the Appellate Body

---

72 Tams (n 67) 27ff.
73 EFILA Task Force Paper (n 30) 50.
74 Howse (n 66) 17ff; see also Kurtz (n 51) 262.

giving additional explanations of its approach and some guidance on what could be considered as in compliance with the covered agreements in the future.[75]

In contrast, remedies under the ICS normally take the form of monetary damages and are applied retrospectively from the date of breach on.[76] I would doubt that in the case of a high damages award against a state, providing additional reasons without reversing the initial award would be sufficient to pour oil on the troubled waters and restore trust in the dispute settlement system. Appellate proceedings could equally have the reverse effect by prolonging the public attention to the dispute and thus intensifying the criticism.

I would therefore conclude that the legitimacy argument can – if at all – only provide very limited support for a two-tiered court system.

IV. Accountability of First Instance

A different but related point has been made by Howse with respect to the accountability of the ICS Tribunals of First Instance.[77] On the basis that accountability is a fundamental principle of the rule of law, he argues that appellate review is particularly important in cases where serious matters such as the propriety of state conduct are at stake.

Even if there is no explicit appeal in international tribunals, their rulings are often still subject to some *de-facto* review or scrutiny by domestic courts deciding how to implement the international tribunal's judgment. In the case of the ICS, however, the awards are designed to be final and not subject to domestic review, set-aside or annulment.[78] This leads Howse to conclude that the *quid pro quo* of making an award final is that the first instance is accountable to an appeal instance within the system.

It is correct that the absence of any review might give rise to accountability concerns. The genesis of the WTO Appellate Body also seems to highlight the need for an appeal instance where states submit to compulsory jurisdiction and binding outcomes. So the argument carries some weight.

Yet, I would qualify it in two regards. First, adding an appeal facility cannot solve the accountability issue but merely shifts it to the next level. Judicial activism can equally occur on the part of the higher instance that is not accountable to another body. This is exacerbated by the fact that the higher institutional status of the ICS Appeal Tribunals is not reflected by higher qualification requirements. It may be doubted whether a body of equals is capable of controlling a lower instance in a meaningful manner.

Second, there are other ways of addressing these accountability concerns. All three treaties establishing the ICS provide for a mechanism that allows the

---

75 Kurtz (n 51) 230.
76 The tribunal can also order the restitution of property; see Article 27 EU–Vietnam FTA; Article 8.39 CETA; Article 28 TTIP-Proposal.
77 Howse (n 66) 16ff.
78 Article 31.1 EU–Vietnam FTA; Article 8.28.9 (d), (e) CETA; Article 30.1 TTIP Proposal.

contracting parties to adopt interpretations of provisions in the investment chapters that are binding upon the ICS Tribunals.[79] A similar approach can be found in the WTO[80] and NAFTA[81] and has also been suggested in the ICSID context as an accountability mechanism.[82] Such binding interpretations are likely to be sufficient to reduce the risk of judicial activism and ensure that tribunals remain committed and responsive to the intentions of the parties.

This leads me to conclude that any accountability concerns can be addressed by the interpretive commissions and do not necessitate an appeal instance.

D. Reasons against Establishing Two Permanent Tiers

Whereas there is only limited support for a two-tiered ICS, I will now turn to the arguments against establishing two permanent instances and show that a second instance could have negative effects on the functioning of the ICS.

I. Enforceability of Awards under the ICSID Convention

The introduction of an appeal mechanism might render final awards unenforceable under the ICSID Convention.

Imagine a dispute is submitted under the ICSID Rules.[83] If enforcement of the final award is then sought in another member state of the ICSID Convention that is not a party to the bilateral ICS treaty, its domestic courts might refuse enforcement on the grounds that the state would be subject to a transformed enforcement obligation under Article 54.1 it has not consented to.

The ICS provisions derogate from two key provisions of the ICSID Convention. First, the ICS provisions exclude the right to request the review, annulment or set-aside of the final award and thereby opt out of the annulment procedure under Article 52 ICSID Convention.[84] Second, the ICS provides for an appeal facility although Article 53.1 ICSID Convention explicitly prohibits any appeal including bilateral appeal mechanisms.[85]

The replacement of annulment by an appeal mechanism is therefore clearly incompatible with the terms of the ICSID Convention. Articles 52 and 53.1 ICSID Convention are modified *inter se* by the parties of the ICS treaty.[86]

---

79   Article 16.4 EU–Vietnam FTA; Article 8.31.3 CETA; Article 13.5 TTIP Proposal.
80   Article IX (2) Marrakesh Agreement.
81   Article 2001(2) NAFTA.
82   International Institute of Sustainable Development (IISD), *Comments on ICSID Discussion Paper 'Possible Improvements of the Framework for ICSID Arbitration'* (2004) 5, www.iisd.org/pdf/2004/investment_icsid_response.pdf accessed 1 May 2018.
83   Article 7.2 EU–Vietnam FTA; Article 8.23.2 CETA; Article 6.2 TTIP Proposal.
84   See n 78.
85   Christoph Schreuer, *The ICSID Convention: A Commentary* (2nd edn CUP 2009), Article 53, para 29.
86   August Reinisch, 'Will the EU's Proposal Concerning an Investment Court System for CETA and TTIP Lead to Enforceable Awards? – The Limits of Modifying the ICSID

It has been argued that these modifications do not violate Article 41.1 (b) of the Vienna Convention on the Law of Treaties (VCLT)[87] as they neither affect the rights and obligations of third states nor run counter to the object and purpose of the ICSID Convention.[88] Yet, even if these *inter se* modifications are not precluded by the rules of the VCLT, they can only have effect for and against the bilateral parties of the respective ICS treaty. They cannot impose new or substantially different obligations on third states without their consent as this would run contrary to the fundamental international legal rule of *res inter alios acta* embodied, *inter alia*, in Article 34 VCLT. Third states remain only bound by the original Convention.[89]

Under Article 54.1 ICSID Convention, member states have consented to enforce awards that are the result of the proceedings and remedies provided for in the Convention. Yet, requiring third states to enforce awards that have undergone appeal proceedings agreed upon in a bilateral treaty would subject them to a substantially transformed enforcement obligation they have never consented to.[90]

The ICS rules attempt to work around this issue by determining that only 'final' awards after the completion of the appellate proceedings or the expiry of the cut-off period are to be considered as enforceable awards under the ICSID Convention.[91] Yet, if two states parties were able to define in a bilateral treaty what qualifies as an enforceable award under the ICSID Convention, this would effectively circumvent the principle that a treaty may not create or add to obligations of third states without their consent. Third states can therefore be under no obligation to enforce awards that have been the outcome of fundamentally different proceedings than envisaged in the Convention.

While the ICS might also encounter other difficulties regarding the enforcement of its awards under arbitration conventions,[92] the replacement of annulment by a bilateral appeal mechanism adds an ICSID-specific difficulty to this list. Given the relative ease with which ICSID awards can be enforced in the Convention's

Convention and the Nature of Investment Arbitration' (2016) 19 Journal of International Economic Law 761, 779.

87 Note that the ICSID Convention entered into force before the VCLT so the latter does not apply directly. Yet its rules might be applied as far as they reflect customary international law; see ibid, 771.

88 As the replacement of annulment by a bilateral appeal mechanism does not prevent other ICSID member states and their nationals from having recourse to ICSID annulment – so the argument goes – their rights and obligations are not negatively affected by the *inter se* modifications. Equally, the object and purpose of the Convention may not only be fulfilled by the specific *ad-hoc* annulment procedure provided for in Article 52 but arguably also by other review mechanisms including a permanent appeal facility (as long as there is some second layer of scrutiny); see ibid, 779; Brian McGarry and Josef Ostřanský, *Modifying the ICSID Convention under the Law of Treaties* (2017), www.ejiltalk.org/modifying-the-icsid-convention-under-the-law-of-treaties accessed 1 May 2018.

89 Reinisch (n 86) 781.

90 Reinisch (n 86) 781; McGarry/Ostřanský (n 88).

91 Article 31.8 EU–Vietnam FTA; Article 8.41.6 CETA; Article 30.6 TTIP Proposal.

92 See Reinisch (n 86) 782ff.

153 member states, the non-enforceability of ICS awards under the ICSID Convention would be a major drawback for investors and might lead them to question the effectiveness of the legal protection afforded by the ICS.

II. Acceptance of First-Instance Decisions

A permanent two-tier system risks undermining the authority and acceptance of first-instance decisions as most rulings get appealed.

Although the WTO Appellate Body was originally expected to be used infrequently,[93] statistics on its caseload show that more than two thirds of all Panel decisions get appealed.[94] In light of the high amounts in dispute, one can expect the appeal rate in the ICS to be even higher. Even if the permanent first-instance judges were to render better decisions on average, this would be unlikely to reduce the number of appeals. In fact, there is a strong political economy rationale for states to appeal adverse first-instance decisions as the exhaustion of all remedies helps selling these decisions to domestic political constituencies that are critical of the outcome.[95]

As a result, disputing parties will be less likely to accept first-instance decisions as authoritative.[96] Rather, they might think that the appeal tribunals are the only final arbiters and the provisional award is rather a minor intermediate step on the way to a final decision. Independent of whether the appeal mechanism would actually increase the overall authority of the awards (see p. 172f), the loss of authority of the first-instance decisions would be inevitable.

III. Risk of Judicial Activism of the Appeal Instance

In addition to that, the creation of two similarly qualified bodies bears an inherent risk that the appeal instance engages in judicial activism and reverses first-instance decisions on other grounds than merits to justify its existence.[97]

Assuming that a permanent first instance would be able to remedy some of the flaws of *ad-hoc* tribunals (such as the lack of experience or incoherent decision-making) and produce better decisions on average, there would potentially only be a small scope for meaningful interventions by the appeal instance. Yet, as previously discussed, a second body of similarly qualified judges is not in a better position to produce more accurate decisions than the first instance. This could lead to judicial activism as ICS Appeal Tribunals might wish to leave their own stamp on the evolving jurisprudence and reverse first-instance decisions more frequently than justified on legal grounds.

---

93 McRae (n 12) 372.
94 See Table 2 of the official WTO statistics at www.wto.org/english/tratop_e/dispu_e/stats_e.htm accessed 1 May 2018.
95 Kurtz (n 51) 262.
96 Tams (n 67) 31.
97 See also n 65.

This risk is exacerbated by the fact that the Appeal Tribunals are vested with extensive reviewing powers. The broad wording of the grounds for appeal effectively leaves it to the Appeal Tribunals to determine what falls within the scope of appellate review. Even if they cannot conduct a *de-novo* review, they have wide discretion to examine all parts of the first-instance decision they deem relevant.

Creating an appeal facility with similarly qualified judges and far-reaching reviewing powers might therefore lead to judicial overreach and have the unintended effect of decreasing rather than increasing the overall quality of judgments.

IV. *Length and Costs of Appellate Proceedings*

Finally, an appeal mechanism increases the length and costs of disputes.

As previously discussed, the ICS provides for time limits that attempt to cut the average times of investment proceedings by more than half. This seems fairly ambitious given that appeal proceedings in the ICS are likely to be more complex than ICSID annulment proceedings and the time limits do not include a possible remand of the case to the lower instance. It is yet to be seen how long ICS proceedings will take in practice. Nevertheless, even if proceedings in the ICS were significantly shorter than in the current ICSID system in absolute terms, it is clear that litigation in a two-tier system would take more time than in a system with only one permanent instance.

At the same time, an appeal mechanism drives up the litigation costs. This could create a problem for litigants with limited means such as small or medium-sized investors. Well-resourced states could attempt to outspend such investors by taking every case to appeal.[98] A two-tier ICS might therefore put small litigants at a disadvantage.

V. *Interim Summary*

While the drawbacks on length and costs of proceedings could certainly be outweighed by compelling reasons for establishing an additional instance, they carry significant weight in the absence of such reasons. After all, the length and costs in investor-state arbitration are the subject of some heavy criticism.[99] A two-tier ICS is therefore at odds with the objective of procedural efficiency. This, in conjunction with the unclear enforcement under the ICSID Convention, the loss of authority of first-instance decisions and the risk of judicial activism of the appeal instance, builds a strong case against two permanent tiers.

---

98 Kurtz (n 51) 262.

99 See eg OECD Working Papers on International Investment, *Investor-State Dispute Settlement: A Scoping Paper for the Investment Policy Community* (2012) 9, http://dx. doi.org/10.1787/5k46b1r85j6f-en accessed 1 May 2018.

E. Conclusion

This chapter has compared the design of the ICS with the WTO Dispute Settlement Body. Some key features of the ICS Appeal Tribunals, such as the small number of permanent members, the rotation principle, the requirements of professional independence or the existence of time limits, build upon the WTO Appellate Body. However, the first-instance WTO Panels distinguish themselves from the Appellate Body by the lack of experience and legal expertise among their *ad-hoc* members. In stark contrast, the ICS Tribunals of First Instance mirror the permanent structure and composition of the Appeal Tribunals. On that basis, I have argued that the creation of the WTO Appellate Body must be seen against the backdrop of the GATT tradition of *ad-hoc* Panels and may serve as a model for an ICSID Appeal Facility rather than for a permanent two-tier court system. Common arguments in favour of creating a permanent appeal facility only carry significant weight in conjunction with a non-permanent first instance that has less experience and expertise than the appeal instance. For instance, this could be the case if arbitral tribunals were retained or domestic courts served as first instance.[100] However, these arguments cannot build a strong case for two permanent and similarly qualified instances. Instead, a two-tier system is at odds with procedural efficiency, might lead to non-enforceable awards under the ICSID Convention and risks undermining the authority of first-instance decisions. My conclusion is that a single permanent body can equally be trusted to 'deliver fair and objective judgments' – and reach the goal set out for the ICS by EU Trade Commissioner Cecilia Malmström.[101]

---

100 For the latter proposal see Stephan Schill, *Reforming Investor-State Dispute Settlement (ISDS): Conceptual Framework and Options for the Way Forward* (2015), E15 Task Force on Investment Policy, 7ff, http://e15initiative.org/wp-content/uploads/2015/07/E15-Investment-Schill-FINAL.pdf accessed 1 May 2018.
101 Press release of the European Commission of 29 February 2016, http://europa.eu/rapid/press-release_IP-16-399_en.htm accessed 1 May 2018.

Part III

Practical Issues in Investor State Proceedings

1 The Appropriate Use of Bifurcation as a Means for Promoting Efficiency and Fairness in Investment Arbitration

Dr Jola Gjuzi[1]

A. Introduction

In international arbitration, bifurcation is an essential procedural technique aimed at efficient and fair proceedings. However, in practice, bifurcation of proceedings does not necessarily prove successful in meeting such an aim. The tribunals' decision to bifurcate is hence delicate, triggering the need for them to cautiously exercise their discretion. Focusing on investor-state arbitration, this chapter analyses the issue of bifurcating respondents' jurisdictional objections from the merits, and purports to identify a standard for appropriate (efficient and fair) bifurcation. It does so by reviewing the relevant case-law, which has a major role in arbitration, particularly in the absence of a test for bifurcation in the various arbitration rules.

The chapter starts with an overview of the meaning, rationale and legal basis of bifurcation of jurisdiction in investor-state arbitral proceedings (B.). It then discusses the tribunals' discretion in addressing bifurcation requests, in view of the quest for fair and efficient proceedings (C.). Having set this background, the chapter identifies a number of requirements that tribunals have considered in the effort of making appropriate decisions on bifurcation (D.). This is followed by some conclusions as to a possible standard for bifurcation, and an overview of certain open issues about the application of this standard by tribunals (E.).

B. Bifurcation in Investment Arbitral Proceedings

I. Bifurcation of Jurisdiction

When an arbitral tribunal is faced with a preliminary issue, it has to decide whether to deal with it as a distinct issue in a separate phase of the proceedings, or to join it

1 The Author has a Law Degree from the Law Faculty of the University of Tirana, Albania, and a Master of Law and Business Degree from Bucerius Law School/WHU Otto Beisheim School of Management, Hamburg/Vallendar, Germany. In February 2017, she defended her Dr. Iur Degree at Bucerius Law School, Germany. She is also an Attorney-at-Law admitted in the Tirana Bar since 2005, and currently working as a partner in an Albanian law firm. The Author wishes to express her gratitude to the participants at the 1st Bucerius Law Journal Conference on International Investment Law & Arbitration held in Hamburg on 22–23 April 2016 for their comments to the earlier draft of this chapter.

to the rest of the matters to be resolved by means of a final award. In international arbitration, the former situation refers to 'bifurcation' of proceedings. This can be defined as the procedural technique of separating the arbitral proceedings into two, three, or more distinct phases, each contemplating *ad hoc* pleadings (possibly even hearings), and ending with a decision on a discrete matter.[2] Arbitral proceedings may be split into a procedural/jurisdictional part and a merits part – so that preliminary issues are considered at an early stage and prior to a possible hearing on the merits. The proceedings may also be separated into a liability part and a quantum part – so as to make sure that the tribunal decides first on liability, and only if that decision is affirmative, the tribunal proceeds by hearing the case on damages. In another scenario, the proceedings may be split into a jurisdiction, liability, and quantum part (trifurcation).[3]

In investment disputes, bifurcation usually concerns the preliminary issues or quantum, and less often, the merits.[4] Highly frequent are jurisdictional objections.[5] This chapter focuses on the question of bifurcating such objections, ie where the investor-state tribunal is asked whether to determine a jurisdictional question as a preliminary matter or to join it to the merits.

II. Rationale of Bifurcation: Efficient and Fair Proceedings

Bifurcation is a procedural device aimed at eliminating or decreasing the need to arbitrate the parties' dispute, once it is possible to determine one dispositive or

---

2   See, Thomas J Tallerico and J Adam Behrendt, 'The Use of Bifurcation and Direct Testimony Witness Statements in International Commercial Arbitration Proceedings' (2003) 20(3) Journal of International Arbitration 295; Baiju S Vasani, 'Bi-Trifurcation of Investment Disputes' in Katia Yannaca-Small (ed), *Arbitration Under International Investment Agreements: A Guide to the Key Issues* (OUP 2010) 121; Massimo V Benedettelli, 'To Bifurcate or Not to Bifurcate? That is the (Ambiguous) Question' (2013) 29(3) Arbitration International 493, 495; Vojtěch Trapl, 'Thinking Big – Bifurcation of Arbitration Proceedings – To Bifurcate or Not to Bifurcate' (2013) 4 Czech Yearbook of International Law 267, 268; Andrea Carlevaris, 'Preliminary Matters: Objections, Bi-Furcation, Request for Provisional Matters' in Chiara Giorgetti (gen ed), *International Litigation in Practice Volume 8, Litigating International Investment Disputes: A Practitioner's Guide* (Martinus Nijhoff Publishers 2014) 173, 182; Colin Y C Ong, 'The Bifurcation of Jurisdiction from the Merits, and Merits from Damages' in Barton Legum (ed), *The Investment Treaty Arbitration Review* (Law Business Research Ltd 2016) 59.

3   Proceedings may be separated into more than three phases, in which case the correct term would be 'multifurcation'.

4   This is particularly the case of ICSID tribunals. See for an empirical study, Lucy Greenwood, 'Does Bifurcation Really Promote Efficiency?' (2011) 28(2) Journal of International Arbitration 105, 107.

5   Carlevaris (n 2) 182–183; Thomas H Webster, 'Efficiency in Investment Arbitration: Recent Decisions on Preliminary and Costs Issues' (2009) 25(4) Arbitration International 471, 477; Pierre Lalive, 'Some Objections to Jurisdiction in Investor-State Arbitration' in Albert Jan Van Den Berg (gen ed), *International Council for Commercial Arbitration: International Commercial Arbitration: Important Contemporary Questions* (Kluwer 2003) 376, 381.

essential issue first.[6] For example, a tribunal's determination that it lacks jurisdiction over the matter will obviate the need of trying the remaining issues, thereby dispensing with the parties' need to spend time, legal and other fees, and efforts to proceed with the written pleadings on liability and quantum. The same can be said of the liability part, where failure of the case on liability grounds will result in unnecessary pleadings and expert opinions on the matter of quantification of damages.[7] As one commentator explains,

> Investment cases are often very complex; bifurcation allows the arbitrators to focus on preliminary matters, which, depending on the decision, may render the subsequent phases superfluous (e.g., in case of bifurcation of jurisdictional or statutory limitation issues), or reduce the scope of the dispute (e.g., where the jurisdictional or limitation objection succeeds with respects to certain claims only). In other cases, a separate decision on preliminary issues may allow the parties to focus on the legal or factual elements the tribunal identified as applicable and relevant (e.g., in case of bifurcation of decisions on applicable law or on disputed facts). Bifurcating preliminary issues in these circumstances may result in reducing the duration and the cost of the subsequent phase of the proceedings.[8]

This means that the bifurcation measure should avoid useless procedural acts, so as to result in a quicker and less costly settlement of the dispute.[9] As put by Redfern and Hunter, bifurcation of an objection to jurisdiction 'enables the parties to know where they stand at an early stage; and it will save them spending time and money on arbitral proceedings that prove to be invalid.'[10] The tribunal in *Mesa Power v Canada* also took this position when stating that 'it is good practice … not to impose the burden of full fledged proceedings on a party that disputes being subject to arbitration'.[11]

---

6 Tallerico and Behrendt (n 2) 296; Carlevaris (n 2) 184.

7 Simon Greenberg, Christopher Kee and J Romesh Weeramantry, *International Commercial Arbitration: An Asia-Pacific Perspective* (CUP 2011) 330; Gabrielle Kaufmann-Kohler and Antonio Rigozzi, *International Arbitration: Law and Practice in Switzerland* (1st edn, OUP 2015) 326.

8 Carlevaris (n 2) 183.

9 Benedettelli (n 2) 501; Adam Raviv, 'A Few Steps to a Faster ICSID' 2013 8(5) Global Arbitration Review 23, 25. See also, *Tulip Real Estate and Development Netherlands BV v Turkey*, ICSID Case No ARB/11/28, Decision on Respondent's Request for Bifurcation, 2 November 2012, para 30. All cases referred to herein, except as otherwise indicated, are available in the websites of ICSID and/or Investor-State LawGuide.

10 Alan Redfern and Martin Hunter, *Law and Practice of International Commercial Arbitration* (4th edn, Thomson, Sweet & Maxwell 2004) 257–258. See similarly Gary Born, *International Commercial Arbitration* (Kluwer 2009) 993–994; Sigvard Jarvin, 'Objections to Jurisdiction' in Lawrence W Newman and Richard D Hill (eds), *The Leading Arbitrator's Guide to International Arbitration* (2nd edn, JurisNet 2008) 97, 102.

11 *Mesa Power Group, LLC v Canada*, UNCITRAL, PCA Case No 2012–17, Procedural Order No 2, 18 January 2013, para 16.

By reducing the time and costs of the proceedings, the bifurcation measure is considered efficient.[12] Indeed, procedural economy and efficiency are the broader principles of arbitration upon which a tribunal's decision for bifurcation rests.[13] By employing arguments of procedural economy and efficiency, respondents are the ones who typically ask the tribunal to bifurcate the jurisdictional objections from the merits.[14]

On the other hand, claimants often reject bifurcation of objections to jurisdiction. They fear that a decision on bifurcation will not lead to quicker and less costly proceedings. In fact, should the tribunal dismiss the objections to jurisdiction in an earlier bifurcated phase, then the proceedings shall continue onto liability/quantum, and last even longer than initially planned. Most importantly, claimants fear that a separate consideration of objections to jurisdiction might result prejudicial to claimants' upcoming arguments on the merits of the case, thereby resulting unfair for the whole proceedings. In fact, some tribunals have referred to 'procedural fairness' as another principle underlying the decision to bifurcate the proceedings. In *Apotex v USA*, the tribunal stated that it should decide by 'weighing for both sides the benefits of procedural fairness and efficiency against the risks of delay, wasted expense and prejudice.'[15] Commentators also suggest that, '... an arbitral panel should always consider all economical means by which to resolve the disputes before them fairly. ... the

---

12 Benedettelli (n 2) 497.

13 *Glamis Gold Ltd v USA*, UNCITRAL, Procedural Order No 2 (revised), 31 May 2015, para 12; *Tulip Real Estate v Turkey* (n 9) para 30. See also Christoph Schreuer, *The ICSID Convention: A Commentary* (2nd edn, CUP 2009) 516, 537, para 76:

> The choice between a preliminary decision and a joinder to the merits is a matter of procedural economy. It does not make sense to go through lengthy and costly proceedings dealing with the merits of the case unless the tribunal's jurisdiction has been determined authoritatively.

14 Claimants prefer avoiding bifurcation, so as to circumvent a situation where certain aspects of the case perceived as weak might outweigh the stronger ones. See Tallerico and Behrendt (n 2) 297.

15 *Apotex Holdings Inc and Apotex Inc v USA*, ICSID Case No ARB(AF)/12/1, Procedural Order deciding Bifurcation and Non-bifurcation, 25 January 2013, paras 3, 8, 10; *Guaracachi America Inc and Rurelec PLC v Bolivia*, UNCITRAL, Permanent Court of Arbitration ('PCA') Case No 2011-17, Procedural Order No 6, 30 August 2012, para 7(d) (where claimants argued that, given that respondent's jurisdictional objections could not be divorced from the merits of the dispute, 'bifurcation would lead the Tribunal to address the same facts and arguments twice. This could undermine procedural fairness since there may be a particular danger of prejudging issues before the parties had the opportunity of addressing them in full.'); *Emmis International Holding, BV and others v Hungary*, ICSID Case No ARB/12/2, Decision on Respondent's Application for Bifurcation, 13 June 2013, paras 37, 41, 47; *Accession Mezzanine Capital LP and Danubius Kereskedöház Vagyonkezelö Zrt v Hungary*, ICSID Case No ARB/12/3, Decision on Bifurcation, 8 August 2013, para 39; *Canfor Corporation v USA*, UNCITRAL, Decision on the Place of Arbitration, Filing of a Statement of Defense and Bifurcation of Proceedings, 23 January 2004, para 52.

panel should weigh the desirability of prompt resolution against the risks of an unfair, rushed decision'.[16]

Fairness and equity are hence other principles that should guide tribunals when these latter address bifurcation requests. As one practitioner states in the broader context of arbitral proceedings,

> ... of course, speed is not an unqualified virtue. An arbitrator could quickly decide a case by flipping a coin, but that would be capricious. Thus, speed cannot come at the cost of fairness and justice. Arbitrators should not unfairly limit the opportunity of the parties to present their case solely for the sake of resolving the case quickly.[17]

It follows that bifurcation should not be viewed simply as a strategic instrument that is aimed at limiting the duration and costs of arbitral proceedings as such (thereby making them more efficient), but that it does so while ensuring that the case is fairly managed by the tribunal, and both parties are given a reasonable opportunity to present their case.[18] This approach ultimately contributes to access to justice as another essential principle underlying arbitration.

III. Legal Basis for Bifurcation of Jurisdiction in Investment Arbitration

This chapter addresses bifurcation of jurisdictional matters in investment arbitration conducted under the International Convention for Settlement of Investment Disputes ('ICSID Convention') and ICSID Arbitration Rules, or under the United Nations Commission on International Trade Law ('UNCITRAL') Arbitration Rules. The former constitute today the set of rules most commonly applied

---

16 Tallerico and Behrendt (n 2) 297.

17 John Fellas, 'A Fair and Efficient International Arbitration Process' (2007) *PLI's Course Handbook, International Arbitration* 4–5, www.pli.edu/emktg/all_star/Intl_Arb13.doc accessed 30 June 2017. See more broadly, William Laurence Craig, William W Park and Jan Paulsson, *International Chamber of Commerce Arbitration* (3rd edn, Oceana Publications 2000) 359, 361 (on the role of bifurcation in the 'administration of arbitral justice').

18 See eg UNCITRAL Arbitration Rules (2010), Article 17(1):

> Subject to these Rules, the arbitral tribunal may conduct the arbitration in such manner as it considers appropriate, provided that the parties are treated with equality and that at an appropriate stage of the proceedings each party is given a reasonable opportunity of presenting its case. The arbitral tribunal, in exercising its discretion, shall conduct the proceedings so as to avoid unnecessary delay and expense and to provide a fair and efficient process for resolving the parties' dispute.

Instead of such a general provision, ICSID Rules contain more detailed ones, which ensure equality of treatment, and which provide for a special default procedure should any party fail to appear or present its case. See ICSID Arbitration Rule 42.

in investment arbitration, and the latter are frequently selected by the parties, in case of non-ICSID and *ad hoc* investment arbitration.[19]

Article 41 of the ICSID Convention and Rule 41 of the ICSID Arbitration Rules (2006) constitute the legal basis for an ICSID tribunal to address a bifurcation request, where respondent raises objections to jurisdiction.[20] Article 41(2) of the ICSID Convention reads:

> Any objection by a party to the dispute that that dispute is not within the jurisdiction of the Centre, or for other reasons is not within the competence of the Tribunal, shall be considered by the Tribunal which shall determine whether to deal with it as a preliminary question or to join it to the merits of the dispute.

ICSID Arbitration Rule 41(4) reads: 'The Tribunal ... may deal with the objection [to jurisdiction] as a preliminary question or join it to the merits of the dispute. ...'

Similar language is encountered in Article 23(3) of the UNCITRAL Arbitration Rules (2010):[21] 'The arbitral tribunal may rule on a plea referred to in paragraph 2 [a plea that the arbitral tribunal does not have jurisdiction] either as a preliminary question or in an award on the merits. ...'

C. Tribunals' Discretion to Bifurcate and the Quest for Appropriate Bifurcation

The previously mentioned rules provide for the parties' right to request bifurcation, a right which is typically exercised by respondents.[22] They also confirm

---

19   See eg UNCTAD, IIA Issues Note (May 2015) 'Investor-State Dispute Settlement: Review of Developments in 2014' 2. See generally Rudolf Dolzer and Christoph Schreuer, *Principles of International Investment Law* (2nd edn, OUP 2012) 278.

20   See similarly ICSID Arbitration (Additional Facility) Rules (2006), Article 45(5). Generally speaking, respondent should raise an objection to the tribunal's jurisdiction not later than at the time the filing of the counter-memorial is due. In fact, generally objections are obtained before receipt of the first memorial on the merits. The tribunal may decide to suspend the proceedings on the merits, and resume them after a decision on jurisdiction is made, unless it finds that it has no jurisdiction, thereby rendering an award to that effect. See ICSID Arbitration Rules (2006), Article 41(1, 3, 6) and similarly, UNCITRAL Rules, Article 23(2, 3).

21   Other rules are invoked in non-ICSID cases, such as Article 21(4) of the Permanent Court of Arbitration Optional Rules for Arbitrating Disputes Between Two Parties of Which Only One Is a State (1993); Article 21(4) of the Iran-United States Claims Tribunal Rules of Procedure (1983); Article 18(5) of the Inter-American Commercial Arbitration Commission Rules of Procedure (2002), etc. Some rules are silent about bifurcation (eg those of the International Chamber of Commerce ('ICC') and Stockholm Chamber of Commerce), though the tribunal's power to decide on bifurcation is considered as 'inherent' to its judicial function and implied by its broader powers to conduct the proceeding as it deems appropriate. See Benedettelli (n 2) 505; Carlevaris (n 2) 185.

22   See also (n 14) and accompanying text.

the tribunal's authority and discretion to decide on a request for bifurcation. This is drawn particularly from the verb 'may', which is encountered both in Rule 41(4) of the ICSID Rules (2006) and Article 23(3) of the UNCITRAL Rules (2010). The extensive discretionary power of tribunals is also confirmed by the fact that currently, neither the ICSID Rules nor the UNCITRAL Rules contain a presumption in favour of bifurcation.[23]

Viewed against the broader context of the flexible nature of arbitration, at least two intertwined factors contribute to the discretionary power of arbitral tribunals. First, there is a conscious limitation of the previously mentioned and other arbitration rules to general language.[24] In fact, these rules contain no abstract requirements to be considered by an investor-state tribunal when determining a request for bifurcation.[25] Second, there is an already admitted argument that each case has its own peculiarities, calling for a tailor-made approach from the side of tribunals.[26]

Yet, such an extensive discretion of tribunals on the one side – dependent as it is on the lack of abstract requirements and the specifics of each case – and the general lack of binding arbitral precedent on the other can be responsible for a missing 'test' that could demonstrate 'when bifurcation makes sense'.[27] Ultimately, this discretion has the potential to diminish legal security among disputing parties on the matter of bifurcation. Moreover the arbitral proceedings might be susceptible to arbitrators' subjectivity. As such, they may not only be hardly predictable

---

23 In the ICSID context, compare Arbitration Rules (2006), Article 41(3), with Arbitration Rules (1984), Article 41(3) ('Upon the formal raising of an objection relating to the dispute, the proceeding on the merits *shall be suspended. ...*') (emphasis added). The mandatory suspension implies more than a presumption in favour of bifurcation. See Carlevaris (n 2) 185. In the UNCITRAL context, compare 2010 Rules, Article 23(3) with 1976 Rules, Article 21(4) ('*In general*, the arbitral tribunal *should* rule on a plea concerning jurisdiction as a preliminary question. However, the arbitral tribunal may proceed with the arbitration and rule on such a plea in their final award.') (Emphasis added). See eg *Philip Morris Asia Limited v Australia*, UNCITRAL, PCA Case No 2012–12, Procedural Order No 8, 14 April 2014, para 101 (where the tribunal interpreted the new UNCITRAL Rules as giving it 'a wider discretion and not providing a presumption in favor of bifurcation'). See also Vasani (n 2) 127 and 122 (referring to tribunals' 'full and absolute discretion ... without parameters or limitations'); Benedettelli (n 2) 505 (referring to tribunals' 'wide margin of discretion'); Raviv (n 9) 25 (referring to tribunals' 'considerable discretion').

24 Tallerico and Behrendt (n 2) 296; Catherine Rogers, 'Fit and Function in Legal Ethics: Developing a Code of Attorney Conduct for International Arbitration' (2002) 23 Michigan International Law Journal 341, 412.

25 Vasani (n 2) 121; Tallerico and Behrendt (n 2) 296.

26 Benedettelli (n 2) 493–494, 506; Richard Happ, 'ICSID Rules' in Rolf A Schuetze (ed), *Institutional Arbitration: Article-by-Article Commentary* (Beck/Hart 2013) 978, para 239; Carlevaris (n 2) 184 ('... the question whether to bifurcate a phase of the proceedings cannot be answered in the abstract, but only in light of the specific circumstances of the case.')

27 Tallerico and Behrendt (n 2) 296.

from the disputing parties,[28] but also trigger questions of arbitrariness and lack of legitimacy of the tribunal's decision.[29]

These concerns are extended by the disputed role of bifurcation in bringing about efficient proceedings. As pointed out earlier, a decision to bifurcate should rely on principles of procedural economy, efficiency, and fairness. In practice, however, there is a risk that bifurcation does not result in shorter and less expensive proceedings.

Scholars and practitioners admit that it is questionable whether a tribunal's decision to bifurcate the proceedings indeed leads to efficiency, or rather it risks becoming a source of unnecessary additional costs and delays.[30] Some authors' empirical analyses of ICSID case-law on the matter have already challenged the assumption that, time-wise, bifurcation is always efficient.[31] In fact, bifurcation would result in an increase of the overall duration of the proceedings every time the preliminary objection is rejected and arbitration will have to continue.[32]

In this way, and having regard of its identified rationale, bifurcation of jurisdiction from the merits can be appropriate, only if it increases efficiency and ensures fairness of the proceedings. Efficiency and fairness from bifurcation are in turn not a given. It is a rather difficult task for tribunals to assess whether bifurcation promotes efficiency and fairness in each particular case.[33] This is even more so because of the tribunal's task for making the decision relating to bifurcation ex-ante, ie before assessing the objection as such.

In other words, tribunals need to find good reasons in making their decisions relating to bifurcation requests, which need to be based on the quest for efficiency and fairness of proceedings.[34] As Benedettelli points out in the context of

---

28 See also, Vasani (n 2) 127. See more broadly Kaufmann-Kohler and Rigozzi (n 7) 326–327. Two other factors that are at times encountered in the arbitral practice, namely the lack of public decisions relating to bifurcation and the lack of reasoning therein, contribute to less predictability of the approach of investor-state tribunals relating to bifurcation. For some examples, see (n 36) and (n 37).

29 See also Benedettelli (n 2) 506.

30 ibid 493, 494; Tallerico and Behrendt (n 2) 296; Raviv (n 9) 23; Claudia T Salomon, 'Splitting the Baby in International Arbitration' (2015) The National Law Journal.

31 Greenwood (n 4) 106–107 (finding that, out of the concluded ICSID cases under review, the bifurcated ones took on average 3.62 years, and the non-bifurcated ones, 3.04 years. Out of the concluded ICSID Additional Facility cases, the bifurcated ones took on average 3.39 years, and the non-bifurcated ones, 2.96 years). See similarly Raviv (n 9) 25 (noting that despite ubiquitous jurisdictional objections, most ICSID cases are not dismissed for lack of jurisdiction, which in case of bifurcation results in 'extremely long' proceedings).

32 Carlevaris (n 2) 183; Raviv (n 9) 25; Jack J Coe, 'Pre-Hearing Techniques to Promote Speed and Cost-Effectiveness: Some Thoughts Concerning Arbitral Process Design' (2002) 53(2) Pepperdine Dispute Resolution Law Journal 53, 69–70.

33 Greenwood (n 4) 108 ('... tribunals should be cautious about proceeding with a twin-track approach to a case without good cause. A party may be advocating bifurcation to delay and obstruct the arbitration, rather than to make it more efficient.')

34 A case in point is Suggestion 30 of the ICC Commission Report, 'Controlling Time and Costs in Arbitration' (ICC Publication 2014) 11 ('The arbitral tribunal should consider, or the parties could agree on, bifurcating the proceedings or rendering a

managing arbitral proceedings, '[f]lexibility ... should not mean arbitrariness and criteria should be devised in order to enhance both the legitimacy of the arbitral tribunal's decision and the predictability of the proceedings.'[35]

Against this backdrop, questions arise as to where the issue of bifurcation stands in the practice of investment tribunals. Are tribunals exercising their discretion without limitations/qualifications, thereby contributing to less predictable decisions? Or are they rather cautious enough in this regard and already setting out a possible threshold beyond which bifurcation decisions can indeed ensure efficient and fair proceedings? What are the requirements/criteria that establish a dividing line between bifurcation that is efficient and fair (hence appropriate), and bifurcation that is not?

The identification of requirements for appropriately using bifurcation of jurisdictional issues in investment proceedings is mainly of practical relevance. While it could offer some contribution to the theoretical question of fairly balancing the legitimate interests of claimants for non-bifurcation and those of respondents for bifurcation, in the context of the scope of this chapter, such identification is primarily aimed at assisting arbitrators and parties' counsel in preparing their submissions once the issue of bifurcating the proceedings arises.

D. Requirements for Bifurcation in Investment Case-Law

The following addresses the previous questions by reviewing the relevant investor-state case-law. This is to the extent that decisions on bifurcation (or final awards referring to them) are public,[36] and that tribunals provide reasons for such decisions.[37]

As the review reveals, in order to justify a decision for bifurcation, tribunals have considered a number of requirements,[38] to which it is turned next. The questions underlying the tribunals' decision have been about the likeliness that a bifurcated procedure results in increased procedural economy, efficiency, and fairness to the parties – principles that constitute the rationale of bifurcation.[39]

---

partial award *when* doing so may genuinely be expected to result in a more efficient resolution of the case.') (Emphasis added.)

35 Benedettelli (n 2) 506. See also, Kaufmann-Kohler and Rigozzi (n 7) 326–327.

36 Cf eg *Mamidoil Jetoil Greek Petroleum Products Societe SA v Albania*, ICSID Case No ARB/11/24, Award, 30 March 2015, para 36 (referring to the tribunal's decision against bifurcation, which is, however, not public).

37 See eg *Tokios Tokelés v Ukraine*, ICSID Case No ARB/02/18, Order No 2, 1 July 2003, para 3 (where, after having examined the arguments put forward by the parties regarding the request for bifurcation, the tribunal did not give reasons for its bifurcation decision).

38 Tribunals use various terms regarding these requirements: 'factors' (*Mesa Power v Canada* (n 11) para 17); 'criteria' (*Philip Morris v Australia* (n 23) para 109); 'considerations' (*Glamis Gold v USA* (n 13) para 12(c)). The focus here is on the *requirements* identified, and not on the various *circumstances*, which also play an important role for the decision (eg the timing of the request for bifurcation, the complexity of the case, the chances for settlement, the scope of claim, etc.).

39 See (n 13 and n 15) and accompanying text.

I. The Objection to Jurisdiction is Substantial

In deciding whether the objection to jurisdiction deserves preliminary and discrete consideration, tribunals have assessed the merit of the objection, ie whether it is *prima facie* 'substantial',[40] 'serious',[41] 'proper',[42] 'significant',[43] 'genuinely preliminary',[44] or rather 'frivolous'[45] and 'dilatory'.[46] They have evaluated the element of seriousness by having regard to the fact that the preliminary consideration of a non-substantial (frivolous/dilatory) objection to jurisdiction is very unlikely to reduce the costs or the time of the proceedings.[47] Neither would it be fair in terms of parties' equality.[48]

In *Accession v Hungary*, the tribunal held that the jurisdictional issues raised by respondent, namely that the dispute does not arise out of an investment and it concerns non-existent rights, are 'significant and deserve a focused examination in a separate phase.'[49] In *Mesa Power v Canada*, the tribunal regarded respondent's objection to jurisdiction that claimant did not respect the conditions precedent for submitting a claim to arbitration under Chapter 11 of North American Free Trade Agreement ('NAFTA'), as 'non-frivolous'. It stated that this question is open to evaluation at a later stage, but it could not be denied that respondent's objection 'could have an effect on the tribunal's jurisdiction' if a decision by the tribunal were to be taken in its favour.[50] In *Glamis Gold v USA*, the tribunal found that an objection that claimant has not suffered a loss as a result of certain state measures, in accordance with NAFTA Article 1117(1), is not a plea as to jurisdiction, rather an issue to be examined in the merits.[51]

II. The Objection to Jurisdiction, if Granted, Could Dismiss the Entire Claim or Materially Reduce the Next Phase

Tribunals have also assessed *prima facie* whether the objection(s) to jurisdiction requested to be bifurcated might be successful and lead to an early resolution of the case.[52] As one commentator explains,

---

40 *Glamis Gold v USA* (n 13) para 13(c).
41 *Philip Morris v Australia* (n 23) para 109.
42 *Tulip Real Estate v Turkey* (n 9) para 32.
43 *Accession v Hungary* (n 15) para 39.
44 *Libananco Holdings Co Limited v Turkey*, ICSID Case No Arb/06/8, Award, 2 September 2011, para 33.
45 *Mesa Power v Canada* (n 11) para 16.
46 ibid.
47 *Glamis Gold v USA* (n 13) para 13(c); *Mesa Power v Canada* (n 11) paras 4, 16; *Philip Morris v Australia* (n 23) para 109; *Emmis v Hungary* (n 15) para 37; *Accession v Hungary* (n 15) para 39.
48 See eg Salomon (n 30) ('A party cannot be hindered in making its case, but neither does a dispositive application allow one party to hijack the arbitration process with a weak or meritless claim or defense.').
49 *Accession v Hungary* (n 15) para 39.
50 *Mesa Power v Canada* (n 11) paras 5, 6, 18.
51 *Glamis Gold v USA* (n 13) paras 23–25.
52 *Philip Morris v Australia* (n 23) paras 109, 111.

[i]f a potentially finally dispositive objection, for all or part of the case, fails, this will reflect in an overall increase of the duration of the proceedings. Whether an objection is successful (and therefore whether bifurcating the relevant phase of the proceedings proves to be procedurally efficient) can only be assessed *ex post facto*. However, since the decision whether to bifurcate is obviously taken *ex ante*, the arbitral tribunal will be required to make a *prima facie* assessment of the chances of success of the objection.[53]

Two scenarios have been considered in this respect. First, tribunals have assessed whether a determination of the preliminary objection is capable of resulting in the dismissal of the entire case. In *Libananco v Turkey*, the tribunal found respondent's objection to jurisdiction that claimant's claim did not satisfy the express conditions on Turkey's consent to arbitration as being 'genuinely preliminary' and 'capable of bringing the proceedings to an end'.[54]

Second, tribunals have assessed whether the jurisdictional objection, if granted, results in a material, significant, or essential reduction of the proceedings at the next phase (including its scope and complexity). In *Accession v Hungary*, the tribunal held that the jurisdictional objections that the dispute does not arise out of an investment and that it concerns non-existent rights, 'deserve a focused examination in a separate phase that could either make a merits phase unnecessary or sharpen many factual issues should the Tribunal reach the merits', given that certain rights could possibly qualify as investment, and others not.[55]

III. The Issue of the Objection to Jurisdiction is Intertwined with the Merits

Tribunals have also assessed whether the jurisdictional issue identified may be easily isolated from the merits, or rather it is so intertwined with the merits that it may be difficult to deal with it separately. This is where the objections are closely related to the facts to be fully examined at the merits of the case,[56] involving very

---

53 Carlevaris (n 2) 184. See similarly Webster (n 5) 478.
54 *Libananco v Turkey* (n 44) para 33. See similarly *Philip Morris v Australia* (n 23) para 109.
55 *Accession v Hungary* (n 15) para 39 (further arguing that the nature and incidents of the rights and investments allegedly held by claimants are distinct from the merits question as to whether such rights were expropriated by respondent). See similarly *Tulip Real Estate v Turkey* (n 9) paras 30–31. As put by Salomon (n 30) (one question of the test for assessing when to split the proceedings is whether the issue raised is 'truly dispositive', thereby ending or disposing of the case (or a significant portion thereof)).
56 *Ioannis Kardassopoulos v Georgia*, ICSID Case No ARB/05/18, Decision on Jurisdiction, 6 July 2007, para 257; *Generation Ukraine, Inc v Ukraine*, ICSID Case No ARB/00/9, Award, 16 September 2013, paras 6.3–6.4; *World Duty Free Company Limited v Kenya*, ICSID Case No ARB/00/7, Award, 4 October 2006, para 102; *Methanex v USA*, UNCITRAL, Preliminary Award on Jurisdiction and Liability, 7 August 2002, para 86; *Burimi SRL and Eagle Games SHA v Albania*, ICSID Case No ARB/11/18, Decision on Bifurcation, 18 April 2012, para 13.2.

complex and extensive/full gathering of factual evidence,[57] and being not yet ripe for decision.[58]

In *Tradex v Albania*, consent to ICSID jurisdiction, as offered by the Albanian law, was limited to disputes arising from expropriations. One objection to jurisdiction related to the question of whether the alleged conduct of Albania could be considered an expropriation. The tribunal noted that such a question was relevant for purposes of jurisdiction, but it was also decisive for purposes of the merits of the claim, therefore deciding to join it to the merits.[59]

In *Kardassopoulos v Georgia*, the tribunal regarded respondent's objection to jurisdiction ratione temporis under the Bilateral Investment Treaty ('BIT') as 'clearly not ripe for decision'. In its reasoning,

> ... the Tribunal cannot determine whether the alleged BIT breaches occurred before or after 3 August 1996 without having considered the testimony and other evidence that can only be obtained through a full hearing of the case. A thorough examination of the events which may have led to the expropriation of Claimant's investment in Georgia is necessary to determine whether Article 4 of the BIT was breached and, if so, when it was breached. This must be left to the merits stage of the proceeding when a full evidentiary hearing will take place.[60]

Similarly, in *Iberdrola v Guatemala*, the main dispute was whether the facts alleged by claimant constitute a contract claim or a treaty claim. The ICSID tribunal dismissed respondent's application for bifurcation, holding that the difference is closely linked to the merits of the dispute 'which is difficult to separate from that decision and which requires for its resolution a comprehensive assessment of the facts and evidence.'[61] Commentators agree that if the jurisdictional issues would involve extensive evidentiary activity, including hearing the same witnesses as at the hearing on the merits, then it may not be procedurally efficient to hear the jurisdictional matter at the outset.[62]

Tribunals have considered bifurcation in the previously mentioned situations to be impractical, as it would very unlikely result in any savings in time or costs. In *Glamis Gold v USA*, the tribunal denied respondent's request for bifurcation of its objection that one of claimant's claims should be dismissed, since claimant had not incurred a loss as a result of certain state measures. It stated that it would need to

57 *Generation Ukraine v Ukraine*, ibid para 6.4; *Impregilo SpA v Pakistan*, ICSID Case No ARB/03/3, Decision on Jurisdiction, 22 April 2005, paras 270, 284–285.
58 *Alex Genin, Eastern Credit Limited, Inc and AS Baltoil v Estonia*, ICSID Case No ARB/99/2, Award, 25 June 2001, para 27.
59 *Tradex Hellas SA v Albania*, ICSID Case No ARB/94/2, Decision on Jurisdiction, 24 December 1996, ICSID Review – Foreign Investment Law Journal 185.
60 *Kardassopoulos v Georgia* (n 56) para 257.
61 *Iberdrola Energía SA v Guatemala*, ICSID Case No ARB/09/5, Award, 17 August 2012, para 19.
62 Webster (n 5) 478; Carlevaris (n 2) 184; Benedettelli (n 2) 499–500; Schreuer (n 13) 538–539, para 80.

examine the same facts both when deciding the preliminary objection and the merits.[63]

Taking into account the quest for efficient and fair proceedings, tribunals have opted not to grant requests for bifurcation in such cases. They have done so in order to avoid the risk of having the issues being addressed twice, which might in turn result in inconsistent submissions by the parties, or in prejudicial decisions by the tribunal. In *Philip Morris v Australia*, the tribunal was prepared to use its discretion relating to bifurcation 'in order to ensure that any decision on the preliminary objections neither prejudices the merits nor is taken in the absence of sufficient information.'[64] As rightly put by Tallerico and Behrendt,

> [a]rbitrators must balance the use of hearing potentially dispositive issues first to the extent that it may interfere with the underlying fairness of the hearing and/or a party's right to be heard and to submit its evidence to the panel.[65]

E. A Standard for Appropriate Bifurcation and Some Open Issues about Its Application

I. A Standard for Bifurcation of Jurisdictional Objections

The review shows that tribunals have widely used the previous three requirements when addressing bifurcation requests. In fact, despite the lack of binding precedent in investment arbitration, tribunals have often relied on the reasoning of earlier tribunals when purporting to identify possible requirements for substantiating their decision in favour or against bifurcation.[66]

Notably, the previously identified factors/requirements find support beyond the realm of investment arbitration. They are already present in the practice of non-investment arbitration,[67] as well as in that of the Permanent Court of

---

63 *Glamis Gold v USA* (n 13) paras 22–25. See similarly *Mesa Power v Canada* (n 11) paras 4, 16; *Philip Morris v Australia* (n 23) para 108; *Tulip Real Estate v Turkey* (n 9) paras 30–31; *Emmis v Hungary* (n 15) para 37; *World Duty Free v Kenya* (n 56) para 102; *Kardassopoulos v Georgia* (n 56) para 260.

64 *Philip Morris v Australia* (n 23) para 108.

65 Tallerico and Behrendt (n 2) 297.

66 See eg *Mesa Power v Canada* (n 11) para 17 (where the tribunal relied on the reasoning on bifurcation of the UNCITRAL tribunal in *Glamis Gold v USA* (n 13) para 13(c)); *Accession v Hungary* (n 15) para 39 (where the tribunal considered the analysis on bifurcation in *Emmis v Hungary*, as 'sound' and 'persuasive authority'). The same factors discussed previously are encountered even in other decisions, where no express reliance to earlier awards is mentioned (eg *Philip Morris v Australia* (n 23) para 109; *Burimi v Albania* (n 56) para 13.2; *Apotex v USA* (n 15) paras 9–13).

67 See eg American Arbitration Association, 'Saving Time & Money in Arbitration: Tips for Advocates: A Facilitator's Guide' 2, www.adr.org/cs/idcplg?IdcService=GET_FILE&dID=33940&dDocName=ADRSTAGE2023843 accessed 30 June 2017 (referring to similar factors that arbitrators may consider in determining if a motion for bifurcation should be granted).

International Justice and International Court of Justice.[68] Moreover, scholars and practitioners commenting on the issue of bifurcation offer suggestions along the lines of the investment arbitral practice.[69]

In view of this, the three identified requirements already delineate a standard for appropriate bifurcation, which investor-state tribunals can apply and upon which disputing parties may rely. These requirements would qualify the otherwise 'full' or 'extensive' discretion of tribunals when assessing the appropriateness of bifurcation in terms of efficiency and fairness of proceedings.[70]

II. Open Issues on the Application of the Standard

Beyond the identification of a standard for bifurcation, in terms of its application, the issue is more delicate as it heavily depends on the circumstances of each case.[71]

---

68 See eg *Barcelona Traction, Light and Power Company, Limited*, Preliminary Objections, Judgment ICJ Reports 1964, 6, 46 (where the Court assessed whether the objection to jurisdiction was of a 'preliminary character that can be determined on its own', or rather 'inextricably interwoven with the issues of denial of justice which constitute the major part of the merits'); *Prince von Pless Administration Case*, 1933 Order PCIJ Ser A/B No 52, 14, where the Court considered that the preliminary objection:

> appears to be inextricably bound up with the facts adduced by the Applicant and can only be decided on the basis of a full knowledge of these facts, such as can only be obtained from the proceedings on the merits.

See for a discussion, Lalive (n 5) 378–380.

69 See esp Tallerico and Behrendt (n 2) 296, 298; Carlevaris (n 2) 184–185; Benedettelli (n 2) 497–500; Vasani (n 2) 122–125; Inna Uchkunova and Oleg Temnikov, 'Bifurcation of Proceedings in ICSID Arbitration: Where Do We Stand?' Kluwer Arbitration Blog, 15 August 2013; Nigel Blackaby and others, *Redfern and Hunter on International Arbitration* (6th edn, Kluwer & OUP 2015) paras 5.116 and 5.121; Carolyn Lamm, Chiara Giorgetti, and Mairée Uran-Bidegain, 'International Centre for Settlement of Investment Disputes' in Chiara Giorgetti (gen ed), *International Litigation in Practice Volume 4: The Rules, Practice and Jurisprudence of International Courts and Tribunals* (BRILL 2012) 77, 89, n 70; Greenberg, Kee and Weeramantry (n 7) 211; Schreuer (n 13) 537, para 76; and relevant references in Section D of this chapter.

70 See *Tulip Real Estate v Turkey* (n 9) paras 30–31 (where the tribunal referred to the three considerations and noted that it is 'guided by [them] in the exercise of its discretion whether to grant Respondent's Application for bifurcation.').

71 See (n 26 and n 38) and accompanying text. See *Philip Morris v Australia* (n 23) para 103:

> While the Tribunal agrees that taking into account such other jurisprudence is indeed helpful and appropriate, and will do so in its considerations, the present procedure must be examined in light of its own specific factual and legal circumstances which differ in various ways from the cases addressed by other courts and tribunals.

Borrowing from the general discussion of Kaufmann-Kohler and Rigozzi (n 7) 326–327, paras 6.81–6.82, on standardisation and flexibility in arbitration, it should be pointed out that the delineated standard should serve as a 'default procedure only', and

Given its limited scope, this chapter does not purport to address such an issue *per se*. It rather focuses on the following two factors identified from the review of the arbitral practice, and which might negatively affect the consistent application of the standard and/or contribute to some insecurity relating to the proceedings.

1. Controversies Relating to the Application of Requirements to Jurisdictional Objections

Some objections to jurisdiction appear uncontroversial in meeting the identified requirements for bifurcation. One example is respondents' objection that claimants' claims are contract claims and not treaty claims, and as such they deprive the tribunal of jurisdiction. Tribunals have denied bifurcation of this objection, arguing that the issues that need to be considered in determining such an objection are intimately linked to the merits. This is where there appears to be a close relationship between such an objection, and the factual evidence pertaining to the alleged conduct of respondent.[72]

Other objections, though, could be controversial. Illustrative are the pre-arbitration consultation and negotiation provisions. In *Tulip Real Estate v Turkey*, in question was whether or not such a provision of the applicable BIT referred to a 'mandatory' and 'formalistic' period, thereby depriving the tribunal of jurisdiction to hear the case or making claimant's claim inadmissible.[73] The tribunal ordered bifurcation of this objection, implying the mandatory nature of what constituted a 'pre-condition to arbitration'.[74] In its reasoning, such an objection was capable of being dealt with preliminarily, and if successful, 'it could have the effect of disrupting the entire case by taking the dispute outside the Tribunal's jurisdiction or making the dispute inadmissible...'[75] Other tribunals, however, show a general tendency of treating consultation periods as 'directory and procedural rather than as mandatory and jurisdictional'.[76] They thereby consider compliance with such a requirement as not 'amounting to a condition precedent for the vesting of jurisdiction',[77] and therefore see no need to bifurcate such a jurisdictional objection.

---

should allow arbitrators to make 'adjustments' when this is so required by the circumstances.

72 *Tulip Real Estate v Turkey* (n 9) para 37; *Iberdrola v Guatemala* (n 61) para 19.
73 *Tulip Real Estate v Turkey* (n 9) paras 45–55.
74 ibid para 55(c).
75 ibid para 55(a, b).
76 *SGS Société Générale de Surveillance SA v Pakistan*, ICSID Case No ARB/01/13, Decision on Jurisdiction, 6 August 2003, para 184 (with further reference).
77 ibid para 184. See also *Alps Finance and Trade AG v The Slovak Republic*, UNCITRAL, Award (redacted version), 5 May 2011, para 200. See for a comment Uchkunova and Temnikov (n 69).

2. Tribunals' Occasional Reluctance to Employ Bifurcation

At least two situations are identified where tribunals have shown reluctance when deciding for bifurcation.[78] One relates to the tribunals' reservation to re-join a bifurcated matter to the merits. In *Mesa Power v Canada*, respondent objected jurisdiction alleging claimant's failure to abide by a waiting period provided in Article 1120(1) of NAFTA, which failure resulted in a lack of consent and thus a lack of jurisdiction. The tribunal saw 'potential merit in the requested bifurcation', yet reached the decision in favour of bifurcation 'with a reservation' of having the possibility to re-join to the merits the already bifurcated objection. This was necessary because, although bifurcation might lead to more efficient proceedings, 'the tribunal cannot exclude the possibility that once the issue is explored further with the benefit of the Parties' further briefing, it may transpire that a determination cannot be made without substantially engaging with the merits of the dispute'.[79]

In another situation, tribunals have addressed the issue of additional costs that would result for the parties in case of an inappropriate decision on bifurcation.[80] In *Emmis v Hungary*, the tribunal pointed out that:

> Claimants will not be prejudiced by bifurcation, other than in the increased costs occasioned by the jurisdiction application and consequent delay in the event that they are successful in opposing it. It is within the discretion of the Tribunal, as Respondent accepts, to compensate Claimants for those costs.[81]

Certainly, tribunals might have different perceptions of risk when making a decision in favour of bifurcation for the sake of efficiency and fairness. Yet, given the *ex ante* nature of such a decision and the important role of the circumstances of each case, it cannot be excluded that their bifurcation decision might, at times, prove inappropriate. As the case evolves, one party might miss a reasonable opportunity to fully present its case, if, due to bifurcation, certain objections are heard and decided beforehand and separately. One party might also suffer the longer time and costs involved, where Respondent's objections to jurisdiction are not upheld and the arbitration shall have to continue. The tribunals' reluctance in their bifurcation decision, and/or their preparedness to put the burden on respondent for the additional costs of an extended proceeding resulting from inappropriate bifurcation, might be justified in view of their role of purporting to ensure that ultimately, fairness of proceedings and access to justice prevail for both parties.

---

78 See for a comment Uchkunova and Temnikov (n 69).
79 *Mesa Power v Canada* (n 11) paras 5, 17, 21. See further *Mesa Power v Canada*, Procedural Order No 3, 28 March 2013, paras 73 et seq (where the tribunal discontinued bifurcation arguing that, having had the benefit of claimant's Answer on Jurisdiction, it would not be possible to rule on the application of Article 1120(1) in the abstract, without substantially engaging in the facts of the dispute).
80 *Apotex v USA* (n 15) para 12; *Accession v Hungary* (n 15) para 39. Some practitioners support this approach. See, Raviv (n 9) 25.
81 *Emmis v Hungary* (n 15) para 56.

F. Conclusions

When addressing a request for bifurcating jurisdictional objections from the merits, the essential and practical question that investor-state arbitral tribunals face is how to ensure that the decision promotes procedural economy and fairness. The discretionary authority of tribunals in deciding on such requests, particularly in the context of the amended ICSID and UNCITRAL Rules, is not only a manifestation of the needed flexibility in arbitration, but also a door for possible subjectivity.

Bifurcation is not equal to efficiency and fairness; it can, however, be so if appropriately used. In the absence of a test for bifurcation in the previously mentioned arbitration rules, this chapter looked at the investor-state arbitral practice and identified the following requirements that tribunals widely use in the effort of addressing appropriately requests for bifurcation of jurisdictional objections: (i) the objection is substantial and *prima facie* proper and serious; (ii) the objection, if granted, shall result in the dismissal of the entire claim, or in a material reduction of proceedings at the next phase; and (iii) the objection is closely intertwined with the merits. The rather uniform reference to these requirements, and the broader support they receive from other international fora as well as from commentators, contribute to a sound standard for appropriate bifurcation that tribunals could employ and practitioners could rely upon when building their case.

Beyond the identification of the standard, an open question remains as to its application. While admittedly a decisive role in this regard play the circumstances of each case, from a review of case-law, two issues of application appear upfront, and contribute to some insecurity of proceedings among disputing parties specifically and practitioners generally. It is already controversial as to whether objections, such as the pre-arbitration consultation and negotiation provisions, should be determined preliminarily (hence bifurcated) or not. Moreover, tribunals show some hesitation about their decisions in favour of bifurcation. This is when they reserve their right to re-join to the merits bifurcated objections, should these prove relevant for the merits of the case. This is also when tribunals undertake to use the 'loser-pays-principle', in order to address the financial consequences of a bifurcation decision proven to be inefficient. This latter approach of tribunals, however, might be justified by their role in purporting to ensure efficient and fair proceedings to both disputing parties.

2 Effective Management of Mass Claims[1] Arbitration

What We Could Learn from International Tribunals

Katarzyna Barbara Szczudlik

A. Overview

Mass claims have become a hot topic in investment arbitration since the *Abaclat* case (followed by the *Ambiente Ufficio* and *Giovanni Alemanni* cases) and it is one that will stay with us for a long time, as experts are convinced that the large scale legal injuries ratio will increase in the years ahead.

Unfortunately, no arbitration institution offers a comprehensive set of rules applicable to mass claims investment arbitration. This situation has already caused major difficulties for International Centre for Settlement of Investment Disputes ('ICSID') investment tribunals, which were forced to invent rules on a case-by-case basis, using Article 44 of the ICSID Convention (which reads: '[…] If any question of procedure arises which is not covered by this Section or the Arbitration Rules or any rules agreed by the parties, the Tribunal shall decide the question'). But does it mean that mass claims investment arbitration proceedings are to be conducted differently every time? If so, this constitutes an additional argument for the opponents of international investment arbitration, as it becomes less predictable and more dependent upon the arbitral tribunal selected.

There is therefore a clear and urgent need to write effective rules for mass claims arbitration. The good news is that the arbitration community can draw inspiration from rules created by national arbitration bodies (for instance in the US) and by international tribunals (for example, the Iran–US Claims Tribunal, the United Nations Compensation Commission, the Commission for Real Property Claims of Displaced Persons and Refugees in Bosnia and Herzegovina, the Housing and Property Claims Commission and the Claims Resolution Tribunal for Dormant Accounts in Switzerland).[2] The bad news is that those rules require major adaptation if they are to be of any use at all in the investment arbitration world. It is obvious that not all of the many procedural techniques used by international tribunals can be copy-

---

1 The type of claims covered by this chapter are not mass claims in the traditional sense (namely 'numerosity of claims which have some commonality of legal and factual issues', Hans v Houtte and others, *Post-War Restoration of Property Rights Under International Law*, vol 2 (CUP 2008) 23–25), but the term best reflects their nature.
2 See generally Howard M Holtzmann and Edda Kristjánsdóttir, *International Mass Claims Processes: Legal and Practical Perspectives* (OUP 2007).

pasted into investment arbitration (such as: computerisation, forming groups of claims based on the same/similar legal and factual patterns, using 'cover decisions', using evidentiary presumptions, relaxing the standard of proof and adopting statistical methods). First, it could create jurisdictional problems; second, those techniques were devised for proceedings of a different character.

This chapter gives a systematic overview of procedural legal issues that may arise in the course of arbitrating mass claims. It outlines problems related to mass claims and solutions that were applied in selected fora and assesses their applicability in mass claims investment arbitration, especially under the ICSID Convention. Techniques used by international tribunals and in national legislation are described one by one; each of these descriptions concludes with an attempt to answer whether any, and if so, what, objections may arise because of their application and the resulting risk (if any) of an award being set aside. The chapter glances at ICSID Tribunals' decisions to date, with special attention paid to any observations concerning the possible use of mass claims handling techniques. Finally, procedural techniques are suggested that should be applied so that mass claims investment arbitration can be conducted effectively and legitimately. The chapter concludes with a summary.

B. Introduction

First, one needs to analyse why mass claims handling techniques were adopted in some legal systems, both in Europe and in the US, and in international tribunals. There are multiple rationales for mass claims, mostly related to efficiency and number of claimants. In many cases, including those described in this chapter, lack of recourse to, for example, a relaxed standard of proof and cover decisions would result in complete blockage of a court/tribunal because of the flood of cases. However, many states have decided not to allow them, citing numerous drawbacks, mostly of a procedural nature, for both claimant and respondent. The main objection is that usage of mass claims handling techniques run contrary to the right to due process of every party to a dispute. Some aspects of this counterargument are addressed in this chapter.

C. Representative and Aggregate Proceedings – Differences

Proceedings involving several claimants are not homogenous. Before turning to the main topic of this chapter there is a need to explain the differences between two types of mass claims: representative and aggregate proceedings.

Class actions are the most important type of representative proceedings. They are initiated by a member or agent of a class on behalf of the whole class. Its key feature is that in the end a tribunal resolves one claim, but with many claimants. The representative/agent acts on behalf of the whole class of claimants that are automatically bound by the award of the court/tribunal.[3]

---

3 Maciej Zachariasiewicz, 'Kilka refleksji w odniesieniu do możliwości rozwoju postępowań grupowych w arbitrażu w Polsce' [2014] ADR ARBITRAŻ I MEDIACJA

In turn, aggregate proceedings entail several separate, individual claims that are based upon the same or a significantly similar fact pattern. This type of procedure exists in the UK, where a common registry is created and a common judge assigned for those similar cases, and in the US, where claims are consolidated only at the pre-trial stage – as a result, during this initial phase a court may enjoy economies of scale. After that, each case is dealt with separately, as to both liability and/or damages.[4] In the aggregate procedure 'plaintiffs must 'opt in' or intervene in the lawsuit, in order to be bound'.[5] Therefore it is up to a claimant to express his willingness to have a judgment applicable to him. Contrary to class actions, there is no joint dealing with the cases. The aggregate element, at least in the US and UK, exists only at the pre-trial stage. At the time of the actual proceedings, cases are treated as separate. It needs to be stressed that the mass claims resolution system as it stands right now encourages aggregate instead of collective proceedings.[6]

D. Procedural Problems Related to Mass Claims

Rules applicable to arbitration of investment disputes under ICSID are set out in the Convention on the Settlement of Investment Disputes between States and Nationals of Other States (hereinafter '**ICSID Convention**')[7] and the Rules of Procedure for Arbitration Proceedings (hereinafter '**ICSID Arbitration Rules**').[8] The problem is that they do not contain any provision that concerns mass claims, nor do the relevant bilateral investment treaties (BITs). Consequently, when the first mass claim case (*Abaclat and others v Argentine Republic, 'Abaclat'*)[9] was

70; note that in general in Europe it is not acceptable that a claimant who neither files a suit nor joins mass claims proceedings is bound by an arbitral award issued in such proceedings, see ibid 70; Katarzyna B Szczudlik, 'Mass Claims under ICSID' (2014), 4 Wroclaw Review of Law, Administration & Economics, available at, http://wrlae. prawo.uni.wroc.pl/index.php/wrlae/Article/view/84 accessed 1 May 2018.

4 Stacy I Strong, 'From Class to Collective: The De-Americanization of Class Arbitration' (2010) 26 Arbitration International 504.

5 Veijo Heiskanen, 'Arbitrating Mass Investor Claims: Lessons of International Claims Commissions' in Permanent Court of Arbitration (ed), *Multiple Party Actions in International Arbitration* (OUP 2009) 298.

6 Michael D Nolan, Frederic G Sourgens and Hugh Carlson, 'Leviathan on Life Support? Restructuring Sovereign Debt and International Investment Protection after Abaclat' in Carl P Sauvant (ed), *Yearbook on International Investment Law & Policy 2011–2012* (OUP 2013) 534.

7 https://icsid.worldbank.org/ICSID/StaticFiles/basicdoc/CRR_English-final.pdf accessed 1 May 2018.

8 https://icsid.worldbank.org/ICSID/StaticFiles/basicdoc/CRR_English-final.pdf accessed 1 May 2018.

9 *Abaclat and others v Argentine Republic*, ICSID Case No ARB/07/5, Decision on Jurisdiction and Admissibility, 4 August 2011, www.italaw.com/sites/default/files/case-documents/ita0236.pdf accessed 1 May 2018.

initiated before ICSID, the Tribunal appointed to resolve the case faced a real problem of admissibility[10] of such claims before ICSID.

While the *Abaclat* Tribunal's findings on the admissibility of mass claims are interesting in themselves, space constraints mean we will not deal with them here. Instead, we look at procedural problems that occurred before ICSID Tribunals in three cases: *Abaclat, Ambiente Ufficio SpA others v Argentine Republic* ('*Ambiente Ufficio*')[11] and *Giovanni Alemanni and others v Argentine Republic* ('*Giovanni Alemanni*').[12]

Importantly, despite the lack of express provisions concerning mass claims in the ICSID Convention and ICSID Rules, ICSID Tribunals found in them a gateway that opened up the whole discussion about mass claims under ICSID – ie Article 44 of the ICSID Convention and Article 19 of the ICSID Arbitration Rules. Article 44 of the ICSID Convention reads: 'any question of procedure arises which is not covered by this Section or the Arbitration Rules or any rules agreed by the parties, the Tribunal shall decide the question' while Article 19 of the ICSID Arbitration Rules reads: 'the Tribunal shall make orders required for the conduct of the proceedings'. Using those provisions the Tribunals concluded that since the ICSID Convention does not regulate the question of conducting mass claims, this lacuna shall be filled by ICSID Tribunal.[13] According to the Tribunal, this lack of regulation does not constitute a qualified silence, ie that the contracting states, when creating ICSID Convention, did not omit the issue of mass claims on purpose. This particular *Abaclat* Tribunal's finding is critical since while a Tribunal may fill a gap in the rules, it cannot modify the rules without the consent[14] of the parties, as was correctly pointed out in *Abaclat*.[15]

However, the finding that both the ICSID Convention and ICSID Arbitration Rules allow for the processing of mass claims is not a solution to a problem with mass claims, but just the beginning of a series of difficulties. Arbitrations involving multiple claimants, if conducted in the same way as any other ICSID arbitration, would be extremely time-consuming and in fact, in a case involving several thousand claimants,

---

10 On this particular problem see for example Samuel Wordsworth, 'Abaclat and Others v Argentine Republic. Jurisdiction, Admissibility and Pre-condition to Arbitration' (2012), 27 ICSID Review 255–260.

11 *Ambiente Ufficio SpA and others (Case formerly known as Giordano Alpi and Others) v Argentine Republic*, ICSID Case No ARB/08/9, Decision on Jurisdiction and Admissibility, 8 February 2013, https://icsid.worldbank.org/ICSID/FrontServlet?requestType=CasesRH&actionVal=showDoc&docId=DC2992_En&caseId=C340 accessed 1 May 2018.

12 *Giovanni Alemanni and others v Argentine Republic*, ICSID Case No ARB/07/8, Decision on Jurisdiction and Admissibility, 17 November 2014, www.italaw.com/sites/default/files/case-documents/italaw4061.pdf accessed 1 May 2018.

13 See for example *Abaclat*, Decision on Jurisdiction and Admissibility (n 9) 534–535, where the Tribunal held that Article 44 of the ICSID Convention and Article 19 of the ICSID Convention empower a Tribunal to apply to proceedings before it any modification needed to enable hearing mass claims, as such changes will not relate to the substance or object of a claim, but to the method of examination and presentation of a claim.

14 On the meaning of consent in ICSID arbitration see Andrea M Steingruber, 'Abaclat and Others v Argentine Republic, Consent in Large-scale Arbitration Proceedings' (2012) 27 ICSID Review 237–246.

15 *Abaclat*, Decision on Jurisdiction and Admissibility (n 9) 522.

impossible to deal with. That is why tribunals deciding mass claims cases have to create a set of rules to help them effectively manage those claims. At the same time, usage of those rules cannot put the award issued after the proceedings at risk of annulment. That is why it is critical to examine how other judicial bodies have tried to manage those difficulties, which I will do in the subsequent section, and subsequently to indicate which of those rules could be 'safely' used in ICSID arbitrations.

E. International Tribunal's Experience with Mass Arbitration Claims

International mass claims have been dealt with for many years by international claims commissions and claims tribunals.[16] Those international bodies multiplied after World War I.[17] Generally, they failed to perform their functions timely and effectively, resulting in this method of dispute resolution being largely abandoned after World War II.[18]

In the relatively recent past the idea of claims commissions and tribunals has had a new lease of life, starting with the Iran–United States Claims Tribunal.[19] Other examples of such tribunals are: the United Nations Compensation Commission, the Commission for Real Property Claims of Displaced Persons and Refugees in Bosnia and Herzegovina, the Housing and Property Claims Commission and the Claims Resolution Tribunal for Dormant Accounts in Switzerland. In this chapter some of these tribunals will be presented – space constraints notwithstanding – together with one or more of the techniques of handling mass claims disputes they use.

I. Iran–United States Claims Tribunal – TEST CASES – BELLWETHER and PILOT

The Iran–United States Claims Tribunal was established in 1981 by the United States of America and the Islamic Republic of Iran. Its objective was to resolve claims by nationals of one state against the other state party and certain claims between the states.[20]

The key feature of this international tribunal is that arbitration is conducted on a case-by-case basis and each case is treated as a separate one.[21] Probably that is why the Iran–United States Claims Tribunal was so extremely slow in deciding the cases put before it.[22] But what is interesting and noteworthy is that the Tribunal, because of

---

16 See for example The International Bureau of the Permanent Court of Arbitration (ed), *Redressing Injustices Through Mass claims Processes* (OUP 2006); Holtzmann and Kristjánsdóttir (n 2).

17 Norbert Wühler, 'Mixed Arbitral Tribunals' in Rudolf Bernhardt (eds), *Encyclopedia of Public International Law* (Elsvier 2000) 143.

18 Heiskanen (n 5) 300 and the sources indicated therein.

19 ibid 301.

20 www.iusct.net/ accessed 1 May 2018.

21 J R Crook, 'Mass Claims Processes: Lessons Learned Over Twenty-Five Years' in International Bureau of the Permanent of Arbitration (ed), *Redressing Injustices Through Mass Claims Processes: Innovative Responses to Unique Challenges* (OUP 2006) 41, 44.

22 See Menno T Kamminga, 'Towards a Permanent International Claims Commission for Victims of Violations of International Humanitarian Law' (2007) 25 Windsor

the significant number of smaller cases filed by the claimants' governments, took a decision to decide a limited amount of selected cases in the first place. The Tribunal thought that the decisions in those cases would encourage direct agreements between the governments to resolve other cases that were similar to those decided.[23]

II. United Nations Compensation Commission – Standard of Proof, Grouping of Claims, Computer Matching, Sampling

The UN Compensation Commission ('UNCC') was created in 1991. It is a subsidiary body of the United Nations Security Council and it was charged with processing claims and paying compensation for damage resulting from Iraq's unlawful invasion and occupation of Kuwait in 1990–91. UNCC was more of a political organ than a court or tribunal[24] and its tasks were of a particular nature, namely to handle an extremely large number of claims fairly and objectively, and at the same time promptly and efficiently.[25] Decisions on particular claims were taken by a panel consisting of commissioners, whose decisions were subsequently approved or rejected by the Governing Council.[26]

Key to understanding the nature and methods of processing claims is the fact that before UNCC made decisions on individual claims, the UN Security Council had found Iraq liable in resolution 687 'for any direct loss, damage, including environmental damage and the depletion of natural resources, or injury to foreign Governments, nationals and corporations'.[27] Once established, Iraq's liability was not re-established in the subsequent proceedings concerning particular claims, which significantly simplified and shortened both the evidentiary phase of the proceeding and the decision-making process.

Procedure before UNCC was regulated by the Provisional Rules for Claims Procedure ('the Rules'), annexed to Governing Council Decision 10, UN

Yearbook of Access to Justice, http://papers.ssrn.com/sol3/papers.cfm?abstract_id=1816463 accessed 1 May 2018.

23 D Prywes, 'The Small Iran Claims: Present Status and Prospects' (1987) 10 Middle East Executive Rep 9, 19.

24 Report of the UN Secretary General pursuant to Paragraph 19 of the Security Council Resolution 687 (1991), S/22559 of 2 May 1991, www.uncc.ch/sites/default/files/attachments/S-22559%20%5B1991%5D_0.pdf accessed 1 May 2018.

25 For an excellent overview of UNCC's activities see for example Fred Wooldridge and Olufemi Elias, 'Humanitarian Considerations in the Work of the United Nations Compensation Commission' (2003) 85 International Review of the Red Cross, available at www.icrc.org/eng/assets/files/other/irrc_851_wooldridge_olufemi.pdf accessed 1 May 2018.

26 For a detailed overview of the UNCC's structure and its origins see for example Michael F Raboin, 'The Provisional Rules for Claims Procedure of the United Nations Compensation Commission: A Practical Approach to Mass Claims Processing' in Richard B Lillich (ed), *The United Nations Compensation Commission: Thirteen Sokol Colloqium* (Irvington, NY/Transnational 1995) 119–153.

27 Resolution 687 (1991) Adopted by the Security Council at its 2981st meeting, on 3 April 1991, available at www.un.org/Depts/unmovic/documents/687.pdf accessed 1 May 2018.

Doc. S/AC.26/1992/10.[28] One particularly interesting feature of UNCC is that it applies an unusual burden of proof. Normally, as is known, the burden of proof is upon claimants, who have to 'make allegations substantiating their claim and to provide evidence in support of it'.[29] In proceedings before UNCC 'claimants did not have to demonstrate that they were victims of a breach by Iraq of an international humanitarian obligation owed to them',[30] and they needed to show only that 'the loss they had suffered was a direct consequence of Iraq's invasion of Kuwait'.[31] Evidence was collected by the very same body that later made a decision[32] and it was done through a search in public and private archives and other sets of documents.[33]

In addition, UNCC applied more mass claims handling techniques, which are described mainly in Articles 37 and 38 of the Rules. Due to the limited space I will not present all the nuances of the Rules, but what is important for the purpose of this chapter is to underline that the claims before UNCC were divided into two main groups and subdivided into smaller groups given alphabet letter titles. Article 37 of the Rules applies to 'urgent claims' (claims A, B and C),[34] generally of lower value and less complicated in terms of factual background. When deciding those claims, the UNCC panels were allowed to, *inter alia*, perform the following tasks:

- match those claims against the information in the computerised database;[35]
- if this was impossible, and if the volume of claims was large, panels could check individual claims on the basis of sampling (ie commissioners took sample claims

---

28 Available at www.uncc.ch/sites/default/files/attachments/S-AC.26-DEC%2010% 20%5B1992%5D.pdf accessed 1 May 2018.

29 Menno T Kamminga, 'Towards a Permanent International Claims Commission for Victims of International Humanitarian Law', http://pub.maastrichtuniversity.nl/ d71f592e-7386-4965-9827-6cd699c607be accessed 1 May 2018

30 Kamminga (n 22) 3.

31 ibid.

32 Heiskanen (n 5) 297, 317.

33 ibid.

34 For an explanation of the nature and amount of particular A, B, C, D, E, F claims see ibid.

35 For more information on usage of computerisation in the early 1990s see Ch S Gibson, 'Mass Claims Processing: Techniques for Processing Over 400 000 Claims for Individual Loss at the United Nations Compensation Commission' in Richard B Lillich (ed), *The United Nations Compensation Commission: Thirteen Sokol Colloqium* (Irvington, NY/Transnational 1995) 184; about computer matching in case of A Claims see UNCC Report and recommendations made by the panel of commissioners concerning the first instalment of claims for departure from Iraq or Kuwait (Category A Claims) S/AC.26/1994/2 of 21 October 1994, 23–40, available at www.uncc.ch/ sites/default/files/attachments/documents/r1994-02.pdf accessed 1 May 2018. According to the Report:

> the goal of the computerised verification process was to determine whether a given claimant appears in one or more of the records that constitute the arrival/Departure Database and which the Panel found to establish departure from Kuwait or Iraq during the relevant jurisdictional period.

from a group of claims and reviewed them individually; for each group of claims the sample size was different as it depended upon, *inter alia*, the number of claims in a group and the factual and legal complexity);[36]

- forward recommendations of panels as to particular claims to the executive secretary within a specified timeframe.

Article 38 of the Rules was applied to claims D, E and F that qualified as urgent matters under Article 37 of the Rules. Under Article 38 of the Rules:

- 'claims with significant common legal and factual issues will be processed together';
- the panel could adopt special procedures appropriate to the character and subject-matter of the particular types of claims.

In addition, those claims 'must be supported by documentary and other appropriate evidence sufficient to demonstrate the circumstances and amount of the claimed loss'.[37] Also the standard of proof was not as relaxed as in the case of claims A, B and C.

Another interesting mechanism, from the ICSID arbitration perspective, used by UNCC, was the concept of *bone fide* nationality. In the case of C claims, claims were not supposed to be considered if filed by/on behalf of Iraqi nationals that do not have *bona fide* nationality of any other state.[38]

The next technique was to limit participation in the proceedings of the parties to the dispute, which was only required 'to the extent that is necessary for the panels of Commissioners to make their determinations on the claims'.[39]

III. The Housing and Property Claims Commission in Kosovo (HPCC) – Sources of Evidence

HPCC was created in 1999[40] to decide individual conflict-related disputes concerning housing/property and to assure 'the safe and unimpeded return of all refugees and displaced persons to their homes'.[41] HPCC was given exclusive jurisdiction over three types of claims: A claims – discrimination, B claims – informal

---

36 ibid 183.

37 Article 35 (3) of the Rules.

38 UNCC Decision No 1, para 16, available at www.uncc.ch/sites/default/files/atta chments/documents/dec_01.pdf accessed 1 May 2018.

39 N Wühler, 'The United Nations Compensation Commission: A New Contribution to the Process of international Claims Resolution', [1999] Journal of International Economic Law 261.

40 UNMIK Regulation No 1999/23 on the Establishment of the Housing and Property Directorate and the Housing and Property Claims Commission, 15 November 1999 (Regulation No 1999/23).

41 UN Security Council Resolution 1244, S/RES/1244, 10 June 1999.

transactions and C claims – displacement.[42] More than 40 000 cases were filed with HPCC, which constantly faced considerable problems with funding and lack of local support, as well as problems with implementation of its decisions.[43]

When performing its tasks, HPCC took into consideration the very special situation of claimants, who were refugees, and therefore did not always have at their disposal the relevant evidence to support their claims. Therefore the Directorate of HPCC could retrieve evidence from any record of a public body, corporate or natural person[44] and hence it had an 'active role in collecting and verifying evidence'.[45]

IV. Eritrea–Ethiopia Claims Commission (EECC) – Dormant Mass Claims Handling Techniques and Statistical Sampling and Modelling

EECC was established in 2000 upon consent between Eritrea and Ethiopia[46] to decide, through arbitration, claims concerning loss, damage or injury caused by governments and nationals of one state to the government and nationals of the other state. At the beginning of EECC's activity, there were some proposals as to how to deal with monetary claims. EECC suggested an approach similar to the one adopted by UNCC – namely to adopt mass claims proceedings 'under which the parties might file claims for fixed amounts for different categories of individual claimants'.[47] This proposal was not accepted, as the governments of the two states eventually decided to pursue 'Government-to-Government claims rather than to attempt an individually-based mass claims procedure'.[48]

One of the proposals for processing mass claims was to use sampling of the filed claims to establish the proportion of invalid claims. At this stage, this determination would impact the total award per group of claims, which would be reduced accordingly by the proportion of the invalid claims.[49]

---

42 Organization for Security and Co-operation in Europe, Mission in Kosovo, 'Challenges in the Resolution of Conflict-Related Claims in Kosovo' (2011) 4, available at www.osce.org/kosovo/80435?download=true accessed 1 May 2018.

43 ibid 14.

44 On Residential Property Claims and the Rules of Procedure and Evidence of the Housing and Property Directorate and the HPCC, UNMIK/REG/2000/60, available at www.kpaonline.org/hpd/Laws%20and%20regulations/04%20RE%202000-60.pdf accessed 1 May 2018.

45 Hans v Houtte and Iasson Yi, 'Due Process in International Mass Claims' (2008) 1 Erasmus Law Review 235 (quoting A Dodson and V Heiskanen, 'Housing and Property Restitution in Kosovo' in Scott Leckie (ed), *Returning Home: Housing and Property Restitution Rights of Refugees and Displaced Persons* (Transnational Publishers 2003)).

46 www.haguejusticeportal.net/index.php?id=6161 accessed 1 May 2018

47 ibid; Decision Number 5: Multiple Claims in the Mass Claims Process, Fixed-Sum Compensation at the $500 and $1500 Levels, Multiplier for Household Claims (Erit-Eth), available at www.pcacases.com/web/sendAttach/773 accessed 1 May 2018.

48 Holtzmann and Kristjánsdóttir (n 2) 168.

49 ibid.

V. First and Second Claims Resolution Tribunal for Dormant Accounts ('CRT') in Switzerland

The first CRT was established in 1997 and its duty was to decide claims regarding the entitlement of non-Swiss nationals to accounts held in Swiss banks.[50] Under Article 22 (Relaxed Standard of Proof) of the CRT Rules of Procedure[51] a claimant was obliged to 'show that it is plausible in the light of all the circumstances that he or she is entitled, in whole or in part, to the dormant account'.[52] In the latter part of this chapter of the Rules of Procedure it is explained what an arbitrator should take into account when deciding whether the plausibility standard was met by a particular claimant. A similar standard was adopted in the rules of the Second CRT established in 2001,[53] but it was supplemented by several evidentiary presumptions.[54]

F. ICSID Tribunal Decisions – The Techniques Already Accepted

As was indicated earlier, the Tribunal in *Abaclat*, using Articles 19 and 44 of the ICSID Convention, held that it needed to fill the gaps in the ICSID Convention and ICSID Arbitration Rules when facing a necessity to hear a mass claims case.[55] Filling the gaps consisted in making some adoptions to the ICSID legal framework and not creating a brand-new set of rules applicable to mass claims.[56] The techniques used by the *Abaclat* Tribunal were in particular: admittance of scanned identification documents instead of the originals[57] and taking into consideration, while no actually using, the implementation, in the future, of sampling procedures to replace examination of all the documents,[58] as well as bellwether and pilot-case proceedings.[59]

Due to the number of claimants, the usage of computerised data management was inevitable in this case. It helped the Tribunal to group the claimants and issues into subgroups and consequently make decisions on broadly applicable problems more efficiently.[60] Usage of this mechanism certainly will not be subject of any objections of the parties, as generally it does not affect the decision-making process of a tribunal.[61]

---

50 Jacomijn van Haersolte-van Hof, 'Innovations to Speed Mass Claims: News Standards of Proof' in Permanent Court of Arbitration (ed), *Redressing Injustice Through Mass Claims Processes* (OUP 2006) 17.
51 Available at www.crt-ii.org/_crt-i/frame.html accessed 1 May 2018.
52 ibid.
53 ibid 18.
54 ibid 19.
55 *Abaclat*, Decision on Jurisdiction and Admissibility (n 9) 522.
56 ibid 524, 529.
57 ibid 531, 540.
58 ibid 666.
59 ibid.
60 *Abaclat*, Decision on Jurisdiction and Admissibility (n 9) 227, 669.
61 Donald F Donovan, 'Abaclat and others v Argentine Republic as a Collective Claims Proceedings' (2012), 27 ICSID Review 262.

Anticipating future problems in the merits phase, the Tribunal observed that it 'would need to implement mechanisms allowing a simplified verification of evidentiary material'[62] which might 'concern either the depth of examination of a document [...] or the number of evidentiary documents to be examined', and if so their selection process (ie random selection of samples instead of a serial examination of each document).[63] The Tribunal underlined a distinction between 'such a simplification of the examination process [...] from the failure to proceed with such examination'.[64]

The Tribunal took into consideration the use of statistical sampling and modelling, but its findings in that regard were far from decisive, as the Tribunal underlined that some jurisdictional and merits issues could be claimant-specific.[65]

The merits phase will be, according to the *Abaclat* Tribunal's decision, divided in two parts – first, the Tribunal will identify 'the core issues' and 'the conditions [that] would need to be required' for the purpose of resolution of the claims; second, the Tribunal will decide what is the best way to address those 'issues and conditions'.[66] Also to a moment when having an overview of the merits of the case the Tribunal postponed a decision concerning possible usage of pilot cases or bellwether proceedings (which technique is widely recognised in mass tort cases in the US).[67] As to use of this technique, Georges Abi-Saab in his dissenting opinion emphasised that:

> to the extent that the individual claims in the mass differ from each other, it is the absolute due process right of the defence, and the obligation of the Tribunal, to have them examined individually and adversarially by the Tribunal,[68]

with a possibility to examine the cases on a group basis if they were identical if 'in spite of the multitude of the claimants, totally safeguarding the due process rights of the respondent'.[69]

In sum, the Tribunal's approach to the case was that the proceedings were collective rather than representative (in the American style). That resulted in numerous restraints on the use of mass claims handling techniques, as virtually all controversial issues had to be resolved, at the end of the day, on an individual basis.

---

62   *Abaclat*, Decision on Jurisdiction and Admissibility (n 9) 531.

63   ibid.

64   ibid.

65   See for example *Abaclat*, Decision on Jurisdiction and Admissibility (n 9) 531, 666, 227, 669.

66   ibid 668.

67   On bellwether proceedings and pilot cases in the US see for example Eldon E Fallon, Jeremy Grabill and Robert P Wynee, 'Bellwether Trials in Multidistrict Litigation' (2008), 82 Tul L Rev 2323, 2330–2342.

68   *Abaclat and others v Argentine Republic*, ICSID Case No ARB /07/5, Decision on Jurisdiction and Admissibility, Dissenting Opinion, Georges Abi-Saab, para 238, 28 October 2011 (*Abaclat*, Dissent), available at www.italaw.com/documents/Abaclat_Dissenting_Opinion.pdf accessed 1 May 2018.

69   ibid 237.

In *Ambiente Ufficio* there were 90 Italian claimants in a very similar legal and factual position against Argentina.

As to the issue of application of the ICSID legal framework to mass claims and possible modifications of that framework in the light of lack of express consent of the respondent state to mass arbitration, the Tribunal decided, in keeping with the *Abaclat* Tribunal, that 'the mass aspect of the present proceedings related to the modalities and implementation of the ICSID proceedings and not to the question whether respondent consented to ICSID arbitration'.[70]

Argentina was of an opinion that claimants had to prove 'all aspects of the nationality and domicile requirements, namely the positive nationality requirements and negative nationality requirements',[71] while claimants contended that they had to prove Italian requirements, but they bore no burden of proving they did not have Argentinian nationality.[72] The Tribunal, using the International Court of Justice decision in *Avena* [73] held, as was submitted by claimants, that they were obliged to establish their Italian nationality, but 'the burden of disapproving the negative elements – ie not being Argentine (or, for that matter, dual) nationals and not being domiciled in Argentina for more than two years – would fall on the Respondent's side'.[74] Moreover, the Tribunal did not:

> consider that the mere number of claimants in the present case would make the proceedings unmanageable [...] or would violate fundamental principles of due process or would be unfair to Respondent, neither in the present jurisdictional phase nor in the merits phase of the proceedings.[75]

The third case where a tribunal had to address an issue of mass claims was *Giovanni Alemanni*, also under the Italy–Argentina BIT as in the two earlier cases.[76] What differentiates this case from *Ambiente Ufficio* and *Abaclat* though is that in their case the Tribunal unanimously decided to proceed with the claim,[77] which could be treated as a trend toward a more accommodating approach to mass claims in investment arbitration. When addressing the issue of the number of claimants, the Tribunal quoted the earlier finding of the *Ambiente Ufficio* Tribunal as indicated that it 'sees no good reason for reaching a conclusion any different from that arrived at by the *Ambiente Ufficio* tribunal'.[78]

---

70 *Ambiente Ufficio* (n 11) 492.
71 ibid 348.
72 ibid 312.
73 *Avena and other Mexican Nationals (Mexico v USA)*, Judgement, ICJ Reports 2004, 12.
74 *Ambiente Ufficio* (n 11) 312; *Ambiente*, Santiago Torres Bernandez, Dissenting Opinion of 2 May 2013, 137.
75 *Ambiente Ufficio* (n 11) 166–170.
76 Available at http://investmentpolicyhub.unctad.org/IIA/country/8/treaty/135 accessed 1 May 2018.
77 *Giovanni Alemanni* (n 12) 167–168.
78 ibid 324.

G. Mass Claims Handling Techniques that Could be Applied by ICSID Tribunals

When conducting an analysis concerning the rules that could potentially be applicable to mass claims proceedings, one should always bear in mind that in no case could those techniques be inconsistent with the ICSID Convention or ICSID Arbitration Rules, as any such contravention would result in a possible annulment of a decision issued after such proceedings pursuant to Article 52 (d) of the ICSID Convention.

It is also crucial to take into consideration that all the bodies listed earlier in section E were supposed to achieve their goals in a short period of time and at a lower cost than ordinary dispute resolutions mechanisms.[79] Therefore some restrictions on the normal course of litigation are inherent in their procedures, but the countries that helped set them up consented to those constraints on due process rules at the very beginning. Therefore it is fair to conclude that 'they knew what they were doing'.

The key question to be asked is whether the investment arbitration community truly wants to follow the path of 'democratisation' of investment arbitration. If the answer is affirmative, then the arbitrators, practitioners and state parties involved have to accept limitation of some rights (especially of the respondents) and principles to date inherent for ICSID arbitrations. Leaving aside the merits of Georges Abi-Saab's statement from his *Abaclat* dissenting opinion that allowing the verification method proposed by the majority would infringe Argentina's due process guarantees,[80] mass claims investment proceedings would certainly have great advantages of speed when compared to domestic litigation. And besides, taking into consideration the costs of investment arbitration, there is no compelling reason to prohibit individual claimants from getting together to reduce them.

Only after one accepts this statement could one proceed with creating a list of mass claims management techniques that might be of help in ICSID investment arbitration.

The following list sets out all the techniques addressed in this chapter, indicates whether they might be used in ICSID arbitration and points out their pros and cons.

I. Deciding One Case to Encourage Resolution of Other Claims

This technique has the advantage of shifting responsibility for deciding a significant part of the claims from the tribunal to the parties to the dispute. However, normally it takes a lot of time to even decide one claim before an ICSID Tribunal, leaving aside possible annulment proceedings. In addition, it seems unlikely that after two or more years of heated proceedings the losing party would be willing to

---

79   Hans v Houtte and others (n 1) 5.
80   *Abaclat* (n 9) Dissent 120.

resolve the other cases in the same manner as in the case it lost. Therefore this technique cannot be applied in ICSID arbitration.

II. Statistical Sampling and Modelling

When tribunals are faced with similar numbers of claimants as in *Abaclat*, statistical sampling might look tempting. For example, in a jurisdictional issue a sample would be selected from the pool of claimants and examined to discover what portion of them fails to meet the jurisdictional criteria. In the latter stages of proceedings the overall award[81] for all the claimants would be reduced by the same portion.

This technique could only be used in ICSID arbitration if the very model of this arbitration was re-thought. It would probably entail the introduction of a new set of rules applicable especially to individual, small investors that due to circumstances similar to *Abaclat* lost their life savings, as was often the case in disputes resolved by international courts and tribunals. In their current form both the ICSID Convention and the ICSID Arbitration Rules do not allow for such limitation of assessment of jurisdictional criteria and merits of the case as would be necessary for effective implementation of statistical sampling.

However, if some forms of statistical sampling were accepted, arbitral tribunals would benefit greatly from assistance by professionals skilled in mathematical methods, as the key issue is to select the right sampling group.

III. Grouping

It seems far more feasible to apply grouping in investment arbitration than statistical sampling. Careful formation of the groups of claimants and claims around particular problematic issues would allow a tribunal to proceed swiftly, while not violating the due process right or any rules of procedure. However, correct grouping requires thorough knowledge about the merits of the case, so a tribunal would need very detailed and clearly drafted input from both claimants and respondents. Provided this requirement is met, it seems there are no *prima facie* obstacles to grouping in ICSID arbitration.

IV. Computer Matching

Computerised methods have greatly helped international tribunals to decide some key issues in cases. In ICSID arbitration, besides very complicated legal or factual issues, there are some more straightforward problems, such as concerning claimants' compliance with a jurisdictional requirement of nationality. Provided the appropriate software is used and the relevant data introduced, the tribunals could check the nationality of claimants against computer databases. In this context, the *bona fide* nationality concept deserves consideration, but of course always with due

---

81 Assuming that the award would be awarded for the whole group of claimants and not for every claimant individually, which seems to be unlikely.

attention paid to the importance of the nationality requirement for the jurisdiction of ICSID Tribunals.

V. Standardised Verification and Valuation

It seems that ICSID Tribunals are allowed to use simplified evidentiary rules as they are, pursuant to Article 34 (1) of the ICSID Arbitration Rules, to 'judge the admissibility of any evidence adduced and of its probative value'. Having said that, tribunals' discretion in this regard is not limitless, as it could give rise to objections of an overly simplistic examination of particular issues, which could lead to violation of due process rights.

VI. Panels and Recommendations

This idea would be revolutionary in ICSID arbitration and for the time being is impossible to implement due to the impossibility of delegating the arbitrator's obligations to hear a case to other persons. However, it would match up very well with implementation of the 'grouping' technique. The idea would be to allow arbitrators' assistants (or 'deputy arbitrators') to conduct a preliminary assessment of a case, identify the main problematic issues, preliminarily group the claims and claimants around those issues and then issue recommendations for further proceedings with the case. An arbitral tribunal would assess those recommendations and would either opt to proceed accordingly or revert the case to a panel for reconsideration, indicating the elements that should be changed. While this procedure would involve more people than at present, it would be the 'price' that claimants need to pay for having their claims heard in investment arbitration.

VII. Other Techniques – Electronic and Communication Technology, Preservation of Papers and a Method of Submission

Electronic and communication technology as methods of preservation of papers and a method of submission in the form available nowadays were not available at the time of intense activity of the tribunals and commissions described in this chapter. However, when addressing a topic of this nature, it is impossible to escape deliberations of their meaning for future mass claims arbitrations before ICSID Tribunals. If these methods were combined with computer matching and highly advanced software, it would greatly enhance the efficiency of arbitrating mass claims. It would be appropriate to eliminate altogether hard copy submissions, as this form of submission would completely paralyse both the arbitrators and ICSID.

H. Conclusion

As demonstrated in this chapter, international court and commissions have achieved much in terms of effective management of cases involving large numbers of claimants. Helping them was the very specific type of cases, often involving refugees or people who suffered because of war. That is why states were more willing to limit some of their procedural rights in proceedings initiated by those claimants. The situation has been different in investment arbitration, as claimants wanted to retrieve money they lost because of sovereign default. At the same time, very often those claimants are not wealthy, institutional investors, but individuals who put their savings into investments and lost out due to the respondent state's actions. Bearing that in mind, the possibility of using mass claims techniques seems more acceptable.

To date, no arbitral tribunal has truly faced the problem of handling mass claims in the merits phase of the proceedings and all findings of ICSID Tribunals on mass claims handling techniques are evasive and they postponed final decisions to the merits phase. Given the fact that *Giovani Alemanni* and *Ambiente Ufficio* were discontinued[82] and *Abaclat* was settled,[83] at the end of the day, the arbitral community has to wait for any conclusive decision in this regard. The list of promising methods presented in this chapter will be, in the future, a good starting point for performing this task.

---

82 *Giovani Alemanni*, Order of the Tribunal Discontinuing the Proceeding, 14 December 2015, www.italaw.com/sites/default/files/case-documents/ITA%20LAW% 207009.pdf accessed 1 May 2018; *Ambiente Ufficio*, Order on Discontinuance of the Proceedings, 28 May 2015, www.italaw.com/sites/default/files/case-documents/ita law4289.pdf accessed 1 May 2018.
83 *Abaclat*, Consent Award Under ICSID Arbitration Rule 43(2), 29 December 2016, www.italaw.com/sites/default/files/case-documents/italaw8024.pdf accessed 1 May 2018.

3 The Impact of the Economic and Political Situation Prevailing in the Host State on Compensation and Damages under International Investment Law

Dr Sven Lange[1]

It is a truism that the development and success of an investment, and thus its profitability, will be strongly influenced by a range of circumstances prevailing in the state in which the investment is made (the 'host state'). Chiefly among such circumstances is the economic and political situation. Accordingly, even the least sophisticated investor will assess economic and political factors applying in the host state before making an investment.[2] These factors may include such diverse elements as the robustness of the economy, the respect for the rule of law, the host state's general stance on foreign investment or the existing tax regime.

Against this background, it comes as no surprise that investment arbitration tribunals have frequently been faced with the question of how to take into account the host state's economic and political climate in their assessment of the quantum of investor claims. In particular, in a number of recent cases brought against Venezuela, tribunals were faced with the difficult question of how an adverse change of the economic and political climate, brought about mainly by the adoption of an expropriation policy, should be accounted for in a discounted cash flow ('DCF') analysis.[3]

---

1 The author is an associate at Allen & Overy LLP in Frankfurt, Germany. The views expressed in this chapter are those of the author alone and do not necessarily reflect those of the firm with which he is affiliated, or its clients.

2 Cf *Himpurna California Energy Ltd v PT (Persero) Perusahaan Listruik Negara*, Final Award, 4 May 1999 (2000), 25 YBCA 11, para 364.

3 *Gold Reserve Inc v Bolivarian Republic of Venezuela*, ICSID Case No ARB(AF)/09/1, Award, 22 September 2014; *Venezuela Holdings BV and others v Bolivarian Republic of Venezuela*, ICSID Case No ARB/07/27, Award, 9 October 2014; *Flughafen Zürich AG and others v Bolivarian Republic of Venezuela*, ICSID Case No ARB/10/19, Award, 18 November 2014; *Tidewater Inc and others v Bolivarian Republic of Venezuela*, ICSID Case No ARB/10/5, Award, 13 March 2015; *Tenaris SA and others v Bolivarian Republic of Venezuela*, ICSID Case No ARB/12/23, Award, 29 January 2016; *Saint-Gobain Performance Plastics Europe v Bolivarian Republic of Venezuela*, ICSID Case No ARB/12/13, Decision on Liability and the Principles of Quantum, 30 December 2016.

In addressing this topic, the present chapter will first outline some of the basic principles and methods underlying quantum determinations in investment arbitration (section A.) and will then elaborate how tribunals have dealt with economic and political circumstances in the host state when assessing quantum (section B.). Special attention shall then be given to the recent Venezuela cases (section C.). Thereafter, some of the practical aspects of taking into account the so-called country risk in a DCF analysis shall be discussed (section D.).

A. Basic Principles of Quantum in International Investment Law

Any quantum analysis in investment arbitration will always start with the determination of whether the host state legally expropriated the investor (section I.) or whether the host state breached the applicable Bilateral Investment Treaty (BIT) (be it by illegal expropriation or breach of another treaty standard – section II.).[4] For the specific calculation of the appropriate quantum, tribunals may then draw on various valuation methods. This chapter will however only address the DCF method (section III.).

I. Compensation for Legal Expropriation

The customary law standard for the compensation due upon legal expropriation was subject to controversy for a long time.[5] Developed countries have continuously insisted on the so-called *Hull* formula, providing for prompt, adequate and effective compensation[6] – and thus generally advocating for the award of the 'fair market value' of the investment immediately before the lawful taking.[7] Fair market value is typically defined by reference to the price a willing buyer would normally pay to a willing seller for the investment.[8] Developing countries, on the other hand, have argued that compensation should only be 'appropriate' and should be calculated based on the laws and regulations of the host state.[9]

It was the advent of international investment treaties (IITs) which ultimately settled the debate. IITs typically contain an express reference to the *Hull* formula

---

4 The need to distinguish the two was already stressed by the Permanent Court of International Justice, cf *Case Concerning the Factory at Chorzów*, PCIJ Series A (No 17) 47.

5 Irmgard Marboe, *Calculation of Compensation and Damages in International Investment Law* (OUP 2009) para 3.07.

6 *CME Czech Republic BV v The Czech Republic*, UNCITRAL, Final Award, 14 March 2003, para 497.

7 Borzu Sabahi and Nicholas J Birch, 'Comparative Compensation for Expropriation' in Stephan W Schill (ed), *International Investment Law and Comparative Public Law* (OUP 2010) 755, 761.

8 Cf World Bank Guidelines on the Treatment of Foreign Direct Investment, Section IV.5.

9 Cf 'Charter of Economic Rights and Duties of States', UN General Assembly Resolution A/RES/29/3281 of 12 December 1974.

or include comparative phrasing.[10] Since, today, investor protection is almost exclusively achieved by way of IITs, the typical measure of compensation is the fair market value of the investment immediately before the expropriation has occurred or has become publicly known.[11] Indeed, the use of the *Hull* formula in investment treaties is so widespread that tribunals consider the formula to have become the customary international law standard for compensation upon expropriation.[12]

The approach historically advocated by developing countries allowed for various factors to play a role in the determination of compensation – including the host state's ability to pay or other economic and political circumstances prevailing in the host state.[13] However, this does not mean that, under the *Hull* formula, the economic and political circumstances prevailing in the host state would be disregarded. To the contrary, the fair market value of an investment will naturally be affected by economic and political factors. After all, these factors can have a direct impact on the profitability of an investment.[14]

II. Full Reparation

The standard of full reparation was formulated most famously in the *Chorzów Factory* case in which the PCIJ determined that:

> reparation must, as far as possible, wipe out all the consequences of the illegal act and reestablish the situation which would, in all probability, have existed if that act had not been committed. Restitution in kind, or, if this is not possible, payment of a sum corresponding to the value which a restitution in kind would bear [...] – such are the principles which should serve to determine the amount of compensation due for an act contrary to international law.[15]

Full reparation may therefore go beyond compensation for legal expropriation because it must take account of all financially assessable damage.[16] However, in some cases, the distinction might be inconsequential. In particular, where the damage claimed by the investor is simply the complete loss of the investment, full reparation and compensation for legal expropriation will typically be the same.

---

10 Kaj Hobér, 'Remedies in Investment Disputes' in Andrea K Bjorklund, Ian A Laird and Sergey Ripinsky (eds), *Investment Treaty Law: Current Issues III* (BIICL 2009) 3, 10.

11 Cf Article 5(2) Austria/Iran BIT; Article 5(2) Slovenia/Denmark BIT; Article 6(2) Azerbaijan/Finland BIT.

12 *CME* (n 6) Final Award, 14 March 2003, para 498.

13 Cf Sergey Ripinsky and Kevin Williams, *Damages in International Investment Law* (BIICL 2008) 74.

14 The exact manner in which tribunals have taken account of such factors will be discussed in section B of this chapter.

15 *Chorzów Factory* (n 4) 47.

16 *Siemens AG v The Argentine Republic*, ICSID Case No ARB/02/8, Award, 17 January 2007, para 352.

Indeed, many tribunals have explicitly relied on the fair market value of the investment even when applying the full reparation standard.[17]

III. The DCF Valuation Method

Investment tribunals have applied various methods for valuing investments, such as the stock market approach (relying on the price of publicly traded shares),[18] the comparable companies approach (relying on the share price of comparable companies)[19] or the book value approach (relying on information in a company's balance sheet).[20] However, the method that has been applied most commonly – at least where future cash flows could be projected with reasonable certainty[21] – is the DCF method. The assumption underlying the DCF method is that an asset's value is equal to the present value of the cash flows that will be generated by the asset in the future.[22] Thus, in a DCF analysis, the future free cash flows of the investment are estimated based on certain assumptions; these cash flows are then discounted by way of a discount rate.[23] The rationale behind the discount is that future cash flows are worth less than current cash flows, given that they cannot immediately be reinvested.[24] The discount rate is typically equated to the so-called cost of capital which is often calculated as the weighted average of the cost of equity and the cost of debt applying to the investment.[25] Since riskier investments entail a higher cost of capital, the discount is generally higher where the investment is exposed to more risk.[26]

In the context of DCF valuations, the typical way for tribunals to take into account the economic and political situation in the host state is the so-called country risk.[27] Country risk is a variable that is used in the calculation of an

17 Cf *Gold Reserve* (n 3) paras 678ff, 681; *Tenaris* (n 3) paras 514, 519; *CME* (n 6) Partial Award, 13 September 2001, para 618. This approach has however not remained without criticism, cf José Alberro, 'Should Expropriation Risk Be Part of the Discount Rate?' (2016) 33 JIntlArb 525, 526.

18 Cf *Crystallex International Corporation v Bolivarian Republic of Venezuela*, ICSID Case No ARB(AF)/11/2, Award, 4 April 2016, para 889.

19 Cf *Yukos Universal Limited (Isle of Man) v The Russian Federation*, UNCITRAL, PCA Case No AA 227, Award, 18 July 2014, para 1784 (annulled on unrelated grounds).

20 *Siemens* (n 16) paras 355, 362ff.

21 Cf *Metalclad Corporation v The United Mexican States*, ICSID Case No ARB(AF)/97/1, Award, 30 August 2000, paras 119ff; *Siemens* (n 16) para 355.

22 Ripinsky and Williams (n 13) 195.

23 *Amoco International Finance v Iran and others*, 15 Iran-US CTR (1987) 189, para 213.

24 Marboe (n 5) para 5.193; Ripinsky and Williams (n 13) 197.

25 Richard Walck, 'Methods of Valuing Losses' in Marc Bungenberg and others (eds), *International Investment Law* (Beck 2015) 1045, 1051; PwC, 'Rewarding expropriation?' 4, www.pwc.co.uk/assets/pdf/rewarding-expropriation.pdf accessed 15 June 2017.

26 James Searby, 'The Country Risk Premium in International Arbitration' [2019] European and Middle Eastern Arbitration Review 19.

27 *EDF International SA and others v Argentine Republic*, ICSID Case No ARB/03/23, Award, 11 June 2012, para 1262.

investment's cost of capital.[28] It broadly combines a variety of risk factors applicable in the host state, including in particular political risk (eg policy changes, expropriation), macroeconomic risk (eg inflation, high levels of public debt) and environmental risk (eg civil unrest, natural disaster).[29] For certain countries, such as the USA or Switzerland, generally no country risk is assumed.[30] For other countries, a 'country risk premium' will be added in the cost of capital calculation. This, in turn, entails a higher discount rate, and, accordingly, a lower valuation of the investment.[31]

B. General Relevance of Adverse Economic and Political Circumstances for Quantum

Any valuation, be it in case of legal expropriation or in case of a treaty breach, is based on a 'but-for-scenario', ie an assumption as to how the investment would have developed but for the legal taking or the breach of the IIT, respectively. In constructing this scenario, it is clear that all effects of the specific legal taking or breach of the IIT need to be disregarded.[32] What is however more complex is the question to which extent general economic and political circumstances in the host state need to be included in the but-for-scenario. Two different approaches are conceivable. For one, it could be argued that any and all economic and political circumstances in the host state need to be taken into account. Alternatively, all economic and political circumstances in the host state could in principal be taken into account, with the exception of circumstances which themselves constitute a violation of international law. In the author's view, only the latter approach makes sense. After all, the tribunal will be constructing the but-for-scenario for the purpose of assessing damages under an IIT. It would therefore be contradictory to assume a but-for-scenario in which the host state is not acting in accordance with the IIT. Accordingly, this approach, which in the following shall be referred to as the 'legality differentiation', has found overwhelming support in investment case law.

Early examples for the legality differentiation can be found in the jurisprudence of the Iran–US Claims Tribunal (IUCT). In the late 1970s, the Iranian revolution

---

28 Searby (n 26) 20.
29 Florin A Dorobantu, Natasha Dupont and M Alexis Maniatis, 'Country Risk and Damages in Investment Arbitration' (2016) 31 ICSID Review 219, 221; Searby (n 26) 19; PwC, 'How is Expropriation Risk Captured in a Valuation?' www.pwc.co.uk/services/forensic-services/disputes/how-is-expropriation-risk-captured-in-a-valuation.html accessed 15 June 2017.
30 That is not to say that, for these countries, these risk factors do not exist. Rather, other elements of the cost of capital determination already account for the (limited) relevance of these risks, cf Searby (n 26) 20.
31 PwC (n 29); Searby (n 26) 23.
32 For legal takings, this follows from the formulation of compensation clauses in IITs which typically refer to the fair market value of the investment immediately before the expropriation has occurred or has become publicly known, cf n 11. For breaches of international law, this follows from the *Chorzów Factory* standard, cf (n 4).

led both to the expropriation of foreign property and to more general changes to the economic and political framework.[33] For the IUCT, the latter could not be ignored at the quantum stage. Thus, in *AIG v Iran*, the IUCT held that:

> [i]n ascertaining the going concern value of an enterprise at a previous point in time for purposes of establishing the appropriate quantum of compensation for nationalization, it is [...] necessary to exclude the effects of actions taken by the nationalizing state in relation to the enterprise which actions may have depressed its value. [...] On the other hand, prior changes in the general political, social and economic conditions which might have affected the enterprise's business prospects as of the date the enterprise was taken should be considered.[34]

According to the IUCT, economic and political circumstances hence need to be taken into account for valuation purposes unless these circumstances (i) in themselves constitute instances of nationalisation; or (ii) have only materialised after the date of expropriation.[35]

In modern investment case law, the case of *Occidental v Ecuador* is exemplary for the legality differentiation. In this case, the investor and Ecuador had entered into a participation contract regarding the production of oil.[36] Ecuador eventually terminated this participation contract,[37] which the tribunal deemed a breach of the fair and equitable treatment standard as well as an unlawful indirect expropriation pursuant to the US/Ecuador BIT.[38] Prior to and unconnected to this breach, Ecuador had issued the so-called Law 42 which required all companies operating under participation contracts to contribute 50% of their windfall revenues to the host state.[39] According to Ecuador, this needed to be taken into account in the calculation of quantum. The consequence could have been a reduction of the DCF value in an amount of USD 800 million compared to the investor's claim.[40]

The tribunal undertook a detailed analysis of Law 42, ultimately finding that this law was in breach of the participation contract and of the guarantee of fair and

---

33 For example, due to socio-economic changes, the market for certain products, such as eg western music, basically collapsed, cf *CBS v Iran and others*, 25 Iran-US CTR (1990) 131, para 52.

34 *American International Group v Iran*, 4 Iran-US CTR (1983) 96, 107.

35 Cf also *Khosrowshahi v Iran*, 30 Iran-US CTR (1994) 76, paras 49ff; cf also Marboe (n 5) paras 5.138ff for further references.

36 *Occidental Petroleum Corporation and others v The Republic of Ecuador*, ICSID Case No ARB/06/11, Decision on Annulment of the Award, 2 November 2015, paras 5ff.

37 ibid para 22.

38 *Occidental* (n 36) Award, 5 October 2012, paras 452, 455.

39 *Occidental* (n 36) Decision on Annulment of the Award, 2 November 2015, para 23.

40 ibid para 469. The tribunal eventually awarded USD 1,769,625,000, cf Award, 5 October 2012, para 876. The amount was later reduced by an annulment committee on unrelated grounds to USD 1,061,775,000, cf Decision on Annulment of the Award, 2 November 2015, para 586.

equitable treatment.[41] Based on this finding, the tribunal held that Law 42 could not be taken into account in the quantum analysis.[42] In that regard, the tribunal held that 'a State cannot reduce its liability for a wrongful act [...] on the basis of another wrongful act [...].'[43] Moreover, the tribunal explicitly differentiated between 'changes in the general political, social and economic conditions' prior to the treaty breach on the one hand, and the host state's breaches of its obligations towards the investor on the other hand. While the former should be considered as a matter of quantum, the latter cannot be taken into account.[44] Any other approach would 'allow the Respondent to profit from its own wrongdoing, contrary to the general principles of international law explicitly proscribing this.'[45]

Case law thus indicates that the dividing line for economic and political circumstances is indeed the legality differentiation set out previously.[46] This approach has also found support in commentary.[47]

C. Recent Case Law in Relation to the DCF Valuation Approach

In recent cases against Venezuela, the economic and political circumstances prevailing in the host state played a very prominent role at the quantum stage, both with regard to the applicability of the DCF valuation approach as such (section I.) and with regard to the country risk premium applied in the DCF analysis (section II.). A detailed analysis is therefore warranted so as to determine how these cases relate to the legality differentiation (section III.).

I. Applicability of DCF Approach in Light of Economic and Political Circumstances

Concerning the influence that economic and political circumstances in the host state may have on the applicability of the DCF valuation approach in general, the award in *Tenaris v Venezuela* is noteworthy. In this case, the tribunal had found

---

41 *Occidental* (n 36) Award, 5 October 2012, para 527. Note however the opposite finding by dissenting arbitrator *Stern*, Dissenting Opinion, 20 September 2012, para 12.

42 *Occidental* (n 36) Award, 5 October 2012, para 546.

43 ibid para 541.

44 ibid para 543ff.

45 ibid para 546.

46 Notably, numerous tribunals held that economic and political circumstances prevailing in the host state needed to be taken into account at the valuation stage without explicitly analysing whether these circumstances were in line with the international law obligations of the host state, cf *CME* (n 6) Final Award, 14 March 2003, paras 561ff; *American Manufacturing & Trading, Inc v Republic of Zaire*, ICSID Case No ARB/93/1, Award, 21 February 1997, para 7.13ff; *Sempra Energy International v The Argentine Republic*, ICSID Case No ARB/02/16, Award, 28 September 2007, para 397 (annulled on unrelated grounds). However, this can be explained by the fact that, in these cases, there were no indications for the circumstances in question being in breach of international law obligations.

47 Marboe (n 5) paras 3.258, 5.138ff.

that Venezuela had illegally expropriated the investor,[48] and set out to assess the fair market value of the investment.[49] Notably, the parties and their experts agreed on the DCF method as being the most appropriate methodology for measuring future income.[50] Nonetheless, the tribunal discarded this method, instead awarding the price paid for the investment in a transaction undertaken several years prior to the illegal expropriation.[51]

In arriving at this conclusion, the tribunal identified a number of factors that made it difficult to identify future cash flows with the necessary reasonable certainty, among them a relatively short period of past performance and uncertainty regarding future supplies.[52] However, the tribunal also included the economic and political situation in Venezuela in this mix of factors – including the adoption of an expropriation policy towards foreign investment. Specifically, the tribunal stated that the existing uncertainties 'are compounded by other government interventions in the market place, as well as unstable inventories and shortages of a wide range of products in the Venezuelan market.'[53] According to the tribunal, the:

> general economic conditions in Venezuela as well as the business situation [of the investment] did not, at the time of expropriation – or later – give rise to the likelihood that [the investment's] free cash flows could be projected with reasonable certainty.[54]

Notably, the tribunal itself acknowledged that by relying on the historic price rather than the DCF method, the quantum determined was 'probably quite depressed'.[55] Moreover, the tribunal also accepted that it was in particular the expropriation policy adopted by the host state which had 'contributed to an environment in which the traditional approaches to establishing fair market value [ie the DCF analysis] confront serious difficulties.'[56] Nonetheless, the tribunal was apparently not prepared to set a less demanding threshold for the certainty required to apply the DCF method.

II. Country Risk Premium as Part of the DCF Analysis

In the wake of Venezuela adopting expropriation policies in key industrial sectors, the state's country risk was generally seen as having increased considerably. As explained earlier, a higher country risk leads to a higher discount rate, and thus, to a decrease of the claim. Hence, in a number of cases brought against Venezuela, it

---

48 *Tenaris* (n 3) paras 494ff.
49 ibid paras 514, 519.
50 ibid para 520.
51 ibid paras 550ff.
52 ibid paras 525ff.
53 ibid para 527.
54 ibid.
55 ibid para 567.
56 ibid.

was discussed whether, and to what extent, political risk may be taken into account as part of the country risk in a DCF valuation. Investors regularly argued that this may not happen since otherwise, Venezuela would profit from its expropriation policy due to lower awards of compensation or damages.[57]

In *Gold Reserve v Venezuela*, the tribunal had to deal with a dispute under the Canada/Venezuela BIT arising out of an investment in Venezuela's mining industry.[58] The specific object of the dispute was the revocation of the investment's mining concessions and the subsequent takeover of the investment's assets,[59] which the tribunal deemed to be in breach of the fair and equitable treatment standard.[60] Invoking the *Chorzów Factory* case and the standard of full reparation, the tribunal determined that applying a 'fair market value methodology' was appropriate in the case, given that the investor was totally deprived of the investment.[61] To determine the fair market value, the tribunal opted for the DCF method.[62] The parties disagreed on the discount rate, largely because of the country risk premium to be applied in the calculation of the cost of capital.

The tribunal found that the country risk premium advocated by the host state was too high since it was based on the 'generic country risk' including the state's 'policy of ousting North American companies from the mining sector'.[63] According to the tribunal, a country risk premium should not 'reflect the market's perception that a State might have a propensity to expropriate investments in breach of BIT obligations'.[64] At the same time, the tribunal also concluded that the country risk premium suggested by the investor was not high enough. That was because the investor's country risk premium only took into account 'labor risks and not other genuine risks that should be accounted for – including political risk, other than expropriation.'[65] Thus, the tribunal took a middle-of-the-road approach, insisting both on the inclusion of general political risks and the exclusion of the expropriation risk.

In practice, the tribunal's determination caused a problem since neither of the parties' quantum experts had calculated a discount rate on the basis of the tribunal's country risk assumptions. In consequence, the tribunal had to free-handedly adopt a discount rate of its own, between the discount rates determined by the quantum experts.[66] Moreover, since the tribunal could not conduct its own calculations on the basis of this discount rate, it decided to use the investor's calculation and deducted a certain amount therefrom – an approach which the tribunal freely admitted to be 'rough' and 'back of the envelope'.[67]

---

57 Cf with regard to this argument in more general terms Searby (n 26) 23ff.
58 *Gold Reserve* (n 3) paras 3ff.
59 ibid paras 26ff.
60 ibid para 564.
61 ibid paras 678ff, 681.
62 ibid para 831.
63 ibid para 840.
64 ibid para 841.
65 ibid.
66 ibid paras 839, 840, 842.
67 ibid para 842.

The tribunal in *Tidewater v Venezuela* did not follow this precedent. This case concerned an investment company providing maritime support services for hydrocarbon extraction to Venezuela's national oil company.[68] In 2009, Venezuela seized the investment company's assets.[69] The tribunal determined that Venezuela's actions constituted expropriation within the meaning of the applicable Barbados/Venezuela BIT, and further held that the expropriation was lawful since it was only lacking compensation.[70] Accordingly, the tribunal set out to determine the 'market value' of the investment (as prescribed by Article 5 of the applicable Barbados/Venezuela BIT).[71] In so doing, the tribunal opted for a DCF valuation.[72]

Concerning the details of the DCF valuation, both the parties and the tribunal put particular focus on the country risk premium. The investor argued for a comparatively low country risk premium of 1.5%, noting that political risk should not be included in the assessment. According to the investor, the state could otherwise threaten businesses, thus lower their value and ultimately take over foreign investment at a discount.[73] This would run counter to the legal implications of the existence of the investment protections in the BIT and would constitute an illegitimate benefit to the state.[74]

The tribunal rejected the investor's approach. According to the tribunal, only the specific measure at issue in the case at hand needed to be disregarded in the quantum analysis.[75] Conversely, 'general risks, including political risks, of doing business in the particular country' had to be taken into account as part of the country risk.[76] In arriving at this finding, the tribunal made explicit reference to the willing-buyer-willing-seller definition of the term 'market value' and noted that 'one element that a buyer would consider is the risk associated with investing in a particular country.'[77] Moreover, the tribunal explicitly rejected that, by including political risk as part of the country risk, the host state might be profiting from its own wrong.[78] In a nutshell, the tribunal summarised its position by stating that the applicable BIT was 'not an insurance policy or guarantee against all political or other risks associated with such investment.'[79]

---

68 *Tidewater* (n 3) paras 13ff.
69 ibid paras 24ff.
70 ibid paras 121, 146. There is considerable controversy as to whether an expropriation can be considered lawful if it is enacted without compensation, cf Marboe (n 5) paras 3.32ff.
71 ibid para 151.
72 ibid para 165.
73 ibid para 183.
74 ibid.
75 ibid para 186.
76 ibid.
77 ibid.
78 ibid.
79 ibid para 184. Incidentally, in calculating compensation, the tribunal failed to properly apply its determinations on the country risk premium. That is because the tribunal (involuntarily) relied on a number provided by the investor's expert that had been

The case *Venezuela Holdings et al v Venezuela*, brought under the Netherlands/Venezuela BIT, was decided in a similar vein. The case concerned a variety of measures taken by Venezuela against an investment in the oil production sector, culminating in the ultimate takeover of the investment by the state.[80] The tribunal determined that an expropriation had occurred but deemed this expropriation lawful since only compensation was missing and since it had not been shown that the state's offers for compensation were inappropriate.[81]

The tribunal's starting point regarding quantum was that the standard of compensation as set out in the BIT had to be applied.[82] The BIT provided for 'just compensation', more specifically defined as 'the market value of the investments affected immediately before the measures were taken or the impending measures became public knowledge, whichever is the earlier'.[83] Since the parties agreed that a DCF valuation should be conducted, the tribunal needed to decide on the applicable discount rate.[84] The investor argued that 'the country risk is largely composed of the risk of uncompensated expropriation, which cannot be taken into consideration'.[85] Specifically, the investor contended that 'a valuation of the expropriated property that complies with the Treaty cannot include the risk that the property right be expropriated later without the compensation required by the Treaty'.[86]

The tribunal rejected the investor's argument. What appears to have been decisive in that regard was that the BIT required compensation of the market value. Making explicit reference to the willing-buyer-willing-seller formula, the tribunal postulated that a hypothetical willing buyer would take into account the risk of a potential expropriation when determining the amount he was willing to pay.[87] Accordingly, 'the confiscation risk remains part of the country risk and must be taken into account in the determination of the discount rate.'[88]

The views adopted in *Gold Reserve* and in *Tidewater* and *Venezuela Holdings* collided head on in the case of *Saint-Gobain v Venezuela* decided under the France/Venezuela BIT. The subject of this case was Venezuela's expropriation without compensation of a proppants plant indirectly owned by the claimant.[89] The tribunal opted not to determine whether the expropriation was lawful or unlawful and instead contended itself with finding that the compensation should

---

calculated based on a country risk premium excluding political risk. The award was partially annulled for this reason, cf Decision on Annulment, 27 December 2016, paras 181ff.
80 *Venezuela Holdings* (n 3) paras 45ff, 86.
81 ibid paras 288, 301, 305, 306.
82 ibid para 306.
83 ibid para 307.
84 ibid paras 308ff.
85 ibid para 363.
86 ibid para 364.
87 ibid para 365.
88 ibid.
89 *Saint-Gobain* (n 3) para 5.

reflect the fair market value of the investment.[90] Within the application of the DCF method, the country risk premium once again became contentious. While the claimant's expert relied on a method which he said excluded the 'risk of uncompensated expropriation', the respondent's experts advocated two methods which did not.[91]

Faced with this issue, the tribunal was ultimately not able to reach a unanimous decision. The majority of the tribunal decided to include the risk of expropriation without compensation in the country risk premium.[92] Citing *Tidewater*, the majority relied on the willing-buyer-willing-seller formula and argued that the willing buyer would have taken into account all risks.[93] According to the majority, the 'notion of fair market value [...] requires the elimination of the specific measure that was subject of the Tribunal's finding on liability' but not 'a correction of the economic willing-buyer perspective on the basis of normative considerations'.[94] The applicable BIT could not serve as insurance against the general risks of investing in Venezuela that a willing buyer would take into account when investing.[95]

In his dissenting opinion, Judge Brower strongly criticised the majority view. Citing *Gold Reserve*, Judge Brower argued that including the risk of uncompensated expropriation, of which the investor is purportedly being relieved, is equivalent to denying the investor the full compensation to which it is entitled. In his words, '[i]t is like undertaking to restore to the owner of a severely damaged automobile a perfectly repaired and restored vehicle but then leaving parts of it missing because it just might be damaged again in the future.'[96]

Finally, for yet another approach, reference can be made to the case of *Flughafen Zürich et al v Venezuela*, brought under both the Switzerland/Venezuela and Chile/Venezuela BITs. In 2004, the investors in this case had obtained a 20-year operating license for an airport in Venezuela.[97] At the end of 2005, the state seized the airport.[98] The tribunal determined that the state's actions constituted illegal direct expropriation[99] and that the market value was the relevant measure for reparation.[100] Since the tribunal, in accordance with the parties, opted for a DCF valuation,[101] the country risk needed to be discussed.

In the course of this discussion, the investors put forward a very low country risk premium, basically providing only for the risk of increases in labour costs.[102]

---

90 ibid paras 602, 614, 627.
91 ibid paras 698–700, 725, 734.
92 ibid para 723.
93 ibid para 717.
94 ibid para 719.
95 ibid.
96 *Saint-Gobain* (n 3), Concurring and Dissenting Opinion of Judge Charles N Brower, para 3.
97 *Flughafen Zürich* (n 3) para 971.
98 ibid.
99 ibid paras 509, 511.
100 ibid paras 740, 744.
101 ibid paras 780ff.
102 ibid para 890.

According to the investors, legal, regulatory and political risks could not be included because this would allow host states to decrease the damages due in case of an expropriation by increasing the level of country risk after the making of the investment.[103] Interestingly, the tribunal in principle agreed with this line of argument. According to the tribunal, a state that increases the country risk through the adoption of new policies after the making of the investment cannot benefit from this increase when it comes to damages for an internationally wrongful act.[104]

However, this finding ultimately did not help the investors. In the tribunal's view, a considerable country risk due to political and legal uncertainties had already existed when the investors had made their investment.[105] Thus, there was no increase of the country risk after the making of the investment, and, accordingly, a country risk premium including the full country risk, taking into account all political, legal and regulatory factors, needed to be applied.[106] Practically, the tribunal thus distinguished between different levels of country risk over time; however, it did not distinguish between risks relating to legal and illegal conduct.[107]

III. Analysis

The recent jurisprudence regarding Venezuela's expropriation policies shows very different approaches to the question of how the economic and political circumstances prevailing in the host state should be accounted for at the quantum stage. The consequences of these variations can be staggering. For example, commentators have noted with regard to the determination of the country risk premium that including the expropriation risk may lead to a considerable reduction of compensation or damages – up to one third, depending on the circumstances.[108]

Arguably, most of the awards cited previously are hardly reconcilable with the legality differentiation. To begin with, the findings of the *Tenaris* tribunal regarding the applicability of the DCF valuation approach seem questionable. The tribunal relied *inter alia* on the uncertainties following from the state's expropriation policy to justify its decision not to apply the DCF method and to award a

---

103 ibid para 898.
104 ibid para 905.
105 ibid para 907.
106 ibid.
107 Incidentally, the claimant in the *OI European Group* case also argued for a reduction of the country risk premium in light of a state policy of expropriation. However, whether such a reduction was appropriate in principle was not addressed in this case. Rather, the tribunal rejected the proposal because it held that the country risk premium put forward by the respondent had not been calculated based on input data that could have been influenced by the state's expropriation policy, cf *OI European Group BV v Bolivarian Republic of Venezuela*, ICSID Case No ARB/11/25, Award, 10 March 2015, paras 775ff.
108 Dorobantu, Dupont and Maniatis (n 29) 220; PwC (n 25) 6.

'probably quite depressed' amount of damages.[109] Under the legality differentiation, the tribunal should however have discarded the expropriation policy and all consequences following from it, given that specific implementations of the expropriation policy had been found to be in breach of international law both by the tribunal in the case and by tribunals in other cases.[110] Accordingly, the tribunal could not use any uncertainty flowing from Venezuela's expropriation policy to argue that there was insufficient certainty regarding future cash flows. Admittedly, this might not have made a difference in the concrete case. After all, the tribunal also stressed various other factors creating uncertainty, such as the short period of past performance and shortages of a wide range of products on the Venezuelan market.[111] These factors on their own may already have been sufficient for rejecting the DCF approach as being too uncertain.

Regarding the determinations of the country risk premium, the awards in *Tidewater, Venezuela Holdings* and *Saint-Gobain* are also at odds with the legality differentiation. All three tribunals declined to exclude the risk of host state measures in breach of international law from the calculation of the country risk premium. Admittedly, the previously cited case law concerning the legality differentiation is not directly applicable because it relates to disregarding specific breaches of international law and not to disregarding the *risk* of breaches of international law. However, a consistent application of the legality differentiation requires extending its effects to the level of risks as part of the country risk premium analysis. After all, IITs determine that, as a matter of international law, the risk of certain host state measures directed against an investment must not materialise. Yet, if these risks may not materialise, it would be inconsistent to take them into account in the but-for-scenario on which the valuation is based. The *Tidewater* and *Saint-Gobain* tribunals did not recognise this latter point when they argued that the applicable BITs were not 'insurance' against all political or other risks associated with an investment.[112] While this statement is correct, it fails to recognise that IITs are indeed insurance policies against certain political risks, namely the risks of expropriation without compensation, unfair and inequitable treatment, etc. For such risks, there is no place in the but-for-scenario.

Tidewater, Venezuela Holdings and *Saint-Gobain* highlighted one further reason why it is supposedly necessary to have all risks covered within the country risk premium. According to these tribunals, all risks would be factored in by a willing buyer and a willing seller (ie the hypothetical persons relevant pursuant to the fair market value standard) when assessing the value of the investment.[113] In raising this argument, the tribunals however overstated the relevance of the willing-buyer-willing-seller formula. The tribunals assumed that the willing-buyer-willing-seller formula helps in determining which circumstances form part of the but-for-

---

109 *Tenaris* (n 3) para 567.
110 ibid paras 494ff; *Flughafen Zürich* (n 3) paras 509, 511.
111 *Tenaris* (n 3) paras 525ff.
112 *Tidewater* (n 3) para 184; *Saint-Gobain* (n 3) para 719.
113 Cf *Tidewater* (n 3) para 186; *Venezuela Holdings* (n 3) para 365; *Saint-Gobain* (n 3) para 717.

scenario. In fact, however, the but-for-scenario needs to be determined first, with the legality differentiation as its sole basis. It is only once the but-for-scenario is determined (with the risk of breaches of international law being disregarded) that the willing-buyer-willing-seller formula comes in and serves as a valuation tool for the benefit of the tribunal.[114]

The *Flughafen Zürich* case also runs counter to the legality differentiation. The tribunal in the case did not differentiate between the risk of expropriation and other political, legal and regulatory risks. Instead, the tribunal differentiated between risks arisen before and after the making of the investment. Taken at face value, this line of reasoning would mean that general economic and political circumstances may be disregarded for the determination of the country risk premium, even if they follow from legal conduct of the host state, as long as these circumstances came into existence after the making of the investment. Thus, under the tribunal's approach, the effects of eg a tort reform for the benefit of consumers, while not illegal under international law, could still be excluded from the country risk premium. Arguably, this approach cannot be the right one, as it would indeed turn IITs into general insurance policies against all political risk.

Hence, the only case which can be reconciled with the legality differentiation is *Gold Reserve*. Here, the tribunal drew a clear line between general economic and political circumstances on the one hand and the risk of breaches of international law on the other. This approach to determining the country risk premium is consistent with previous investment jurisprudence and leads to appropriate results. Specifically, it ensures that the host state is not rewarded with reduced damage awards after adopting policies in breach of international law. At the same time, moral hazard is avoided because IITs are not turned into general insurance policies against any and all general economic and political circumstances in the host state.

Incidentally, some have argued that the lawfulness or unlawfulness of the expropriation is decisive when determining whether to include the risk of breaches of international law in the country risk premium.[115] This view should be rejected. In that regard, it is correct that those tribunals which had explicitly deemed the expropriations lawful (ie the ones in *Tidewater* and *Venezuela Holdings*) then moved on to include this risk in the country risk premium. However, these tribunals did not expressly rely on their findings of a lawful expropriation in that regard. Moreover, both in cases of lawful and of unlawful expropriation, tribunals are called upon to determine a hypothetical scenario without the legal taking or the breach of the IIT, respectively. There is no reason why this hypothetical scenario should include the risk of breaches of international law in the former case and exclude it in the latter.

D. Practical Aspects of Determining the Country Risk Premium

The previous analysis is limited to the theoretical side of the country risk premium analysis – namely the question of which risks may be taken into account as a

---

114 Cf Dorobantu, Dupont and Maniatis (n 29) 224.
115 Cf Alberro (n 17) 546.

matter of law. How can these considerations be applied in the practical determination of the country risk premium? Unfortunately, there is no one-size-fits-all answer to this question.

There are various techniques for determining country risk premiums.[116] The most typical approach is some form of derivation from market data regarding the host state's sovereign bond yield ('sovereign risk method') or the volatility of the host state's equity markets ('equity market risk method').[117] Under these approaches, it is inherently difficult to isolate the risk of breaches of international law from other country risk factors.[118] The sovereign risk method and the equity market risk method simply rely on market data and thus automatically include, without distinction, all country risk factors, as they are perceived by the market.[119] Under these methods, it is therefore necessary to reduce the country risk by way of an estimate, making an assumption to which extent the risk perceived by the market is made up of the risk of breaches of international law.[120]

Alternatively, it is also possible to model the country risk premium by specific reference to the various elements of country risk and combining them into one country risk premium ('specific factor risk method').[121] For that purpose, rating agencies publish country risk ratings representing a combined assessment of political, economic and financial risks.[122] This method is not based on market data at all but exclusively relies on judgement calls.[123]

As these explanations show, it will almost always be impossible to determine on a purely empirical basis a country risk premium that excludes the risk of breaches of international law. Judgement calls will become necessary. The ensuing subjectivity may be considered unfortunate – but does not undermine the analysis as such. Tribunals need not establish quantum with scientific certainty but may use approximations and estimates.[124] In the view of the author, tribunals should make use of this power when determining the country risk premium, so as to ensure that the risk of breaches of international law is excluded from the analysis.

---

116 For a brief summary of the most common methods cf. PwC (n 25) 8 and Marboe (n 5) para 5.206. For an analysis of country risk premiums for various countries pursuant to such methods cf *Damodaran*, 'Country Default Spreads and Risk Premiums', http://pages.stern.nyu.edu/~adamodar/New_Home_Page/datafile/ctryprem.html accessed 15 June 2017.

117 Searby (n 26) 20ff. For a discussion of the merits of these two approaches with a view to a country facing a high risk of sovereign default cf. *EDF* (n 27) paras 1263ff.

118 PwC (n 29) 9.

119 Dorobantu, Dupont and Maniatis (n 29) 231.

120 Cf PwC (n 29) 9.

121 Searby (n 26) 22.

122 Cf International Country Risk Guide, www.prsgroup.com/about-us/our-two-methodologies/icrg accessed 15 June 2017.

123 Searby (n 26) 22.

124 *Khan Resources Inc and others v Government of Mongolia*, UNCTIRAL, Award on the Merits, 2 March 2015, para 375; *Quasar de Valors SICAV SA and others v Russian Federation*, SCC Case No 24/2007, Award, 20 July 2012, para 215.

Procedurally, tribunals depend on expert input in order to determine the appropriate country risk premium. Unfortunately, in many arbitrations, tribunals only start considering quantum matters in detail once the file is closed and reports by the party-appointed experts have been submitted. This can lead to the less than ideal situation illustrated by the *Gold Reserve* case. Here, the tribunal found that no expert had provided a country risk premium (and, accordingly, a damage calculation) in line with the tribunal's risk assumptions, thus forcing the tribunal to make its own 'back of the envelope' calculation.[125] More precision could be achieved by tribunals proactively instructing the valuation experts of both sides at an early stage to run calculations both including and excluding relevant risk elements.[126] This would allow the tribunal to choose from a set of numbers that are backed by at least one of the party's experts and hence increase the reliability of the ultimate damage number.[127]

E. Conclusion

In the author's view, the recent awards in the cases against Venezuela are evidence of two conflicting interests: On the one hand, tribunals want to avoid moral hazard. From this viewpoint, investment treaties shall not be turned into insurance policies protecting investors from all risk emanating from the economic and political situation prevailing in the host state, and thus liberating investors from conducting their own due diligence. On the other hand, tribunals equally want to avoid a situation in which host states are rewarded for behaviour that is in breach of the applicable IITs. Tribunals have taken different approaches in order to strike a balance between the two sides of the argument. In the author's view, the appropriate approach is to follow a strict legality differentiation, including all circumstances and risks in the hypothetical but-for-scenario, except those that are in themselves not in accordance with international law. Unfortunately, when it comes to the determination of the country risk premium for the purposes of a DCF valuation, this will not be possible based on empirical data alone and will instead require judgement calls. Tribunals should be aware of this early on and pro-actively communicate to the parties and their experts that numbers for different risk assumptions should be provided. This will allow the tribunal to pick the appropriate numbers in the end and avoid unsatisfactory 'back of the envelope' calculations.

125 *Gold Reserve* (n 3) paras 839 et seq.
126 Dorobantu, Dupont and Maniatis (n 29) 228.
127 Cf also PwC (n 29) 6.

4 The Impact of Third-Party Funding on an ICSID Tribunal's Decision on Security for Costs

Dr Alexander Hoffmann

A. Introduction

'Only in the jurisprudence of an imaginary Wonderland would this make sense.' This statement was issued by the dissenting arbitrator in the case *RSM Production Corporation v Saint Lucia* [1] before the International Centre for Settlement of Investment Disputes ('ICSID'). In this proceeding, the arbitral tribunal – for the first time in the history of ICSID arbitration – had granted the request of the respondent state to order the claimant investor to provide security for costs.[2] The dissenting arbitrator not only questioned the tribunal's authority to order security for costs, but also criticised that the majority had taken the admitted existence of a third-party funding agreement on the claimant's side into account when assessing the respondent's application.[3]

The question of whether and under which circumstances ICSID tribunals may order security for costs is highly controversial. With the recent advent of third-party funding, a new element has been added to the debate raising the issue of whether this factor should be taken into account by ICSID tribunals assessing applications for security for costs.

This chapter will address this issue. After having briefly explained the object and purpose of security for costs, the author will show that ICSID tribunals have general authority to order this provisional measure. The chapter will then turn to the question of which requirements need to be met before an ICSID tribunal may order security for costs. Applying these standards the author will finally – after having given a brief overview on the concept of third-party funding – evaluate the role third-party funding may play in an ICSID tribunal's decision on security for costs.

---

1 *RSM Production Corporation v Saint Lucia*, ICSID Case No ARB/12/10, Decision on Saint Lucia's Request for Security for Costs of 13 August 2014, Dissenting Opinion of Edward Nottingham of 12 August 2014, para 8.
2 The tribunal ordered the claimant to post security for costs in the amount of USD 750,000.
3 *RSM v Saint Lucia* (n 1), Dissenting Opinion of Edward Nottingham of 12 August 2014, para 17.

B. What is an Order for Security for Costs?

A security for costs order is a special form of interim relief requiring the party bringing a claim (or counter-claim) to provide sufficient security to cover the respondent's legal costs that may be awarded against the claimant should the claim be dismissed.[4] This interim measure is usually requested by a respondent who fears that the claimant might be unable or unwilling to honor an adverse costs award and who wants to preserve the ability to recover its costs incurred in defending the claim.[5] The security can take various forms but is typically provided by way of a bank guarantee or a payment into escrow.[6]

C. Does an ICSID Tribunal Have Authority to Order Security for Costs?

I. The Lack of Express Wording

Under the ICSID regime[7], no provision explicitly addresses an ICSID tribunal's power to order security for costs. Some arbitrators have taken this lack of express wording as a reason to generally question the authority of an ICSID tribunal to grant such measures.[8] However, a large number of arbitration tribunals have ruled that security for costs orders do not fall outside an ICSID tribunal's power, classifying them as a subset of general provisional measures mentioned in Article 47 ICSID Convention and ICSID Arbitration Rule 39.[9]

---

4 Jeff Waincymer, *Procedure and Evidence in International Arbitration* (Kluwer Law International 2012) 642; Noah Rubins, 'In God we Trust, All Others Pay Cash: Security for Costs in International Commercial Arbitration' (2000) 11 Am Rev Int'l Arb 307, 310; Blackaby and others, *Redfern and Hunter on International Arbitration* (6h edn, OUP 2015) 5.35.

5 Jean E Kalicki, 'Security for Costs in International Arbitration' (2006) 3(5) TDM; Joe Tirado and Max Stein, 'Security for Costs in International Arbitration – A Briefing Note' (2012), 9(4) TDM.

6 Jonas von Goeler, *Third-Party Funding in International Arbitration and its Impact on Procedure* (Kluwer Law International 2016) 333; Wendy Miles and Duncan Speller, 'Security for Costs in International Arbitration – Emerging Consensus or Continuing Difference' (2007), The European Arbitration Review, 32; Waincymer (n 4) 652.

7 By 'ICSID regime' the author refers to the Convention on the Settlement of Investment Disputes between States and Nationals of Other States ('ICSID Convention') and the ICSID Rules of Procedure for Arbitration Proceedings ('ICSID Arbitration Rules').

8 *RSM v Saint Lucia* (n 1), Dissenting Opinion of Edward Nottingham of 12 August 2014, para 8.

9 *Atlantic Triton v Guinea*, cited in Paul D Friedland, 'Provisional Measures and ICSID Arbitration' (1986) 2 Arb Int'l 335, 347; *Emilio Agustin Maffezini v Kingdom of Spain*, ICSID Case No ARB/97/7, Procedural Order No 2 of 28 October 1999, paras 6–8; *Rachel S Grynberg, Stephen M Grynberg, Miriam Z. Grynberg and RSM Production Corporation v Grenada*, ICSID Case No ARB/10/6, Decision on Respondent's Application for Security for Costs of 14 October 2010, para 5.16; *RSM v Saint Lucia* (n 1) para 52; this view has been supported by scholars and commentators as well, see von

In *RSM Production Corporation v Saint Lucia*, the ICSID tribunal tried to explain the fact that security for costs was not expressly mentioned and listed as a separate provisional measure in these provisions.[10] It held that the provisions on interim measures were phrased broadly on purpose in order to leave it to the tribunal's discretion which concrete measure it finds necessary and appropriate under the circumstances of the individual case.[11]

II. The Meaning of the Word 'Recommend'

Apart from the lack of express wording, an ICSID tribunal's authority to order security for costs has also been challenged with regard to the meaning 'recommend' used both in Article 47 ICSID Convention and ICSID Arbitration Rule 39. For instance, the dissenting arbitrator in *RSM Production Corporation v Saint Lucia* has pointed out that the drafters of the ICSID Convention omitted the term 'order' intentionally since they did not want provisional measures – such as security for costs – to be binding on the parties.[12]

Despite this objection, ICSID tribunals have held on many occasions that the term 'recommend' must be understood as meaning 'order'. In *Maffezini v Spain*, the tribunal took the view that 'the difference is more apparent than real' and that the parties to the ICSID Convention did not mean 'to create a substantial difference in the effect of these two words'.[13] Consequently, the tribunal considered its authority to rule on provisional measures 'no less binding than that of a final award'.[14] Subsequent ICSID tribunals dealing with provisional measures have confirmed and adopted this line of reasoning.[15] This jurisprudence has also been embraced by commentators pointing out that a doctrine under which provisional measures have binding effects on the parties will serve the purpose of promoting the effective enforcement of awards and upholding the integrity of the arbitral process.[16]

Goeler (n 6) 335; Tirado and Stein (n 5); Rubins (n 4) 346; Christoph Schreuer, *The ICSID Convention – A Commentary* (2nd edn, CUP 2009) 784.

10 *RSM v Saint Lucia* (n 1) para 54.

11 ibid.

12 See *RSM v Saint Lucia* (n 1), Dissenting Opinion of Edward Nottingham of 12 August 2014, para 13.

13 *Maffezini* (n 9) para 9.

14 ibid.

15 *Pey Casado v Chile*, ICSID Case No ARB/98/2, Decision on Request for Provisional Measures of 25 September 2001, paras 17–20; *Tokios Tokelés v Ukraine*, ICSID Case No ARB/02/18, Procedural Order No 1 of 1 July 2003, para 4; *Occidental Petroleum Corporation and Occidental Exploration and Production Company v Republic of Ecuador*, ICSID Case No ARB/06/11, Decision on Provisional Measures of 17 August 2007, para 58.

16 Zannis Mavrogordato and Gabriel Sidere, 'The Nature and Enforceability of ICSID Provisional Measures' (2009), 75(1) Arbitration 38, 42.

III. No Enforceability

In this context, it should be clarified, however, that provisional measures issued by an ICSID tribunal do not have a 'binding' effect in terms of being enforceable through the ICSID Convention because recommendations under ICSID Arbitration Rule 39 do not qualify as final awards within the meaning of Article 54 ICSID Convention.[17] Nevertheless, parties should not underestimate the authority attached to these recommendations since an ICSID tribunal, in its final award, can take into account the behaviour of the parties and draw adverse inferences from the non-compliance with provisional measures.[18]

D. Which Requirements must be Met before an ICSID Tribunal may Grant Security for Costs?

After having clarified that ICSID tribunals generally have the power to order security for costs, we now turn to the question of which requirements must be met before an ICSID tribunal may grant such measures.

I. General Criteria for Provisional Measures

Given the fact that security for costs orders are commonly classified as a subset of provisional measures pursuant to Article 47 ICSID Convention, it seems plausible to first take a look at the criteria used by arbitral tribunals to assess applications for general provisional measures.

In this context, it should be highlighted that neither the ICSID Convention nor the ICSID Arbitration Rules lay down conditions upon which tribunals may order provisional measures.[19] Consequently, the decision to grant provisional measures is left to the discretion of each ICSID tribunal without the ICSID regime providing any guidance as to how this discretion should be exercised.[20] However, a review of ICSID jurisprudence reveals that they may only be granted if the respondent can show that they are necessary, urgent, and needed in order to avoid irreparable harm.[21]

---

17 Gabrielle Kaufmann-Kohler and Aurélia Antonietti, 'Interim Relief in International Investment Agreements' in Katia Yannaca-Small (eds), *Arbitration under International Investment Agreements – A Guide to the Key Issues* (OUP 2010) 546; *RSM v Saint Lucia* (n 1) para 50.
18 Kaufmann-Kohler and Antonietti (n 17) 546; Loretta Malintoppi, 'Provisional Measures in Recent ICSID Proceedings: What Parties Request and What Tribunals Order' in Christina Binder and others (eds), *International Investment Law for the 21st Century: Essays in Honour of Christoph Schreuer* (OUP 2009) 180–181; Schreuer (n 9) 758.
19 ICCA-Queen Mary Task Force on Third Party Funding in International Arbitration, Subcommittee on Security for Costs and Costs, Draft Report of 1 November 2015, 13, www.arbitration-icca.org/media/6/09700416080661/tpf_taskforce_security_for_costs_and_costs_draft_report_november_2015.pdf accessed 25 June 2017.
20 Kaufmann-Kohler and Antonietti (n 17) 514; Blackaby (n 4) 310; von Goeler (n 6).
21 Schreuer (n 9) 776; Malintoppi (n 18) 161; Kaufmann-Kohler and Antonietti (n 17) 529.

II. Higher Threshold for Security for Costs Orders

Unfortunately, the criteria outlined by ICSID tribunals for ordinary provisional measures are of little help in determining requirements concerning the assessment of applications for security for costs. This is because, although security for costs fall into the category of general provisional measures pursuant to Article 47 ICSID Convention, they represent a special form of interim relief raising particular issues that necessitate a higher threshold for the assessment of respective applications.[22]

The main reason for this higher threshold is that orders for security for costs have an impact on the claimant's ability to get access to justice. It is a general concern of practitioners and scholars in international arbitration that an order for security for costs might constitute a financial impediment preventing a claimant who cannot afford to provide the ordered security from pursuing a meritorious claim.[23] This concern is even more justified if the claimant's impecuniosity has been caused by the actions of the respondent that are the very subject matter of the dispute between the parties.[24] Allegations to this effect are particularly frequent in the context of disputes between private investors and states where the respondent state is often accused of having unlawfully expropriated the claimant, thereby leaving the claimant with little funds to pursue costly investment arbitration.[25] In these cases, it would seem inappropriate and unfair to place an additional financial burden on the claimant by granting security for costs only because of circumstances the claimant may not even be responsible for.[26]

III. Hurdles to Develop a Uniform Test

In the light of the previously mentioned, it is not surprising that ICSID tribunals have been generally very reluctant to grant security for costs. In *Libananco v Turkey*, the tribunal took the view 'that it would only be in the most extreme cases – one in which an essential interest of either Party stood in danger of irreparable damage – that the possibility of granting security for costs should be entertained at all'.[27] However, apart from handling requests for security for costs with extreme caution, ICSID tribunals have not yet managed to develop a uniform test or specific conditions upon which such measures may be ordered. One ICSID tribunal admitted that 'it is difficult, in the abstract, to formulate a rule of general application against which to measure whether the making of an order for security for costs might be reasonable'.[28]

---

22 Blackaby (n 4) 5.35; Waincymer (n 4) 647; von Goeler (n 6) 336; *Pey Casado v Chile* (n 15) para 86.
23 Waincymer (n 4) 643; Miles and Speller (n 6) 32; Blackaby (n 4) 5.35.
24 Waincymer (n 4) 643; Blackaby (n 4) 5.35 Weixa Gu, 'Security for Costs in International Commercial Arbitration' (2005) 22(3) Journal of International Arbitration 167, 185.
25 von Goeler (n 6) 337.
26 Rubins (n 4) 362; von Goeler (n 6) 337.
27 *Libananco Holdings Co Limited v Republic of Turkey*, ICSID Case No ARB/06/8, Decision on Preliminary Issues of 23 June 2008, para 57.
28 *RSM v Grenada* (n 9) para 5.20.

Creating a uniform standard is even more difficult as some criteria used for the assessment of applications for security for costs in commercial arbitration do not apply in investment treaty arbitration.

Commentators emphasise that, in international commercial arbitration, the parties voluntarily chose to engage in a business relationship including an agreement to arbitrate. Therefore, by the time the agreement was closed, each party must be assumed to have accepted any risks inherent in the other party's nationality, creditworthiness, and trustworthiness.[29] As a consequence, it is not sufficient for a respondent requesting security for costs in commercial arbitration proceedings to simply point to an alleged impecuniosity of the claimant which might prevent him from paying a potential adverse costs award since the possibility of a business partner's credit standing changing over time is generally considered a normal commercial risk.[30] Rather, to justify a security for costs order, the respondent must show that the financial situation of the claimant has materially and unforeseeably changed since the conclusion of the arbitration agreement.[31]

This test, however, cannot be transferred to the system of treaty-based and legislation-based arbitration since the respondent state, in these cases, has not entered into an arbitration agreement with a particular claimant investor.[32] Therefore, it cannot be said that the respondent state – not even knowing his potential counterpart in a future arbitration proceeding – has, at some point, accepted the risk of transacting with a financially unstable claimant entity.

IV. Key Requirements Demanded by ICSID Tribunals

Despite these difficulties to develop a uniform test with regard to specific criteria for security for costs orders, it is possible – by reviewing ICSID jurisprudence – to extract certain key requirements that ICSID tribunals generally deem necessary before they consider ordering security for costs.

1. The Claimant's Impecuniosity

As a first step in their assessment of applications for security for costs, ICSID tribunals usually examine the financial situation of the claimant investor and evaluate if the respondent state has brought sufficient evidence showing that the claimant is impecunious and therefore unable to pay a potential adverse costs award.[33]

---

29 Alastair Henderson, 'Security for Costs in Arbitration in Singapore' (2011) 7(1) Asian International Arbitration Journal 54, 69.

30 ICCA-Queen Mary Task Force Draft Report (n 19) 13; Waincymer (n 4) 650.

31 ICC Case No 10032, Procedural Order of 9 November 1999, para 45, cited in Pierre A Karrer and Marcus Desax, 'Security for Costs in International Arbitration – Why, When, and What If ...' in Robert Briner and others (eds), *Liber Amicorum Karl-Heinz Böckstiegel* (Carl Heymanns Verlag 2001) 339, 348; Henderson (n 29) 69; Gu (n 24).

32 ICCA-Queen Mary Task Force Draft Report (n 19) 14.

33 *Commerce Group Corp & San Sebastian Gold Mines, Inc v Republic of El Salvador*, ICSID Case No ARB/09/17, Decision on El Salvador's Application for Security for

However, ICSID tribunals have emphasised that in order to justify an order for security for costs 'more should be required than a simple showing of the likely inability of a claimant to pay a possible costs award.'[34] In their opinion, 'it is simply not part of the ICSID dispute resolution system that an investor's claim should be heard only upon the establishment of a sufficient financial standing of the investor to meet a possible costs award'.[35]

2. 'Exceptional Circumstances'

In addition to the claimant's impecuniosity, ICSID tribunals have considered evidence of 'exceptional circumstances' a prerequisite for granting security for costs.[36] While the term 'exceptional circumstances' has not yet been defined in the abstract, one tribunal, in an attempt to at least narrow down the threshold of exceptional circumstances, named 'abuse or serious misconduct' as elements that had to be evidenced on the claimant side before security for costs could be granted.[37] These examples have been taken up in subsequent ICSID decisions[38] and have also been approved by scholars adding that the claimant's behaviour, in this context, may involve elements of bad faith as well.[39] It therefore appears valid to state that the threshold for 'exceptional circumstances' is met where the claimant conducts an arbitration proceeding abusively or in bad faith.

E. Which Role does Third-Party Funding Play in the Assessment of Security for Costs Requests?

Against the background, the author will now evaluate the role third-party funding may play in an ICSID tribunal's decision on security for costs.

I. A Brief Overview on Third-Party Funding

First, a short overview will be provided on the concept of third-party funding, its use and funding terms relevant in the context of security for costs.

Costs, 20 September 2012, para 51; *RSM v Grenada* (n 9) para 5.18; *RSM v Saint Lucia* (n 1) para 82.
34 *RSM v Grenada* (n 9) para 5.20; *EuroGas Inc and Belmont Resources Inc v Slovak Republic*, ICSID Case No ARB/14/14, Procedural Order No 3 – Decision on the Parties' Request for Provisional Measures of 23 June 2015, para 120.
35 *RSM v Grenada* (n 9) para 5.19; *EuroGas v Slovak Republic* (n 34) para 120; *Pey Casado v Chile* (n 15) para 86.
36 *EuroGas v Slovak Republic* (n 34) para 121; *RSM v Saint Lucia* (n 1) para 75; *Libananco Holdings Co Limited v Republic of Turkey*, ICSID Case No ARB/06/8, Decision on Preliminary Issues of 23 June 2008, para 57; *Commerce Group v El Salvador* (n 33), para 45; *RSM v Grenada* (n 9) para 5.17.
37 *Commerce Group v El Salvador* (n 33) para 45.
38 *EuroGas v Slovak Republic* (n 34) para 121.
39 von Goeler (n 6) 356; ICCA-Queen Mary Task Force Draft Report (n 19) 17.

1. The Concept of Third-Party Funding

Third-party funding[40] can appear in various shapes and forms, but there is one model which largely predominates in international arbitration.[41] According to this model, third-party funding can broadly be described as an arrangement whereby an outside entity otherwise unconnected with a legal action agrees to pay the claimant's costs associated with pursuing its case.[42] In return for financing the claimant's legal representation in the dispute, the outside entity – the third-party funder – receives a percentage or fraction of the proceeds from the case if the claimant wins.[43] However, if the case is unsuccessful, the claimant has no obligation to repay the funder meaning that the funder has lost its investment in the claimant's case.[44]

2. The Use of Third-Party Funding

Third-party funding is often praised as a medium to facilitate access to justice by enabling claimants with insufficient financial resources to pursue their claims in arbitration proceedings.[45] This benefit is particularly relevant in the context of investor-state arbitration where the claimant investor's impecuniosity may result from actions taken by the host state leaving the investor financially incapable to sue the host state for compensation in a costly investment arbitration proceeding. Nevertheless, third-party funding is also used by financially stable claimants that are in a position to pay for the costs of arbitration themselves but that prefer to outsource the costs of arbitration in order to maintain liquidity.[46]

3. Relevant Funding Terms in the Context of Security for Costs

The terms of third-party funding products available for the financing of international arbitration proceedings vary from funder to funder.[47] It would go beyond

---

40 Some scholars and commentators use slightly different terms – such as 'third-party financing' – to describe the same phenomenon.

41 Victoria Shannon Sahani and Lisa Bench Nieuwveld, *Third-Party Funding in International Arbitration* (Kluwer Law International 2012) 5; Catherine Rogers, *Ethics in International Arbitration* (OUP 2014) 185.

42 Victoria Shannon Sahani, 'Judging Third-Party Funding' (2016) 63 UCLA Law Review 388, 392; von Goeler (n 6) 73; Cento Veljanovski, 'Third-Party Litigation Funding in Europe' (2012) 8(3) Journal of Law, Economics & Policy 405.

43 Shannon Sahani and Bench Nieuwveld (n 41) 392; von Goeler (n 6) 73; Rogers (n 41) 185.

44 Veljanovski (n 42) 405; von Goeler (n 6) 73; Shannon Sahani (n 42).

45 Susanna Khouri, Kate Hurford and Clive Bowman, 'Third Party Funding in International Commercial and Treaty Arbitration – A Panacea or a Plague? A Discussion of the Risks and Benefits of Third Party Funding' (2011) 8(4) TDM.

46 von Goeler (n 6) 83–84; Yasmin Mohammad (Senior Counsel with Vannin Capital), 'A Partial Commentary of the *RSM Production Corporation v Saint Lucia* Decision on Security for Costs', http://emailing.iccwbo.org/events/Yasmin-Mohammad.pdf accessed 25 June 2017.

47 Aren Goldsmith and Lorenzo Melchionda, 'Third Party Funding in International Arbitration: Everything You Ever Wanted to Know (But Were Afraid to Ask)' (2012)

the scope of this chapter to describe all possible contract structures underlying third-party funding agreements. However, it is worth highlighting some common funding terms that can shed light on a funder's contractual liability for adverse costs and that may, thus, play a role in the decision of an ICSID tribunal to grant a security for costs application.

Funding terms that first come to mind in this context concern clauses explicitly excluding the funder's liability for adverse costs.[48] Such clauses would naturally draw the attention of an arbitral tribunal deciding upon security for costs since they indicate that the funder will definitely not take responsibility for the respondent's costs if the claim fails.

Other terms that may be relevant in this context concern provisions entitling the funder to terminate the funding agreement. While basically all third-party funders insist on including such provisions in their funding agreements, the design of such terms varies across the industry.[49] Some termination clauses allow the funder to cease funding at its sole discretion; other terms require material changes in circumstances or a material breach committed by the funded party.[50] Depending on how easily a funder can terminate a funding agreement, it may happen that a claimant will be left in a proceeding without funding on short notice leaving the claimant incapable of paying adverse costs.[51]

Finally, ICSID tribunals may also center their attention on terms regarding the budget limit reflecting the maximum amount of capital that the third-party funder is willing to invest in the case and that is usually determined at the outset of the funding agreement.[52] Once the budget limit is reached, the funder is contractually not obliged to expand its financial commitment and to pay for costs above this limit. Expenses resulting from adverse costs awards issued at the very end of a proceeding, meaning at a time where the budget will probably be almost spent, might therefore exceed the case budget with the consequence that these costs will most likely not be covered by the third-party funder.

II. The Debate

Among the arbitration community, there is a heated debate as to what role third-party funding should play in an arbitral tribunal's assessment on a security for costs request.

53 International Business Law Journal 53, 56; Shannon Sahani and Bench Nieuwveld (n 41) 28.

48 ICCA-Queen Mary Task Force Draft Report (n 19) 18.

49 Maxi Scherer, Aren Goldsmith, and Camille Flechet, 'RDAI/IBLLJ Roundtable 2012: Third Party Funding in International Arbitration in Europe (Part 1: Funders' Perspective)' (2012) 2 International Business Law Journal; von Goeler (n 6) 35.

50 Scherer, Goldsmith, and Flechet (n 49); von Goeler (n 6) 35; Christopher Hodges, John Peysner, and Angus Nurse, 'Litigation Funding: Status and Issues' (Legal Research Paper Series, July 2012, Paper No 49) 55, http://papers.ssrn.com/sol3/papers.cfm?abstract_id=2126506 accessed 25 June 2017.

51 von Goeler (n 6) 340.

52 Shannon Sahani and Bench Nieuwveld (n 41) 27; von Goeler (n 6) 29.

Some scholars take exception to the idea that funders provide impecunious investors with the necessary means to sue states and participate in the proceeds if the claimant wins but – as third parties to the action – cannot be held liable to meet any award of costs that might be made against the claimant if it loses.[53] This scenario has been entitled 'arbitral hit and run' and described as 'particularly compelling grounds for security for costs'.[54] Given the fact that arbitral tribunals are powerless to issue costs orders against the third-party funder, commentators have argued that a security for costs order should be used as leverage to ensure that the third-party funder will be made to contribute.[55] In line with this rationale, the assenting arbitrator in *RSM v Saint Lucia* opined that the presence of a third-party funder on the claimant side alone should allow a tribunal to order security for costs unless the claimant proves its ability and willingness to pay adverse costs in the event that the tribunal finds for the respondent.[56]

This proposal, however, has been criticised as 'too drastic or misconceived' by other commentators and especially by representatives of the funding industry.[57] They have argued that it would be 'unfair and discriminatory' to treat specialist funding firms differently from other financial support in arbitration such as insurance companies or attorneys working on a contingency-fee basis.[58]

III. Investment Arbitration Case Law

The impact of third-party funding on security for costs decisions has also been evaluated by arbitral tribunals in several investment arbitration proceedings.[59]

1. Cases

A) *GUARACACHI AND RURELEC V BOLIVA*

One of the first cases where an investment arbitration tribunal had to consider the existence of a third-party funding agreement when assessing an application for security for costs was *Guaracachi and Rurelec v Bolivia*. [60] In this proceeding, where the UNCITRAL Arbitration Rules applied, the arbitral tribunal rejected the respondent state's request to order security for costs stressing the 'very rare and

---

53 Kalicki (n 5).
54 ibid.
55 David Howell, cited in Alison Ross, 'The Dynamics of Third Party Funding' (2012) 7 Global Arbitration Review 12; William Kirtley and Koralie Wietrzykowski, 'Should an Arbitral Tribunal Order Security for Costs When an Impecunious Claimant is Relying upon Third-Party Funding?' (2013) 30(1) Journal of International Arbitration 17, 20.
56 *RSM v Saint Lucia* (n 1), assenting opinion of 12 August 2014, para 16.
57 Alison Ross, 'A Storm Over St Lucia' (2014) 9(5) Global Arbitration Review 12, 14.
58 Christopher Bogart, 'Why the Majority Got it Wrong on Security for Costs' (2014) 9 (5) Global Arbitration Review 16; Todd Weiler, cited in Ross (n 57) 14.
59 Cases have only been taken into consideration until June 2017.
60 *Guaracachi America, Inc (USA) and Rurelec plc (United Kingdom) v Plurinational State of Bolivia*, PCA Case No 2011–17, Procedural Order No 14, 11 March 2013.

exceptional' nature of the requested measure. The tribunal held that the respondent had not been able to demonstrate that the claimants would be unable to pay an eventual adverse costs award and underlined that the mere existence of third-party funding on the claimants' side would not automatically support the conclusion that the claimants lack the means to pay a costs award rendered against them.[61]

B) *RSM PRODUCTION CORPORATION V SAINT LUCIA*

The next relevant case concerned the already mentioned ICSID case *RSM Production Corporation v Saint Lucia*.[62] In this proceeding, the tribunal ordered the claimant investor, for the first time in the history of investment arbitration, to provide security for costs. Highlighting that the provisional measure of security for costs required evidence of 'exceptional circumstances', the tribunal held by majority that this threshold was reached for two reasons: First, the claimant had a proven record of non-compliance with prior decisions and failure to make advance payments. Second, the presence of a third-party funder on the claimant side further supported the tribunal's concern that the claimant would not comply with an adverse cost award.[63] The tribunal reasoned that it was unfair to the respondent state to burden it with that uncertainty and risk.[64]

C) *EUROGAS INC AND BELMONT RESOURCES INC V SLOVAK REPUBLIC*

A third reported decision was rendered in *EuroGas and Belmont v Slovak Republic*[65] in 2015. In this ICSID proceeding, the tribunal denied the request of the respondent state to order the claimant to provide security for costs finding that no exceptional circumstances had been evidenced which would have urged such a measure. The tribunal stated that 'financial difficulties and third-party funding – which has become a common practice – do not necessarily constitute *per se* exceptional circumstances justifying that the Respondent be granted an order of security for costs'.

D) *SOUTH AMERICAN SILVER LIMITED V BOLIVIA*

Based on very similar considerations, the arbitral tribunal rejected the respondent's request for security for costs in *South American Silver Limited v Bolivia*.[66] Like arbitral tribunals before, the tribunal in *South American Silver Limited v Bolivia* stressed the exceptional nature of this provisional measure and its high threshold. Against this background, the tribunal found that the respondent state had not

---

61 *Guaracachi v Boliva* (n 59) para 7.
62 *RSM v Saint Lucia* (n 1).
63 ibid para 86.
64 ibid para 83.
65 *EuroGas v Slovak Republic* (n 34).
66 *South American Silver Limited v The Plurinational State of Bolivia*, PCA Case No 2013–15, Procedural Order No 10, 11 January 2016.

brought sufficient evidence showing that the claimant investor was impecunious and therefore financially not able to satisfy an adverse cost award.[67] The mere support by a third-party funder was not considered proof for the claimant investor's impecuniosity, as funding solutions were not only used by financially instable claimants. An investor's reliance on third-party funding might be taken into consideration by an arbitral tribunal in the context of its decision making process as one factor among others; the funder's mere presence, however, was not considered sufficient to grant a request for security for costs.[68]

2. Interpretation

Analysing the foregoing decisions, it can be noted that all tribunals applied the same standards in their assessments on request for security for costs. Being aware of the exceptional nature of this provisional measure, all tribunals stressed the high threshold for ordering security for costs – 'exceptional circumstances' – and confirmed that financial limitations on the claimant side alone could not justify an award for security for costs. Therefore, it may come as no surprise that none of the arbitral tribunals considered the mere presence of a third-party funder on the side of a claimant investor, on its own, reason enough to grant a request for security for costs.

This conclusion is even truer with regard to the case of *RSM v Saint Lucia* where the majority based its decision to order security for costs in part on the fact that the claimant investor had relied on third-party funding. However, it does not appear as if the admitted involvement of a funder had played a decisive role in the assessment of the tribunal since the main reason for the tribunal's decision was the claimant's proven history of non-compliance with costs orders that the tribunal considered as sufficient evidence of bad faith. The claimant's reliance on third-party funding seemed to be used by the tribunal as a rather supportive argument.[69]

IV. Analysis

Keeping in mind this position of ICSID tribunals affirming the high threshold for security for costs that requires evidence of not only the claimant's impecuniosity but also of exceptional circumstances, the author will now analyse the impact of third-party funding on an ICSID tribunal's assessment regarding an application for security for costs.

1. The Claimant's Impecuniosity

Given that the claimant's impecuniosity appears to be one condition for ordering security for costs, it is important to highlight that a claimant's reliance on third-party funding, on its own, should not automatically lead an ICSID tribunal to the

---

67 *South American Silver Limited v The Plurinational State of Bolivia* (n 65) paras 66–67.
68 *South American Silver Limited v The Plurinational State of Bolivia* (n 65) paras 75–77.
69 *RSM v Saint Lucia* (n 1) para 83; see von Goeler (n 6) 353.

conclusion that a funded claimant is impecunious. This is because third-party funding is not only relied on by financially distressed claimant investors but also used by solvent parties that are in a position to pay for the costs of arbitration themselves and seek recourse to third-party funding in order to share costs risks or to remain financially liquid.[70] Therefore, an ICSID tribunal may see a claimant's reliance on third-party funding as a first indication of the funded party's general financial situation. This, however, should not end the tribunal's review for impecuniosity. Instead, it should verify that the claimant is, in fact, financially distressed. This can be accomplished by reviewing other financial records in order to assess whether a funded claimant is impecunious.[71]

2. Exceptional Circumstances

As already mentioned, in addition to the claimant's impecuniosity, evidence of exceptional circumstances is a prerequisite for ordering security for costs. Thus, the question is whether the presence of a third-party funder constitutes a circumstance which is so exceptional that it can warrant an order of this provisional measure.

Given the fact that ICSID tribunals require evidence of abuse or an element of bad faith on the claimant side for the threshold of exceptional circumstances to be met[72], it appears that in order to classify the recourse to third-party funding as 'exceptional', it has to be put on the same level as conducting investment arbitration abusively or in bad faith.

A) RECOURSE TO THIRD-PARTY FUNDING AS AN ELEMENT OF BAD FAITH OR ABUSE?

In the context of bad faith or abuse related to honoring cost awards issued in arbitration proceedings, commentators often refer to a scenario where the claimant investor, before launching its claim, takes deliberate action in order to shield itself against potential liability for adverse costs.[73]

One way of doing this is to assign a claim to a legal entity that does not hold any assets and that may not even have the financial means to pursue the claim in an arbitration proceeding. This legal entity constitutes a so-called 'empty shell' whose costs and expenses incurred during the proceeding are covered by an unrelated but financially solid third party.[74] In this context, the nominal claimant operates as a mere procedural vehicle that will collect the proceeds if the case is won but that will be incapable of paying adverse costs if the case is lost and a costs award is issued in the respondent's favour.[75]

---

70 See section E. I. 2.
71 See ICCA-Queen Mary Task Force Draft Report (n 19) 17.
72 See section D. IV.; see also von Goeler (n 6) 356; ICCA-Queen Mary Task Force Draft Report (n 19) 14.
73 Kirtley and Wietrzykowski (n 55); von Goeler (n 6) 357; Kalicki (n 5).
74 Rubins (n 4) 361.
75 von Goeler (n 6) 358.

Is such behaviour – that may serve as a reference point for abuse or bad faith – comparable to the situation where an impecunious claimant investor relies on the financial support of a third-party funder to bring a claim against a respondent state?

B) TWO SCENARIOS WITH A DIFFERENT EVIDENTIARY BASIS

In order to answer this question, it is helpful to distinguish between two scenarios that ICSID tribunals may be faced with in investment arbitration proceedings and that differ with regard to the evidentiary basis ICSID tribunals will have for their assessments of security for costs requests.

aa) The First Scenario   In the first scenario, an ICSID tribunal may have notice of an impecunious claimant's recourse to third-party funding without, however, knowing the exact terms of the arrangement underlying the funding relationship.

In this situation, an ICSID tribunal has to make its decision on whether or not to order security for costs on a factual basis that is not very solid. The only information which the ICSID tribunal has with regard to third-party funding and which the tribunal may include in its assessment is the fact that a funder is actually involved in the financing of the case on the side of an impecunious claimant.[76] Further information regarding the nature or the terms of the funding agreements are not available – either because the tribunal does not deem it necessary to make further inquiries or because the funded claimant refuses to disclose details of the funding arrangement.

Can, in this scenario, the mere recourse of an impecunious claimant to third-party funding be compared to the previously described constellation where a claimant deliberately circumvents liability for adverse costs by assigning its claims to an 'empty shell'? Hardly, because an impecunious claimant's reliance on third-party funding does not even mean that a respondent will not be able to recover its costs if the claimant is unsuccessful. While certainly not all third-party funders offer coverage for future adverse costs awards as a standard part of their funding packages, some funders are prepared to assume responsibility for adverse costs depending on the contract and the pricing structure used.[77] For instance, one representative of the funding industry recently confirmed in an article that its firm offered After the Event Insurance (ATE insurance) that provides an indemnity for the opponent's costs if the claim fails.[78] It was added that such insurance 'naturally come at a premium which is to be borne by the claimant'.[79]

If and to what extent a funder will cover adverse costs is usually laid down in the funding terms. Therefore, it is true that, in ignorance of the exact terms of a

---

76 The presence of a third-party funder may be admitted by the funded party, as experienced in the ICSID case *RSM v Saint Lucia* (n 1).
77 Scherer, Goldsmith, and Flechet (n 49).
78 Mohammad (46).
79 ibid.

funding agreement, an ICSID tribunal will not know for sure whether or not a claimant has arranged for adverse costs being covered if its case is lost. In this context, some commentators and arbitrators have opined that, due to this uncertainty, the burden of proof should be on the funded claimant to 'disclose all relevant factors' and that it should be up to the claimant to 'make a case why security for costs orders should not be made'.[80] This approach, however, is misleading. It is generally accepted that the party requesting security for costs has the burden of proof.[81] There is no reason why the mere recourse of a claimant to third-party funding should, as a general rule, shift the burden of proof to the claimant.[82]

As an interim result, one can state that, in situations where an ICSID tribunal's evidentiary basis for its decision on security for costs is – with regard to the factor 'third-party funding' – limited to the information that a funder is involved in the financing of the impecunious claimant's case, this information should, on its own, not prompt an ICSID tribunal to order security for costs.

bb) The Second Scenario This brings us to a second scenario where an ICSID tribunal may not only be aware of the presence of a third-party funder on the impecunious claimant's side but may also have knowledge of the terms of the funding agreement showing that the funder will not assume responsibility for adverse costs. In this situation, an ICSID tribunal can make its decision on security for costs on a better evidentiary basis. The tribunal may have knowledge of the terms of the funding agreement, for example because the funded claimant chose to come forward and to disclose the funding terms voluntarily.[83] By reviewing the funding terms the tribunal then finds out that the funder is not contractually liable for potential adverse costs. As outlined earlier, an ICSID tribunal may arrive at this conclusion due to funding terms explicitly excluding the funder's responsibility for adverse costs, provisions entitling the funder to terminate the funding agreement, or clauses setting a certain budget limit for the case.[84]

An ICSID tribunal faced with an impecunious claimant relying on the financial support of a third-party funder that is evidently not willing to cover adverse costs might find this situation comparable to the previously described situation where the claimant tries to escape liability using an 'empty shell'. In both situations the

---

80 Such a proposition was made, for instance, by the assenting arbitrator Mr Gavan Griffith in the ICSID case *RSM v Saint Lucia* (n 1), Assenting opinion of 12 August 2014, para 18.

81 Schreuer (n 9) 776; Romesh Weeramantry and Montse Ferrer, 'RSM Production Corporation v Saint Lucia: Security for Costs – A New Frontier?' (2015) 30(1) ICSID Review 30, 32.

82 von Goeler (n 6) 354.

83 The terms of a funding agreement may also be disclosed following an order of an ICSID tribunal. An order to this effect has been issued by the ICSID tribunal in *Muhammet Çap & Sehil Insaat Endustri ve Ticaret Ltd Sti v Turkmenistan*, ICSID Case No ARB/12/6, Procedural Order No 3 of 12 June 2015.

84 See section E. I. 3.

claimant chooses to bring a claim knowing from the beginning of the proceeding that the respondent will not be able to recover its costs if the claim fails.

Even if these situations appear to be similar in this regard, they are, nevertheless, not comparable. In the scenario involving the 'empty shell' model, the original claimholder takes active steps to assign its claim to an entity not holding any assets in order to frustrate a potential costs award rendered against it; the claimant investor's sole intention behind the deliberate assignment of claims is to circumvent procedural duties by escaping future liability for adverse costs. The situation where an impecunious claimant takes recourse to a third-party funder that is not responsible for adverse costs is different. Unlike in the previously described situation, the claimholder here has not taken any active steps to cause its own impecuniosity. Neither has the claimholder assigned its claim to another corporate entity with insufficient assets to satisfy an adverse costs award nor has the claimant deliberately disposed of its assets to become impecunious and thereby rendered itself unable to pay adverse costs. Rather, the impecunious claimant's predominant motif is to enable itself to arbitrate. If this goal can only be reached with the help of a third-party funder that is willing to fund the case but not willing to pay for adverse costs, a claimant's recourse to such funder may not be considered as acting abusively or in bad faith. Because under these circumstances the fact that the respondent is not able to recover its costs if the claim fails is not caused on purpose. It simply occurs as a side effect – one might even say as a 'necessary evil' – of the claimant's recourse to a legitimate financial solution that may be the only option of an impecunious investor to get access to justice.[85]

For these reasons, it can be stated that, even if an ICSID tribunal is aware of the terms of a funding agreement showing that the funder will not take responsibility for an adverse costs award, this fact should not prompt the tribunal to order the claimant to provide security for costs. As pointed out by one commentator, it may seem unfair that a respondent state will see itself faced with a claim brought by an impecunious claimant investor that is financially supported by a third-party funder and can thereby arbitrate as if it was solvent. Such a claimant does not have to assume any economic risk and may leave the respondent unable to recover its costs if the claim fails.[86] However, as highlighted by other scholars and practitioners, the investment treaty dispute resolution mechanisms were primarily designed to protect investors and their investments – not the contracting states.[87] Against this background, it appears to be justified to prioritise the capability of claimant investors to get access to justice in order to invoke a possible violation of rights conferred on them under a treaty over the ability of respondent states to recover their costs.

85 See von Goeler (n 6) 359.
86 von Goeler (n 6) 359.
87 Mohammad (n 46).

F. Conclusion

An ICSID tribunal's assessment on a request for security for costs is a careful balance between the legitimate interests of the claimant investor and the respondent state. While the respondent state – using public funds to defend the claim – wishes to remain in a position enabling it to recover its costs if the claim fails, the claimant investor seeks effective access to international justice.

So far, no uniform test as to when security for costs may be granted has been established. Rather, ICSID tribunals tend to assess applications for security for costs by taking into account the specific circumstances of each case. However, it appears that the potential insolvency of a claimant investor is not sufficient to grant security for costs. Because of the mentioned policy concerns, namely the risk to stifle a meritorious claim and thereby denying a claimant investor access to justice, ICSID tribunals require, in addition to the claimant's proven lack of financial resources, evidence of exceptional circumstances such as abusive behaviour or a similar element of bad faith on the claimant side.

In the author's opinion, an impecunious claimant's recourse to third-party funding does not meet this high threshold of bad faith or abusive behaviour. Therefore, an ICSID tribunal should not be prompted to order security for costs, irrespective of whether the tribunal is only aware of the presence of a funder on the claimant's side or whether it knows the terms of an underlying funding agreement showing that the funder will not take responsibility for adverse costs.

Rationalising Costs in International Arbitration

A Tall Order?[1]

Neil Kaplan QC CBE SBS

I am delighted to have been invited to address you at the opening of this fascinating conference organised by the Bucerius Law Journal. The programme is a very interesting one and I hope you will benefit from it as well as enjoy it.

It is also a great pleasure to be able to return to Hamburg for my second visit. You might be a little surprised that I have chosen the topic of costs for this opening speech. I know it does not feature large during the course of study on arbitration where more academic and fascinating topics catch the attention of students and teachers alike.

But to ignore the issue of cost is a grave mistake as the topic permeates the whole process. It raises important access to justice issues. The high cost of many international arbitrations, including treaty arbitrations, is the black mark we need to erase. It also raises issues of over-lawyering and professional integrity and perhaps more importantly it impacts on whether you can get a job and if so at what salary.

It is also a very difficult problem for arbitrators themselves. The issue of who should pay the costs and at what amount is not as easy as counsel think it is. Furthermore, and most significantly, the cost of arbitration has prompted certain procedural innovations designed to ameliorate the cost and we can expect more in the future.

So let me begin with access to justice. When the Labour government won the election in England in 1945 it began to set up the Welfare State. Free medical care for everyone became a right. As did education. The 1945 Rushcliffe Report recommended the introduction of legal aid, which came into force through the Legal Aid and Advice Act in 1949. This changed the face of litigation in England. By 1950 it applied to both criminal and civil cases. However, things have gone downhill since 1950. In that year the legal aid scheme provided around 80% of the population with a means-tested entitlement to legal aid. By 1973, this had dropped to 40% and by 2008 it was just under 30%. I suspect that recent cost cutting by the government has reduced this even further.

---

1 This chapter is a transcript of a speech given by Mr Kaplan at the 1st Bucerius Law Journal Conference on International Investment Law & Arbitration.

No longer would the ironic statement that the doors of the law courts are open to all, just like the Ritz hotel, be true.

Coming to the Bar in England in the mid-1960s I was a beneficiary of legal aid. The generation of barristers before me went for ages without work. My generation was funded largely by the state and in those days generously so. But today with economic caution, the legal aid system has been largely dismantled. The government cannot dismantle the right to free medical care or education, but constant tinkering with the legal aid system takes place without riots in the streets. Allegedly 'fat cat' lawyers do not attract sympathy nor accurate reporting. Free representation for all child molesters, for example, is not an election issue that governments want to fight on.

In more recent times it could be said that only the very poor and the very rich could afford litigation. The former funded by the state and the latter by themselves. It was the large chunk in the middle that was left out. However, today the poorer members of society do not receive the largesse they once received and the group in the middle has grown in size.

But access to justice is crucial in a civilised society. All societies have needed some form of dispute resolution apart from violence. That is why arbitration has been used for millennia. The Assyrians, the Egyptians, the Greeks, and the Romans all used arbitration. It was the only game in town in the Middle Ages because state courts, as we know them today, did not exist. Arbitration flourished in Elizabethan England and on into the seventeenth and eighteenth centuries. The first English Arbitration Act of 1698 was drafted by John Locke, the philosopher, who wanted disputes settled without legal entanglement. He would be sorely disappointed if he read my emails.

So to counter the diminution of legal aid and the rising cost of litigation and arbitration, we have seen more use made of insurance, conditional fee agreements (no win–no fee agreements with lawyers introduced in 1990). The regulation on conditional fee agreements was substantially liberalised by the Access to Justice Act in 1999, partly to mitigate the reductions in legal aid made that year.

What we see today, particularly in large arbitrations, is the advent of litigation funders who provide funding in exchange for a share of the proceeds if the action is successful.

Contingency fees have always been part of the American system and have been the substitute for legal aid. It has been experimented with recently in England, but several authors have suggested that the introduction of contingency fees has led to unprofessional conduct and that the system ought not to be extended.[2] We must not think that only impecunious parties resort to third party funding. The fact is, many large organisations would prefer to pass on part of their entitlement in exchange for reducing risk.

---

2 For example David G Green, 'Abolish Contingency Fees and Conditional Fee Agreements' in *Democratic Civilisation or Judicial Supremacy? A Discussion of Parliamentary Sovereignty and the Reform of Human Rights Laws* (Civitas 2016).

I now need to deal with a little history. The common law had set itself against the notion of third party funding of litigation. In the Middle Ages powerful people would buy litigation and use their position to influence the result. This was thought to be against the public interest and accordingly, champerty and maintenance, as this was called, was rendered unlawful by the Statute of Westminster in 1275. Maintenance is 'the procurement, by direct or indirect financial assistance, of another person to institute, or carry on or defend civil proceedings without lawful justification'.[3] Champerty is an aggravated form of maintenance where the maintainer receives 'a share of the proceeds of the action or suit or other contentious proceeding where property is in dispute'.[4]

As society developed during the centuries and regular courts of justice were set up, the need for this prohibition seemed questionable.

So bit-by-bit, the courts whittled down these laws until 1967, when in England champerty and maintenance were abolished as crimes and torts. They didn't disappear altogether because there was a saving provision, which said that the act did not affect 'any rule of law as to the cases in which a contract is to be treated as contrary to public policy or otherwise illegal'.[5]

In 1994 the point came before me when I was a judge. A claims consultant agreed to prepare a claim in arbitration for a contractor. It was agreed that the consultant would be paid a percentage of the award. The contractor settled the case and failed to pay the consultant who sued for his fees. He was met by the argument that this agreement was unlawful because it was champertous. The issue I had to decide was whether the public interest in Hong Kong in 1994 required the enforcement of such a rule in the context of arbitration as opposed to litigation. I held that the doctrine of champerty did not apply in arbitration, which is a private dispute resolution system. I could see no public policy requirement for the doctrine's extension to arbitration.

In 2007, the Court of Final Appeal upheld the validity of a third party funding agreement conducted in a foreign jurisdiction where the doctrine of champerty and maintenance did not apply. Justice Ribeiro concluded his ruling by stating that he would 'leave open the question whether maintenance and champerty apply to agreements concerning arbitrations taking place in Hong Kong'.[6]

If third party funding is to gain hold, then the doctrine of champerty will need to be relaxed in Hong Kong and other places. This is precisely what the Hong Kong Law Reform Commission subcommittee on the subject has recommended.[7] I might add that in Singapore, the Court of Appeal took a different view and thus third party funding for litigation or arbitration in Singapore is not permissible.

3 Law Commission, Proposals for the Reform of the Law Relating to Maintenance and Champerty (1966) at [9], www.bailii.org/ew/other/EWLC/1966/7.html accessed 1 May 2018; *Hill v Archbold* [1968] 1 QB 686.
4 ibid.
5 Criminal Law Act 1967, Section 14 (2).
6 *Unruh v Seeberger* (2007) 10 HKCFAR 31, para 123 (*per* Ribeiro PJ).
7 Third Party Funding for Arbitration Sub-Committee of the Law Reform Commission, Consultation Paper, October 2015.

As far as civil law systems are concerned, the situation is not always clear. For instance, France does not know the concept of champerty or maintenance. However, because French law did not provide a specific regulation regarding third party funding, funders were – at least at first – reluctant to fund arbitration in France. In 2006, Versailles Court of Appeal partially allayed funder's uncertainty by giving a legal qualification to the contract between the funder and the party to the arbitration. Indeed, the court decided that it is an agreement *sui generis*. By doing so, French judges also confirmed that third party funding is allowed in France.

I must also mention Germany, where there is no doctrine of champerty and maintenance either, and where the contract between the funder and the party is considered as a simple partnership without any specific regulation or restriction. Therefore, there is no obstacle to the growth of this industry there.

In the international context one has to think out of the box and consider what the position might be under a different system of law and in different places. This sort of problem is what makes international arbitration so fascinating.

All this is relevant to the issue of cost because tribunals may have to consider whether those who fund arbitration should pay the whole or any part of the costs if the party who is funded loses.

Many years ago, if you asked what were the advantages of arbitration, you would be told: cost, speed, expertise, flexibility, privacy, and maybe enforcement would be mentioned.

Let's examine these briefly.

It is true that the flexible nature of arbitration enables a very quick result if both parties cooperate. But if they do not and in the absence of any summary judgement procedure, arbitration can often take longer than a court hearing in an efficient jurisdiction. However, I know one case in Hong Kong that started at noon and the award was delivered at 4pm. Unfortunately, I know more cases where the arbitration has taken many years.

I accept that not all jurisdictions are efficient. In some parts of the world we see long delays in courts. In two cases where I was sole arbitrator, it took ten years for my award to be enforced by the relevant Supreme Court.

In arbitrations with three arbitrators, dates can be harder to fix. BIT cases traditionally take a long time often due to procedural generosity offered to state parties.

So on balance, speed cannot be claimed as an advantage.

Expertise is another matter. By being able to choose your tribunal you can ensure subject matter expertise on the tribunal. In more immature jurisdictions where judges are not appointed from the ranks of experienced practitioners this is a great advantage.

This concern about subject matter expertise is anything but new. In 1601, Mr Francis Bacon – later to be Viscount St Albans and a Lord Chancellor – stood up in the House of Commons as a mere Member of Parliament and proposed a bill on marine insurance. He had chaired the committee that prepared the bill and he recommended it to the House on the basis that merchants would not take risks without insurance, and if they did not take risks the economy would suffer. He pointed out to the House that the bill made provisions for dealing with any disputes under it by arbitration. He explained that the committee proposed arbitration as opposed to litigation because the courts were too slow and judges lacked subject matter expertise. *Plus ça change*!

Interestingly, he was probably the first arbitrator to be removed for misconduct because he took bribes. It was not much mitigation that he took bribes from both sides. Although today, this might be seen as transparency.

Another advantage of arbitration is its flexibility. Arbitrators are not bound by rules of court, and can and should fashion an appropriate procedure for each case. This can impact on speed and cost.

Privacy is an advantage. No one can be present unless agreed by the parties. No journalists.

Confidentiality on the other hand cannot be guaranteed. It depends on the local law. In the UK, arbitration proceedings are deemed to be confidential. In Australia, absent agreement they are not. Some jurisdictions like Hong Kong and New Zealand have a statutory confidentiality provision, others, such as Germany, do not. In France, there is a dual system where only domestic arbitration proceedings are confidential except if otherwise agreed by the parties. So the only certain way to ensure confidentiality is by agreement.

Today, enforcement is the major advantage of international arbitration. The New York Convention applies in over 1,574 states or territories. It is easier to enforce an arbitral award than a judgement of a local court.

Hong Kong is a good example of a pro-enforcement jurisdiction. In a recent decision (*Kb v S*, 5 / 12 (HCCT 13/2015)), the Hong Kong Court of First Instance rejected an application to set aside an order to enforce an arbitral award and stated that 'the primary aim of the court is to facilitate the arbitral process and to assist with enforcement of arbitral awards'. The ten principles set out in this decision are not new, but the arbitration community has acknowledged that this decision was a positive sign of Hong Kong's unchanged support to arbitration.

A. What is the Role of the Arbitral Tribunal with Regard to Costs?

So I now turn to the vexed issue of costs. One differing feature of arbitration costs is that provision has to be made for paying the arbitrators and renting the hearing rooms while the judge and courtroom come relatively free.

What about legal fees? In many countries the principle that costs follow the event has no application. In most common law systems it does and my experience as a common law arbitrator is that, in the cases in which I am involved, the basic attitude of the tribunal is that costs follow the event. In some cases, it can be hard to decide what is the 'event'.

However, it is worth pointing out that there is no costs regime in arbitration so far as legal costs are concerned. Most laws and rules give the tribunal a wide discretion with regard to the allocation of costs. However most institutional rules do limit arbitrators' fees. This is strange when one notes that around 90% of the cost of an arbitration comprise the cost of legal representation and expert witnesses. The ICC and other institutions pay arbitrators on the basis of an *ad valorem* system. In theory, the more money at stake the higher the fee. But it does not always work that way and in any event a $100 million case may be a lot easier than a $1 million case.

I have seen arbitrations where the total costs of both sides were in excess of $75 million. Both sides claimed their costs and the arbitrators had to work out a reasonable result.

However, in most court systems there is a regime for the recovery of costs. Rules of court proscribe what can and cannot be recovered. In common law countries, there are judges called taxing masters, whose sole job is to rule on what may and may not be recovered and in what amount.

French law is slightly different because legal costs – eg lawyer's fees – are not recoverable as such. However, French judges may order the losing party to pay a certain amount of money to cover the winning party's legal costs. When doing so, French judges have the duty to take the financial situation of the losing party into consideration.

Germany has fixed tariffs for major costs items in litigation, which makes the allocation of costs much easier.

Arbitration provides – again – a different system.

What I find interesting is that no rules have been introduced for an *ad valorem* system for the recovery of legal costs. If it's appropriate for arbitrators then why not for counsel? You can spend what you like but you will only recover from the loser the sum specified in the scale.

The 1996 Arbitration Act in England gave power to arbitrators to fix the amount of recoverable costs at the beginning of the case subject to later revision. However, I am not aware that this power has been much used.

There is then the issue of whether the loser should pay the costs. That is the general rule in England, Australia, Hong Kong, Singapore and I believe Switzerland and Germany. It is not the rule in US litigation, nor is it in France. The question then arises whether the loser pays doctrine, justified on the basis that the winner should be fully indemnified for all consequential losses, has negative consequences in that it has the effect of increasing the cost and whether it stands as a disincentive to settling. In some cases, it is the amount of costs that keeps the case alive. It can be argued that the risk of having to pay the other parties' costs in addition to your own has caused parties to leave no stone unturned to ensure the other party pays them, and this leads to a hugely expensive legal system.

Let's look at this situation from the arbitrator's viewpoint. We can take, for example, a case between two large multinationals where each spends £15 million on its case. One side wins and both had claimed their costs. The tribunal has a wide discretion. Why should it refuse the winner the bulk of its costs when the loser was claiming the same sum in the event it won? What is the role of the tribunal in those circumstances? Should it act as a costs policeman knocking down the winner's costs because it thinks the case was over-lawyered or the hourly rates were too high? Most of the time, the award will not be published, so whatever strictures the tribunal states, it will have no effect outside this case.

Now, if we take the same case and instead of two multinationals pit one multinational against a small poorly funded company or an individual who is not overly wealthy. The multinational spends the same £15 million but the other party only spends £2.5 million. I should add that we know these figures because we ask for both sides' costs schedules before they know the result.

In this case, let's assume the multinational wins. Should it receive £15 million? Or should the tribunal recognise the inequality of arms and reduce the £15 million by a substantial percentage. Assume when thinking about this that the multinational was correct and behaved impeccably, and that the defence was a try-on. Does this make any difference? Would it make any difference if you knew that a costs order would bankrupt the respondent?

If we now assume a case where a claimant's substantive claims amount to $10 million. This sum comprises five claims of $2 million each. The hearing lasts five days. The claimant wins on one head of claim only. Should the claimant recover all his costs or just a proportion? Some arbitrators might say that in the absence of an acceptable offer the claimant had to go to arbitration to get $2 million and the fact that it claimed more is irrelevant. Others would say that four-fifths of the hearing time was wasted and would award costs accordingly, ie deprive the claimant of four-fifths of its costs. Others might say that as respondent won on four out of five issues, it should get its costs on the issues upon which they won. Others might say that as both parties had some success there should be no order and each party should bear their own costs.

Another interesting issue is where there is third party funding, should the premium paid to the funder be recoverable in whole or part by the successful party as part of its costs? This occurred in an ICC arbitration led by Sir Philip Otton. The English court declined to interfere.[8] Indeed, according to the High Court's decision, the recovery of third party funding is permitted in principle under Section 59 (1)(c) of the Arbitration Act 1996 and Article 31(1) of the ICC Rules.

There are very wide parameters for the exercise of discretion in dealing with costs.

There are of course no easy or correct answers to these questions. I pose them only to emphasise that difficult questions arise when considering cost issues.

Many other issues may arise. In the multinational's example, let's assume that they had three in-house counsel working on the case. Should their salaries be an allowable legal cost? One party wishes to test its case through a mock arbitration before another arbitrator. Should these costs be allowed? One party has its witnesses trained not as to what to say but how to say it. Is it allowable?

These questions lead to my next point. To what extent can the tribunal control and ultimately reduce the costs allocated to the winning party?

---

8 *CL-2016–000188 Essar Oilfield Services Limited v Norscot Rig Management Pvt Limited* (15 September 2016). See also 'Landmark Decision, High Court Appeal Allows Recovery of Third Party Funding Costs in Arbitration Proceedings.', 4 New Square (15 September 2016).

First, it is worth emphasising that no institution has ever taken the initiative to control legal representation costs (ie counsel's fees) in the past and, considering the actual tendency to blame arbitrators for the costs and delays in arbitration, one doubts that such initiative will arise in the future. Therefore, the tribunal is the only body able to control costs.

The tribunal knows how the parties handled the dispute and whether they were willing to cooperate. Thus, it can easily ascertain whether a case was over-lawyered for instance. Considering what I said before about equality of arms, it is clear that the tribunal is also in a better position than the institution to determine whether it would be pertinent to divert from the winning-party-recovers-its-costs-rule.

This being said, we must be very careful that the costs phase does not lead to further arguments between the parties. At the end of a case, when deciding on the allocation of costs, the tribunal knows exactly which procedural application was fully justified (even if it was not successful) and which party created unnecessary difficulties leading to a costs increase. The parties must trust that the tribunal is able to decide on this question without requiring lengthy arguments.

I think that the best way to get the parties on board with this is to include provisions on costs management in Procedural Order No 1. One should not forget that party-autonomy is at the heart of the arbitration process and for this very reason, the parties should be consulted at an early stage and agree the procedure regarding costs management. At the first meeting with the parties, the issue of costs should be discussed and following that discussion, Procedural Order No 1 could state that:

1) The parties shall act in a cost-effective manner throughout the entire proceedings;
2) The tribunal may issue decisions on costs at any time of the proceedings if it deems necessary and order payment;[9]
3) The tribunal may not necessarily apply the rule that the losing party bears the costs.

Once the framework is formally set out in an order, the parties know what to expect if they unnecessarily increase the costs of the proceedings. There is no doubt that this will encourage counsel to think carefully before investing huge monies on a case.

B. What Can Arbitral Tribunals Do to Reduce Costs in Arbitration?

It is within the power of arbitrators to run the case in a cost efficient manner. In fact, in some jurisdictions the tribunal is placed under a statutory duty to achieve

---

9 the ICC rules provide the tribunal with such power. I think that tribunals should use this prerogative more often!

this. This is covered in the legislation in England and Hong Kong and doubtless elsewhere too. Section 46 of the Hong Kong Arbitration Ordinance provides:

> When conducting arbitral proceedings or exercising any of the powers conferred on an arbitral tribunal by this ordinance or by the parties to any of those arbitral proceedings, the arbitral tribunal is required to use procedures that are appropriate to the particular case, avoiding unnecessary delay or expense, so as to provide a fair means for resolving the dispute to which the arbitral proceedings relate.[10]

These duties should not be overlooked, and tribunals should be robust and not suffer from due process paranoia, which is a major complaint.

Three easy measures can be adopted in order to reduce costs.

First, early openings. I have promoted this initiative and used it for quite a long time. The early opening is a hearing held at the beginning of a case, often after the first round of written submissions. During this short hearing, both sides have the opportunity to present their respective cases before the tribunal. It is also an opportunity for the tribunal to discuss procedural issues that may arise at an early stage.

One of the problems we face at the present time is that there is an absence of arbitral triage – in other words, parties throw everything, good and bad, at the tribunal and leave it to them to sort out. This is a very wasteful exercise and expensive, too. Tribunals must be rigorous in identifying bad points that can be decided early in the proceedings and get rid of it quickly. Further thoughts need to be given to introduce into arbitration rules a system of summary judgement, to enable bad claims and defences to be dealt with quickly and efficiently.

There is another issue that I need to touch upon. What is the best way to sanction frivolous claims? This question has been debated at length by arbitration practitioners specialising in investment arbitration. The allocation of costs is certainly the right stage to address this issue. The threat of having to bear the additional costs relating to a frivolous claim might discourage a party to submit such a claim, but is it sufficient to contain this trend in investment arbitration? Time will tell.

Another great advantage of the early opening is that it ensures that all three members of the tribunal get on top of the case at an early stage rather than just the presiding arbitrator. This meets the requirement of the Reed retreat proposal in which Lucy Reed suggests that the three arbitrators should take time before the commencement of the hearing to lock themselves away for a couple of days and go through the issues so that they are well prepared for the main hearing.

The second proposal that I want to submit today deals with expert evidence. When one approaches the issue of reducing costs in arbitration, one has to consider the three main categories of costs: legal counsel's fees, experts' fees, and the tribunal costs. Although the latter is a smaller cost item when compared to the

---

10 See also section 33 of the English 1996 Arbitration Act.

two former categories, tribunal costs are often more scrutinised. Why don't counsel's fees and experts' fees receive the same attention? It is probably because the onus of deciding to use experts, for instance, lies with the parties, therefore the additional costs related to this decision is commonly accepted and considered as reasonable. It is certainly more difficult to blame a party for doing everything possible to win a case.

However, the use of expert evidence can be pointless and even burdensome for the tribunal especially when experts are not fully aware of their role. For instance, I have seen experts acting like an additional member of one party's legal team during a hearing. This lack of neutrality is a real problem because, at the end of the day, experts are there to help the tribunal understand questions that are not in their scope of expertise. The tribunal will make no use of the testimony of a biased expert. In this situation, the use of experts is just pouring money down the drain. This is why experts need to be instructed, as soon as they are appointed, that their role is not so much to help their appointed-party win at all costs but to assist the tribunal in understanding the technicality of the dispute.

There are many problems with the use of party appointed expert witnesses and it is essential for the tribunal to get to grips with the issue of expert evidence at a very early stage. Obviously, the tribunal has to make clear to the experts that they are the tribunal's experts and that they are there to assist the tribunal regardless of which party is paying them.

It is really important that the experts are asked the same question or questions. If they are asked different questions, as is frequently the case, then they are shooting at different targets and their reports will be of no assistance to the tribunal.

Third, I think it would be really helpful if at the very least the presiding arbitrator has regular telephone calls with the experts to see how they are getting on and to head off any possible problems. This regular contact with the tribunal helps to underscore that the experts are in fact working for the benefit of the tribunal.

At the end of a case, where there is contested accounting evidence, the tribunal is often left in a quandary. There may be ten points of difference between two highly distinguished experts dealing with discounted cash flow for instance. If the tribunal accepts that expert A is right on all ten, then they just have to adopt his figures. But what is to happen if they accept five propositions from expert A and five propositions from expert B and thus do not accept either expert's bottom line. This is a really common occurrence.

What I have done to deal with this problem is to invite the parties and the experts to agree at the end of the hearing that once the written closing submissions have been completed, the experts will become the experts solely of the tribunal and will work only with the tribunal in a confidential manner without any reference to their former client or instructing counsel. The tribunal can then tell the experts that they want the damages calculated on the following bases and then invariably both experts will have no difficulty in coming up with a jointly agreed figure. Some of the calculations of damages, particularly of discounted cash flow analyses, are extremely complicated and it is unfair and unreasonable to expect a tribunal to work it out themselves. This idea of converting the experts into the tribunal's experts in a confidential manner is a really cost effective way of proceeding with accuracy and speed.

C. Conclusion

I hope I have made good my proposition that the issue of costs permeates the whole arbitral process. We must all strive to give the parties to arbitration a better deal. We must use cutting edge techniques. We must accept that arbitrators should exercise more case management functions and the parties should trust experienced arbitrators who have, after all, been there many times before to fashion an appropriate procedure for the particular case. We should be aware of over-lawyering and although, of course, running a legal practice is a business as well as a service, parties themselves, as well as in-house counsel, should exercise more control over what is done and spent in their name.

The present manner of preparation, which involves extremely lengthy written submissions in numerous rounds, lengthy witness statements, huge battles over discovery, enormous experts' reports, needs looking at very carefully. The temptation to throw the kitchen sink at the arbitral tribunal (for fear of missing something) is an unedifying approach. There needs to be more arbitral triage exercised so that the good points are not diluted by the bad. If more time were spent in attempting to achieve this state of affairs, the total cost would be reduced and the speed with which the arbitrators would be able to answer the questions posed to them would be increased.

I hope I have satisfied you that the issues of cost and costs are extremely important issues, which you need to bear in mind throughout your career as a litigator, arbitrator, or judge.

Index

For Product Safety Concerns and Information please contact our EU
representative GPSR@taylorandfrancis.com Taylor & Francis Verlag GmbH,
Kaufingerstraße 24, 80331 München, Germany

Printed and bound by CPI Group (UK) Ltd, Croydon, CR0 4YY
08/05/2025
01864327-0005